The European Union Green Deal in Southeast Asia

One of the first book-length works that critically examines the discourses and implementation of the European Union Green Deal (EGD) in Southeast Asia, this volume charts the complex mix of controversies, ambiguities, and opportunities that EGD policies present for Southeast Asian countries.

Tasked with making the European Union (EU) climate-neutral by 2050 through green transformation, the EGD has generated controversy through a lack of clarity over implementation details and caused considerable uncertainty for countries concerned about its economic and social impact. Controversies stem from its unilateral nature, rooted in power imbalances between the EU and Southeast Asia, which give rise to perceptions of inequity and create political and economic strains. Drawing on different theoretical approaches and detailed empirical analyses of key aspects of the EGD, the chapters present critical contributions from a diverse group of established and emerging Southeast Asian and European scholars investigating the tension and complexity of EGD policy implementation and discourse.

Demonstrating how foreign policy implementation can lead not only to contestation but also to convergence and collaboration, this book will be of interest to researchers, postgraduates, and scholars in the fields of environmental policy, EU policy, and Southeast Asian politics and policy.

Otto Hospes is Associate Professor of Public Administration and Policy at Wageningen University, the Netherlands, and Adjunct Professor of the Politics of Global Value Chains at IPB University, Indonesia. His research focuses on the international politics of sustainable food and agriculture, particularly the contestation between state and non-state actors from the Global South and Global North over sustainability governance. He has published widely on the governance of sustainable palm oil in Indonesia, including the Roundtable on Sustainable Palm Oil (RSPO) and Indonesia Sustainable Palm Oil (ISPO), and conflicts between communities and companies. He is co-author of *Rightless Resistance: Postcolonial Citizenship, Palm Oil, and Land Grabbing in Indonesia*. His recent work examines debates between the EU and countries in the Global South over EU "green" legislation on renewable energy, deforestation, and due diligence, as well as the idea of norm subsidiarity as an alternative to regulatory unilateralism.

Arya Hadi Dharmawan is Professor in Political Ecology in the Faculty of Human Ecology, IPB University, Indonesia. He primarily researches the topics of agricultural expansion, rural livelihoods, farm household livelihood resilience and vulnerability, agrarian changes, natural resources, and environmental governance. His recent work focuses on Indonesia Sustainable Palm Oil (ISPO) in Indonesia, the Oil Palm Adaptive Landscape (OPAL), and the impact of European Union Deforestation Regulation (EUDR) Policy in Indonesia.

Athiqah Nur Alami is Senior Researcher at the Research Center for Politics, the National Research and Innovation Agency (Badan Riset dan Inovasi Nasional [BRIN]), Indonesia. Her main interests are Indonesia's labour migration, foreign policy, and gender in International Relations. She has been part of the research team on Indonesia's foreign policy for the last ten years. In the last three years, Athiqah and her team have been conducting research on Indonesia in the Indo-Pacific, gender in Indonesia's foreign policy, education for displaced children, and forced migration. Her publication with the research team, "Indonesia's engagement in the climate change negotiations: building national resilience," as part of the edited volume on *Climate Change, Community Response and Resilience*, was published in 2023.

Helen E.S. Nesadurai is Professor of International Political Economy at Monash University Malaysia in the School of Arts and Social Sciences. From an original interest in the IPE of regional integration, governance, and state-based institutional architectures in Southeast Asia/ASEAN and the Asia Pacific, she has expanded her work to study non-state modes of transnational governance and their intersection with state authority in this region. Her recent work, "Challenging the EU Deforestation Regulation: Sovereignty Games as Authority Contests in Global Governance," has been accepted for publication in *International Affairs* in 2026.

Politics in Asia

Japan and the As-If International Systems
Strategic Performance in a Plural World
Kenki Adachi

The Braking Mechanism in Mao-era Politics
Actions by Military Leaders after 1958
Jia Gao

Buffer Thinking in Chinese Foreign and Security Policy
The Reasoning behind China's Policies toward North Korea, Taiwan, and Mongolia
Yu-Hua Chen

Myanmar's Post-Coup Foreign Policy
Weathering Isolation and Sanctions
Andrea Passeri

Strategic Silences and Narrative Power in International Relations
Ambiguity and Non-verbal Diplomacy in Reframing Central Asian Agency
Timur Dadabaev and Shigeto Sonoda

China and the Liberal International Order
Roots of A Plural World Order
Xiaoming Huang

The European Union Green Deal in Southeast Asia
Critical Approaches to Policy Discourse and Implementation
Edited by Otto Hospes, Arya Hadi Dharmawan, Athiqah Nur Alami and Helen E.S. Nesadurai

For more information about this series, please visit: www.routledge.com/Politics-in-Asia/book-series/PIA

The European Union Green Deal in Southeast Asia

Critical Approaches to Policy Discourse and Implementation

Edited by
Otto Hospes, Arya Hadi Dharmawan, Athiqah Nur Alami and Helen E.S. Nesadurai

Routledge
Taylor & Francis Group
LONDON AND NEW YORK

First published 2027
by Routledge
4 Park Square, Milton Park, Abingdon, Oxon OX14 4RN

and by Routledge
605 Third Avenue, New York, NY 10158

Routledge is an imprint of the Taylor & Francis Group, an informa business

British Library Cataloguing-in-Publication Data
A catalogue record for this book is available from the British Library

Library of Congress Cataloging-in-Publication Data
Names: Hospes, Otto editor | Dharmawan, Arya-Hadi editor | Alami, Athiqah Nur editor | Nesadurai, Helen Sharmini editor
Title: The European Union Green Deal in Southeast Asia : critical approaches to policy discourse and implementation / edited by Otto Hospes, Arya Hadi Dharmawan, Athiqah Nur Alami, Helen E.S. Nesadurai.
Description: Abingdon, Oxon ; New York, NY : Routledge, 2027. | Series: Politics in Asia | Includes bibliographical references and index.
Identifiers: LCCN 2026018044 (print) | LCCN 2026018045 (ebook) | ISBN 9781041324294 hardback | ISBN 9781041324331 paperback | ISBN 9781003783176 ebook
Subjects: LCSH: Green New Deal—Southeast Asia | Green New Deal—European Union countries | Environmental policy—Southeast Asia | Environmental policy—European Union countries | Environmental policy—International cooperation | European Union countries—Foreign economic relations—Southeast Asia | Southeast Asia—Foreign economic relations—European Union countries
Classification: LCC GE190.S635 E87 2027 (print) | LCC GE190.S635 (ebook) | DDC 333.72094—dc23/eng/20260603
LC record available at https://lccn.loc.gov/2026018044
LC ebook record available at https://lccn.loc.gov/2026018045

ISBN: 978-1-041-32429-4 (hbk)
ISBN: 978-1-041-32433-1 (pbk)
ISBN: 978-1-003-78317-6 (ebk)

DOI: 10.4324/9781003783176

Typeset in Times New Roman
by Apex CoVantage, LLC

Contents

Contributors

1. **Ata, Asad**, Lecturer, the Asia School of Business, Kuala Lumpur, Malaysia.
2. **Azhara, Nadia Fausta**, alumna of Wageningen University and Research, the Netherlands.
3. **Dini, Inggit Kartika**, Lecturer, Department of International Relations, Faculty of Social and Political Science, Universitas Gadjah Mada, Yogyakarta, Indonesia.
4. **Guillermo, Gerald John Cabanilla**, Lecturer, the College of Law, University of the Philippines Diliman, Quezon City, the Philippines.
5. **Handitya, Binov**, Researcher, Research Center for Law, the National Research and Innovation Agency (Badan Riset dan Inovasi Nasional [BRIN]), Indonesia.
6. **Hapsari, Maharani**, Lecturer, the Department of International Relations, Faculty of Social and Political Science, Universitas Gadjah Mada, Yogyakarta, Indonesia.
7. **Juniyanti, Lila**, Researcher, Center for International Forestry Research-World Agroforestry Center (CIFOR-ICRAF), Indonesia, and the Research Center for Population, National Research and Innovation Agency (BRIN), Indonesia.
8. **Kartini, Indriana**, Researcher, Research Center for Politics, the National Research and Innovation Agency (Badan Riset dan Inovasi Nasional [BRIN]), Indonesia.
9. **Kusumadewi, Sonya Dyah**, Researcher, Center for International Forestry Research-World Agroforestry Center (CIFOR-ICRAF), Indonesia.
10. **Malim, Dinna Dayana La Ode**, Researcher, Research Center for Law, the National Research and Innovation Agency (Badan Riset dan Inovasi Nasional [BRIN]), Indonesia.
11. **Nawireja, Iman K.**, Assistant Professor in Rural Sociology, IPB University, Indonesia.

12. **Nurhidayah, Laely**, Researcher, Research Center for Law, the National Research and Innovation Agency (Badan Riset dan Inovasi Nasional [BRIN]), Indonesia.
13. **Okarda, Beni**, Researcher, the Center for International Forestry Research-World Agroforestry Center (CIFOR-ICRAF), Indonesia.
14. **Permana, Yogi Setya**, Researcher, Research Center for Politics, the National Research and Innovation Agency (Badan Riset dan Inovasi Nasional [BRIN]), Indonesia.
15. **Pramudya, Eusebius Pantja**, Lecturer, the Faculty of Business and Economics, Universitas Prasetiya Mulya, Indonesia.
16. **Purnomo, Herry**, Researcher, Center for International Forestry Research-World Agroforestry Center (CIFOR-ICRAF), Indonesia, and the Faculty of Forestry and Environment, IPB University, Indonesia.
17. **Puspitaloka, Dyah**, Researcher, the Center for International Forestry Research-World Agroforestry Center (CIFOR-ICRAF), Indonesia.
18. **Ramadhan, Edwin Mahatir Muhammad**, PhD Candidate in the Public Administration and Policy Group at Wageningen University, the Netherlands
19. **Ramadhan, Ghilandy**, Lecturer, IPB University, Indonesia.
20. **Rethel, Lena**, Professor, Department of Politics and International Studies, University of Warwick, United Kingdom.
21. **Stek, Pieter E., Lecturer,** the Asia School of Business, Kuala Lumpur, Malaysia.
22. **Simons, Apolline**, Independent Researcher based in the United Kingdom.
23. **Suntoro, Agus**, Researcher, Research Center for Law, the National Research and Innovation Agency (Badan Riset dan Inovasi Nasional [BRIN]), Indonesia.
24. **Termeer, Catrien J. A. M.,** Professor of Public Administration and Policy at Wageningen University, the Netherlands.

Preface and Acknowledgments

The European Union Green Deal (EGD) is more than a regional policy framework; it is a global benchmark for systemic transformation. However, as its legislative ripples reach the shores of Southeast Asia, they encounter a complex landscape of diverse developmental priorities, energy dependencies, and ecological sensitivities. This volume arrives at a critical juncture, offering a rigorous examination of how European climate leadership intersects with the aspirations and realities of the Southeast Asia region.

By bridging the gap between Brussels' ambitions and Southeast Asian perspectives, this collection offers essential insights for policymakers, scholars, and practitioners alike. It not only highlights key points of friction in trade and regulation but also underscores the immense potential for a collaborative, interregional response to the most pressing crisis of our time.

The book's central aim is to examine the complex mix of controversies, ambiguities, and opportunities that EGD policies present for Southeast Asian countries. It does so by unpacking how these policies are framed, applied, adapted, embraced, or contested at different levels by a range of Southeast Asian stakeholders, including governments, businesses, civil society organizations, and smallholders. This book is the first to examine the EGD in the context of Southeast Asia, a major developing region of the Global South.

This volume is the culmination of a collaborative journey between the Research Organization for Social Sciences and Humanities of Indonesia's National Research and Innovation Agency (BRIN), Wageningen University, Monash University Malaysia, and IPB University, that began during a workshop titled "The EU Green Deal and ASEAN: Controversies, Ambiguities, and Opportunities" on 3–4 December 2024 in Indonesia.

The transition from workshop proceedings to a formal edited volume was guided by a commitment to academic excellence. Therefore, this book has encountered quality control mechanisms through a series of editorial processes, including peer review and copyediting.

As a final note, we would like to deliver our heartfelt gratitude to everyone who took part in the process of this book. We are deeply indebted to the four organizing institutions whose vision and resources made this book possible. Their commitment to interdisciplinary research provided the necessary foundation for this project.

We would like to express our sincere gratitude to the speakers of the workshop and the reviewers of the book proposal, whose critical insights and constructive feedback significantly sharpened the arguments presented in these chapters. Their intellectual rigor ensured that this volume met the highest standards of scholarship.

We also extend our thanks to the editorial and production teams for their meticulous copyediting and design work, transforming a diverse set of papers into a cohesive and polished manuscript.

Finally, our deepest appreciation goes to the contributing authors. Their expertise, patience through the revision process, and dedication to exploring the nuances of EU-Southeast Asia relations are what make this book a vital contribution to the field.

Otto Hospes
Arya Hadi Dharmawan
Athiqah Nur Alami
Helen E.S. Nesadurai

1 Introduction

The Ambiguities, Controversies, and Opportunities of the European Union Green Deal in Southeast Asia

Otto Hospes, Arya Hadi Dharmawan, Athiqah Nur Alami and Helen E.S. Nesadurai

Background and Aim

Many have concluded that to prevent a bleak future for our planet, we must radically change the way we live, consume, and produce – moving decisively towards sustainability. It has been argued that the agricultural, economic, institutional, political, financial, and cultural systems that underpin our societies need to undergo fundamental change in system goals, values, and paradigms; in other words, they must transform.

The European Union Green Deal (EGD), launched in 2019, is widely regarded as one of the most ambitious political efforts to realize sustainability transformations, both in Europe and beyond. The EGD is the European Union's (EU) strategy to achieve climate neutrality by 2050 through green transformation, focusing on renewable energy, biodiversity, circular economy, and sustainable development. The deal is not just a domestic policy but also a vision to realize sustainable transformation at a global scale. The EU seeks to lead by example and influence international partners through trade agreements, development aid, and climate diplomacy. Each of the wide range of policy instruments of the EGD is not only meant to contribute to transformational change of food systems, the corporate sector, and value chains within the EU but also beyond. On top of that, the EGD is also aimed at a just transformation, as evidenced by the slogan "Leaving No One Behind."

The scale and scope of the EGD have also made it one of the most controversial initiatives aimed at achieving sustainability transformation across the globe. Political leadership across the Global South and Europe-based development non-governmental organizations have strongly voiced their dissent on the unilateral design of the EGD policy instruments, giving rise to external accountability gaps (Hadjiyianni, 2021). Both scholars and stakeholders claim that the European Commission has consulted too little with governments, producers, and other stakeholders from the Global South in the preparation and legislative decisions of EGD laws. There is a widely shared concern among these stakeholders about the lack of attention to the effects of EGD regulations on hundreds of millions of smallholders. Finally, while the targets and norms of different EGD instruments are quite specific, there is a lot of uncertainty and ambiguity about their implementation in

DOI: 10.4324/9781003783176-1

the Global South, prompting many bilateral controversies between EU agencies and Global South countries.

Next to these concerns that do not question the EGD as such, more fundamental critiques have evolved about the drivers and nature of the EGD. Both political leadership from Global South countries and Western scholars have qualified the EGD as a neocolonial endeavour. Almeida et al. (2023) conclude that the EGD is a discursive strategy imbricated in neocolonial motivations and emphasizing the EU's wish for continued economic and political leadership: the EGD is an EU-first agenda. The authors argue that the EGD uses this deal to 'turn ecological crises into profitable opportunities' for private investors and business (Almeida et al., 2023, p. 1). In a way, this should not come as a surprise, as the EGD was presented at its very launch as a 'new growth strategy that aims to transform the EU into a fair and prosperous society, with a modern, resource-efficient and competitive economy' (European Commission, 2025). At a public event in June 2024, the head of the European Commission's climate department said that the EGD is "an agenda of economic modernisation" rather than an ecological agenda. This framing of the nature of the EGD is in sync with the ambition of the Clean Industrial Deal of the EU, launched in February 2025, outlining concrete actions to turn decarbonization into a driver of growth for European industries (European Commission, 2025).

The dual nature of the EGD– as a project aimed at driving global sustainability transformation while simultaneously promoting the EU's economic modernization – creates a political landscape marked by controversy, ambiguity, and uncertainty. Yet this complexity also generates opportunities for countries in the Global South, particularly in areas such as green technology cooperation, sustainable finance, and access to climate-related investments. Through joint task forces, strategic partnerships, and collaboration with the EU on green innovation and clean technologies, these countries can forge their own "green deals" with the EU and its member states – advancing their economic development while contributing to environmental protection and social progress.

While the EGD seeks to have a global impact, and its policy instruments exert extraterritorial reach and effects, not a single book on the EGD adequately addresses how countries and actors in the Global South, at various levels, engage with the tensions, ambiguities, and challenges these instruments present. Dyrhauge and Kurze (2024) and Gródek-Szostak et al. (2024) focus on the role and challenges of the EGD for the process of European integration, that is, the political, legal, social, regional, and economic integration of states wholly or partially in Europe, or nearby. The central question of Eritja and Fernández-Pons (2024) is how the EU can strengthen the impact of its normative power on international environmental governance. All these books, featuring contributions from scholars based at European universities, show elements of Eurocentrism and lack grounding in the social realities, agronomic landscapes, legal complexities, and political contexts of Global South countries.

This book is the first to examine the EGD in the context of Southeast Asia, a major developing region of the Global South. It covers not only the world's fastest-growing economic group of countries, with a combined gross domestic product exceeding $3.6 trillion in 2022 and a population of over 650 million, but is also home to critical biodiversity hotspots, such as Indonesia's rainforests and Malaysia's peatlands. While the production and export of agricultural commodities, like oil palm, and the mineral industry (e.g., coal, tin, nickel) have driven economic growth, they also form threats to the preservation of these ecosystems and pose significant challenges to the commitments of each country to reduce national emissions. This makes the EGD and, in particular, the policy instruments of the European Union Deforestation Regulation (EUDR) (European Union, 2023a), EU taxonomy for sustainable activities (European Union, 2020a), and the Carbon Border Adjustment Mechanism (CBAM) (European Union, 2023b), very important for Southeast Asian countries as partners of the EU in trade, innovation, and energy projects.

The main aim of this book is to examine the complex mix of controversies, ambiguities, and opportunities that EGD policies present for Southeast Asian countries. It does so by unpacking how these policies are framed, applied, adapted, embraced, or contested at different levels by a range of Southeast Asian stakeholders, including governments, businesses, civil society organizations, and smallholders. For this purpose, we distinguish three levels or fields in which Southeast Asian stakeholders address controversies, ambiguities, and opportunities of the EGD. The first level or field is international relations between the EU and Southeast Asian countries. The second level or field is the legal and institutional complexities of Southeast Asian countries. The third level or field is on the ground: it is about forests, smallholders, plantations, and companies. Our book is organized into three parts, each corresponding to one of the three levels or fields. However, each part reveals that controversies, ambiguities, and opportunities abound within every field and are interconnected in complex ways. Controversies may lead to deadlock, yet they can also open up new opportunities for dialogue and change. Ambiguities often provoke controversies, yet they can also open space for reinterpretation, the emergence of new institutional frameworks, and the development of innovative governance arrangements. By contrast, recognizing and pursuing opportunities may help to resolve existing controversies, yet can simultaneously generate new ambiguities in the process.

The remainder of this introduction consists of two parts: first, we generally outline controversies, ambiguities, and opportunities that EGD policies present for Southeast Asian countries; second, we introduce the different contributions to our book per part. The introduction concludes with a brief outline of the Afterword and an explanation of the book's wider relevance.

Controversies, Ambiguities, and Opportunities

Many of the controversies surrounding EGD policies in Southeast Asian countries stem from their unilateral nature and reliance on the standard model of democratic accountability. While the EGD's policies, including the EUDR and the CBAM, aim to address global climate challenges, these policies reflect unilateralism: Southeast Asian countries have not been engaged in a process of co-creation of EGD policies with EU agencies. The European Commission has enabled EU citizens and stakeholders to give their views on the Commission's initiatives through public consultation but not organized policy deliberation on normative contents of EGD policies with those affected by these policies outside the EU. The public consultation on the EUDR attracted 1.2 million views, of which 7 were from Southeast Asia (European Union, 2020b). This consultation is based on the standard model of democratic accountability (Goodhart, 2011), considering citizens and voters within the EU as the demos rather than all those affected by political decisions to constitute a new kind of demos.

The EGD's unilateral policies are often perceived in Southeast Asia as neocolonial, both in the sense of imposing European environmental standards and protecting European agriculture and industries. The Indonesian government, for instance, accused the EU of "regulatory imperialism," infringing its domestic sovereignty and not regarding local context (Jakarta Post, 2023). Nguyen et al. (2025, p. 175) state that the implementation of the EU's CBAM in Vietnam and other Southeast Asian countries "imposes regulatory standards beyond its borders, potentially encroaching on other countries' sovereignty and self-determination in tackling their environmental issues." The EU legislators seem to assume that the regulatory and legal environments of each Southeast Asian country are void or not relevant. In terms of colonial history, EGD policies are not even based on the concept of indirect rule, where domestic authorities outside the EU would be granted certain administrative, legal, and other powers.

A final source of controversy for Southeast Asian countries and stakeholders is the focus of EGD policies on the risks of deforestation, greenhouse gas emissions, and biodiversity loss, rather than on the risks faced by millions of smallholders who often have insecure land rights and lack the means to comply with the data requirements and norms of these policies. The EUDR acknowledges the importance of addressing the needs and challenges of smallholders, Indigenous peoples, and local communities – but only in the implementation of EGD policies, rather than as a guiding design principle for those policies.

Many of the ambiguities that EGD policies present for Southeast Asian countries stem from the processes of norm diffusion and localization – more specifically, from a failure to critically examine how norms set by EU agencies are interpreted and translated into Southeast Asian contexts. Admittedly, EGD policy documents do offer definitions of processes and actors, but these are often presented in abstract, technical, bureaucratic, and non-localized terms. While the overall direction of the transformation that EGD policies aim to achieve – such as decarbonization and deforestation-free supply chains – is clear, the policies themselves are not truly SMART: specific, measurable, achievable, realistic, and time-bound. The EGD policies provide normative contents and procedural criteria, but it is unclear or confusing how norms and steps should be applied across the diverse economic, agricultural, political, and legal contexts of Southeast Asia. There is hardly any policy deliberation, for instance, on how EGD policies can be linked to and reinforce domestic laws on stopping deforestation and preserving biodiversity hotspots or support domestic policy initiatives under the Nationally Determined Contribution under the Paris Agreement.

Even more critically, it is often ambiguous who holds the responsibility – or the legitimacy – to interpret and translate norms and steps of EGD policies into locally meaningful frameworks. While the EU has engaged ASEAN through high-level platforms such as the EU-ASEAN Strategic Partnership and the Climate Change Dialogue, these interactions remain predominantly government-to-government. Such forums often lack meaningful inclusion of diverse stakeholders – particularly those most affected by environmental and trade policies, such as smallholder farmers. This limited consultation reinforces existing power imbalances and undermines the legitimacy and effectiveness of EU external governance in the region.

Ambiguities also stem from the portrayal of EGD policies as a neutral, linear, legal-rational process – one that conceals the complex power dynamics and political struggles inherent in policy design and implementation. "A key feature of modern power," Shore and Wright (1997) contended, is the "masking of the political under the cloak of neutrality" (p. 7). EGD policy documents are not merely bureaucratic texts; they are instruments of discursive power, deeply embedded in and amplified by the EU's broader regulatory and economic power. Southeast Asian countries and their stakeholders find themselves participating in a discursive struggle with EU institutions, one shaped by unequal capacities to define norms and implement policies.

Furthermore, in the context of implementing EGD policies in Southeast Asian countries, there is a marked lack of attention to power – both in terms of power dynamics in society and implementation capacities – which in turn generates significant ambiguity in practice. Policy implementation in Southeast Asian countries is deeply influenced by domestic power configurations – including the political economy, the robustness of democratic institutions, and the role of civil society. These internal dynamics fundamentally shape how EGD policies are interpreted, adapted, and ultimately realized on the ground. In addition, there is limited recognition of the varying capacities among Southeast Asian countries to implement EGD-related policies – challenges that begin with fundamental difficulties in understanding the policies themselves. This is particularly evident in relation to complex reporting requirements set out by instruments such as the CBAM and the Corporate Sustainability Due Diligence Directive. For example, steel exporters in Vietnam have struggled to understand the reporting requirements under CBAM, leading to confusion and limited awareness. Lower-middle-income countries in Southeast Asia – such as Cambodia and Myanmar – face a disproportionate burden compared to more advanced economies in the region due to limited resources and technical expertise needed to navigate the uncertainties of EGD policy frameworks. Similarly, Indonesia's palm oil sector faces significant challenges in complying with the EUDR, particularly regarding geolocation requirements and the legal status of land ownership. The one-size-fits-all approach embedded in these EGD policies fails to account for such contextual differences, thereby generating ambiguity around how the EGD should be interpreted and implemented across the region.

The controversies and ambiguities presented by EGD policies to Southeast Asian countries and stakeholders could easily lead to continuous criticism of EU agencies. While there are valid reasons for such criticism, these policies also present opportunities for these countries and stakeholders. More importantly, the controversies and ambiguities themselves can be reframed as opportunities – both for EU agencies and Southeast Asian countries – if there is sufficient commitment, ambition, and dedication to engage constructively and collaboratively and to provide adequate resources (time, money, and expertise).

Outline of the Book: Chapter Contributions and Afterword

The issues and observations highlighted above are unpacked in more detail in the eleven empirical chapters of this book. These chapters are organized in three parts, each addressing a distinct level or field. The first presents a complex mix of controversies, ambiguities, and opportunities for Southeast Asian countries. The first level or field is International Relations between the EU and Southeast Asian countries. The second level or field focuses on legal and institutional complexities and ambiguities. The third level or field directs attention to on-the-ground practices and impacts. Each part and chapter offers a distinctive contribution to the book, bringing together original empirical insights and diverse theoretical perspectives. The result is not only a rich and detailed palette of insights into controversies and ambiguities but also ideas and lessons for stakeholders and policymakers.

Part 1: Controversies of the EGD as a Unilateral Measure

This first part of the book examines how the unilateralism of the EGD and various derived policies and instruments creates significant tensions in International Relations, bringing back earlier debates about imperialism and the sovereign equality of states, the question of environmental justice, and the impact of these unilateral policies on external countries. Three chapters take these discussions forward in innovative ways as they highlight several complexities raised by the EGD for the existing state of International Relations between the EU, its member states, and Southeast Asian countries. Importantly, the three chapters also explore the opportunities the EGD presents for collaboration and jointly designed mechanisms between EU and Southeast Asian countries.

In **Chapter 2, Edwin Mahatir Muhammad Ramadhan, Otto Hospes, and Catrien J. A. M. Termeer** explore how a set of government actors positioned between national political leaders and bureaucratic officials – namely, diplomats and diplomatic missions – are able to act as important interlocutors between rule-making and rule-taking entities. In studying the interventions of Indonesian diplomats based in Brussels and Berlin with respect to the EUDR through an environmental justice lens, Ramadhan and colleagues go beyond the more common approach of regarding groups such as smallholders and local communities as the subjects of environmental justice. They make a strong case for considering governments as subjects of justice given their responsibility for the social and economic welfare of peoples living and working in their jurisdictions. Paying attention to diplomats and diplomatic missions as interlocutors makes analytical and policy sense, as these actors can interact far more frequently with EU actors in ways that national governments located halfway across the world may find difficult to do. The analysis in this chapter offers important insights into the different diplomatic strategies conducted at this level of engagement and the extent to which these are able to mitigate the controversies of the EUDR by charting more productive courses of joint action to aid national governments. In some ways, argue the authors, these diplomats and their diplomatic interactions go some way towards adding elements of multilateral engagement into the unilateralist EUDR.

Opportunities for collaboration – specifically in the form of co-designed approaches – forms the theme of **Chapter 3 by Gerald John Cabanilla Guillermo** on decolonizing climate action. Using the lens of climate colonialism, Guillermo emphasizes the neocolonial control at the heart of the CBAM and the EUDR, which are integral elements of the EGD. Although the CBAM and the EUDR have generally been perceived as trade protectionism disguised as green climate action, Guillermo questions this perspective by analyzing the ways in which the CBAM and EUDR operate as climate colonialism rather than as mere protectionism. He thus makes an important analytical distinction between climate colonialism and trade protectionism, showing also that the CBAM and EUDR repeat the historical patterns of political inequality in International Relations between the Global North and Global South, this time through climate governance frameworks framed as universal and morally right that overlook the South as a source of insight and policy perspectives. But rather than seeing Global South states as passive rule-takers or simple resistors of externally imposed rules and standards, this chapter examines how EU–ASEAN cooperative frameworks that already exist might be employed to offset these neocolonial dynamics in the climate governance space.

In **Chapter 4, Athiqah Nur Alami and Indriana Kartini** point to an additional layer of complexity that scholars should pay attention to when considering how policies and programmes adopted by powerful regional actors impact external, rule-taking countries like Indonesia. Despite being a supranational entity, the EU is also an organization made up of member states. This at once reveals an added level of interaction as the EGD and other EU policies do not just impact on relations between the EU as an entity and individual external countries but also impact on, and unfold through, the bilateral relations between individual EU member states and other states outside the EU, especially in the Global South. Many of these long-standing bilateral relationships built over decades are now having to confront controversial EU projects such as the EGD. Will such relationships be negatively impacted as a result, even unravelling, or could these relations prove to be an asset? These authors apply Putnam's two-level game framework to examine the long-standing relationship built between Indonesia and Germany, showing that there is an added game level here as Germany and Indonesia face the need to reconcile their positions on EU matters with their bilateral relationship. In this case, the authors find that these countries' bilateral relations, focused on areas of development, environmental protection, and renewable energy, can function as an asset, helping Indonesia to meet EGD requirements despite the controversies generated by EGD unilateralism. The authors show that the bilateral level can become a crucial mediating level depending on the nature and content of previous and ongoing bilateral collaborations.

Part 2: Regulatory and Legal Ambiguities – Norms, Discourses, and Taxonomies

Part 2 of the book focuses on how the EGD contributes to the regulatory and legal ambiguities that have emerged as EGD implementation looms. Four chapters explore these ambiguities as they are reflected in the norms, taxonomies, and discourses that surround the EGD, which may involve target countries making local/national adjustments to existing laws and policies, or generating new ones, or offering distinct understandings of climate-related norms and discourses rooted in local experiences and realities. The chapters take novel approaches to this task, but a shared feature is to bring the material into direct conversation with the ideational. These works show how the deeply intertwined material-ideational nexuses become central factors shaping the fate of the EGD as it unfolds in target countries and regions.

In **Chapter 5, Maharani Hapsari, Eusebius Pantja Pramudya, and Inggit Kartika Dini** analyze the EGD in the Southeast Asian region as a case of international norm diffusion across interregional entities, a process that encounters the complex political economic settings in three palm-oil-producing countries as they face the prospect of complying with the EUDR, part of the EGD. Their analysis reveals the deeper and complex structural relations connecting the two regions rooted in, and highly dependent on, international commodity production networks. By juxtaposing Amitav Acharya's concept of constitutive localization and Robert Cox's historical structure analysis, the authors argue that the three countries studied – Indonesia, Malaysia, and Thailand – reveal diverging paths of normative localization, shaped by the centrality of palm oil in local, national, and regional production structures that sustain the economies of these countries. Their integration of constructivist and historical materialist theoretical frameworks has broader theoretical implications beyond this work, which reveals norm localization as a process that encounters not only local ideational frameworks at the heart of constructivist analytical processes but also has to contend with deeply embedded material structures of production and consumption as well.

In **Chapter 6, Agus Suntoro, Laely Nurhidayah, Binov Handitya, and Dinna Dayana La Ode Malim** focus on the law, asking what the legal implications of the EUDR mean for Indonesia's environmental laws and policies as the country wrestles with the challenge of meeting EUDR obligations so that exports of these commodities are enabled rather than jeopardized. Undertaking legal analyses and case studies at the local level, their chapter finds Indonesian laws that conflict with the EUDR as well as those that better align with and comply with the EUDR. Ultimately, the authors point to the significant challenges to harmonizing the EUDR and environmental governance in Indonesia. They call for political will on the part of the Indonesian government to adjust its current approach to ecological governance, revise regulations to support implementation of sustainability at local levels, and continue negotiations with the EU to assist smallholders to meet EUDR requirements. Although harmonizing laws and regulations is an important means to address some of the challenges of responding to the EGD and related policies, the discursive construction of the various concepts and terms underpinning climate law and policy can create openings for both unintended and instrumentalized ambiguities that undermine the very objectives aimed for.

Green transition, which is at the heart of the EGD, is nowhere more material than in the story of green finance. As **Apolline Simons and Lena Rethel explain in Chapter 7**, the question of how to finance ambitious green transitions is among the key challenges for both ASEAN and the EU. But before funding can be directed to green projects and investments, they must be identified and categorized as activities that meet necessary green objectives, shining a spotlight on sustainable finance taxonomies as categorization tools that guide capital to these activities. Green finance taxonomies are thus vital in a world of regulatory differences among countries and regions competing to attract capital to fund their respective green transitions. When examining regional-level efforts to develop green taxonomies for green finance, respectively, by ASEAN and the EU, Simons and Rethel also highlight instances of difference between the ASEAN taxonomy and the EU taxonomy. Although the former references the latter in several areas to enhance interoperability, the ASEAN taxonomy also shows regional innovations that pay special attention to regional diversity, socio-economic development stages, and regionally inflected understandings of the purpose of green finance. Referencing constructivism in International Relations, the authors suggest that the development of sustainable finance taxonomies in Southeast Asia thus presents an important case of not only norm localization but also norm subsidiarity.

In **Chapter 8, Nadia Fausta Azhara** argues that concepts and terms such as deforestation, biodiversity, emissions, human rights, land rights, and Indigenous people, can be defined differently, thus making it difficult to monitor companies' commitment to compliance, especially if companies commit to standards with underlying definitions that better cater to their corporate interests. Studying nickel mining in Indonesia in the context of clean energy transition, she argues that ambiguous definitions, for instance, on avoiding deforestation, can be leveraged by mining companies to show that they have complied with the best practices in responsible mining on the one hand, while on the other hand, these claims of compliance trigger unending conflict with civil society organizations (CSOs), the community, and even the general public as to whether the companies have indeed complied with the appropriate standards. Because their respective discourses comprise contending definitions, these debates operate on different grounds and in some ways seem irreconcilable. However, being transparent about underlying definitions and terminologies, the author suggests, is a way to get past unproductive debates rooted in divergent discourses and perhaps even pave the way towards new, shared understandings of what should constitute responsible climate action in diverse contexts.

Part 3: Environmental and Social Impacts – Controversies and Opportunities

Authors writing in Part 3 turn towards examining the environmental and social impacts of the EGD on the ground in Southeast Asian countries for governments, producer companies and small farmers, local and Indigenous communities, and other stakeholders. In four insightful chapters, they unpack the controversies generated by the EGD, going beyond direct impacts resulting from stringent regulations and standards that affect local production processes and trade. These chapters also acknowledge that these regulations and standards can be marshalled by more powerful actors to support actions that lead to further marginalization of less powerful groups and, ironically, of nature and the environment that the EGD and its policies were designed to protect.

Yogi Setya Permana in Chapter 9 takes a critical view of energy transition projects, which have noble aims to address the pressing issue of climate change but which also have the capacity to generate injustices for people while further destroying nature and the environment. Studying the case of the geothermal project in Poco Leok, Nusa Tenggara Timur, Indonesia, he asks whether land-grabbing practices unfolding in such projects are analogous to practices common in authoritarian regimes that largely employ coercion and violence as methods of dispossession to enforce land grabs and suppress resistance. Thus, he locates the social and environmental impacts of energy transition projects within political contexts. In his chapter, he asks how green grabbing manifests in a country like Indonesia experiencing democratic regression, which he defines as one that has not fully devolved into authoritarianism but has not yet attained the stability characteristic of a mature liberal democracy. The chapter identifies the use of the law to facilitate such land grabbing in Indonesia, institutionalized and legitimized through Indonesia's legal frameworks for land appropriation and the legal criminalization of resistance. Thus, practices that would otherwise be deemed illegal or illegitimate become legalized, while resistance is cast as criminal. As a result, climate vulnerability is exacerbated for grassroots populations as extractive activities are extended into biodiversity-rich conservation areas and food-producing lands that would otherwise support local livelihoods.

In **Chapter 10, Pieter E. Stek and Asad Ata** draw important attention to the costly traceability measures required by the EUDR that they argue will lead to the exclusion of small farmers. They attribute a good part of this anticipated outcome to the dependence of independent smallholders on middlemen. In Peninsular Malaysia, which the authors focus on in this chapter, independent small farmers cannot sell directly to mills, and they are therefore forced to use middlemen, which increases the complexity of the supply chain. With middlemen usually uncertified and traceability relatively costly for small farmers to obtain, it is likely they will become marginalized within local palm oil supply chains, making it almost inevitable that EU buyers would have to source their palm oil purchases from large plantations to ensure compliance with the EUDR. Moreover, the EUDR requires that every producer in the supply chain, large or small, must be traced to the farm level and shown to conform to EUDR requirements. Applying a techno-political analysis to the EUDR, which operates as a tripartite standards regime comprising standard-setting, accreditation, and certification stages, the authors argue that such a regime tends to operate as a community of practice among larger producers to develop closed standards that do not meet the needs of weaker, marginal producers. With the beneficiaries of the EUDR likely to be large producers who can comply more easily with these regulations, this chapter suggests that sustainability regulations may therefore act as an unintended force driving producer consolidation, thus further exacerbating the exclusion of small farmers from a significant income-generating sector.

Continuing the discussion of the impact of the EUDR on small farmers, **Iman K. Nawireja, Eusebius Pantja Pramudya, Ghilandy Ramadhan, and Maharani Hapsari in Chapter 11** trace the range of sustainability governance instruments such as standards, pledges, commitments, and locally developed regulations. Consequently, smallholders, who constitute the second-largest oil palm producer community in Southeast Asia, are emplaced in what the authors deem an "unending labyrinth" of distinct and often mutually exclusive requirements. With smallholders rarely consulted during the standards development phase, a point highlighted in several chapters, insufficient attention is paid to local contexts when the final version of standards is developed. To overcome this gap, efforts are needed to streamline EUDR requirements, encourage collaboration between standard bodies, and provide financial and technical assistance as well as include smallholder voices in standard setting.

Chapter 12 turns our attention to a systematic analysis of the impact of the EUDR in Southeast Asia. Employing system dynamic simulation and scenario development, **Herry Purnomo, Beni Okarda, Lila Juniyanti, Sonya Dyah Kusumadewi, and Dyah Puspitaloka** identify the opportunities and threats presented by the EUDR and suggest actions that might be adopted to create fairness for both regions. Despite revisions in the EUDR that reduce its negative impacts and present opportunities to improve local sustainability practices, implementing the EUDR will still incur production and livelihood costs for small farmers. The authors return us to the theme of unilateralism that began this edited book, and the importance of prior consultation, negotiations, and diplomacy. Drawing lessons from the past, namely the extended bilateral negotiations between the EU and Indonesia that saw the adoption of the timber legality regime, the chapter emphasizes that both the ASEAN and EU sides learn from such consultative practices and negotiate in good faith to ensure the EUDR can be implemented in ways that are fair and that contribute to both the social and environmental/nature dimensions of the Sustainable Development Goals (SDGs).

In the **Afterword** of this book, we pull together main points from the book chapters and propose principles for (re)design and implementation of the EGD policies. We end with a brief reflection on the future of the EGD and what's next for Southeast Asian states.

A final word on the wider relevance of our book: while our book focuses on the implications of the EGD in Southeast Asia, we believe its relevance extends to governments, individuals, and groups across other regions of the Global South that are also grappling with EGD-related policies. We hope this volume encourages stakeholders in these regions to critically engage with EU institutions on the design and implementation of the EGD, advancing context-sensitive approaches and advocating for norm subsidiarity. We further hope it inspires scholars – particularly those in and from Latin America, Africa, and other parts of Asia – to join us in developing theories and methodologies that not only unpack the complexities and uncertainties of Europe's regulatory governance but also enhance the agency of Global South actors in shaping more equitable global environmental governance.

Reference List

Almeida, Diana Vela, Vijay Kolinjivadi, Tomaso Ferrando, Brototi Roy, Héctor Herrera, Marcela Vecchione Gonçalves and Gert Van Hecken (2023). The "Greening" of Empire: The European Green Deal as the EU First Agenda. *Political Geography* 105, 102925. https://doi.org/10.1016/j.polgeo.2023.102925

Dyrhauge, Helene and Kristina Kurze (2024). *Making the European Green Deal Work: EU Sustainability Politics at Home and Abroad*. Routledge.

Eritja, Mar-Campins and Xavier Fernández-Pons (2024). *Deploying the European Green Deal: Protecting the Environment Beyond the EU Borders*. Routledge.

European Commission (2025). *The Clean Industrial Deal*. Brussels: European Commission. https://commission.europa.eu/document/download/9db1c5c8-9e82-467b-ab6a-905feeb4b6b0_en?filename=Communication%20-%20Clean%20Industrial%20Deal_en.pdf

European Union (2020a). *Regulation (EU) 2020/852 of the European Parliament and of the Council*. Brussels: European Union. https://eur-lex.europa.eu/legal-content/EN/TXT/PDF/?uri=CELEX:32020R0852&from=EN

European Union (2020b). *Deforestation and Forest Degradation: Reducing the Impact of Products Placed on the EU Market*. https://ec.europa.eu/info/law/better-regulation/have-your-say/initiatives/12137-Deforestation-and-forest-degradation-reducing-the-impact-of-products-placed-on-the-EU-market/public-consultation_en

European Union (2023a). *Regulation (EU) 2023/1115 of the European Parliament and of the Council*. Brussels: European Union. https://eur-lex.europa.eu/legal-content/EN/TXT/PDF/?uri=CELEX:32023R1115

European Union (2023b). *Regulation (EU) 2023/956 of the European Parliament and of the Council*. Brussels: European Union. https://eur-lex.europa.eu/legal-content/EN/TXT/PDF/?uri=CELEX:32023R0956

Goodhart, M. (2011). Democratic Accountability in Global Politics: Norms, Not Agents. *The Journal of Politics* 73(1), 45–60. www.jstor.org/stable/pdf/10.1017/s002238161000085x.pdf?refreqid=excelsior%3Af5035085a7e0a520b7f87c925c598e69

Gródek-Szostak, Zofia, Jadwiga Adamczyk, Karolina Kotulewicz-Wisińska, Agata Niemczyk, Karolina Wanda Olszowska and Anna Szeląg-Sikora (2024). *The European Green Deal and the Eastern Partnership: Towards Resilient, Sustainable and Integrated Economies*. Routledge.

Hadjiyianni, Ioanna (2021). *The EU as a Global Regulator for Environmental Protection: A Legitimacy Perspective*. Bloomsbury Publishing.

Jakarta Post (2023). *Indonesia Accuses EU of 'Regulatory Imperialism' with Deforestation Law*. www.thejakartapost.com/business/2023/06/09/indonesia-accuses-eu-of-regulatory-imperialism-with-deforestation-law.html

Nguyen, Thi Kim Anh, Hoang Thai Hy Nguyen and Xuan My Hien Nguyen (2025). Carbon Border Adjustment Mechanism: From a Green Vision to Fading Alignment with the WTO and EVFTA: Bridging Divergences between the EU and Developing Countries. *TalTech Journal of European Studies* 15(2), 174–192. https://reference-global.com/article/10.2478/bjes-2025-0027

Shore, Cris and Susan Wright (1997). *Anthropology of Public Policy: Critical Perspectives on Governance and Power*. London: Routledge.

Part 1

Controversies of the EGD as a Unilateral Measure

2 Navigating between Conformist and Decolonial Justice

The Case of Indonesian Diplomats Addressing the European Union Deforestation Regulation

Edwin Mahatir Muhammad Ramadhan, Otto Hospes and Catrien J. A. M. Termeer

Introduction

The European Union Green Deal (EGD) is one of the most ambitious efforts to realize sustainable transformation on a global scale (Dobbs et al., 2021; Samper et al., 2021). Many of the policy instruments adopted by the European Union (EU) over the past seven years are intended not only to contribute to transformational change in food systems and value chains within the EU, but also beyond it (Paleari, 2022; Schunz, 2022). One of the key policy instruments for externalizing the EGD across EU borders is the Regulation on Deforestation-Free Products, also known as the European Union Deforestation Regulation (henceforth EUDR), which aims to restrict the import of global commodities when contributing to deforestation or forest degradation (Bradford, 2015; European Commission, 2021b). All seven targeted commodities by the EUDR – palm oil, soy, wood, cocoa, coffee, cattle, and rubber – are mainly produced in the Global South (European Commission, 2023).

While the EUDR aims to curb deforestation and eliminate unsustainable practices globally, it is also an example of unilateral policymaking that extends the EU's regulatory reach beyond its borders, exerting an extraterritorial effect on non-EU member states (Bradford, 2020; Mata Diz & de Paiva Araújo, 2021). The extraterritorial reach of the EUDR imposes sustainability requirements on commodity production and trade practices in territories and production systems outside the EU's jurisdiction, potentially infringing on the sovereignty of producer countries (Schouten & Hospes, 2018; Thorens et al., 2025). Echoing Hadjiyianni's (2017) earlier warnings that unilateral measures of the EU in the field of environmental protection and corporate accountability "may give rise to external accountability gaps" (p. 519), Berning and Sotirov (2023) conclude that research on the EUDR's legitimacy beyond the EU borders is needed. They argue that "improvements in external governmental accountability, as in enhancing the inclusion of external stakeholders in the policy process, are required for legitimate governance beyond EU borders" (Berning & Sotirov, 2023, p. 886).

DOI: 10.4324/9781003783176-3

While we sympathize with these scholars' critical arguments, we also think the call to close external accountability gaps is a bit naive and sweeping. First, closing these gaps is very difficult and would require fundamental changes in EU policy-making processes. It is not very realistic to expect that the EU's external accountability will become on par with its internal accountability to member states, citizens, and interest groups. Second, there are many different types of external stakeholders. The call for external governmental accountability is not grounded in research on external stakeholders, their views, strategies, and contexts.

In this chapter, we focus on the government of a Global South country as a major type of external stakeholder that is often overlooked in debates over the legitimacy of the EUDR beyond EU borders. Much of this debate is about the impact of the EUDR on smallholders, and this makes a lot of sense: The contributions of Nawireja *et al.* (Chapter 11), Stek and Ata (Chapter 10), and Suntoro et al. (Chapter 6) in this book show that the EUDR can do more harm than good to smallholders despite its commitment "to strengthening the rights of forest-dependent communities, *including smallholders*, local communities, and Indigenous peoples through partnerships with producer countries" (European Commission, 2023, art. 30.3, our italics). However, restricting the debate on the legitimacy of the EUDR to its impact on smallholders is to be blind to the "elephant in the room": the governments of countries in the Global South. These governments consider themselves the legitimate authority over all producers in their territories and as the logical partners of the EU in discussions on deforestation policies. Many of these governments have worked for years with the EU in programs and partnerships to curb illegal logging and stop deforestation, like, for instance, the EU Forest Law Enforcement, Governance and Trade (FLEGT) programme (Acheampong & Maryudi, 2020; Verhaeghe, 2023). It is difficult to see how the EU's benchmarking of countries and parts of them on deforestation risks can contribute to external governmental accountability without partnering with governments in the Global South.

This chapter aims to contribute to the policy and scientific debate on the legitimacy of the EUDR from the perspective of Global South states. For this purpose, we first review debates on environmental justice. In this review, we bring Global South states back into the analysis and argue that these debates could benefit from a stronger perspective on International Relations and diplomacy. Second, we provide an insight into the world of diplomats from the Global South who work in Europe to voice concerns and organize dialogue with EU policymakers on the EUDR. These diplomats embody and articulate the perspectives of Global South states, making them well-suited as objects of study for our purposes. Not being a formal part of EU policymaking processes, they can be seen as "soft powers" trying to address the EUDR on behalf of their country via ideas, framing, and consultation rather than coercion or force (Nye, 2008). In this chapter, we focus on diplomats in Europe who represent the world's largest producer and exporter of palm oil: Indonesia. Our set of questions is: How do Indonesian diplomats perceive the EUDR in terms of environmental justice? What actions have they taken to address any environmental injustice arising from the EUDR? And what achievements have they achieved?

The remainder of this chapter has been structured as follows. In section two, we review three generations of debates on environmental justice and distinguish two modes of seeking justice by diplomats of Global South countries in coping with the EUDR. In section three, we present our qualitative methods for data collection and data analysis. In the fourth section, we present our results in three steps: First, we examine diplomats' views; second, we describe their actions; and third, we analyze their achievements. We end with a discussion and conclusion.

Conceptual Review of Environmental Justice Debates

The concept of environmental justice (EJ) "dates back to the 1980s, with the confluence of a large set of political movements in the United States, increasingly aware of the unequal distribution of environmental degradation along class, racial, cultural, and gender divides" (Álvarez & Coolsaet, 2020, pp. 53–54). Gradually, this first generation of EJ studies gave way to a second generation that increasingly focused on regions and countries in the Global South (Álvarez & Coolsaet, 2020; Ramcilovic-Suominen, 2023). Theoretically, Schlosberg (2004) emphasized that this second generation of EJ studies holds that justice is "a concept with multiple, integrated meanings" (p. 536). Next to distributional justice, the concept includes "recognition of cultural identity and for full participatory democratic rights as integral demands for justice" (p. 537). The threefold distinction of distribution, recognition, and participatory justice has become a popular analytical framework ever since, with different emphases and scopes for each element, and it also pervades other research fields, such as the food system (de Bruin et al., 2024). For instance, some scholars use the term "procedural justice" instead of "participatory justice" (Ramcilovic-Suominen et al., 2024; San Martín & Wood, 2022). But in all this, the emphasis has remained on marginalized or vulnerable groups, such as Indigenous communities or smallholders, or more generally, all those who are – potentially or actually – negatively affected by policies but whose voices and values are hardly recognized, heard, or given a say in policymaking processes.

Decolonial environmental justice (DEJ) has emerged as a fundamental critique of the three-dimensional EJ framework and can be seen as a third generation of EJ studies. DEJ scholars hold that this three-dimensional framework is based on Western or Eurocentric worldviews, imaginaries, and politics, which do not fit those in many countries in the Global South where Eurocentric EJ is commonly applied (Álvarez & Coolsaet, 2020; Ramcilovic-Suominen, 2023; Rodriguez, 2020; Temper et al., 2018). They offer alternative ways to conceptualize each dimension of the threefold EJ framework: First, DEJ scholars give a different meaning to distribution justice, pointing to the need to rethink the idea of objectifying and exploiting nature. They emphasize that humans are an intrinsic and embedded part of the natural world and consider the idea of nature as a resource and service provider to be exploited by humans to be Eurocentric and to ignore ontologies of Indigenous and non-Indigenous local groups. Second, DEJ scholars give recognition and participative justice another meaning by placing greater emphasis on epistemic justice. Using epistemic justice as a lens, these scholars point to the lack of recognition of local knowledge by policymakers and the lack of participation of local knowers in decision-making procedures. But this is not all; they also find that terms such as "procedural" and "participatory justice" assume the supremacy of Western policies and procedures. Because procedural and participatory justice are grounded in state-centered assumptions, DEJ scholars advance a third critique, arguing that such calls for procedural justice confirm the supremacy of formal state systems and overlook self-governance and self-governing authority. They point to "the need to go beyond participation and towards the self-governing authority of informal indigenous or other customary structures and authorities, which exist in parallel with formal state systems" (Ramcilovic-Suominen, 2023, p. 713).

Each of the three generations of EJ studies offers a conceptualization of EJ that can address the legitimacy of the EUDR beyond EU borders, but it also has limitations in doing so. The first generation learns that the unequal distribution of environmental degradation reflects power inequalities. While the first generation of EJ studies has a limited geographical scope, this insight helps reflect on the EUDR's unilateral character, which imposes sustainability requirements on producers in the Global South. One could say that the distribution of the task of stopping deforestation is unequally assigned to these non-EU producers and reflects the EU's regulatory and economic power.

The second generation of EJ studies provides us with a practical three-dimensional framework of EJ but is again geographically limited, not to the USA, but to countries and regions in the Global South. The notion of stakeholder is limited to marginalized or vulnerable groups. For instance, the call by San Martín and Wood (2022) to pluralize planetary justice beyond the North-South divide focuses on communities and organizations. Environmental justice is not problematized and conceptualized as part of and reflecting controversies and power struggles between states over what is just sustainable transformation and why, as in our case, the EU can claim some sovereignty, or at least regulatory power, over foreign producers, and bypass foreign governments.

The third generation of EJ studies draws on the ontologies and epistemologies of Indigenous and other local groups to reconceptualize the distribution and recognition of justice. To this generation, procedural justice is not about organizing better participation of Indigenous and other local groups in formal state systems but challenging these systems and recognizing Indigenous authorities. Though the third generation is not very helpful in overcoming the limited geographical scope of the first two generations and also not addressing environmental justice in power struggles between states, the emphasis on onto-epistemological justice and self-governing authority of the third generation EJ scholars can be transplanted and used for exploring contestation between Global South states and the EU over the EUDR. We could consider different framings of forests and commodities, the recognition (or lack thereof) of the laws and regulations of a Global South state, and the acknowledgement (or lack thereof) of Global South states as the ultimate authority over forests and producers on their territory. All this can have huge implications for understanding the legitimacy of the EUDR from the perspective of Global South states.

In this chapter, we use the second and third generations of EJ to distinguish two ways of framing injustice, which we apply to analyze how diplomats from Global South states perceive the EUDR's EJ: The conformist and decolonial framing of injustice (see Table 2.1). With the conformist framing, diplomats are (a) emphasizing the unequal and

Table 2.1 Two ways of framing injustice by diplomats from the Global South

Type of Environmental Justice	*Conformist Framing of Injustice*	*Decolonial Framing of Injustice*
Distributive justice	Pointing at the unequal and disproportionate burden on Global South countries, their sectors, and their producers	Challenging the centrality of nonhumans over humans
Recognition justice	Calling to consider smallholders and Indigenous communities as the main subjects of justice	Calling for recognition of domestic laws and regulations
Procedural justice	Calling for the inclusion of stakeholders, especially from the Global South, in EUDR decision-making and implementation	Challenging the authority of the EU

disproportionate burden put on Global South countries, their sectors, and producers; (b) calling for recognition of smallholders as the main subjects of justice; and (c) calling for inclusion of governments of Global South states in decision-making processes on the EUDR and its implementation in the Global South. With the decolonial framing, diplomats are (a) challenging the way in which the EUDR centralizes nonhumans over humans and nature conservation over smallholder development; (b) calling for recognition of laws and regulations of a Global South state; and (c) challenging the authority of the EU to regulate producers beyond their borders.

Methodology

Object of Study

This chapter focuses on Indonesian diplomats stationed at two Indonesian embassies (Kedutaan Besar Republik Indonesia, hereafter KBRI) in Brussels and Berlin. Brussels is not only the capital of Belgium but also the venue for key environmental policy decisions at the EU level. KBRI Brussels is at the forefront of engaging with EU policymakers and advocating for Indonesia's interests. KBRI Brussels has hosted several EUDR-related events, including developing a South-South coalition, the Like-Minded Countries (LMC), and serving as the liaison for the Indonesia-Malaysia Joint Mission to the EU under the auspices of the Council of Palm Oil Producing Countries (CPOPC). Similarly, Berlin is another strategic location for Indonesia to engage, given Germany's influential role within the EU and its status as a significant market for Indonesian palm oil exports. KBRI Berlin is well-positioned to advance Indonesia's interests in the context of the EUDR by engaging with German authorities and German-based companies.

Positionality

The first author's dual position, as a civil servant in the Government of Indonesia and a researcher at a renowned Dutch research university, presents both advantages and challenges. Familiarizing oneself with Indonesia's government culture, networks, and political landscape deepens understanding of the nuances in Indonesian diplomats' perspectives and actions. This cultural and contextual familiarity facilitates more nuanced interviews and observations, and access to internal documents can lead to richer data. However, this same background introduces potential biases. Being an Indonesian official might lead to an unconscious preference for Indonesia's standpoint or to assumptions about diplomats' viewpoints based on shared national perspectives. Additionally, the authors' affiliation may influence participants' responses, as they may perceive the research as an extension of national or international political agendas. The diplomats could perceive this situation as prompting caution, especially regarding matters that may have adverse implications for Indonesia's foreign policy.

Data Collection

The data collection process for this chapter is both unique and challenging, given the sensitive nature of the data and the complex dynamics of foreign policy. Working with diplomats requires understanding the nuances of International Relations and diplomacy, as well as the geopolitical implications of the EUDR. Diplomats often operate within a framework of confidentiality and political sensitivity, making it essential that the data-collection process respect these boundaries. The sensitive topics discussed, particularly those relating to trade, national interests, and international policy disagreements, require that all discussions be conducted in a manner that does not jeopardize the interests or professional standing of diplomats, research participants, and the researcher.

Data collection about and from Indonesian diplomats requires a mix of qualitative methods, but foremost, it must be an approach that is tailored to diplomacy itself. Access to these diplomats, particularly high-ranking ones, is challenging due to stringent embassy protocols, limited time availability, and potential diplomatic sensitivities. Furthermore, interpreting diplomatic actions and their effects is inherently challenging because diplomatic activities are complex and often confidential. Data were collected by staying at the embassy, participating in events, conducting semi-structured interviews, and analyzing documents.

The first author stayed at the KBRI in Brussels from May to June 2024, gaining comprehensive and detailed insights into Indonesian diplomatic actions and strategies regarding the EUDR. The observational data were documented via notes and recordings. This data provided valuable insights and offered a deeper understanding by revealing non-verbal communication, informal interactions, and behind-the-scenes dynamics among the diplomats. For instance, informal conversations and interactions during breaks or after events with diplomats may have revealed unspoken nuances, unvoiced concerns, and candid reflections that were not readily expressed in formal interviews. We participated in EUDR-related events in 2023 and 2024, during which Indonesian diplomats served as speakers, organizers, or participants (see Table 2.2).

We conducted semi-structured interviews with six Indonesian diplomats of different ranks between June and October 2024. Participants were purposively selected based on their involvement in, and institutional responsibility for, the

Table 2.2 Overview of events (in which the first author presents)

Code	*Event*	*Place*	*Organizer*	*Date*
O1	The Joint Mission of Indonesia and Malaysia to the EU	Brussels	KBRI Brussels and CPOPC	30 May–31 May 2023
O2	Palm Oil Global Community Meeting on the Adoption of EUDR and Consumer Perception	Brussels	KBRI Brussels and CPOPC	24 October 2023
O3	Observation at the embassy	Brussels	First author	5 May–28 June 2024
O4	The Sustainable Palm Oil Dialogue (SPOD) 2024	Brussels	Roundtable on Sustainable Palm Oil (RSPO), the Sustainable Trade Initiative (IDH), and Action for Sustainable Derivatives (ASD)	22 May 2024
O5	The third Sustainable Vegetable Oil Conference (SVOC)	Rotterdam	CPOPC and MVO (the Netherlands Oils and Fats Industry)	10 September 2024
O6	The International Conference Governing Sustainability Transformation: The Panel on the Politics of the EUDR	Wageningen	Wageningen Center for Sustainable Governance	16 October 2024

European Union Deforestation Regulation (EUDR) dossier. The interview process began with the first author's stay at the Indonesian Embassy in Brussels (KBRI Brussels), which facilitated trust-building through daily interaction and informal engagement. We subsequently identified and recruited diplomats at the Indonesian Embassy in Berlin (KBRI Berlin) through snowball sampling. An overview of the interviewed diplomats is provided in Table 2.3.

During interviews, participants were asked about their understanding of the EUDR context, views, and actions. All interviews were recorded as audio and transcribed into text files. For document analysis, we collected relevant public and internal documents. The public documents, including two joint letters, a press release, and two online news articles, also include a booklet presented by an ambassador at an EUDR-related event. The unpublished internal documents included diplomatic cables and meeting minutes (see Table 2.4 for an overview of document analysis).

Data Analysis

For structuring the presentation of our results, we use the three-dimensional framework of EJ. For data analysis, we draw on insights from Table 2.1 regarding

Table 2.3 List of interviewees

Code	*Diplomatic Rank*	*Office*	*Date of Interview*	*Mode of Interview*
R1	First Secretary	Brussels	4 June 2024	Face-to-face
R2	Third Secretary	Brussels	22 June 2024	Face-to-face
R3	Ambassador	Brussels	17 July 2024	Face-to-face
R4	Attaché	Brussels	8 August 2024	Online
R5	Minister Counsellor	Berlin	15 August 2024	Online
R6	Ambassador	Berlin	2 October 2024	Online

two ways Indonesian diplomats frame injustice. Descriptive analysis of interview transcripts and observational notes to map the emerging patterns and relations of their views, actions, and the Indonesian diplomats' stances on the EUDR using ATLAS.ti software. Deductive coding was guided by EJ themes – recognition, distributive, and procedural justice – as well as considerations of DEJ. This approach was instrumental in analyzing the data and capturing nuanced insights into the diplomats' strategies, motivations, and the dynamics of their engagements with the EUDR.

We employed document analysis to unravel Indonesian diplomats' narratives, arguments, and framing in official communications, press releases, and news coverage. Through this multilayered analysis, we aimed to provide a comprehensive understanding of the Indonesian diplomats' perspectives and efforts in addressing the EUDR policy process.

Results

Indonesian Diplomats' Views on (in)Justice in the EUDR

Distributive Justice

In addressing the implications of the EUDR, Indonesian diplomats in Europe were immediately struck by what they perceived as a significant imbalance. The regulation appeared to impose a disproportionate compliance burden on those least able to manage it. During the interview, a diplomat expressed deep concern: "Our coffee farmer cooperatives in West Java and Flores should have the exact legal requirement and obligation as the big American exporter of soybeans; this is unfair" (R6). This asymmetry underscored the disconnect between the EUDR's regulatory design and the lived realities of producers in the Global South.

Although the regulation formally targets EU-based operators, Indonesian diplomats anticipated that compliance responsibilities would inevitably cascade down to local producers in countries like Indonesia. As one diplomat noted, "EU operators will later on, of course, oblige the producers in our country to comply. So, it's an extension of their obligation as well" (R1). The EUDR's requirements are not only technically overwhelming but also administratively burdensome. The diplomat further elaborated: "There is a complexity regarding book shipment and mass balance supply. So, one shipment consists

Table 2.4 Reviewed documents

Code	*Type and Title of Document*	*Date of Document*	*Source*
	Public: published		
D1	Joint Letter: European Union Proposal for a Regulation on Deforestation-Free Products	27 July 2022	KBRI Brussels
D2	Press Release: Joint Mission to Brussels	31 May 2023	CPOPC
D3	Online News: European Regulation Imperialism	8 June 2023	Kompas
D4	Joint Letter: Concern regarding the recent entry into force of the EUDR	7 September 2023	KBRI Brussels
D5	Online News: Why Indonesia is pushing back against EU rules	30 May 2024	DW News
D6	Booklet: Legal Implications and Challenges of EUDR: How to Decimate Smallholders of the Global South	10 September 2024	KBRI Berlin
	Internal: unpublished		
D7	Diplomatic Cable: Report of LMC Meeting in Response to EUDR Implementation	22 June 2023	KBRI Brussels
D8	Diplomatic Cable: Report of the 20th Multi-Stakeholder Platform Meeting on Deforestation	17 October 2023	KBRI Brussels
D9	Minutes of Meeting: Palm Oil Global Community Meeting on the Adoption of the EUDR and Consumers' Perception	24 October 2023	CPOPC
D10	Minutes of Meeting: CPOPC meeting with DG-ENV, DG-TRADE, and INTPA	25 October 2023	CPOPC
D11	Diplomatic Cable: Special Report of Engagement with LMC Palm Oil Global Community Meeting Organized by the Colombian Embassy in Brussels	4 June 2024	KBRI Brussels

of various plantations, mills, and refineries. Well, that will be a nightmare for logistics" (R1). According to another Indonesian diplomat, the due diligence documents mandated by the EUDR could disproportionately burden business operators:

> The implementation of the EUDR will significantly increase exporters' administrative burden. The process will be lengthy and require extensive documentation, such as geolocation data and product traceability, even for a

> single shipment location. These requirements will be particularly challenging for exporters, who may have to manage multiple documents for a single shipping container. Consequently, exporters will face long port delays and incur substantially higher costs, which will ultimately be passed on to consumers.
>
> (R5)

While many Indonesian diplomats challenged the EUDR on its burdens and economic impact, others went a step further, questioning the regulation's ideological core. In interviews, two diplomats reflected on the policy's impact and its underlying worldview. To them, the EUDR wasn't simply a regulation. It was a projection of Western environmental ideology, cloaked in legal text and intended for export to the Global South. A diplomat offered an intriguing analogy: "In the European mindset, environmental concerns are almost a second religion, with issues like deforestation receiving immense attention. Perhaps this is why there is substantial interest" (R3). This analogy was not a dismissal of the environment but a call for balance, an appeal to recognize that environmental governance must consider livelihoods, history, and context. Another one is more direct: "The problem always comes with 'the ideologues' sitting in small rooms in Brussels, people with green ideologies who want to decide everything for the whole world" (R6). In these remarks, the diplomats weren't just critiquing the distribution of burdens. They were challenging the legitimacy of a system that places abstract ideals over human realities, sees forests but not farmers, and presumes the Global North knows best.

Recognition Justice

The concept of recognition justice centres on the extent to which the actor becomes the main subject of justice, with their roles, needs, and perspectives fully acknowledged and accounted for. In this regard, a diplomat said:

> The most substantial issue in the EUDR is the exclusion of smallholder farmers, a significant concern that impacts the livelihoods of many people. For instance, around 40 percent of palm oil production comes from smallholders. Similarly, the coffee industry relies heavily on smallholder farmers, with 90% of production coming from them. The same applies to cocoa, rubber, and other commodity crops.
>
> (R1)

The EUDR is perceived as predominantly catering to the interests of business operators, dominated by export-import companies and large companies, without adequately addressing the realities and challenges faced by small-scale producers and smallholder farmers in the supply chain. As one diplomat said, "This legislation will impact our exports to the EU. Because of the due diligence system, the cut-off date, and countries' benchmarking. That is the kind of thing that may have some issues with us, especially for the smallholder farmers" (R3).

Indonesian diplomats have consistently emphasized the need to give special attention to smallholder farmers, framing them as a particularly vulnerable group within the EUDR. The second joint letter of the LMC, in which Indonesian diplomats participated in drafting, clearly identified smallholders as vulnerable and called for support in navigating the regulation's requirements. Further evidence of this prioritization appears in a diplomatic cable, which indicates that the Indonesian government strongly emphasizes addressing smallholder-specific challenges in its broader engagement with the EUDR. Among all justice-related concerns raised by Indonesian diplomats, the difficulties faced by smallholder farmers emerge as the most prominent and recurring theme.

In a different way, Indonesian diplomats have reservations about the EUDR's lack of recognition of Indonesia's national laws and regulations on sustainability, particularly in palm oil and timber. They perceive this as undermining Indonesia's sovereignty and autonomy in developing its sustainability standards. There are two palm oil sustainability certifications in Indonesia: The mandatory Indonesian Sustainable Palm Oil (ISPO) and the voluntary Roundtable on Sustainable Palm Oil (RSPO). One diplomat remarked:

> We suggest engaging in dialogue to ensure the implementation of this legislation does not significantly harm our interests. Additionally, we would like to emphasize our certification system and ensure that approximately 99% of the palm oil we export to the European market is sustainable.
>
> (R3)

In the area of timber legality, Indonesia is one of 15 countries that have successfully negotiated a voluntary partnership agreement with the EU under the FLEGT initiative (FLEGT Independent Market Monitor, 2024). This bilateral agreement was designed to combat illegal logging and promote sustainable forest management, with the EU formally recognizing Indonesia's national timber legality assurance system. Following the FLEGT agreement, Indonesia established the Timber Legality Verification System (Sistem Verifikasi Legalitas Kayu, SVLK). Indonesian diplomats have frequently referenced this agreement as a potential model for more inclusive and cooperative approaches to deforestation governance. However, they express disappointment that the EUDR appears to disregard both the spirit and substance of this existing collaboration. As one diplomat pointedly asked during an interview:

> I can also counter-argue: Why is the EU willing to negotiate with Indonesia on timber certifications? Is it not the same? Do you want to stop deforestation in Indonesia by acknowledging the international certification system? Why don't you work with us? Why don't you work with the international community?
>
> (R6)

Indonesian diplomats also argue that their country has made considerable progress in tackling deforestation through national regulations, sustainability certifications, and international cooperation. They are concerned that the EU has not sufficiently acknowledged these efforts in formulating the EUDR. One diplomat cited a reference: "A study by Gaveau et al. (2022) showed that deforestation in Indonesia has been declining" (R4), attributing this to strengthened sustainability practices and the increasing uptake of certification schemes, especially in the palm oil sector. Another added: "Our aims are pretty aligned. Indonesia does not want deforestation either. In fact, given our large forest, I would say our efforts to tackle deforestation have been even more persistent than the EU's. The results already show that deforestation rates are going down" (R2).

Furthermore, in their first joint letter on 27 July 2022, Indonesian and other LMC diplomats strongly protested to the EU regarding the adoption of the EUDR proposal. The letter, signed by fourteen Global South ambassadors, stated:

> It disregards the local conditions and national legislation of developing and producing countries, as well as their efforts to combat deforestation. It recalls the principle of common but differentiated responsibilities, as well as the EU Member States' own historical role in deforestation activities and climate change. (D1)

From the diplomats' perspective, the EUDR adopts a rigid, "one-size-fits-all" approach that fails to account for the specific progress and contextual realities of producer countries like Indonesia. Despite ongoing national regulations and a demonstrated commitment to sustainable forest governance, the EUDR is perceived to insufficiently recognize or build upon existing sustainability frameworks such as ISPO and SVLK, thereby undermining trust and cooperation between the EU and its Global South partners.

Procedural Justice

The European Commission's online public consultation on deforestation, which attracted nearly 1.2 million participants, was the second-most-popular in EU history (European Commission, 2021a). Through platforms such as "the Have Your Say" initiative and various multi-stakeholder platform (MSP) meetings, the EU presented an image of inclusive policy development for the EUDR. These mechanisms allowed affected stakeholders, including producer countries, to share perspectives and influence the regulation's formulation (European Commission, 2020). In this regard, Indonesian diplomats questioned the extent to which these consultations genuinely reflected the voices of the Global South. One diplomat noted, "At first, they were incredibly proud. This may be one of the most extensive public consultations on environmental issues, or the second-largest after GDPR. However, they must admit that the process is not going well" (R3).

Despite the formal availability of consultation channels, several diplomats shared the perception that these opportunities amounted to little more than procedural formalities. One diplomat explained, "The process has been more about ticking the box of stakeholder consultation rather than genuine dialogue and incorporating diverse perspectives" (R1). These concerns were further intensified by the perception that the EUDR selectively targets certain commodities, such as palm oil and soy, while excluding European-produced alternatives, such as rapeseed, sunflower, and linseed oil. "If you talk about vegetable oils, then you need to treat all vegetable oils equally, not just palm oil or soybean" (R6), another diplomat argued, recalling discussions with EU officials.

The perceived lack of inclusivity was also evident during the joint mission of Indonesia and Malaysia to the EU on 30 May 2023. A senior Indonesian official expressed his shock at the rapid process of the EUDR. He said, "We were surprised when Brussels launched the EUDR while we in Jakarta were still sleeping" (O2). In contrast, diplomats pointed to the FLEGT initiative as a more equitable engagement model. They recalled that the FLEGT-VPAs emerged from a long, iterative negotiation process prioritizing alignment with partner countries' specific contexts and interests. As one diplomat reflected, "It is totally different when we talk about wood or timber. FLEGT was a long process and discussion. However, I think this one totally lacks consultation. So we were just informed by the EU that they will have this legislation two weeks before the commission launches it" (R3).

The diplomats viewed this abrupt and unilateral process as emblematic of a broader asymmetry in global environmental governance. They noted that the EUDR appeared to have been developed with limited regard for the Global South's operational, socio-political, and regulatory conditions. Rather than building on existing collaborative frameworks, the EU unilaterally extended its regulatory authority beyond its borders. As one diplomat stated, "We all adhere to the Paris Agreement. Each of us has our own Nationally Determined Contributions. Indonesia commits. However, this proposal and regulation disregard these collective commitments and instead try to push their own standards" (R1).

From the perspective of Indonesian diplomats, the EUDR thus symbolizes a lack of procedural justice and a broader challenge to multilateralism and national sovereignty. It represents a case in which decisions made by a powerful actor in the Global North are imposed on producing countries in the Global South that are already undertaking their own sustainability transitions, yet are excluded from shaping the global rules that govern them.

Indonesian Diplomats' Actions to Address the EUDR

Addressing Distributive Justice

In collaboration with LMC, Indonesian diplomats in Brussels issued two joint letters addressed to four EU institutions, in which they expressed unified opposition to several provisions of the EUDR. Central to their critique were the regulation's disproportionate economic burdens on smallholder farmers and the absence of meaningful consultation with producer countries during the policy development process (D1). Notably, the group's advocacy extended beyond EU institutions to global platforms such as the World Trade Organization (WTO). As one diplomat explained, "The first and second joint letters have now been officially recorded in the WTO. The WTO has incorporated these documents, which were submitted to the Committee on Agriculture. Therefore, it is not just the loose documents but an official submission" (R1). This shift from bilateral lobbying to multilateral diplomatic engagement reflects a deliberate effort to elevate Global South perspectives within international legal and trade frameworks.

In parallel with institutional lobbying, Indonesian diplomats pursued targeted engagement with private-sector stakeholders to better understand how the EUDR might affect commercial operations across the supply chain. In one instance, a diplomat met with major European palm oil importers to discuss the practical implications of the regulation on trade flows, smallholder participation, and compliance with traceability requirements (O1). During the meeting, he stressed the regulation's complexity, stating, "The EU needs to understand the complexity and additional administrative burden to implement the EUDR among palm oil producing countries" (D9). Simultaneously, Indonesian diplomats in Berlin strengthened ties with Forum Nachhaltiges Palmöl (FONAP), a leading German MSP composed of approximately 50 members, including corporations, civil society organizations, trade associations, and state agencies (R5). These engagements allowed Indonesian diplomats to grasp the perspectives of European business operators while also articulating the practical constraints faced by producers in the Global South, particularly those related to technological readiness and compliance costs.

Together, these initiatives form part of a multipronged diplomatic strategy that combines institutional lobbying, coalition-building, and transnational networking. Indonesian diplomats have used this approach to challenge what they perceive as unequal and disproportionate regulatory burdens and to advocate for a more inclusive and balanced form of global environmental governance. By engaging a broad group of EU stakeholders, from policymakers to industry representatives, they seek to promote regulatory frameworks that are transparent, context-sensitive, and equitable, especially for smallholder-dominated commodity sectors. Their efforts highlight a broader structural issue: The asymmetrical distribution of compliance responsibilities across global supply chains, which disproportionately penalizes producers in the Global South.

Addressing Recognition Justice

Efforts to position smallholders as central subjects of justice have been undertaken through various diplomatic and multilateral channels. According to an internal embassy document, one MSP meeting convened a diverse range of participants – including Portuguese business operators, German public authorities, representatives of Indonesian palm oil smallholders, Brazilian Indigenous leaders, and a Côte d'Ivoire-based NGO – each of whom presented the specific challenges faced by their respective communities (D8). However, the forum's perceived inclusivity was met with skepticism because it lacked representation from state actors in the Global

South. As one diplomat observed, "It did not represent the whole picture of the problem. The MSP is just like a formality" (R2).

Beyond multilateral advocacy, Indonesia and Malaysia have also coordinated joint missions under the auspices of CPOPC to ensure greater international recognition of national sustainability certifications, such as ISPO and Malaysian Sustainable Palm Oil (MSPO). These joint missions aim to strengthen the credibility of national palm oil governance systems and affirm the right of producer countries to define sustainability standards in line with their own legal, environmental, and socio-economic contexts. As one diplomat involved in the founding of CPOPC explained, "I was involved in creating the CPOPC, which aims to make strong networks and to increase the acceptance of the national palm oil sustainability certification in the global market" (R6).

During the negotiation on the Comprehensive Economic Partnership Agreement (CEPA) between the EU and Indonesia, the first author engaged in an informal discussion with one of the negotiators – a diplomat from Jakarta – to get another perspective regarding the ISPO recognition effort. The diplomat remarked, "We are still working to ensure that the palm oil issue becomes a central focus within the Trade and Sustainable Development chapter, particularly concerning environmental protection. One of the strategies we are exploring involves using a product standard and certification-based approach" (O3).

Addressing Procedural Justice

Indonesia cannot directly participate in or appeal the decision-making process for the EUDR, but its diplomats have attempted to engage with EU officials and agencies through the MSP and other diplomatic channels, such as Ambassadors' meetings with the EU. However, the diplomats argue that their concerns have not been adequately addressed. Indonesian diplomats have also raised concerns about insufficient information regarding the technicalities and clarity of the guidelines. A diplomat narrated his experience when he encountered an EU official from the Directorate General for Environment: "They (the EU) asked us to submit written questions. I asked my staff to read the whole legislation, and then we submitted 46 questions. It took them six months to reply, and they offered only a few general responses. Most of our questions went unanswered" (R3).

The diplomat also raised critical questions about the EUDR's methodology for assigning country-specific risk categories, noting the lack of transparent, consistent criteria. Mimicking his exchange with a member of the European Parliament, he explained:

> I said to him, "You are not a rating agency, you are not S&P or Moody's or Fitch. You do not have any right. When you introduce benchmarking or high-risk classifications, can you explain how this will work? Indonesia is a large and diverse country, so is the risk assessed by region, commodity, or something else?"
>
> (R3)

In May 2023, the joint mission of Indonesia and Malaysia to Brussels resulted in the establishment of an Ad Hoc Joint Task Force (JTF) on the EUDR. This task force brings together experts and stakeholders from government, industry, and civil society across Indonesia, Malaysia, and the EU (O2). The JTF has played a key role in developing coordinated, evidence-based responses to the EUDR, enabling diplomats to present more nuanced and constructive arguments to EU counterparts. By drawing on diverse expertise, the JTF serves as a platform for policy alignment and a mechanism to promote greater inclusivity and dialogue. Functioning as a form of mini-multilateralism, the JTF seeks to bridge key technical and interpretative gaps – particularly the lack of clarity regarding the benchmarking system, geolocation, and smallholders' position – that have generated considerable uncertainty for producer countries preparing for compliance. This concern was expressed during a conversation at the Indonesian embassy, where one diplomat remarked, "Without clear and transparent guidelines, it becomes difficult for us as producing countries, particularly for our producers, to prepare for and adapt to the regulation" (O3).

In addition to conventional diplomatic channels, some Indonesian diplomats have adopted more assertive public-facing strategies. One diplomat, for instance, authored an op-ed in a national Indonesian newspaper criticizing the EUDR as a form of European regulatory imperialism (D3). By engaging public media, this intervention aimed not only to raise domestic awareness of the EUDR's implications but also to challenge the regulation's legitimacy in international debates. The same diplomat later reinforced this position in an interview with a European media outlet, where he was asked to reflect on parallels between the EUDR and the WTO ruling on Indonesia's nickel export policy.

Diplomat: . . . We are open to discussion. If you want to be part of the discussion that is inclusive and non-colonial, you know, just extend your hand.

Interviewer: So you say the EU is behaving in a colonial manner?

Diplomat: It's not colonialism. It's just imperialism (D5).

Through such public interventions, Indonesian diplomats have moved beyond formal diplomacy to engage in discursive contestation, challenging EU environmental governance's normative and epistemic authority. These formal and rhetorical efforts signal an increasingly confident Global South diplomacy that seeks to resist regulatory asymmetries and reclaim space in shaping the global sustainability agenda.

Achievements of Indonesian Diplomats' Efforts on the EUDR Policy Process

We identified three achievements that the Indonesian diplomats achieved through their efforts. First, one Indonesian diplomat said they lobbied EU officials regarding the deforestation cut-off date. He stated, "Initially, NGOs were very strong in making the deforestation cut-off date in the regulation from 2014–2015" (R1). The diplomat then met with one of the central policymakers of the EUDR and proposed that the deforestation cut-off date be set in 2024 or when the regulation is implemented. Although the EU finally decided on a 2022 deadline, the diplomat's lobbying efforts influenced the officials not to accept the initial proposal from the non-governmental organizations (NGOs).

Second, the joint letters of the LMC marked a significant diplomatic achievement for Indonesia, demonstrating its ability to coordinate international resistance against what they perceived as unfair and unilateral EU trade policies. The first joint letter, submitted on 27 July 2022, was initiated by Indonesian diplomats in coordination with key producer countries, including Malaysia, Brazil, Colombia, and Ghana. This letter was a collective response from 14 embassies to the EUDR's perceived lack of fairness, transparency, and inclusivity in its formulation. Following the limited EU response to the first letter, Indonesian diplomats led the drafting of a second joint letter, submitted on 7 September 2023, with a broader coalition of 17 Ambassador signatories that now included other commodity-exporting countries, such as Thailand, for the rubber industry, which in the EUDR proposal is not being targeted. Nevertheless, the effect of these joint letters needs to be further observed (D7).

Third, Indonesian diplomats have called for increased transparency and more inclusive stakeholder engagement in developing and implementing the EUDR. They have emphasized the need for meaningful consultation with governments and affected stakeholders in producer countries, including smallholder farmers and local communities. With the CPOPC and ministries from the capital, the diplomats have proposed establishing the Ad Hoc JTF between the EU, Indonesia, and Malaysia to address these concerns. This Ad Hoc JTF would provide a platform for ongoing dialogue, information sharing, and collaborative decision-making throughout the EUDR policy process (D10). The diplomats believe such a mechanism could help ensure that the regulation is developed and implemented fairly, equitably, and in a manner responsive to the unique circumstances and priorities of the producer countries. By fostering greater transparency and inclusive participation, the diplomats aim to secure a more balanced, mutually beneficial approach to addressing deforestation and environmental concerns in the EU's supply chains.

Discussion

Framing of Injustice, Actions Taken, and Achievements

This study shows that Indonesian diplomats' responses to the EUDR go beyond technical concerns. Their engagement with the EUDR reveals an insistence on being seen not only as policy subjects but primarily as political actors. The diplomats' critiques on the EUDR encompass all three key dimensions of environmental justice – distribution, recognition, and procedural. With each dimension, diplomats use both a conformist and a decolonial frame. Table 2.5 provides an overview of how Indonesian diplomats framed injustices related to the EUDR and the actions they pursued in response across the types of EJ.

These framing shapes inspired different kinds of diplomatic action. Conformist framings have prompted lobbying for smallholder inclusion or for technical adjustments through formal platforms such as CEPA or the JTF. In contrast, decolonial framings have elicited strong criticism from diplomats who have qualified the

Table 2.5 Overview of Indonesian diplomats' framings of injustice and actions taken in the context of the EUDR

Type of Environmental Justice	*Framing of Injustice*	*Actions Taken*
Distributive justice	Conformist: Advocating for fairer economic and administrative burden-sharing between smallholders in the Global South and large producers/exporters in the Global North	Conformist: Lobbied EU officials to reconsider the strict deforestation cut-off date; engaged with German stakeholders to raise awareness about Indonesian producers' technological readiness and compliance costs
	Decolonial: Critiquing environmental concerns as driven by a Eurocentric mindset that seeks to dictate global sustainability norms unilaterally	Decolonial: Issued protest letters to the EU (together with Global South Embassies of LMC) and notice of objection with the WTO
Recognition justice	Conformist: Highlighting smallholders as the most vulnerable group negatively affected by the EUDR and advocating for their special consideration	Conformist: Advocated for smallholder inclusion in the MSP meeting
	Decolonial: Advocating recognition of Indonesia's local context (e.g., forest area definition) and certification systems (e.g., ISPO and SVLK) against Eurocentric standards	Decolonial: Promoted ISPO and SVLK beyond the EUDR framework, such as bilateral negotiation (e.g., CEPA), multistakeholder forum (e.g., FONAP), and public dialogues (e.g., SPOD and SVOC)
Procedural justice	Conformist: Demanding more inclusive and transparent consultation processes, similar to the FLEGT-VPA model	Conformist: Established the Ad Hoc JTF with the EU and Malaysia; submitted technical questions; engaged in Ambassador meetings
	Decolonial: Critiquing EUDR methodology and transparency in the country benchmarking system	Decolonial: Used public dialogues (e.g., SPOD and SVOC) and media to challenge EU decision-making and regulatory imperialism

EUDR as "imperialist." These decolonial framings have also fueled the formation of the LMC coalition, a group of countries from the Global South that has publicly criticized the EUDR. The promotion of national certification systems like ISPO and SVLK is a concrete way to demonstrate that their own systems can serve as an alternative to the EUDR.

Given the complexity of the issues and the many officials and stakeholders involved, it is difficult to assess the achievements of Indonesian diplomats. Some of the observed achievements, such as the reconsideration of the deforestation cut-off date and the postponement of the EUDR application from December 2024 to December 2025, cannot be solely attributed to Indonesian diplomatic efforts. Multiple actors, including NGO advocacy, lobbying by other producer countries, political changes, and internal debates within the EU, shaped these developments. While Indonesian diplomats did contribute to these shifts through targeted lobbying, they were part of a broader coalition of influence.

However, in the case of the establishment of the LMC and the Ad Hoc JTF with the EU and Malaysia, it is fair to say that this was very much the result of the diplomatic efforts of Indonesia. The LMC initiative represents a coordinated South-South platform aimed at challenging the perceived epistemic and procedural biases of the EUDR. It reflects Indonesia's decolonial diplomatic posture by aligning with other Global South producers to assert a collective voice against normative impositions from the Global North.

Meanwhile, the JTF serves as a formal trilateral dialogue mechanism created to address implementation challenges of the EUDR. Initiated following joint ministerial visits to Brussels in May 2023, the JTF works through five key workstreams: smallholder inclusivity, alignment of national certification systems (e.g., ISPO and MSPO), traceability tools, scientific data development, and data privacy concerns. This initiative, coordinated by Indonesian diplomats in collaboration with their capital, has enabled Indonesia to institutionalize a more balanced and inclusive negotiation space with the EU. The JTF not only exemplifies Indonesia's hybrid strategy of conformist engagement and decolonial critique but also marks a shift in its diplomacy, from reactive protest to proactive rule-shaping.

Together, the LMC and JTF illustrate how Indonesia has leveraged both regional solidarity and structured dialogue to enhance its influence in transnational regulatory settings. These initiatives reflect a diplomatic strategy that combines technical pragmatism with normative assertiveness, seeking not just to comply with global rules but also to co-author them. Nevertheless, the long-term effectiveness of both the LMC and the JTF remains to be seen. As these platforms are still in development, their impact will likely depend on how they adapt over time to shifting political conditions and the evolving interests of the countries involved.

Future Challenges of Indonesia's Diplomats

Indonesia's dual approach, combining conformist engagement with decolonial critique, has enabled its diplomats to work simultaneously within existing international structures while challenging their underlying assumptions. The first challenge of Indonesia's diplomats will be to navigate between these two framings, conformist and decolonial. Overreliance on engagement without critique risks reinforcing an unjust global system, while pursuing only radical alternatives without building alliances may reduce Indonesia's diplomatic influence. An adjusted strategy combining pragmatic negotiation with visionary leadership will allow Indonesia to defend its immediate interests while contributing to a more equitable and inclusive global environmental order. In this context, Indonesia's diplomatic engagement around the EUDR should be seen not as a singular episode but as part of a broader repositioning of the country within global sustainability debates, aiming to move from passive compliance to active agenda-setting on behalf of the Global South. The second challenge is the need for active, assertive engagement by Indonesian diplomats in multilateral platforms, which can be strategically important for Indonesia and other Global South countries to review unilateral policies and promote rule-based multilateral governance. Leveraging frameworks such as the Rio Declaration, the Paris Agreement, and WTO principles provides a legitimate basis for demanding that future environmental regulations be negotiated transparently, with meaningful participation from producer countries. Strengthening alliances with other Global South states remains essential to amplify Indonesia's voice and present a united front against unilateral policymaking by robust economies.

While engaging in multilateral platforms and strengthening alliances with other Global South states, the third challenge is to develop a more assertive global sustainability narrative. Beyond contesting specific provisions of regulations like the EUDR, Indonesia has an opportunity to promote alternative governance models grounded in epistemological plurality, relational understandings of human-nature relationships, and recognition of Indigenous and local knowledge systems. This shift would require Indonesia to resist externally imposed standards and propose positive alternatives that challenge the dominant Eurocentric sustainability models.

Limitations of the Study

It is important to acknowledge several of the study's methodological limitations. First, the number of Indonesian diplomats with specific knowledge and a formal mandate to address the EUDR dossier was relatively limited. This limitation reflects both the recent introduction of the policy and the rotational staffing system within Indonesia's Ministry of Foreign Affairs. The research captures the perspectives of diplomats serving during the 2023–2024 period, a critical phase in the early implementation of the EUDR, but does not include the views of those who may have been involved in earlier negotiations or initial diplomatic responses. Supplementing interviews with internal and publicly available documents could help recover institutional memory and provide a more comprehensive, historically grounded account of Indonesia's engagement with the EUDR.

Second, the study's focus on interviews and observations involving only Indonesian diplomats necessarily narrows the range of perspectives analyzed. The absence of insights from other relevant stakeholders, such as EU officials, NGOs, smallholder representatives, or producer associations, limits a more comprehensive understanding of the diplomatic landscape. Additionally, the first author's positionality, with prior experience in the Indonesian civil service, may have influenced both data collection and interpretation. While this insider perspective enhances access and depth, it also introduces potential bias that must be transparently acknowledged. However, collaborative authorship by scholars from both the Global South and the Global North provides a valuable counterbalance, contributing to a more nuanced and critically engaged interpretation of the findings.

Finally, the confidential and strategic nature of diplomatic work means that some views and experiences may have been underreported or expressed cautiously. Nevertheless, the diplomats interviewed were key actors in Indonesia's engagement with the EUDR and provided important testimony regarding the strategies and normative orientations shaping the country's justice-seeking diplomacy. Future research could build on these findings by tracing how diplomatic narratives and practices develop over time, incorporating a broader array of stakeholders, and conducting comparative analyses with other Global South countries navigating similar regulatory frameworks. These approaches would offer a richer and more multidimensional understanding of transnational environmental diplomacy.

Conclusion

By applying a justice framework centered on distributive, recognition, and procedural dimensions, we have shown that Indonesian diplomats perceive the EUDR as an unjust regulation due to its unilateral character and its imposition of disproportionate burdens on Global South producers, particularly smallholder farmers, in policymaking. Indonesian diplomats have used a mix of conformist and decolonial frames in their responses to the EUDR. Conformist strategies involve working within formal institutions such as the EU Parliament, the WTO, and CEPA negotiations to advocate for fair treatment of smallholders and greater involvement of Global South governments. At the same time, they also take a decolonial approach by challenging the EU's authority to impose sustainability rules unilaterally and defending their right to define their own standards. A key part of their strategy is to place greater emphasis on multilateral arenas and policymaking. For instance, they send joint letters to the WTO as a litigation strategy for trade impacts, CEPA to negotiate recognition of national certification schemes, and platforms like the JTF, LMC, and CPOPC to build alliances and promote dialogue. This approach helps Indonesian diplomats gain more influence by choosing the most effective venues for each issue.

The case of Indonesian diplomacy illustrates that justice is not just a matter of compliance or technical adjustment but of political recognition and fair governance.

As global environmental governance continues to expand in scope and ambition, the effectiveness and legitimacy of such frameworks will depend not only on their goals but also on the processes through which they are created and implemented, including the voices they include, the burdens they impose, and the partnerships they honour.

Reference List

Acheampong, E., & Maryudi, A. (2020). Avoiding legality: Timber producers' strategies and motivations under FLEGT in Ghana and Indonesia. *Forest Policy and Economics*, *111*, 102047. https://doi.org/10.1016/j.forpol.2019.102047

Álvarez, L., & Coolsaet, B. (2020). Decolonizing environmental justice studies: A Latin American perspective. *Capitalism Nature Socialism*, *31*(2), 50–69. https://doi.org/10.1080/10455752.2018.1558272

Berning, L., & Sotirov, M. (2023). Hardening corporate accountability in commodity supply chains under the European Union deforestation regulation. *Regulation & Governance*, *17*(4), 870–890. https://doi.org/10.1111/rego.12540

Bradford, A. (2015). Exporting standards: The externalization of the EU's regulatory power via markets. *International Review of Law and Economics*, *42*, 158–173. https://doi.org/10.1016/j.irle.2014.09.004

Bradford, A. (2020). *The Brussels effect: How the European Union rules the world*. Oxford University Press. https://doi.org/10.1093/oso/9780190088583.001.0001

de Bruin, A., de Boer, I. J. M., Faber, N. R., de Jong, G., Termeer, K. J. A. M., & de Olde, E. M. (2024). Easier said than defined? Conceptualizing justice in food system transitions. *Agriculture and Human Values*, *41*(1), 345–362. https://doi.org/10.1007/s10460-023-10482-y

Dobbs, M., Gravey, V., & Petetin, L. (2021). Driving the European Green Deal in turbulent times. *Politics and Governance*, *9*(3), 316–326. https://doi.org/10.17645/pag.v9i3.4321

European Commission. (2020). *Deforestation and forest degradation – reducing the impact of products placed on the EU market*. https://ec.europa.eu/info/law/better-regulation/have-your-say/initiatives/12137-Deforestation-and-forest-degradation-reducing-the-impact-of-products-placed-on-the-EU-market_en

European Commission. (2021a). *Commission staff working document impact assessment: Minimizing the risk of deforestation and forest degradation associated with products placed on the EU market*. https://eur-lex.europa.eu/legal-content/EN/TXT/?uri=celex:52021SC0326

European Commission. (2021b). *Proposal for a regulation of the European Parliament and of the Council on the making available on the Union market as well as export from the Union of certain commodities and products associated with deforestation and forest degradation and repealing Regulation (EU) no 995/2010*. https://eur-lex.europa.eu/legal-content/EN/TXT/?uri=CELEX%3A52021PC0706

European Commission. (2023). *Regulation no 2023/1115 of the European Parliament and of the Council of 31 May 2023 on the making available on the Union market and the export from the Union of certain commodities and products associated with deforestation and forest degradation and repealing Regulation no 995/2010*. https://eur-lex.europa.eu/legal-content/EN/TXT/?uri=CELEX:32023R1115

FLEGT Independent Market Monitor. (2024). *Key EU countries and FLEGT VPA partners*. https://flegtimm.eu/country-profiles/

Gaveau, D. L. A., Locatelli, B., Salim, M. A., Husnayaen, Manurung, T., Descals, A., Angelsen, A., Meijaard, E., & Sheil, D. (2022). Slowing deforestation in Indonesia follows declining oil palm expansion and lower oil prices. *PLoS One*, *17*(3), 1–19. https://doi.org/10.1371/journal.pone.0266178

Hadjiyianni, I., Weber, M., & Fellow, P. (2017). The extraterritorial reach of EU environmental law and access to justice by third country actors. *European Papers*, *2*(2), 519–542. https://doi.org/10.15166/2499-8249/167

Mata Diz, J. B., & de Paiva Araújo, H. E. (2021). Extraterritoriality and the impact of EU regulatory authority: Environmental protection as soft power. In N. Cunha Rodrigues (Ed.), *Extraterritoriality of EU economic law: European Union and its neighbours in a globalized world* (Vol. 4, pp. 319–333). Springer, Cham. https://doi.org/10.1007/978-3-030-82291-0_15

Nye, J. S. (2008). Public diplomacy and soft power. *The ANNALS of the American Academy of Political and Social Science*, *616*(1), 94–109. https://doi.org/10.1177/0002716207311699

Paleari, S. (2022). The impact of the European Green Deal on EU environmental policy. *The Journal of Environment & Development*, *31*(2), 196–220. https://doi.org/10.1177/10704965221082222

Ramcilovic-Suominen, S. (2023). Envisioning just transformations in and beyond the EU bioeconomy: Inspirations from decolonial environmental justice and degrowth. *Sustainability Science*, *18*(2), 707–722. https://doi.org/10.1007/s11625-022-01091-5

Ramcilovic-Suominen, S., Chomba, S., Larson, A. M., & Sinclair, F. (2024). Decolonial environmental justice in landscape restoration. In P. Katila, C. J. P. Colfer, W. de Jong, G. Galloway, P. Pacheco, & G. Winkel (Eds.), *Restoring forests and trees for sustainable development: Policies, practices, impacts, and ways forward* (pp. 74–101). Oxford University Press. https://doi.org/10.1093/9780197683958.003.0004

Rodriguez, I. (2020). Latin American decolonial environmental justice. In B. Coolsaet (Ed.), *Environmental justice: Key issues* (pp. 78–93). Routledge. https://doi.org/10.4324/9780429029585-8

Samper, J. A., Schockling, A., & Islar, M. (2021). Climate politics in green deals: Exposing the political frontiers of the European Green Deal. *Politics and Governance*, *9*(2), 8–16. https://doi.org/10.17645/pag.v9i2.3853

San Martín, W., & Wood, N. (2022). Pluralizing planetary justice beyond the North-South divide: Recentring procedural, epistemic, and recognition-based justice in earth-systems governance. *Environmental Science & Policy*, *128*, 256–263. https://doi.org/10.1016/j.envsci.2021.12.002

Schlosberg, D. (2004). Reconceiving environmental justice: Global movements and political theories. *Environmental Politics*, *13*(3), 517–540. https://doi.org/10.1080/0964401042000229025

Schouten, G., & Hospes, O. (2018). Public and private governance in interaction: Changing interpretations of sovereignty in the field of sustainable palm oil. *Sustainability*, *10*(12), 4811. https://doi.org/10.3390/su10124811

Schunz, S. (2022). The 'European Green Deal' – a paradigm shift? Transformations in the European Union's sustainability meta-discourse. *Political Research Exchange*, *4*(1). https://doi.org/10.1080/2474736X.2022.2085121

Temper, L., Walter, M., Rodriguez, I., Kothari, A., & Turhan, E. (2018). A perspective on radical transformations to sustainability: Resistances, movements and alternatives. *Sustainability Science*, *13*(3), 747–764. https://doi.org/10.1007/s11625-018-0543-8

Thorens, M., Bernaz, N., & Hospes, O. (2025). Advocating for the EU corporate sustainability due diligence directive against the odds: Strategies and legitimation. *JCMS: Journal of Common Market Studies*, *63*(2), 606–623. https://doi.org/10.1111/jcms.13623

Verhaeghe, E. (2023). Recognition on whose terms? Indigenous justice struggles in the EU-Honduran FLEGT voluntary partnership agreement. *Geoforum*, *141*, 103718. https://doi.org/10.1016/j.geoforum.2023.103718

Acknowledgements

The authors gratefully acknowledge the support of the Indonesia Endowment Fund for Education (Lembaga Pengelola Dana Pendidikan), the Ministry of Foreign Affairs, and the Coordinating Ministry for Economic Affairs, the Republic of Indonesia.

3 Rethinking the European Union Green Deal in ASEAN

Decolonizing Climate Action Perspectives for an Equitable Future

Gerald John Cabanilla Guillermo

Introduction

On 15 January 2020, the European Parliament approved the European Union Green Deal (EGD), the European Union's (EU) ambitious roadmap to achieve climate neutrality by 2050 (European Parliament, 2020). As a comprehensive strategy, the EGD sets out to reduce greenhouse gas (GHG) emissions by at least 55% by 2030 compared to 1990 levels and ultimately reach net-zero emissions by mid-century. It promotes clean energy, biodiversity, sustainable mobility, and circular economy principles, aligning with the EU's commitments under the 2016 Paris Agreement (EU in ASEAN, n.d.; United Nations Framework Convention on Climate Change, n.d.). Initially launched just before the global onset of COVID-19, the EGD was repackaged as a dual-purpose economic and climate recovery strategy, backed by the €1.8 trillion NextGenerationEU Recovery Plan (Bongardt & Torres, 2022; European Commission, n.d.-a).

The EGD's central mechanisms include the "Fit for 55 Package," which features reforms such as expanding the EU Emissions Trading System (ETS), establishing a Social Climate Fund, and introducing two controversial instruments: the Carbon Border Adjustment Mechanism (CBAM) and the European Union Deforestation Regulation (EUDR) (European Commission, n.d.-b; European Parliament, 2022). These measures aim to globalize the EU's climate standards by regulating carbon-intensive imports and ensuring commodities are sustainably sourced. For instance, the CBAM imposes a carbon price on imports to prevent carbon leakage, replacing free ETS allowances with import tariffs on goods such as cement and steel (European Commission, 2024; Benson et al., 2023). Meanwhile, the EUDR mandates traceability and due diligence on supply chains for commodities like palm oil, cocoa, and timber, barring market access to non-compliant goods (European Commission, n.d.-c).

While framed as environmentally responsible and legally consistent with World Trade Organization rules, these measures have provoked sharp criticism from trading partners, particularly in the Global South. Southeast Asian nations, many of which are heavily reliant on exports of regulated goods, have expressed concern that such policies may function as non-tariff trade barriers (Teja, 2023; Jayaswal, 2024). Smallholders and small and medium-sized enterprises (SMEs) in Southeast

DOI: 10.4324/9781003783176-4

Asia face disproportionate compliance burdens due to a lack of infrastructure, technical capacity, and financial resources (Ülgen, 2023). As such, what is framed as "green leadership" by the EU may translate into exclusion, marginalization, and reassertion of structural inequalities.

This chapter responds to these critiques by asking: In what ways do the CBAM and EUDR operate as instruments of climate colonialism rather than mere trade protectionism? And how might EU–Association of Southeast Asian Nations (ASEAN) cooperative frameworks help counteract these colonial dynamics? To answer these questions, the chapter adopts a climate colonialism lens, defined here as the contemporary reproduction of geopolitical and economic power asymmetries through environmental regulation. Unlike trade protectionism, which primarily serves to shield domestic industries, climate colonialism critiques the normative and extraterritorial reach of Global North climate governance, especially when imposed without adequate dialogue or capacity support (Savic, 2024; Humphrey, 2023; DeBoom, 2021; Hanaček et al., 2024).

The chapter is structured as follows. First, it situates the concept of climate colonialism in environmental governance literature and explains its relevance to the EU's climate agenda. Second, it examines the CBAM and EUDR as case studies, analyzing how they function in practice and affect Southeast Asian countries' trade position, with a focus on Indonesia and Malaysia. Third, it explores alternative pathways for more equitable climate cooperation between the EU and ASEAN, rooted in mutual recognition and differentiated responsibilities. Lastly, it offers conclusions on how the EU might recalibrate its climate diplomacy to align ambition with equity and climate justice.

Mapping the Climate Colonialism Debate

The concept of climate colonialism has emerged as a critical lens to examine how contemporary climate action, especially as led by the Global North, perpetuates historical power asymmetries, extractivist logics, and systems of dispossession. Drawing from postcolonial and neocolonial theory, climate colonialism can be broadly defined as the imposition of climate agendas from the Global North on countries in the Global South through unequal power relations. This includes policies, technologies, and solutions that fail to consider the historical responsibility of the Global North for the climate crisis, while disproportionately shifting the socio-environmental burdens of mitigation and adaptation onto the Global South.

At the heart of climate colonialism is what Hamouchene (2022) describes as the "extension of colonial relations of plunder and dispossession. . . to the green era." In this formulation, climate colonialism involves the transfer of environmental and social costs that are previously associated with extractivist colonial economies into the realm of renewable energy, green technology, and climate policy. He emphasizes that the current green transition displaces socio-environmental burdens under the guise of sustainability, making "green" not synonymous with just or equitable. Similarly, dominant focus on carbon metrics and emissions reductions conceals broader ecological and justice-based concerns, particularly when climate mitigation strategies are pursued through "green recovery measures," reframing the narrative as recovery rather than emphasizing green megaprojects and the increase in consumption that goes with such a recovery (Valdivieso, 2012, as cited in Jerez et al., 2021). As a result, the Global South's traditional role as a raw material provider for the Global North's energy transition is maintained and reinforced. This phenomenon, termed "green extractivism" (Dunlap, 2017), is highlighted in the Global North's pursuit of "zero-carbon lifestyles," which increasingly depends on the ecological sacrifice zones of the Global South, resulting in new forms of resource dependency and displacement of environmental harms (Gobel, 2013, as cited in Jerez et al., 2021).

Building on these critiques, Sovacool et al. (2020) introduce the concept of the "decarbonisation divide" to describe the structural disparities in the ability of different regions to decarbonize equitably. While the Global North reaps the benefits of cleaner air and more sustainable production systems, these gains are frequently achieved by displacing the environmental and social costs onto the Global South. This divide is multifaceted. First, at the epistemic level, decarbonization strategies often prioritize technological innovation and diffusion, yet overlook the uneven and harmful effects embedded across global value chains, particularly those that burden the Global South. In addition, geographically, clean technologies are predominantly deployed in wealthier economies such as those in East Asia, Europe, and North America, whereas the extraction of raw materials, pollution, and toxic waste are concentrated in economically poorer regions, including many parts of Africa, Southeast Asia, and Latin America. Moreover, the divide is also environmental: while the Global North experiences ecological gains, the Global South is left to grapple with deforestation, water contamination, and land degradation associated with extractive industries and industrial agriculture. Most critically, Sovacool et al. (2020) underscore the developmental dimension of this divide, wherein Global South countries are often locked into asymmetrical economic relationships with wealthier states or multinational corporations. These relationships promise investment and development in the short term but ultimately reinforce cycles of dependency, inequality, and structural disadvantage. As such, the global push for decarbonization not only reproduces old hierarchies under new green imperatives but also risks marginalizing the very regions most vulnerable to the climate crisis and least responsible for its origins.

From a geopolitical standpoint, scholars such as Táíwò (2019) and Sultana (2022) conceptualize climate colonialism as a mode of deepened domination wherein climate mitigation policies, such as carbon offsetting, afforestation, and reforestation, are formulated in the Global North and exported to the Global South in ways that undermine local sovereignty, displace communities, and privilege foreign profit over local well-being. These interventions, though framed as necessary for addressing the climate crisis, often reproduce colonial patterns of dispossession and surveillance. Lee (2023) documents how such practices have led to human rights abuses in Africa, Latin America, and Southeast Asia, where communities are subjected to projects that disrupt traditional land use without meaningful consultation or consent.

This dynamic is not confined to international relations alone but can also manifest within countries. Normann (2020) describes such processes as "green colonialism," illustrating how renewable energy initiatives, like wind farm developments in Norway, have intensified the dispossession of Indigenous lands, in this case, the Southern Saami. More broadly, climate colonialism exposes the asymmetry wherein those least responsible for global warming, including Indigenous peoples, ethnic minorities, and impoverished populations, bear the greatest burden of its impacts. Indeed, climate colonialism manifests in melting glaciers, rising sea levels, and intensifying storms, which disproportionately affect these marginalized groups, further entrenching global and local inequalities under the guise of environmental progress (Landrum & Holland, 2020; Naykanchina, 2012, as cited in Hanaček et al., 2024).

Lewis (2023) offers a dual perspective: first, situating the environmental emergency as a legacy of colonialism, given that the Global North is responsible for roughly 92% of historical carbon emissions; and second, understanding climate colonialism as the continued exploitation of Global South resources to fuel the North's climate agenda. Bandera (2024) further underscores this asymmetry, arguing that climate colonialism operates not only through resource extraction but also through the power of prescription, where the Global North defines the terms of acceptable climate governance, often unilaterally, and in ways that benefit itself economically. Policies such as strict deforestation-free certification standards or carbon pricing systems may appear environmentally sound, yet they disproportionately disadvantage producers in developing countries who lack the infrastructure, institutional capacity, or capital to comply. As such, these mechanisms function as instruments of regulatory domination, cloaked in the moral language of climate responsibility.

As a result, climate colonialism is increasingly understood as a form of neocolonial control in which developed nations impose environmental standards and policies without accounting for the differentiated capacities, needs, and historical responsibilities of developing countries. This dynamic reflects broader patterns of geopolitical inequality and challenges the legitimacy of Global North-led climate governance structures that marginalize Global South voices and overlook historical injustices. When climate action is pursued without a commitment to equity and justice, it risks reproducing colonial power imbalances under the guise of environmentalism. As Bhambra and Newell (2022) argue, climate colonialism is "more than a metaphor." Rather, it is a material expression of power, shaped by control over land, resources, and knowledge. This is evident in the export of Western environmental solutions that disregard local contexts, such as large-scale carbon offset plantations in the Global South that displace and disenfranchise local communities.

In addition, climate colonialism is not merely about the unequal exposure of the Global South to the adverse impacts of climate change, but also about the structural reproduction of inequality and exploitation through the mechanisms and discourse of climate action. It differs from trade or regulatory protectionism in its deeper historical and epistemological foundations. While protectionist policies are typically focused on defending domestic industries from foreign competition, often through tariffs, quotas, subsidies, or standards, climate colonialism implicates broader and more enduring power asymmetries rooted in centuries of colonial extraction and dispossession. As defined by Abboushi (2010), protectionism refers to a set of government trade policies designed to support domestic producers, usually by increasing the cost of imported goods, reducing production costs for domestic firms, or restricting foreign competitors' access to the domestic market. Although protectionist measures may be controversial, they are typically framed in the technocratic language of economic efficiency, national interest, or market regulation and do not necessarily claim to serve global public goods such as climate justice.

By contrast, climate colonialism unveils how climate mitigation strategies, especially when unilaterally imposed by the Global North, can operate as vehicles of control, extraction, and exclusion under the guise of planetary stewardship. What distinguishes it is its reliance on historical and epistemic asymmetries, that is, the idea that dominant climate policies and paradigms are shaped by Global North experiences, values, and priorities, while marginalizing or subjugating Global South knowledges, development needs, and socio-political contexts. Climate colonialism critiques the instrumentalization of climate action as a new frontier of dominance, wherein environmental regulations such as carbon pricing or deforestation-free certifications are exported to the Global South without meaningful consultation or support, thereby perpetuating economic dependency and reinforcing geopolitical hierarchies. It draws attention not just to what is being regulated, but how and by whom, exposing how mechanisms intended for the global good may instead re-entrench global injustice. In short, while protectionism is primarily economic and inward-looking, climate colonialism is political, historical, and transnational, questioning the legitimacy of imposing "universal" standards in a deeply unequal world. It demands not merely fairer trade rules or technical adjustments, but a rethinking of the power relations embedded in global climate governance, including who sets the agenda, who bears the costs, and who benefits from the so-called green transition.

However, the line between climate colonialism and trade protectionism has become increasingly blurred. Although analytically distinct, the operational overlap between the two is growing, particularly as climate policies are embedded within international trade regimes. As the Economist Intelligence Unit (2023) observes, the rise of climate-oriented regulations has fueled a new wave of trade protectionism, where environmental goals are deployed to justify trade barriers that disproportionately burden developing economies. For example, subsidy-driven industrial policies for renewable energy technologies in advanced economies may distort markets, while carbon border adjustments and product standards risk becoming de facto barriers to trade. Lottici et al. (2014) refer to this phenomenon as "green trade protectionism," wherein environmental objectives are mobilized to mask protectionist intent, allowing industrialized countries to preserve competitive advantages while enjoying broader social legitimacy. They argue that such policies now manifest in key areas like green growth, climate mitigation, and the liberalization of environmental goods and services. In this way, climate colonialism and trade protectionism converge in practice, as climate norms become instruments for asserting economic and political dominance under a green guise. Therefore, this convergence demands a more critical interrogation of how environmental imperatives are operationalized within global governance and whose interests are served or sacrificed in the process.

In addition, financial and technical aid, while often framed as benevolent tools for supporting climate mitigation and adaptation, can in practice function as instruments of neocolonial control. Donor-driven climate finance frequently comes with conditions that steer recipient countries towards donor-defined priorities, limiting policy autonomy and reinforcing dependency. Umar (2024) argues that the international climate finance regime, though ostensibly designed to support vulnerable nations, imposes debt-based financing and restrictive conditions that burden already struggling economies. These requirements often compel developing countries to scale back fossil fuel-based development, which is critical to their economic growth, without providing viable alternatives, thereby entrenching structural inequalities. Malherbe and Oladejo (2024) similarly assert that the structure of climate aid reflects "climate aid colonialism," as it continues to be funneled through traditional aid channels under neoliberal conditions, subordinating the Global South's development agendas to the market-oriented logic of donor nations. Moreover, Ciplet et al. (2022) demonstrate how climate finance often reinforces existing spatial hierarchies within the global system, mirroring the core-periphery dependencies long critiqued by world-systems theory. Indeed, these critiques highlight that without structural reform, climate finance risks reproducing the very global inequalities it purports to address.

Methodology

This chapter adopts a qualitative interpretive methodology rooted in critical legal and postcolonial inquiry. It draws on documentary analysis of primary and secondary sources to examine how the EU's climate legislation, specifically the EGD, the CBAM, and the EUDR, is received and interpreted by Southeast Asian stakeholders. The data includes EU legal texts, official communications, regulatory documents, ASEAN government statements, position papers from affected states, industry responses, and civil society commentaries. Academic literature, policy reports, and media coverage were selected based on their relevance to ongoing debates on climate governance, environmental justice, and trade equity. Particular attention was given to ASEAN responses due to the region's economic interdependence with the EU and its centrality in current critiques of regulatory extraterritoriality.

In analyzing these materials, the study employs a critical theoretical lens informed by postcolonial and critical development theory. The concept of climate colonialism is used to interrogate how well-meaning climate policies may replicate historical hierarchies, impose Northern standards, and shape global norms in exclusionary ways. Drawing from recent scholarship (e.g., Dunlap & Laratte, 2022; Vela Almeida et al., 2023; Bassey et al., 2023), the analysis considers how environmental regulations such as the CBAM and EUDR may function as instruments of regulatory imperialism or green extractivism. These lenses are applied to unpack the discursive, legal, and material implications of EU climate policy for ASEAN states, especially where burdens are transferred without proportionate consultation or support. Ultimately, the chapter examines how these climate instruments may serve not only to govern emissions but to structure global environmental governance along historically unequal lines, reinforcing rather than redressing colonial legacies.

Climate Colonialism in EU Environmental Governance

The EU's climate policies, particularly the EGD, have increasingly been scrutinized through the lens of climate colonialism (Douo, 2021; Bassey et al., 2023). While the EGD is often framed as a progressive blueprint for achieving climate neutrality and ecological sustainability, a growing body of critical scholarship argues that it reproduces entrenched colonial logics under the guise of environmental responsibility. In this context, climate colonialism is not limited to historical emissions or differential exposure to climate risks, but it also refers to the contemporary reproduction of power asymmetries through climate mitigation mechanisms that extend geopolitical, economic, and epistemic control over the Global South. Rather than facilitating an equitable global transition, the EGD has been critiqued for operating within a necropolitical framework; that is, policies ostensibly aimed at climate protection determine which communities thrive under green development and which are rendered expendable (DeBoom, 2021; Hanaček et al., 2024). By setting stringent sustainability standards and exporting its regulatory regime via external trade and environmental rules such as the CBAM and EUDR, the EU consolidates its normative dominance while shifting the burden of decarbonization onto regions with less economic and technological capacity.

Scholars argue that far from fostering systemic ecological transformation, the EGD reinforces global hierarchies through infrastructural colonization, intensified extraction, and the expansion of market-based energy systems (Dunlap & Laratte, 2022). By promoting green growth without addressing the structural necessity of degrowth (Mastini et al., 2021), the EGD legitimizes widespread socio-ecological destruction. The development of so-called clean infrastructures, such as wind farms, high-voltage power lines, and energy exchange markets, depends on extractive practices that displace communities, destroy ecosystems, and perpetuate colonial patterns of resource exploitation. In this way, the EGD exemplifies a necropolitical economy, cloaked in a sustainability narrative, that continues to impose multidimensional extractivism (Dunlap & Laratte, 2022). This contradiction is highlighted by Vela Almeida et al. (2023) when they characterized the EGD as a continuation of the EU's empire-building under a green banner. According to their analysis, the EGD constitutes a form of "green imperialism" that not only opens new markets for European corporations but also reinscribes extractive and racialized power relations through the globalization of environmental governance. The discursive framing of the EU as a global climate leader legitimizes interventions in non-European territories, often under conditions that marginalize local knowledge, suppress indigenous sovereignty, and reinforce dependency on European technologies and norms. As they argue, such policies leave little room for anti-colonial ecologies or alternative visions of sustainability beyond the technocratic, growth-oriented paradigm advanced by the EU. For instance, Claar (2022) explained how the EGD preserves the asymmetric relationship between Africa and the EU, marked by a continuity of dependency.

Therefore, while the EGD signals a bold commitment to climate action, its underlying logic, which is rooted in extractivism, technocracy, and market expansion, risks perpetuating the very inequalities that the climate crisis demands we dismantle. Thus, the EGD stands as a paradigmatic case of how climate policy, when decoupled from historical justice and democratic participation, can function as a tool of climate colonialism rather than a framework for global ecological equity.

While the CBAM is formally intended to prevent carbon leakage and promote global decarbonization, it has drawn significant criticism for functioning as a mechanism of climate colonialism. First, while aiming to incentivize foreign countries to transition to less carbon-intensive production, the CBAM unilaterally extends the EU's carbon accounting standards to foreign producers, effectively exporting EU environmental norms without sufficient consideration of the disparate technical and administrative capacities of trading partners, leading to trade access limitations (Benson et al., 2023). By requiring non-EU producers to purchase carbon certificates or prove equivalent compliance, the mechanism increases production costs for exporters in developing countries, many of whom need more robust climate regulations or administrative systems to meet these standards. Exporters who are unable to provide information regarding GHG emissions may risk losing their business to competitors with lower-emission products (Szucko, 2024). This norm imposition disproportionately affects Southeast Asian exporters, particularly small producers in countries that often lack the tools, infrastructure, or institutional support to comply with such exacting carbon tracking requirements. One of the concerns about the CBAM is that it may "disproportionately harm developing countries" by establishing compliance burdens that exceed local capacities, while future expansion of the mechanism's scope threatens to deepen these inequities (Magacho et al., 2023).

Second, the CBAM reinforces global power asymmetries by replicating a dual standard that privileges the Global North. While EU producers have historically benefited from free emissions allowances under the ETS, exporters from the Global South are required to either purchase carbon certificates or prove the existence of equivalent carbon pricing mechanisms in their home countries. This disparity not only reflects the EU's historical advantage in shaping global environmental norms but also institutionalizes a form of environmental gatekeeping, wherein access to EU markets is contingent upon compliance with standards designed around Global North capacities. Martinus and Laopirun (2023) underscore how such mechanisms function as non-tariff barriers that disproportionately penalize developing countries, many of which lack the financial resources and technological infrastructure to transition to lower-carbon production. Consequently, the CBAM deepens the "decarbonization divide," enabling wealthier nations to reap the benefits of clean transitions while burdening less-resourced economies with compliance costs they are structurally unequipped to meet.

Finally, while the EU has expressed a willingness to provide transitional financial and technical support to affected partners, the scope, timing, and governance of such assistance remain unclear. In the absence of concrete, co-designed, and inclusive mechanisms, such conditional aid risks reinforcing rather than redressing long-standing patterns of dependency. The CBAM could ultimately undermine investments in green transitions by exacerbating job losses and reducing domestic revenue mobilization in developing countries (Putaturo, n.d., as cited in Schauenberg, 2022). The lack of comprehensive financial support for external stakeholders reinforces the perception of environmental imperialism, where the EU imposes its climate agenda without adequately addressing the socio-economic capacities of its global partners.

This is further compounded by the CBAM's failure to distinguish among countries with varying levels of development. The mechanism does not differentiate between developed, middle-income, and least-developed countries in terms of their ability to monitor and report GHG, thus imposing uniform compliance expectations that ignore asymmetrical capacities (Szucko, 2024). In the Southeast Asian context, the CBAM's initial scope targets key exports such as cement and aluminum, which collectively accounted for 10% of total exports of covered goods to the EU between 2019 and 2022 (Teja, 2023). As a result, this could result in a projected 0.12% decline in ASEAN's regional gross domestic product (GDP) by 2030. More worryingly, if the CBAM expands to cover additional products and indirect emissions, the economic damage could intensify, potentially slashing ASEAN exports to the EU by 10% and reducing the region's GDP by as much as 0.2% by 2033 (Hinojales, n.d., as cited in Teja, 2023). As such, the CBAM reflects how climate policy can reproduce structural inequalities under the guise of environmental leadership. By unilaterally imposing EU norms without adequate differentiation or support, it risks entrenching a "decarbonization divide" that burdens Southeast Asian exporters, particularly small producers, with compliance costs they are ill-equipped to meet. This dynamic illustrates the core of climate colonialism, that is, exporting responsibility without sharing power.

Similarly, the EUDR draws accusations of climate colonialism and regulatory protectionism, particularly from countries with large agricultural sectors tied to exports (Suroyo et al., 2023). First, its selective scope disproportionately targets commodities sourced from tropical regions, such as palm oil, timber, and cocoa, while applying no equivalent scrutiny to similar products originating within the EU. This asymmetric focus, as Szucko (2024) notes, reproduces colonial patterns of Global South resource extraction, where environmental burdens are placed on the Global South, while Global North economies retain regulatory privilege. By constructing deforestation as a problem of the tropics, the regulation externalizes environmental responsibility and reinforces a North-to-South hierarchy of ecological governance.

Second, the compliance burden imposed by the EUDR is especially severe for smallholder producers in countries like Indonesia and Malaysia, where agricultural exports play a central role in local economies. These smallholder farmers often lack formal land titles, digital traceability systems, or the financial resources necessary to meet stringent due diligence requirements (Jong, 2025). While the EUDR is justified as stopping global deforestation, it risks de facto privileging the EU and large commercial producers who can absorb compliance costs at the expense of small Southeast Asian farmers. As Cohen (2024) explains, such conditions risk excluding independent producers from global supply chains, thereby undermining local sovereignty and reinforcing Global North environmental standards as global defaults. Additionally, demanding geolocation data from Indonesian farmers under the EUDR while strict privacy laws apply in Europe and without comparable demands on EU firms is an example of ignoring Global South stakeholders' sovereignty and reinforcement of the legacy of hierarchical control. While the EUDR is framed as a step towards sustainable trade, its implementation reveals a deeper colonial logic, one in which environmental goals are pursued at the expense of development equity, effectively forcing compliance without meaningful consultation or reciprocal responsibility.

Importantly, this analysis does not dismiss the EU's stated climate objectives or the legitimacy of its environmental commitments. Instruments like the CBAM and EUDR are formally framed as tools to meet global climate goals, notably the targets set out in the Paris Agreement. The EU has emphasized that such measures are intended to prevent carbon leakage, halt global deforestation, and create a level playing field for climate-conscious producers. For instance, the EU has also expressed willingness to engage in dialogue and extend technical support, particularly in response to concerns raised by ASEAN Member States (AMS) (Jong, 2025), signaling openness to clarify EUDR requirements and provide capacity-building support to smallholder producers in Indonesia.

Nevertheless, while these aims are normatively laudable, their implementation raises urgent questions of equity, legitimacy, and power. As this chapter has argued, the CBAM and EUDR can function not merely as regulatory instruments but as mechanisms of climate colonialism, through unilaterally exporting EU standards and compliance obligations without sufficient attention to local capacities, histories, or voices. While protectionism may seek to secure economic advantage through trade barriers, climate colonialism goes further: it invokes normative authority, historical responsibility, and global environmental leadership to justify asymmetrical enforcement and external governance. The result is not simply market distortion, but the imposition of new hierarchies under the guise of sustainability. Particularly in Southeast Asia, these dynamics materialize as increased compliance costs, exclusion from high-value markets, and diminished sovereignty over environmental governance. The absence of tailored support mechanisms, inclusive rule-making, and recognition of local contexts exacerbates these challenges. Hence, the CBAM and EUDR reflect a deeper tension in global climate governance: who sets the rules, who bears the costs, and who benefits from the green transition.

Redesigning EU–ASEAN Climate Partnerships

In light of the critiques of the EGD, CBAM, and EUDR as mechanisms of climate colonialism, it becomes imperative to rethink the architecture of EU–ASEAN relations in the domain of climate governance. Instead of replicating North–South hierarchies through normative imposition and uneven regulatory enforcement, both regions must move towards a partnership grounded in mutual respect, co-creation, and equitable climate responsibility.

To address concerns about the EGD's climate colonialist dimensions, the EU must move beyond a prescriptive model of environmental governance and instead foster frameworks that facilitate equitable trade and climate investment. One promising avenue is the Green Team Europe Initiative, launched during the Third ASEAN–EU Dialogue on Sustainable Development in 2021. This initiative outlines a shared vision for a "greener and more sustainable future" (EU in ASEAN, n.d.) and pledges support across priority areas such as clean energy, circular economy, sustainable food systems, and smart cities. Among its contributions is €783 million allocated for the ASEAN Catalytic Green Finance Facility, funding for green city development, youth-oriented environmental education, and support for ASEAN businesses to engage in the green transition (European Union, n.d.).

These efforts can be reinforced by aligning with other EU–ASEAN mechanisms, particularly the Sustainable Connectivity Package (SCOPE), adopted in April 2023. Within SCOPE, the SCOPE-Trade programme aims to enhance institutional capacities for sustainable value chains and resilient trade (EU in ASEAN, 2024a). Such a platform could be mobilized to assist AMS' governments and independent producers in adjusting to the regulatory expectations of the EGD, including the CBAM and EUDR. Notably, farmers' associations and non-governmental organizations (NGOs) in ASEAN have expressed support for due diligence and traceability mechanisms like the EUDR, provided they receive financial and technical assistance to meet the requirements (Cohen, 2024). Similarly, the SCOPE-Higher Education (SCOPE-HE) initiative facilitates green transition research and academic exchange, which can be leveraged to build institutional and human capacity for localizing the EGD's objectives without reinforcing dependency (EU in ASEAN, 2024b).

In parallel, the Enhanced Regional EU–ASEAN Dialogue Instrument (E-READI) fosters mutual learning and policy dialogue. It supports the implementation of the ASEAN Community Blueprints and contributes to regional integration by drawing from the EU's experience through establishing contacts, strengthening networks, conducting studies, organizing seminars, workshops, and meetings, and facilitating knowledge exchange and participation (EU in ASEAN, 2024a). The EU can use E-READI's existing thematic dialogues on SDG Partnerships on Dialogue on Carbon Neutrality in Agriculture and under the Environment and Climate Change on Carbon Pricing Instruments in ASEAN to collaboratively define standards and implementation pathways. This transforms EGD-related engagement from a unilateral process into a dialogic one. In this way, CBAM and EUDR are no longer mere instruments of norm export, but potential outcomes of regionally coordinated consensus.

The ASEAN–EU Strategic Partnership (2023–2027) provides a formal vehicle for advancing such collaboration. Built upon earlier Plans of Action, this Partnership identifies food security, sustainable agriculture and forestry, and environmental cooperation as focal areas. Its existing commitment to establishing a Joint Working Group on Palm Oil (ASEAN, 2022) could serve as a template for addressing

CBAM and EUDR through joint ASEAN–EU implementation forums. However, current commitments remain largely aspirational and often fail to directly address the mechanisms of climate regulation and trade. Strengthening these forums by expanding their mandates to include discussions on CBAM implementation assistance or EUDR exemptions for smallholders would ensure that Southeast Asia's voice is meaningfully included in regulatory processes that deeply affect its economies. In addition, the Regional–ASEAN Forest Governance Support Programme 2020–2023, which focused on sustainable timber production and trade (EU in ASEAN, 2022), can be expanded or replicated for broader commodities affected by the EUDR. Such programmes could ensure that trade measures reflect not only EU climate goals but also Southeast Asian development realities.

Beyond reforming EU-driven programmes, Southeast Asia must proactively assert its own vision for climate governance. The ASEAN Community Vision 2045 offers a pivotal opportunity to institutionalize regional priorities centered on climate justice, economic diversification, and inclusive sustainability. The recent adoption of the ASEAN Strategy for Carbon Neutrality by ASEAN Economic Ministers (ASEAN, 2023) marks a significant step in this direction, laying the groundwork for a regionally tailored approach to carbon neutrality. This strategy, which aligns with AMS' contributions under the Paris Agreement, emphasizes cooperation with global partners to advance an inclusive and strategic green transition, which also capitalizes on emerging economic and labour opportunities. Central to the strategy are harmonized Monitoring, Reporting, and Verification (MRV) systems and interoperable carbon markets, which together can form the foundation for an ASEAN-wide "Green Deal." Such a deal would not only strengthen regional coordination but also enhance ASEAN's ability to negotiate with external partners on equal footing, ensuring that climate alignment supports rather than undermines economic inclusion and regional sovereignty.

Elder et al. (2025) recommend four key negotiation points for ASEAN: (i) mutual recognition of AMS' domestic carbon pricing to offset CBAM adjustments; (ii) simplification of reporting requirements; (iii) EU support for ASEAN's MRV and CBAM systems; and (iv) deeper integration into international platforms like the Climate Club, where Southeast Asia can shape emerging global standards. With Indonesia, Singapore, and Thailand already participating in the Climate Club, Southeast Asia has a strategic opening to amplify its influence and protect its economic interests.

Crucially, Southeast Asia's capacity to localize and implement its sustainability vision depends on financial autonomy and decolonial resourcing. The experience of Indigenous-led climate funds, such as the Mesoamerican Territorial Fund (Goering, 2024), demonstrates how direct, flexible, and community-driven finance can bypass bureaucratic bottlenecks and empower local actors. These models offer a compelling alternative to traditional multilateral funding channels, which often impose rigid documentation requirements and fail to reach frontline communities. The EU should explore partnerships with such funds and replicate their governance models for Southeast Asian-based indigenous and local organizations. Additionally, regional advocacy for climate reparations and South–South solidarity can counterbalance Northern dominance (Malherbe & Oladejo, 2024). These frameworks reimagine climate finance not as conditional aid but as restitution for historical emissions and structural exclusion. By embedding these principles into Southeast Asia's strategic climate engagements, the region can move from reactive compliance towards proactive agenda-setting.

Lessons for Equitable Green Transitions

The intensifying critiques of climate colonialism compel a fundamental rethinking, not only of specific instruments like the EGD, CBAM, and EUDR, but of the very architecture of global climate governance. At stake is not simply the efficacy of emissions reduction policies, but the legitimacy of the values, histories, and power structures that underpin them. As Bhambra and Newell (2022) argue, confronting climate change requires more than just paying for present-day losses and damages; it demands reckoning with the colonial and extractive systems that enabled the Global North to accumulate wealth through high-emission development. These systems, which are built on the theft of land, labour, and resources, continue to shape the global economy, and their legacies are far from the past.

While the EGD is often hailed as a transformative framework for climate neutrality, this chapter has shown how its implementation risks reproducing global hierarchies under a green banner. Mechanisms like the CBAM and EUDR, though aimed at fostering decarbonization and forest protection, can operate as tools of normative imposition and market exclusion when applied without adequate differentiation or support for developing partners. In Southeast Asia, particularly in AMS, these mechanisms burden small producers with compliance costs they are structurally ill-equipped to bear, thus reinforcing the "decarbonization divide."

To ensure that the EGD does not become a vehicle for climate colonialism or regulatory protectionism, the EU must embrace a genuinely cooperative approach that acknowledges its historical responsibility and redistributes climate governance. This includes co-designing policies with affected partners, tailoring standards to diverse capacities, and investing in the infrastructures of compliance and resilience. Fortunately, the institutional foundations for such a shift already exist. Frameworks like the EU–ASEAN Green Initiative, SCOPE, and E-READI offer pathways for joint climate action through capacity-building, knowledge exchange, and inclusive economic cooperation. If reformed and expanded through ASEAN-led priority setting and transparent mechanisms, these initiatives could operationalize a fairer model of green transition.

At the same time, Southeast Asia must assert its agency. The region's evolving climate frameworks, such as the ASEAN Strategy for Carbon Neutrality and the ASEAN Community Vision 2045, reflect a growing readiness to shape its own development trajectory. By formulating an ASEAN Green Deal, the bloc can articulate a regional climate agenda grounded in local needs, indigenous knowledge, and inclusive growth. This would not only rebalance the terms of engagement with the EU but also position Southeast Asia as a leader in defining just and context-sensitive pathways to sustainability.

Ultimately, climate action must not replicate the inequities it seeks to resolve. If the EU and Southeast Asia are to become equitable partners in the green transition, they must move beyond normative export and towards co-production of ideas, policies, and futures. Without a shift towards genuinely inclusive and historically grounded cooperation, well-intentioned climate policies risk entrenching the very injustices they aim to undo. But with mutual recognition, shared leadership, and a commitment to justice, both regions can help shape a more equitable and sustainable global order.

Reference List

Abboushi, S. (2010). Trade protectionism: Reasons and outcomes. *Competitiveness Review*, *20*(5), 384–394. https://doi.org/10.1108/10595421011080760

ASEAN. (2022). *Plan of action to implement the ASEAN-EU strategic partnership (2023–2027)*. https://asean.org/wp-content/uploads/2022/08/ASEAN-EU-Plan-of-Action-2023-2027-FINAL.pdf

ASEAN. (2023, August 19). *ASEAN charts course for a sustainable future with ambitious ASEAN strategy for carbon neutrality* [Press release]. https://asean.org/asean-charts-course-for-a-sustainable-future-with-ambitious-asean-strategy-for-carbon-neutrality/

Bandera, G. (2024, July 21). How climate colonialism affects the Global South. *FairPlanet*. www.fairplanet.org/story/how-climate-colonialism-affects-the-global-south/

Bassey, N., Bringel, B., Buitrago, L., Kumar, M., Naidu, K., Ramasar, V., & Svampa, M. (2023, July 11). Beware Europe's new green colonialism. *Rosa Luxemburg Stiftung*. www.rosalux.de/en/news/id/50690/beware-europes-new-green-colonialism

Benson, E., Majkut, J., Reinsch, W. A., & Steinberg, F. (2023). *Analyzing the European Union's carbon border adjustment mechanism*. Center for Strategic and International Studies. www.csis.org/analysis/analyzing-european-unions-carbon-border-adjustment-mechanism

Bhambra, G. K., & Newell, P. (2022). More than a metaphor: 'Climate colonialism' in perspective. *Global Social Challenges Journal*, *2*(3), 179–187. https://doi.org/10.1332/EIEM6688

Bongardt, A., & Torres, F. (2022). The European Green Deal: More than an exit strategy to the pandemic crisis. *JCMS: Journal of Common Market Studies*, *60*(1), 170–185. https://doi.org/10.1111/jcms.13264

Ciplet, D., Falzon, D., Uri, I., Robinson, S., Weikmans, R., & Roberts, J. T. (2022). The unequal geographies of climate finance. *Political Geography*, *99*, 102769. https://doi.org/10.1016/j.polgeo.2022.102769

Claar, S. (2022). Green colonialism in the European Green Deal. *Culture, Practice & Europeanization*, *7*(2), 262–274. https://doi.org/10.5771/2566-7742-2022-2-262

Cohen, P. (2024, September 19). Backlash erupts over Europe's anti-deforestation law. *The New York Times*. www.nytimes.com/2024/09/19/business/european-union-deforestation.html

DeBoom, M. J. (2021). Climate necropolitics. *Annals of the American Association of Geographers*, *111*(3), 900–912. https://doi.org/10.1080/24694452.2020.1843995

Douo, M. (2021, June 23). Climate colonialism and the EU's Green Deal. *Al Jazeera*. www.aljazeera.com/opinions/2021/6/23/the-eus-green-deal-could-propagate-climate-colonialism

Dunlap, A. (2017). The 'solution' is now the 'problem'. *The International Journal of Human Rights*, *22*(4), 550–573. https://doi.org/10.1080/13642987.2017.1397633

Dunlap, A., & Laratte, L. (2022). European Green Deal necropolitics. *Political Geography*, *97*, 102640. https://doi.org/10.1016/j.polgeo.2022.102640

Economist Intelligence Unit. (2023). *Climate ambitions threaten a new wave of trade protectionism*. www.eiu.com/n/climate-ambitions-threaten-a-new-wave-of-trade-protectionism/

Elder, M., Hopkinson, S., Zhou, X., Arino, Y., & Matsushita, K. (2025). *Implications of the EU's carbon border adjustment mechanism (CBAM) for ASEAN*. Institute for Global Environmental Strategies. www.iges.or.jp/en/pub/asean-cbam-implications/en

EU in ASEAN. (2022, November 8). *FLEGT Asia: Regional-ASEAN forest governance support programme*. www.eeas.europa.eu/delegations/association-southeast-asian-nations-asean/flegt-asia-regional-asean-forest-governance-support-programme_en

EU in ASEAN. (2024a, May 7). *EU-ASEAN blue book 2024–2025*. https://euinasean.eu/wp-content/uploads/2023/10/Blue-Book-EU-ASEAN-2023-Content-REV-14d.pdf

EU in ASEAN. (2024b, October 7). *EU-ASEAN sustainable connectivity package – higher education programme (SCOPE-HE)*. www.eeas.europa.eu/delegations/association-southeast-asian-nations-asean/eu-asean-sustainable-connectivity-package-higher-education-programme-scope-he_en?s=47

EU in ASEAN. (n.d.). *Green growth and the environment*. https://euinasean.eu/cooperation/green-growth-and-the-environment/

European Commission. (2024, November 4). *Carbon border adjustment mechanism*. https://taxation-customs.ec.europa.eu/carbon-border-adjustment-mechanism_en

European Commission. (n.d.-a). *The European Green Deal*. https://commission.europa.eu/strategy-and-policy/priorities-2019-2024/european-green-deal_en

European Commission. (n.d.-b). *Delivering the European Green Deal*. https://commission.europa.eu/strategy-and-policy/priorities-2019-2024/european-green-deal/delivering-european-green-deal_en

European Commission. (n.d.-c). *Regulation on deforestation-free products*. https://environment.ec.europa.eu/topics/forests/deforestation/regulation-deforestation-free-products_en

European Parliament. (2020, January 15). *Parliament supports European Green Deal and pushes for even higher ambitions*. www.europarl.europa.eu/news/en/press-room/20200109IPR69902/parliament-supports-european-green-deal-and-pushes-for-even-higher-ambitions

European Parliament. (2022, June 22). *Green Deal: Key to a climate-neutral and sustainable EU*. www.europarl.europa.eu/topics/en/article/20200618STO81513/green-deal-key-to-a-climate-neutral-and-sustainable-eu#the-fit-for-55-package-to-achieve-the-green-deal-objectives-7

European Union. (n.d.). *Green initiative TEI in partnership with ASEAN/South-East Asia*. https://capacity4dev.europa.eu/resources/team-europe-tracker/partner-countries/middle-east-asia-and-pacific/green-initiative-tei-partnership-aseansouth-east-asia_en

Goering, L. (2024, April 17). As donors dither, Indigenous funds seek to decolonise green finance. *Climate Change News*. www.climatechangenews.com/2024/04/17/as-donors-dither-indigenous-funds-seek-to-decolonise-green-finance/

Hamouchene, H. (2022, October 14). *The energy transition in North Africa: Neocolonialism again!* Transnational Institute. www.tni.org/en/article/the-energy-transition-in-north-africa

Hanaček, K., Kröger, M., & Martinez-Alier, J. (2024). Green and climate colonialities. *Journal of Political Ecology*, *31*(1), 538–566. https://doi.org/10.2458/jpe.5512

Humphrey, C. (2023, September 5). Can the European Green Deal be a good deal for ASEAN? *FULCRUM*. https://fulcrum.sg/aseanfocus/can-the-european-green-deal-be-a-good-deal-for-asean/

Jayaswal, R. (2024, October 10). FM terms EU's carbon tax as 'trade barrier'. *Hindustan Times*. www.hindustantimes.com/business/fm-terms-eu-s-carbon-tax-as-trade-barrier-101728501478443.html

Jerez, B., Garcés, I., & Torres, R. (2021). Lithium extractivism and water injustices in the Salar de Atacama, Chile. *Political Geography*, *87*, 102382. https://doi.org/10.1016/j.polgeo.2021.102382

Jong, H. N. (2025, April 17). Indonesia raises concerns over EU deforestation law's impact on smallholders. *Mongabay*. https://news.mongabay.com/2025/04/indonesia-raises-concerns-over-eu-deforestation-laws-impact-on-smallholders/

Lee, C. (2023). Understanding climate colonialism. *FairPlanet*. www.fairplanet.org/story/understanding-climate-colonialism/

Lewis, A. (2023, June 14). What is climate colonialism? *Global Citizen*. www.globalcitizen.org/en/content/what-is-climate-colonialism-explain-climate-change/

Lottici, M. V., Galperín, C., & Hoppstock, J. (2014). "Green trade protectionism". *Chinese Journal of Urban and Environmental Studies*, *2*(2), 1450016. https://doi.org/10.1142/S234574811450016X

Magacho, G., Espagne, E., & Godin, A. (2023). Impacts of the CBAM on EU trade partners. *Climate Policy*. https://doi.org/10.1080/14693062.2023.2200758

Malherbe, N., & Oladejo, A. O. (2024). Against climate aid colonialism. *Africa Spectrum*, *60*(1), 84–105. https://doi.org/10.1177/00020397241285040

Martinus, M., & Laopirun, K. (2023). *The EU's carbon border adjustment mechanism (CBAM)*. ISEAS – Yusof Ishak Institute. www.iseas.edu.sg/wp-content/uploads/2022/11/TRS1_23.pdf

Mastini, R., Kallis, G., & Hickel, J. (2021). A Green New Deal without growth? *Ecological Economics*, *179*, 106832. https://doi.org/10.1016/j.ecolecon.2020.106832

Normann, S. (2020). Green colonialism in the Nordic context. *Journal of Community Psychology*, *49*(1), 77–94. https://doi.org/10.1002/jcop.22422

Savic, B. (2024, July 25). EU deforestation law may push Southeast Asia toward China. *GIS Reports*. www.gisreportsonline.com/r/eu-deforestation-law/

Schauenberg, T. (2022, December 14). CO_2 tax at Europe's border: A revolution for the climate? *DW News*. www.dw.com/en/carbon-border-tax-co2-eu-europe-global-south/a-59987093

Sovacool, B. K., Hook, A., Martiskainen, M., Brock, A., & Turnheim, B. (2020). The decarbonisation divide. *Global Environmental Change*, *60*, 102028. https://doi.org/10.1016/j.gloenvcha.2019.102028

Sultana, F. (2022). The unbearable heaviness of climate coloniality. *Political Geography*, *99*, 102638. https://doi.org/10.1016/j.polgeo.2022.102638

Suroyo, G., Sulaiman, S., & Teresia, A. (2023, June 8). Indonesia accuses EU of 'regulatory imperialism'. *Reuters*. www.reuters.com/business/environment/indonesia-accuses-eu-regulatory-imperialism-with-deforestation-law-2023-06-08/

Szucko, A. (2024, March 26). How green is the EU deal? *Observatorio de Regionalismo*. https://observatorio.repri.org/2024/03/26/how-green-is-the-eu-deal-environmental-protection-or-european-protectionism/

Táíwò, O. O. (2019, February 25). How a Green New Deal could exploit developing countries. *The Conversation*. https://theconversation.com/how-a-green-new-dealcould-exploit-developing-countries-111726

Teja, N. (2023, November 2). ASEAN countries ambivalent about EU CBAM. *Sustainable Views*. www.sustainableviews.com/asean-countries-ambivalent-about-eu-cbam-147bd948/

Ülgen, S. (2023, May 9). A political economy perspective on the EU's carbon border tax. *Carnegie Endowment for International Peace*. https://carnegieendowment.org/research/2023/05/a-political-economy-perspective-on-the-eus-carbon-border-tax?lang=en

Umar, W. (2024, September 14). Climate finance regime, a neo-colonialist tool? *Modern Diplomacy*. https://moderndiplomacy.eu/2024/09/14/climate-finance-regime-a-neo-colonialist-tool/

United Nations Framework Convention on Climate Change. (n.d.). *The Paris agreement*. https://unfccc.int/process-and-meetings/the-paris-agreement

Vela Almeida, D., Kolinjivadi, V., Ferrando, T., Roy, B., Herrera, H., Gonçalves, M. V., & Van Hecken, G. (2023). The "greening" of empire. *Political Geography*, *105*, 102925. https://doi.org/10.1016/j.polgeo.2023.102925

4 The European Union Green Deal in Indonesia – Germany Relations

Navigating Challenges and Seizing Opportunities

Athiqah Nur Alami and Indriana Kartini

Introduction

The European Union Green Deal (EGD), which portrays the European Union (EU) as a leader in reaching climate neutrality by 2050, creates a substantial landscape of opportunities and challenges for the long-standing bilateral partnership between Indonesia and Germany. Both countries, which have very different geographical, political, and economic landscapes, have come together to form a collaborative cooperation in the field of environment. This connection is especially important as both countries navigate their own responsibilities to sustainability and climate action. Indonesia faces unique problems when it comes to striking a balance between its development ambitions and the requirement to decrease carbon emissions and mitigate the implications of climate change. In a similar vein, Germany, which is a world leader in sustainable practices and renewable energy, has a vested interest in aiding Indonesia's efforts to combat climate change by sharing its experience and resources.

The Indonesian government also has addressed some of the key contributors to greenhouse gas emissions, including deforestation, degradation of peatlands, and forest fires, through the implementation of a variety of initiatives. Germany, on the other hand, as a significant member of the EU, has established itself as a pioneer in the transition to a low-carbon economy, with a significant focus on renewable energy and energy efficiency. The country also has been instrumental in the formulation of the EU policies regarding climate change and energy.

A wide variety of efforts, such as the exchange of information, the transfer of technology, and the provision of financial assistance, are included in the scope of the collaboration between Indonesia and Germany in the field of climate change mitigation. Indonesia's attempts to cut greenhouse gas emissions and strengthen its resilience to the consequences of climate change have been aided by the collaboration between the two countries on initiatives that try to avoid forest fires, restore wetlands, and promote sustainable land-use practices. All of these types of projects contribute to Indonesia's efforts. However, the present policy efforts of the EGD, which aim to turn the continent into a modern economy that is resource-efficient and competitive, have the potential to affect the bilateral relations between Germany and Indonesia. Germany is a prominent member of the EU, and as such, it

DOI: 10.4324/9781003783176-5

will be expected to play a significant role in the implementation of the policies and regulations that are outlined in the EGD. Meanwhile, Indonesia, a major economy in Southeast Asia, faces environmental challenges due to its fossil fuel-driven economic growth.

As a result of the significant role that the EGD plays in the relationship between Germany and Indonesia, the purpose of this study is to investigate the degree to which this ambitious plan will influence the two countries' bilateral ties. To understand the implications of the EGD for the Indonesian-German relations in terms of its challenges and opportunities, we utilize Putnam's (1988) idea of two-level games to study the interplay of multilayered relations. Specifically, we look at how the bilateral relations between Indonesia and Germany influence their foreign policy approaches to implementing the EGD, highlighting both the difficulties and the opportunities that come with it. It argues that while two-level games can certainly impede Indonesia and Germany's international efforts to collaborate on green transitions, this chapter contends that the two countries' bilateral relations provide a strong foundation upon which to address the numerous controversies surrounding the EGD and its implementation in Indonesia. To discuss it, this chapter consists of four sections. Following the Introduction, the second section explains the concept of two-level games that serves as the conceptual framework for the analysis. The third section explores the bilateral relations of Indonesia and Germany. The fourth part discusses the extent to which the EGD framework provides challenges and opportunities in the relations of both countries. The last section is the Conclusion.

Theoretical Frameworks: Two-Level Games

According to Putnam (1988), international political negotiations can be seen as a two-level game at the domestic and international levels. Putnam (1988) describes this concept as a way to illustrate the interaction between domestic and international politics. According to him, national leaders operate in a "two-level game": domestically, they work to build alliances among interest groups to maintain their political power; internationally, they aim to negotiate agreements that promote cooperation without jeopardizing their domestic standing. He emphasizes the unique complexity of managing both arenas simultaneously, as a strategic decision that seems wise in one context may be unwise in the other. However, skilled leaders may sometimes identify opportunities where a move in one arena can provoke beneficial shifts in the other, allowing them to accomplish goals that would otherwise be out of reach (Putnam, 1988, pp. 433–434).

Moreover, Putnam (1988) introduces the idea of a "win-set," defined as the range of possible international agreements that can also gain domestic approval from all relevant parties. Putnam outlines three main factors that influence the size of the win-set: the composition and interests of domestic coalitions, the structure of domestic institutions, and the tactics and influence of the international negotiators (Putnam, 1988, pp. 436–437, 442–451). He further notes that the game becomes more complex due to uncertainty (as negotiators may not fully understand each other's domestic political situations), the internal impact of international pressures (which can either help or hinder domestic support), and the subjective role of the chief negotiator, who may not always act as a neutral representative (Putnam, 1988, pp. 452–459).

As Conceição-Heldt and Mello (2017) point out, although two-level game theory shares some common ground with liberal perspectives, it highlights that political leaders possess a degree of independence in their decision-making that isn't solely determined by domestic constituencies. In contrast to realism, the theory also acknowledges the significant role of domestic veto players and institutional limitations. Since its development in the late 1980s, the two-level game framework has inspired a wide body of literature, leading to further theoretical advancements and its application across a range of policy areas.

Instead of using these two levels, this study aims to frame the multilayered game of bilateral relations and regional politics. Putnam's two-level games framework provides a valuable perspective for analyzing the bilateral relations between Indonesia and Germany within the context of the EGD. In this framework, level one pertains to direct diplomatic interactions between the two countries, whereas level two considers the broader political dynamics related to the EGD. This dual perspective elucidates how bilateral and regional political environments intersect, affecting opportunities and challenges for both Indonesia and Germany. Therefore, it further argues that the ability of Indonesia to implement or comply with EGD policies is dependent on solid and long-term bilateral relationships with Germany.

Indonesia-Germany Bilateral Relations

Indonesia and Germany, two nations with long histories yet distinct geopolitical positions, have long maintained a bilateral relationship that has evolved over time to address the changing dynamics of the global landscape. This section will explore the key aspects of their bilateral foreign policy agendas, focusing on the areas of economic cooperation and diplomatic initiatives on environmental issues, including responding to the current EGD.

Although Indonesia and Germany officially established diplomatic relations in 1952, their connections date back to a time before Indonesia's independence. Historical ties between the two nations can be traced to notable figures such as Adolf Bastian, a German ethnologist who introduced the name "Indonesia"; the establishment of Siemens' office in Surabaya in 1854; and Raden Saleh, the renowned Indonesian painter who resided in Germany between 1839 and 1849. In 2012, both countries signed the German-Indonesian Joint Declaration for a Comprehensive Partnership: Shaping Globalization and Sharing Responsibility, commonly called the Jakarta Declaration. The bilateral relationship was further reinforced in 2016 when President Joko Widodo visited Germany, leading to a strategic partnership focused on three key areas: vocational education, renewable energy, and maritime cooperation. Economic and industrial collaboration between the two nations also continues to expand.

Economic cooperation has been a cornerstone of the Indonesia-Germany bilateral relationship, with both countries seeking to expand trade and investment opportunities. Indonesia, as the largest economy in the ASEAN region, has attracted significant interest from German businesses seeking to capitalize on the country's growing consumer market and burgeoning industrial sectors. Efforts to enhance economic ties have included the negotiation of trade agreements, the promotion of foreign direct investment, and the facilitation of joint ventures between Indonesian and German companies. At present, approximately 250 German multinational corporations operate in Indonesia, including Deutsche Post, Robert Bosch, Bayer, VW, Mercedes-Benz, Adidas, Allianz, BASF, and BMW. Indonesia's strategic significance to Germany is also evident in its selection as a partner country for Hannover Messe, the world's largest industrial exhibition, in 1995, 2021, and 2023. Moreover, several tangible initiatives demonstrate the growing cooperation between the two nations. Indonesia is in the process of sending nurses to Germany under a triple-win scheme. Additionally, Germany has allocated IDR 40.7 trillion to support 15 Green Infrastructure Initiative (GII) projects in various Indonesian provinces. As of January 2022, Germany had provided 14,164,460 doses of COVID-19 vaccines to Indonesia, substantially contributing to the total of roughly 29 million doses received from global partners. This assistance also includes donations of medical equipment and supplies (The Embassy of the Republic of Indonesia in Berlin, 2022). According to Indonesian scholar, Muhadi Sugiono, Germany holds a strategic position for Indonesia for two main reasons: (1) Germany can serve as Indonesia's entry point into the European market; (2) Germany possesses a unique character – not only is it an economic powerhouse, but it also has a strong normative orientation towards environmental sustainability. Thus, Indonesia stands to gain dual advantages: not only in terms of economic growth but also in developing an economy that prioritizes environmental sustainability (Sugiono, 2025).

Concerning investment, Indonesia welcomes the establishment of the Indonesia-Germany Joint Economic and Investment Committee. The Government of Indonesia suggests that German investments in Indonesia should prioritize key sectors such as export-oriented industries, renewable energy, and downstream processing. Indonesia recently focused on developing its electric vehicle (EV) industry ecosystem. In particular, 21 strategic mineral commodities with high investment potential were identified, with an estimated value of US$ 545.3 billion. Additionally, Indonesia reported its lowest deforestation rate in the past 20 years, with 23,000 hectares of Green Industrial Estates already developed. The government is also accelerating efforts to phase out coal-based power plants to achieve a faster transition to clean energy (The Coordinating Ministry for Economic Affairs of the Republic of Indonesia, n.d.).

Diplomatic initiatives between Indonesia and Germany have also been a crucial component of their bilateral relationship. Previously, both nations had also served as non-permanent members of the UN Security Council from 2019 to 2020. The two nations have collaborated on a range of global and regional issues, such as climate change and environmental issues. Indonesia and Germany are actively aligning their foreign policy agendas in response to the EGD, focusing on sustainable development and energy transition. Indonesia's responses not only relate to its commitment to sustainable development and green financing but also advance its trade negotiations with the EU, including Germany. Indonesia aims to achieve net-zero emissions by 2060, with a strong emphasis on transitioning to renewable energy. This commitment is part of its broader vision of becoming a major global economy by 2045, termed "Golden Indonesia."

The governments of Indonesia and Germany have collaborated on multiple initiatives in clean and renewable energy. One notable partnership is with Deutsche Gesellschaft für Internationale Zusammenarbeit (GIZ) to promote the adoption of renewable energy in Indonesia, aiming to contribute positively to climate change mitigation. As part of this cooperation, the German government has provided a grant of 3.4 million euros to support capacity-building programmes, facilitation efforts, and pre-feasibility studies for pilot projects. Regarding Indonesia's energy transition, Germany remains committed to supporting the Just Energy Transition Partnership (JETP). This initiative, launched by the G7, includes a financial commitment of US$ 20 billion from G7 member countries. Germany contributes approximately US$ 1 billion to support Indonesia's energy transition projects (CASE for Southeast Asia, 2020). Moreover, at the recent COP29 summit, Indonesia secured €1.2 billion (approximately $1.26 billion) in green financing from Germany's KfW Development Bank for renewable energy infrastructure. This funding will support projects like pumped storage hydropower plants and the development of a smart grid to enhance energy distribution across the archipelago.

The Indonesian government is also focused on integrating community participation and supportive policies to accelerate its renewable energy targets. Through the KfW Development Bank, the German government has also committed to collaborating to finance green transportation in several Indonesian cities. One example of this cooperation is the development of Bus Rapid Transit (BRT) systems in Semarang and Surabaya, as well as railway projects in Surabaya, carried out in partnership with KfW (Beritatrans, 2023). Therefore, the Indonesian government is advocating for adjustments to ensure that these regulations do not impose undue burdens on its agricultural sector. Furthermore, Indonesia seeks recognition of its sustainability efforts, such as its national certification schemes for palm oil and timber, which align with the EU's environmental goals. In this context, it is essential for Indonesia to leverage its economic interests by engaging with EU member states – such as Germany – as a means of accessing the broader European market. As Oegroseno suggests, there is a clear distinction between the EU and Germany. For instance, in the case of critical raw minerals, Germany understands the importance of these resources for Indonesia and recognizes that it is the sovereign right of a state to manage them. Regarding the export of critical raw minerals, Berlin has no objection, as long as the industry is properly developed (Sugiono, 2025).

Meanwhile, Germany has positioned itself as a key partner for Indonesia in achieving sustainable energy goals. To achieve net zero emissions by 2060, the Indonesian government has partnered with Germany under the Clean, Affordable, Secure Energy (CASE) programme to accelerate the transition to renewable energy. Launched by the German government on February 2, 2021, the CASE initiative fosters collaboration between Germany and Southeast Asian nations, including Indonesia, to promote sustainable energy solutions. Through this initiative, Germany provides technical assistance and funding aimed at enhancing Indonesia's renewable energy capabilities. This programme was established in response to Southeast Asia's vast renewable energy potential. Despite this, the region still relies heavily on coal, which accounts for around 40% of its energy consumption, with significant potential for further coal expansion in the future. To counter this trend, the CASE programme aims to boost the adoption of new renewable energy (NRE), supporting sustainable development and meeting the targets of the Paris Agreement. The initiative focuses on the four largest Southeast Asian economies – Indonesia, the Philippines, Thailand, and Vietnam – due to their substantial gross domestic product (GDP) and population size, ensuring a broader regional impact in advancing clean energy transitions (CASE for Southeast Asia, 2020).

The CASE programme is structured around five key components: (1) research on renewable energy sources, (2) mapping transparency in activities and stakeholder engagement, (3) dialogue and action plans involving stakeholders to facilitate the shift to NRE, (4) technical assistance to enhance stakeholder capacity, (5) public discussions on sustainable energy adoption (CASE for Southeast Asia, 2020). On February 2, 2021, the Indonesian and German governments formalized their partnership through a cooperation agreement. Represented by Indonesia's Ministry of National Development Planning (Bappenas) and Germany's Federal Ministry for the Environment, Nature Conservation, Building, and Nuclear Safety, this collaboration aims to accelerate Indonesia's transition to renewable energy. The partnership also involves two key international organizations: the Institute for Essential Services Reform (IESR) (Indonesia) and GIZ (Germany). According to Saputra and Simanjuntak (2021), Germany's interest in collaborating with Indonesia under the CASE programme was driven by two main factors: (1) Indonesia's strategic role as the G20 presidency holder in 2022 and (2) Indonesia's economic influence as one of Southeast Asia's largest economies by GDP. This cooperation seeks to maximize Indonesia's potential in advancing renewable energy adoption across the region (Hariyadi & Suryadipura, 2022).

For Indonesia, the CASE programme presents a significant opportunity to optimize its abundant renewable energy potential. Through bilateral cooperation with Germany, Indonesia can accelerate the provision of affordable and sustainable energy by 2030. The country has set ambitious national targets for its energy transition, aiming for 23% renewable energy usage by 2025, with an annual goal of integrating 1,500 MW (or 4% per year) of renewable energy capacity (EBTKE, 2021). Germany, a global leader in renewable energy adoption with a renewable energy utilization rate exceeding 50%, serves as a key partner in this initiative. The CASE programme allows Indonesia to leverage Germany's expertise, gaining direct support to help achieve its Net Zero Emissions target by 2060. Additionally, through this collaboration, Indonesia aims to halt the construction of new coal-fired power plants after 2025.

However, Indonesia faces considerable challenges in meeting these targets. As of 2021, only 11.5% of the country's energy came from renewable source

(Ministry of Energy and Mineral Resources, 2022). To overcome this gap, the Indonesia-Germany partnership under CASE adopts an inclusive approach, engaging diverse stakeholders to ensure the programme's successful implementation (Hariyadi & Suryadipura, 2022). This cooperation reflects Germany's commitment to fostering international partnerships that align with the EGD objectives. The German government also emphasizes collaborative frameworks that include not only financial support but also knowledge sharing and capacity building in renewable energy technologies. This partnership aims to address challenges such as low investment rates in renewable energy sectors and ineffective budget allocations in Indonesia. Furthermore, Germany's foreign policy agenda aligns closely with the EGD, particularly in promoting sustainable practices and reducing greenhouse gas emissions. By supporting Indonesia's transition through substantial investments and cooperative agreements, Germany reinforces its commitment to global climate goals while also addressing local economic realities in Indonesia.

Based on the explanation above, both Indonesia and Germany are aligning their foreign policy agendas in response to the EGD through strategic partnerships focused on sustainable development and energy transition. While Indonesia seeks to balance its economic needs with environmental responsibilities, Germany plays a crucial role in facilitating this transition through financial support and technical expertise. Their collaboration exemplifies a proactive approach to addressing climate change while considering local socio-economic contexts.

Two-Level Games: Challenges and Opportunities in EGD Implementation

The EGD is a framework for the EU with the goal of achieving carbon neutrality by the year 2050 while simultaneously influencing both bilateral and regional policies. This dichotomy becomes especially apparent when one considers the relationship that exists between the EGD and the respective policies of countries such as Germany and Indonesia. Particularly in the context of energy transition, environmental diplomacy, and sustainable development, the confluence of these policies offers both opportunities and challenges.

Considering the long history of Indonesia-Germany relations, Putnam's two-level games approach offers a significant lens for examining relations within the setting of EGD. At level one, Indonesia and Germany have developed a strong bilateral relationship characterized by cooperation in trade, technology transfer, and development projects. The EGD presents Indonesia with the opportunity to leverage Germany's expertise in sustainable technologies and green energy, which aligns with Indonesia's climate objectives under the Paris Agreement. Germany's commitment to ambitious environmental targets positions it as a suitable partner for Indonesia as it seeks to transition away from fossil fuels while pursuing economic growth. The potential for joint ventures in renewable energy, where Germany can introduce innovative technologies, could enhance bilateral ties and yield significant economic and environmental benefits.

The EGD is also very congruent with national policies of Germany that are geared towards the transition to renewable energy sources. The government of Germany has pledged to establish ambitious climate targets, which are congruent with the aims of the EGD. For instance, Germany's Energiewende (energy transition) policy places an emphasis on the reduction of greenhouse gas emissions and the promotion of renewable energy. This policy is strikingly similar to the objectives of the EGD, which are to cultivate a circular economy and achieve net-zero emissions (Cseres, 2019). According to Asadov and Asadov (2022), the German approach to energy transition is characterized by a robust legislative framework that supports investment in renewable technology. This is essential for reaching climate targets on both the national and EU-wide levels. On the other hand, implementing these policies often faces challenges – such as balancing economic growth with environmental sustainability – which can create tensions within the EU framework.

However, domestic pressures in both countries may hinder the full realization of these opportunities. In Germany, strong public and political support for environmental sustainability fosters a conducive environment for climate initiatives but can also create constraints. Domestic political actors may advocate for strict compliance measures that could complicate negotiations with Indonesia, thus affecting the bilateral relationship. Additionally, rising sentiments of "green protectionism" may lead to hesitancy in extending favourable trade conditions to Indonesian exports that do not align with EU sustainability standards, potentially generating trade tensions that undermine cooperation under the EGD framework.

The implementation of the EGD in Indonesia also brings a different set of problems than other countries' participation. The process of integrating Indonesia's energy policy with the severe standards of the EGD presents considerable challenges for the country, which is still in the process of developing. According to Wahidin and Purnhagen (2018), the implementation of a sustainable energy system necessitates a significant financial commitment as well as the provision of technological assistance. The Indonesian government has stated interest in embracing renewable energy sources, although the pace of this transition is often hampered. Specifically in the areas of agriculture and forestry, the EU places a strong emphasis on sustainable practices. This poses additional challenges for Indonesia, which must navigate the EU's stringent regulations while safeguarding its economic interests – particularly in sectors like palm oil and fisheries (Robertua, 2019).

Furthermore, the complex nature of public perceptions and political discourse related to environmental sustainability in Germany and the EU can complicate bilateral negotiations. Stakeholders in Germany, including environmental advocacy groups, exert pressure on the government to uphold rigorous standards in international agreements. These dynamics not only influence governmental positions but also affect public perceptions of negotiations, necessitating that Indonesian representatives navigate these politically charged environments adeptly to secure favourable outcomes.

A further illustration of the complexity of environmental diplomacy is provided by the junction of the EGD with Indonesia's domestic policies. By campaigning for sustainable practices not just within its borders but also in its economic connections with countries such as Indonesia, the EU has established itself as a forward-thinking leader in the realm of global climate governance. This dynamic is made manifest in the manner in which the EU handles imports of palm oil, where environmental concerns have resulted in trade disputes and accusations of engaging in protectionism. The EU's insistence on high environmental standards can be seen as a double-edged sword: while it can promote environmentally responsible behaviour, it also runs the danger of alienating developing countries who may have difficulty meeting these requirements in the absence of proper support.

A further point to consider is that the ramifications of the EGD for foreign policy go beyond trade relations. One way in which the EU demonstrates its dedication to climate diplomacy is through its efforts to engage with Indonesia on topics such as the loss of biodiversity and deforestation. Collaborative projects that attempt to reduce emissions caused by deforestation and promote sustainable land use are extremely important for both parties involved. According to Wahidin and Purnhagen (2018), the success of these projects is frequently contingent on the EU's capacity to offer Indonesia both financial and technical aid, which would result in the development of a partnership that is more comprehensive and equal.

At level two, the regional politics surrounding the EGD further complicate the dynamics. As a leading advocate for the EGD, Germany's negotiations are shaped by both national interests and regional obligations regarding sustainability and climate change mitigation among EU member states. The EGD's emphasis on stringent carbon accounting and environmental due diligence compels Indonesia to adjust its economic strategies to achieve compliance. This raises concerns in Indonesia, as fulfilling EU standards might necessitate significant alterations in domestic industries, which could provoke domestic unrest or economic challenges if these sectors are not adequately prepared. Moreover, regional dynamics within Southeast Asia, particularly ASEAN's influence, shape Indonesia's strategic engagement in its relationship with Germany and the EU. As Indonesia navigates economic integration and collaboration frameworks within ASEAN, it must reconcile its commitments with broader regional goals while meeting the expectations associated with the EGD. Balancing these dual obligations may lead to conflicts or delays in executing necessary reforms that both parties aspire to accomplish cooperatively.

Nevertheless, as a result of the EGD's emphasis on renewable energy, energy efficiency, and the reduction of greenhouse gas emissions, new opportunities for collaboration between Indonesia and Germany may become available. Because Indonesia has been investigating the possibility of establishing a domestic carbon market, for example, the carbon trading system that the EU has in place, which is designed to encourage reductions in emissions, would be a subject of mutual interest (Rachmaniar et al., 2021). In light of the fact that Indonesia and Germany are working together to combat climate change, the effective implementation of such a system in Indonesia might potentially improve the existing connections between the two nations. At the same time, the push for sustainable supply chains and the reduction of deforestation that is included in the EGD may have an effect on the economic activities that are carried out in Indonesia, notably in the agricultural and forestry sectors. It is possible that Indonesia may view these restrictions as challenges to its economic progress, which could result in difficulties within the international relationship between the two countries. On the other hand, the two nations might be able to establish a middle ground by investigating environmentally friendly and forward-thinking ideas that strike a balance between economic expansion and environmental preservation.

Additionally, the EGD's emphasis on digital transformation and the development of new technologies has the potential to influence the connection between Germany and Indonesia. This is in addition to the environmental considerations. The knowledge and experience that Germany possesses in fields such as digital technologies, energy efficiency, and renewable energy might be utilized to provide assistance to Indonesia's own efforts to achieve sustainable development. Furthermore, the Green Deal's emphasis on workforce upskilling and the promotion of digital skills creates chances for collaboration in education and training that might be created, which could potentially increase the mobility of skilled workers between the two nations.

All in all, the EGD is a prime example of the complex relationship that exists between bilateral and regional policy whenever there is an effort to achieve sustainability. Therefore, both countries' bilateral and regional politics present challenges and opportunities to the full realization of the EGD's global environmental objectives as a result of the bilateral and regional policy nexus.

Conclusion

Indonesia and Germany, two countries with vastly different geographical, political, and economic landscapes, have established a collaborative partnership in climate change mitigation. The EGD, which aims to turn the continent into a resource-efficient and competitive economy, has the potential to affect bilateral relations between Germany and Indonesia. Indonesia and Germany have a long-standing bilateral foreign policy relationship, focusing on economic cooperation, diplomatic initiatives, and environmental issues. Indonesia, the largest economy in the ASEAN region, has attracted German businesses to capitalize on its growing consumer market and industrial sectors. Efforts to enhance economic ties include negotiating trade agreements, promoting foreign direct investment, and facilitating joint ventures between Indonesian and German companies. Diplomatic initiatives between Indonesia and Germany have been crucial, particularly in response to the EGD, focusing on sustainable development and energy transition. Germany is a key partner for Indonesia in achieving sustainable energy goals, providing technical assistance and funding. Their collaboration exemplifies a proactive approach to addressing climate change while considering local socio-economic contexts.

However, the implementation of EGD policies often faces challenges, such as balancing economic growth and environmental sustainability. Indonesia's participation in the EGD presents unique challenges, as it must balance its economic interests with the stringent EU laws in agriculture and forestry. The EU's commitment to high environmental standards can be seen as a double-edged sword, as it promotes environmentally responsible behaviours while alienating developing countries. Finally, the EGD is a complex relationship between bilateral and regional politics. Its implementation is complex, requiring careful navigation of economic, social, and environmental issues. The EU's ability to establish equitable bilateral relations with developing nations and reconcile the different interests of its member states will determine the success of the EGD implementation.

Reference List

Asadov, B. and Asadov, E. 2022. New Environmental Policy of the European Union: Some Aspects of Transition To Green Energy. *Iop Conference Series Earth and Environmental Science* 1096(1), 012034. https://doi.org/10.1088/1755-1315/1096/1/012034.

Beritatrans. 2023, July 21. Menhub Bahas Integrasi Transportasi Perkotaan di Semarang dan Surabaya Bersama KfW Development Bank Jerman. https://www.beritatrans.com/artikel/240407/menhub-bahas-integrasi-transportasi-perkotaan-di-semarang-dan-surabaya-bersama-kfw-development-bank-jerman/

CASE for Southeast Asia. 2020. https://caseforsea.org/about-us/.

Conceição-Heldt, E. and Mello, P. A. 2017. *Two-Level Games in Foreign Policy Analysis. Oxford Research Encyclopedia of Politics*. New York & Oxford: Oxford University Press. https://doi.org/10.1093/acrefore/9780190228637.013.496.

The Coordinating Minister for Economic Affairs of the Republic of Indonesia Holds a Meeting with the Minister of Economic Affairs and Climate Action Germany and Signs the-Indonesia-Germany Joint-Declaration of Intent. n.d. https://ekon.go.id/publikasi/detail/5113/the-coordinating-minister-for-economic-affairs-of-the-republic-of-indonesia-holds-a-meeting-with-the-minister-of-economic-affairs-and-climate-action-germany-and-signs-the-indonesia-germany-joint-declaration-of-intent-jdoi.

Cseres, K. 2019. Consumer Social Responsibility in Dutch Law. *Erasmus Law Review* 12(4), 94–110. https://doi.org/10.5553/elr.000194.

EBTKE. 2021. *Semester I 2021, Kapasitas Pembangkit EBT Tambah 217 MW*. https://ebtke.esdm.go.id/post/2021/08/20/2940/.

The Embassy of Indonesia in Berlin. 2022. *History*. https://indonesianembassy.de/history/.

Germany and Indonesia-Bilateral Relations. n.d. https://ekonomi.uma.ac.id/2020/12/11/germany-and-indonesia-bilateral-relations/.

Hariyadi, F. A. and Suryadipura, D. 2022. Germany Bilateral Cooperation Towards Renewable Energy Transition Through Clean, Affordable, and Secure Energy (Case). *Jurnal Ilmu Sosial* 21(2). https://jis.undip.ac.id.

Indonesia-Germany Bilateral Meeting Mapping the Best Strategy For Sustainable-Development Cooperation. n.d. https://gii.maritim.go.id/indonesia-germany-bilateral-meeting-mapping-the-best-strategy-for-sustainable-development-cooperation/.

Indonesia-Jerman Kerjasama Kembangkan Infrastruktur Transportasi Ramah Lingkungan. n.d. www.menpan.go.id/site/berita-terkini/berita-daerah/indonesia-jerman-kerja-sama-kembangkan-infrastruktur-transportasi-ramah-lingkungan.

Kerjasama Indonesia-Jerman Dukung Pemanfaatan Energi Bersih. n.d. www.esdm.go.id/id/media-center/arsip-berita/kerjasama-indonesia-jerman-dukung-pemanfaatan-energi-bersih.

Ministry of Energy and Mineral Resources. 2022, February 8. Renewables Power Plants COD within Target, Says Officials. Press Release Number: 63.Pers/04/SJI/2022. https://www.esdm.go.id/en/media-cent.

Perkuat Kerja sama Bilateral Indonesia Jerman Akselerasi Penyelesaian Perundingan Perjanjian-IEU-CEPA. n.d. www.ekon.go.id/publikasi/detail/5092/perkuat-kerja-sama-bilateral-indonesia-jerman-akselerasi-penyelesaian-perundingan-perjanjian-ieu-cepa.

Perkuat kerja sama Indonesia dan Jerman Resmikan Logo Peringatan 70 Tahun Hubungan-Diplomatik. n.d. https://indonesianembassy.de/news/perkuat-kerja-sama-indonesia-dan-jerman-resmikan-logo-peringatan-70-tahun-hubungan-diplomatik/.

Putnam, R. D. 1988. Diplomacy and Domestic Politics: The Logic of Two-Level Games. *International Organization* 42(3), 427–460.

Rachmaniar, A. *et al.* 2021. Carbon trading system as a climate mitigation scheme: why Indonesia should adopt it? *IOP Conference Series: Earth and Environmental Science* 739, 012015.

Robertua, V. 2019. Environmental Diplomacy: Case Study of The EU-Indonesia Palm Oil Dispute. *Jurnal Mandala Jurnal Ilmu Hubungan Internasional*, 1–21. https://doi.org/10.33822/mjihi.v2i1.917.

Saputra, G. and Simanjuntak, U. 2021. *Energy Transition in the Electricity Power Sector through the Clean, Affordable, and Secure Energy for Southeast Asia (CASE Program).* https://iesr.or.id/en/indonesia-germany-collaborate-to-accelerate-the-energy-transition-in-the-electricity-power-sector-through-the-clean-affordable-and-secure-energy-for-southeast-asia-case-program/.

Strengthening Bilateral Cooperation Indonesia-Germany Accelerate Completion of IEU-CEPA Agreement Negotiations. n.d. www.ekon.go.id/publikasi/detail/5122/strengthening-bilateral-cooperation-indonesia-germany-accelerate-completion-of-ieu-cepa-agreement-negotiations.

Sugiono, M. 2025. *Peran Strategis Jerman dalam Memperkuat Diplomasi Indonesia di Kawasan Eropa. Presentation at the Debriefing Forum.* Indonesian Ministry of Foreign Affairs, June 18, 2025.

Wahidin, D. and Purnhagen, K. 2018. Improving the Level of Food Safety and Market Access in Developing Countries. *Heliyon* 4(7), e00683. https://doi.org/10.1016/j.heliyon.2018.e00683.

Part 2

Regulatory and Legal Ambiguities – Norms, Discourses, and Taxonomies

5 Making the European Union Green Deal Work Differently

Norm Diffusion and the Resilient Structure of Palm Oil Production in Southeast Asian Countries

Maharani Hapsari, Eusebius Pantja Pramudya and Inggit Kartika Dini

Introduction

The introduction of the EU Green Deal (EGD) reflects the process of international norm diffusion. It reinstated the pursuit of European normative power (Wurzel & Conelly, 2011) in the field of international sustainability politics. The European Union Green Deal (EGD) has sparked heated debate among academia and policymakers in countries that are likely to be affected by its derivative regulations, particularly the EUDR (the European Union Deforestation-free Regulation). The promotion of stringent sustainability standards has evoked international responses, among others regarding its implications for the European Union's (EU) trading partners. One of the affected regional partners is Southeast Asian countries, in which three major producers of palm oil as an important global commodity (namely Indonesia, Malaysia, and Thailand) are currently shaping their domestic sustainability policies and international commitments. Its political consequences warrant critical discussion. Southeast Asian countries, one of the EU's long-standing trade partners, have been affected by sustainability norms socialization and engaged in the current debate that presents both the recognition and critics of the emerging normative and regulatory framework.

This chapter seeks to examine the state of international norm diffusion as manifested in the EGD through the socialization of EU-driven sustainability standards. It captures norm diffusion in the context of interactive regionalism involving the EU and Southeast Asian countries. There are two angles offered in this study as regards how it contributes to the current theoretical debate on EGD and the study on international norm diffusion. *First*, while previous studies have focused more on how the EUDR affects the EU's trading partners individually, this study focuses on the regional impacts of the normative framework by looking at the way palm oil-producing countries in Southeast Asian countries (Indonesia, Malaysia, and Thailand) are currently responding to the EUDR debate. This is mainly concerned with the intraregional trade situation reinforced by the political economic dimensions of the palm oil economy landscape in these three respective countries. In this context, palm oil-producing countries in Southeast Asia are situated as active participants in the international norm-making process. *Second*, rather than only

DOI: 10.4324/9781003783176-7

focusing on the institutional aspects of international norm-making, this study explores the deeper structural context of power relations (especially with respect to Southeast Asian countries as palm oil-producing countries as active norm-makers) that shape the agency of norm makers in their dialectical relations.

This chapter argues that as part of the EGD, the EUDR is in the process of constitutive localization. There are diverging paths of localization, which include indications of moving towards localization, resistance, negotiation, and withdrawal. The way Indonesia, Malaysia, and Thailand are responding to EUDR is influenced by the centrality of palm oil in the local, national, and regional production structures that sustain Southeast Asian countries' economy.

The remainder of this chapter is divided into five sections. Section two discusses the theoretical framework of international norm making. Section three elaborates on the normative framework of the EUDR and its impacts on interregional trade relations. Section four discusses the constitutive localization in the formation of the EGD, particularly following the introduction of EUDR, in Southeast Asian countries. Section five examines the historical production structure facing EGD localization in Southeast Asian countries. Section six presents concluding remarks.

Conceptual Framework

Norm Diffusion and Constitutive Localization

For most of its history, the EU has portrayed itself as a rule-based and normative power that relies more on diplomacy while establishing and forging cultural cooperation with the rest of the world (Kissack, 2010; Wurzel & Conelly, 2011). The recent promotion of EGD is among the latest reflections of such an image. EGD, and particularly EUDR, in itself is a norm, which is in the process of diffusion to the whole globe. It is in this regard that the application of EUDR in the EU-Southeast Asian countries' relations should be taken as a form of norm diffusion. Norm diffusion is a technical term in international relations to describe the transfer of ideas, defined norms, and institutions from one actor to others (Risse et al., 1999). Strongly influenced by the constructivist view, the term suggests the importance of ideas as determinant factors in global politics and economy. Acharya (2009) embraced the view that ideational forces play key roles. However, in his studies on Asian regionalism, Acharya (2009) emphasized that ideas were locally produced. The centrality of the "local" takes into consideration "cognitive prior" – such as identity – of the targeted actor that shapes how regional institutions are built.

The main question is how ideas and norms travel from one actor to the other. The mainstream view is biased towards "moral cosmopolitanism," which presents norm diffusion as moral struggles between good global norms against bad local beliefs and practices (Krause, 1998). Another perspective focuses on the roles of domestic political structures and agents (Cortell & James, 2000). These domestic elements condition the reception of new external norms. Norm diffusion is more successful when there is a cultural match between diffused norms and targeted countries. Diffused norms simply resonate with historically constructed local beliefs and practices. The constructivist approach concentrates on "framing" and "grafting." Framing norm entrepreneurs – usually external actors – highlight and construct issues by relying on familiar language that names and interprets them. Norm entrepreneurs can also use grafting by associating external norms with the existing one that results in similar prohibition and injunction (Klotz, 1995).

Acharya (2009) paid more attention to the agency roles of (local) norm-takers. At the heart of norm diffusion is contestation between emerging new norms – brought by external actors – and existing local traditions – defended by local actors. The outcome of this battle is shaped by the ideas and initiative of the latter. Acharya (2009) proposed "constitutive localization" as a term to explain the process of local norm-takers building congruence between local and external norms. In these lines of argument, new international norms do not enter into a local normative vacuum. The global prominence of external norms and the global reputation of actors who promote norms are hardly sufficient. In addition, congruence between external and local norms is a dynamic process. The localization of new norms and ideas does not wipe out local beliefs and practices.

Constitutive localization seeks to address the issue of legitimate resistance to external norms by local actors (Acharya, 2009). This implies that local actors contribute significantly to norm diffusion. Such diffusion is an evolutionary process and takes into account existing local beliefs and practices. The result is a compromise, which is often coated with moral registers and requires mutual adaptation. In short, constitutive localization is an intervening variable, which shapes local responses to external norms, either resistance rejection, localization, or norm displacement (Acharya, 2009).

The gist of Acharya's argument revolves around his emphasis on locality and the key roles of local actors in shaping norms diffusion. The problem is, however, such a theoretical move tends to, first, essentialize locality and, hence, conceal the (political) dynamic within locality. Locality is never given, basically fragmented, and only emerges as a fully united identity and force during a certain period. In fact, local norms, values, and beliefs imagined by Acharya (2009) are very often the mainstream version of many others and mostly represented by local elites. On the contrary, the orientation of this study is not only to uncover non-mainstream local beliefs and practices but, more importantly, to accentuate the centrality of power struggles in the formation of so-called local norms and local actors. The dynamic of norm diffusion eloquently put by Acharya (2009) is not only because of local actors' active involvement in localizing external norms but also because of the very dynamic power relations involving dominant and less dominant groups and individuals.

Second, even though ideas matter, it is difficult to ignore the importance of material interests in understanding the diffusion of global norms. It does not imply that matter is more important than ideas and vice versa. This study is more about juxtaposing idea and matter, constitutive localization in this regard, and some forms of material structure. The goal is to compare and contrast the two different terrains in order to identify and speculate on both theoretical and practical bases to enrich the understanding of how norms diffuse.

Finally, Acharya's argument presumes a clear and strict distinction between global and local or external and internal. While such presumed distinctions often result in essentializing both sides, in the current globalized world, global and local relations are better represented as a continuum. Within this continuum is a series of overlapped layers of structure that connect global and local at opposite ends.

Coxian Historical Structure

Notwithstanding the aforementioned weaknesses, Acharya's constitutive localization contributes to this study's understanding of how Southeast Asian countries, particularly Indonesia, Malaysia, and Thailand, respond to EUDR. Based on a taxonomy of local responses proposed by Acharya (2009), the three countries seemed to take the path of resistance to EUDR, at least at this initial phase of the norm diffusion process. The ongoing negotiation with the EU regarding palm oil production could result in a compromise as a strategic phase to what Acharya (2009) describes as localization.

Nevertheless, constitutive localization is far from sufficient to explain Indonesia, Malaysia, and Thailand's response. The dominating presence of palm oil production in trade relations between the EU and these countries should also be considered as a determining factor, which conditions the reception of EUDR in this specific area of Southeast Asia. The material interests of palm oil production should shed light on the path of resistance taken by, particularly, Indonesia and Malaysia. It is also the fear of losing revenues and profits from palm oil production that blocks the diffusion of EUDR norms into the region. At this point, Cox's (1987) critical interpretation of the political-economy structure of global order is useful. By using "Coxian structure," this study shall explain the presence of material structure in the recent development of Southeast Asian countries' responses to EUDR.

To begin with, what is material structure? Following Cox (1987), this study treats production as the material foundation for all forms of social existence, including human interactions with their physical surroundings. Human relations in the process of production affect and shape politics, economy, culture, and other aspects of human lives. Production also reduces and increases capacity to exercise power. At the same time, the operation of power determines the way production takes place.

Cox (1987) approached production as the material foundation in two ways. The first is to translate production as the general category into a concrete socio-historical form of how productive processes and activities are organized. His aim was to unveil social relations of production. The second is how the specific forms of power in state and world-order structures shape production relations and are conditioned by the same production relations. These layers of structure for Cox are useful to understand how power relations emerge and transform within production.

In simple Marxian terms, production means creating use-value of things (Harvey, 2010). In a more commercial terms production is a creation of things and services to be sold for profit and this type of things and services is called commodity.

Production lies at the heart of development. Originally, development, or *dèveloppement* in French, meant "making into value" (Bryant & Bailey, 1997). Historically, development was a euphemism for capitalist exploitation – through imperialism – of the developing world during both colonial and postcolonial times. More than a mystification of capitalist production, development was ironically turned into an ideal – a national goal for postcolonial states – imbued with some sort of moral virtues. The urgency of dealing with environmental problems such as deforestation has been putting huge pressure on development and establishing a horror picture of dystopia in the place of development utopianism. Unless development – and hence, production – is halted, controlled, and modified, an unimaginable ecological catastrophe is waiting in the very near future.

EGD is a challenge to the existing development and, hence, production system in Southeast Asian countries. EUDR in particular, for countries such as Indonesia, Malaysia, and Thailand, is a real threat to their respective palm oil production. This study is an attempt to juxtapose the resistance to environmental norms transmitted through EUDR and the resilient structure of palm oil production in these countries.

The resilient structure is composed of overlapped layers of structure that shape – and in return are shaped by – palm oil production (Hapsari, 2012). The first layer of structure is the concrete form of how palm oil production takes place and is organized. The formation of social relations of production occurs at this micro level of the larger structure. The second layer is concerned with state power, which allows and facilitates or transforms palm oil production. State power also shapes and is reshaped by social relations of palm oil production. The third layer is tendencies at the level of global order that affect state power and palm oil production.

At this stage, the application of EUDR should be understood as norm diffusion. The path of resistance taken by Indonesia and Malaysia in responding to this institutional scheme is part of constitutive localization. The resistance proves that local norm takers' ideas and initiatives are shaping the reception of EUDR. The Indonesian president, Joko Widodo, himself expressed the rejection by mobilizing the idea of sovereignty as practiced by a country that was born out of a three-and-a-half-century traumatic history of colonization. The EUDR is simply taken as the latest bottle of the old imperialism wine.

At the same time, the application of the EUDR will also be detrimental and potentially bring huge damage to the palm oil production in Indonesia, Malaysia, and Thailand. The resistance indicates the degree of resilience of the existing power relations, which have long been forged within layers of palm oil production structure. The EUDR is just another form of pressure often experienced by this production structure. Unless radical transformation occurs within those layers of structure, significant change will hardly take place.

Furthermore, the formulation of the EUDR notably lacks consideration for the dynamics occurring at the community level. The increasing regulatory demands, characterized by the imposition of more complex rules, introduce additional layers of requirements while failing to adequately address the need for building implementation capacity. This oversight spans across communities, bureaucracies, and the diverse perceptions of sustainability practices among the EU's trading partners.

The absence of sufficient provisions for resources, infrastructure, and technology to empower local governments and communities exacerbates disparities. Consequently, the emergence of international sustainability governance through the EUDR widens the global societal gap (Hegde, 2024). Local sustainability practices, often shaped by necessity and aligned with survival strategies, are relegated to marginalized or underprivileged contexts (Zbuchea, 2022). As a result, the behavioural and normative changes expected under sustainability governance primarily serve the interests and well-being of dominant international communities.

EGD/EUDR and Its Impacts on Southeast Asian Countries

The EU has long pursued a leading role in dealing with and tackling global environmental problems. It adopted a climate change strategy as early as 1992. In 1996, it promoted a programme of limiting global warming to 2 degrees Celsius. EGD is simply the latest initiative taken by the EU. The objectives are increasing the EU climate ambition; supplying clean, affordable, and secure energy; building and renovating in an energy- and resource-efficient way; accelerating the shift to sustainable and smart mobility; from "farm to fork" (a fair, healthy, and an environmentally friendly food system); preserving and restoring ecosystems and biodiversity; a zero-pollution ambition for a toxic-free environment; and mobilizing industry for a clean and circular economy (Verhaeghe & Ramcilovic-Suominen, 2024; Almeida et al., 2023; Chikh M'hamed, 2022). EUDR is one of the EGD regulatory frameworks introduced in late 2022. According to this framework, any company that imports the listed commodities or products (cocoa, coffee, soy, palm oil, wood, rubber, and cattle) is required to take reasonable care (known as due diligence) to ensure that they comply with deforestation-free regulation. The company must produce a due diligence statement that includes the company's details, the products it relates to, the quantity, and the geolocations of all plots of land where the commodities were produced (Brack, 2023).

EGD, and particularly EUDR, is oriented internally to affect the economic behaviour and environmental standards of its members. However, because of the economic size of the EU and the importance of the EU market in international trade, this latest initiative will bring global ramifications. Its impacts depend on the nature of a country's trade relations with the EU (Hereau-Morales et al., 2023; Siddi, 2020; Krungsri Research, 2024). Brazil, the world's largest exporter of coffee, relies on the EU's single market. The latter is also the second most important customer of Brazil's soy and palm oil. Other countries in the American continent that will suffer from the stringent EUDR standard are Argentina (for exports of soy, beef, and palm oil), Guatemala (palm oil and coffee), and the United States (soy, wood, rubber, and cattle). Côte d'Ivoire and Ghana are among the countries in Africa that will witness a dramatic decrease in their exports to the EU. Both countries are the most important source of cocoa for the EU.

Asia will share the same fate. As the EU's second most important supplier of EUDR commodities and goods such as products made from wood and rubber, China will experience significant consequences. Southeast Asian countries will also be significantly affected by the deforestation-free regulation. Indonesia and Malaysia will be severely impacted. Both countries account for 85% of palm oil production worldwide and, hence, are the two most important sources of this commodity for the EU. Thailand also exports palm oil to the EU. The country's other main export to the EU is rubber. Vietnam exports coffee to the EU. EUDR will force its domestic coffee industry to deal with challenging environmental standards.

This study focuses on how EUDR affects palm oil production in Indonesia, Malaysia, and Thailand. The EU is a significant importer of palm oil. In 2021, the EU imported 8,000,000 metric tonnes (MT) of palm oil and palm oil products from non-EU countries. Within the category of palm oil-related products, palm oil represented the biggest portion, which accounted for 74% (5.9 million MT) of the total imported volumes and 83% (EUR 5 billion) of total imported values (Chain Reaction Research, 2022). Indonesia and Malaysia are the two largest exporters of palm oil to the EU. In 2021, the EU received 44.6% from Indonesia and 25.2% from Malaysia of its total palm oil imports. This was followed by Guatemala (8.8%), Papua New Guinea (6.6%), Honduras (5.4%), and Colombia (4.1%) (Chain Reaction Research, 2022). The introduction of deforestation-free regulation will certainly bring negative impacts to this sector of production.

Constitutive Localization of EGD in Southeast Asian Countries

The introduction of EUDR is an operation of normative power in a nutshell. This regulatory scheme demonstrates the importance of ideas and norms in shaping the behaviour of other actors by imposing environmental standards worldwide. The EU has been the leading global figure in raising awareness of environmental problems and pioneering climate policy for decades. EGD is the latest initiative with ambitious goals born out of its long endeavour to promote a greener global economy through multilateral environmental diplomacy. The EU also has a material basis to mobilize support for its green goals and, hence, brings the so-called Brussels effect (Bradford, 2012) into reality. The EU is the third largest single market after the United States and China (ERT, 2024). The EU's normative power is significantly linked to the access of its single market. The Brussels effect refers to the global power deployed by the EU through its legal institutions and standards. Such an unprecedented style of power has been successful in implanting the EU's influence on the whole globe. The EU possesses an increasing ability to impose regulations that become embedded in the legal framework of both developed and developing nations.

However, the normative power even supported by a key material basis is hardly sufficient for persuading Southeast Asian countries to adopt deforestation-free commodities regulation. The local norm-takers and the whole localized process of norm-taking are equally important. Indeed, since being passed by the EU Commission in 2022, EUDR has been undergoing a constitutive localized process within the region. The process is marked by the way local norm-takers, particularly in Indonesia, Malaysia, and Thailand, respond to the new environmental standards. The responses have been changing in the last two years and signaled three different attitudes.

Upon the announcement of EUDR, the initial response was concern, which later developed into condemnation. As previously indicated, the main worry was that deforestation regulation will be detrimental to the palm oil exports – but also other commodities such as rubber, wood, coffee, and cocoa – of these countries to the EU's market. EUDR will not only significantly reduce the revenue of palm oil exporting countries but also bring dramatic effects to the welfare of those who generate their wealth along palm oil production chains. The palm oil production in Indonesia and Malaysia involved a large number of smallholders. While the large private corporations might be better equipped to comply with the new regulation, the small-scale farmers will certainly be excluded. Unsurprisingly, the state-sponsored Malaysian Palm Oil Board accused EUDR of establishing a "significant trade barrier" to the affected commodities and forcing the smallholders in the production of those commodities to bear the consequences.

Southeast Asian countries were also concerned with the issue of sovereignty. For the postcolonial states such as Indonesia, Malaysia, and Vietnam, the EUDR is imposing influence on their domestic politics. While national independence is a sacred, non-negotiable dimension of their very existence, these countries are facing pressures to comply with (external) environmental standards, which might not be aligned with their national preferences. This latest regulatory scheme introduced by the EU was then taken as another form of Western imperialism. The president of Indonesia, Joko Widodo, insisted that "there must be no coercion. There can no longer be one side that always dictates to the other and assumes that 'my standard is better than yours'" (Indonesia Palm Oil, 2023).

The existing belief systems and norms of the postcolonial independent nations conditioned the receptiveness of the EUDR. Because of this sort of "cognitive prior" (Acharya, 2009), Southeast Asian countries' first reaction was a pragmatic awareness of their continuing dependence on colonial nations (the West). At the same time, EUDR seemed to have been ironically taken as the old wine of colonialism in a new bottle of global environmental standards. In the latter stage, this mixed reaction developed into criticizing the contents of deforestation-free regulation while recognizing the urgency of a pro-environment attitude. Southeast Asian countries argued that while all countries must address climate change, their responsibilities differ according to their capabilities and historical contributions to global emissions. EUDR hardly recognized this basic principle, which was adopted by the United Nations Framework Convention on Climate Change (UNFCCC) (Tropical Forest Alliance, 2023). In addition, the deforestation-free regulation could potentially constitute a unilateral action, which contradicts the EU's World Trade Organization (WTO) obligation (Krungsri Research, 2024).

It was this bias towards unilateralism that Southeast Asian countries' complained about the lack of consultation between the EU and Southeast Asian countries prior to the introduction of EUDR. There is no dialogue with palm oil production countries on issues such as risk assessment, traceability, and smallholders. Instead, the EU places countries such as Indonesia and Malaysia at a disadvantage without providing support for compliance. The EU is yet to appreciate the existing attempts to reduce deforestation and does not recognize widely adopted palm oil certification schemes such as ISPO and RSPO. In the meantime, the effectiveness of EUDR is increasingly put under scrutiny. Such regulation applied globally can only very marginally reduce deforestation (Busch et al., 2022). More importantly, EUDR could be a new incentive for further deforestation. Palm oil producers of non-compliant producing countries could avoid sustainability measures and sell to markets with less stringent environmental standards.

In the recent development, criticism seemed to have paved the way for Indonesia and Malaysia to open dialogue and negotiation with the EU. Senior government officials of both countries conducted a joint mission to Brussels in May 2023. The mission was followed by a visit from the European Commission to Indonesia and Malaysia in late June 2023. The result of these initial contacts was a three-party agreement to establish an Ad Hoc Joint Task Force on EUDR. The Task Force comprises representatives from the governments and relevant stakeholders, including commodity associations, smallholders, worker associations, and civil society organizations (EIAS, 2024). Despite the ongoing negotiation, Indonesia, Malaysia, and Thailand may take the path of retaliation should the EU continue to stick with the stringent environmental standard. These countries have the potential to open up a new market in Africa and in countries such as China, India, and the United States (Hasan et al., 2022).

Resilient Production Structure Challenging EGD Localization in Southeast Asian Countries

In the following section, this study shall deploy "Coxian structure" to explain the presence of material structure in the recent development of Southeast Asian countries' responses to EUDR. The focus will be on palm oil production and layers of social structure in Indonesia and Malaysia. Both countries are the first and second largest palm oil exporters to the EU.

Smallholders' Struggle for Livelihoods

The palm oil production value chain in Indonesia and Malaysia involves a significant number of smallholders as the main economic actors. They account for about 41% in Indonesia and 27% in Malaysia of total oil palm planted (Solidaridad, 2023). Smallholders account for almost 35%–40% of the global production of palm oil. They are small-scale farmers who grow oil palm as their main source of income. According to *Gabungan Pengusaha Kelapa Sawit Indonesia* (GAPKI) or Indonesia Palm Oil Company Association, EUDR will prevent these small farmers – around 4 million families in Indonesia from accessing the EU market (Indonesia Palm Oil, 2022). The implementation of deforestation free regulation could potentially put the majority of them out of job.

The encounters of palm oil smallholders with international environmental standards can be traced back to the emergence of the Roundtable on Sustainable Palm Oil (RSPO) in 2004. The voluntary certification programme was introduced to international supply chain actors who have been subject to consistent criticism regarding the social and environmental impacts of the palm oil industry. Policy advocacy converging around the issue of deforestation, biodiversity loss, and climate change drives supply chain actors to respond to international public demands. The emergence of RSPO constitutes a convergence of normative frameworks in which sustainable palm oil as an international norm set the landscape of new international sustainability politics governing the global palm oil economy. Following the establishment of the RSPO, there has been a noticeable growth of certification schemes in other agro-industrial commodity sectors with all its consequences on different segments of the related industries.

The main beneficiaries of the RSPO as a voluntary certification are large-scale corporations that mostly afford to invest in the certification scheme. So far, the majority of certified products come from large-scale palm oil companies and their affiliated supply chains. Most of the environmental and social norms integrated into the EUDR are also directed towards practices involving big companies with a significant scope of sustainability impacts. However, smallholders are simultaneously impacted by the increasing market pressure to join the certification scheme. Currently, a very limited number of palm oil smallholders are able to participate substantially in the certification scheme processes (Muthu et al., 2023). Given the high cost incurred in the process of application and the monitoring of principles and criteria implementation, there has been limited participation by smallholders in the adoption of the RSPO certification.

Nevertheless, the absence of a certification attached to the smallholders production scheme does not prevent them from actively struggling for market access. The domestic market, which leaves a substantial space for smallholders to continue their production, remains a promising arena in which the sources of livelihoods are maintained with all its respective structural constraints. The expansion of the global palm oil economy leaves a substantial gap in terms of the mobilization of industrial upgrading opportunities for smallholders in dealing with continuously evolving and deepening sustainability standards. Most of the economic cost borne by smallholders during the transition to the normative sustainability trajectory as envisioned in the EGD, in fact, is beyond the capacity of the institutions supporting the norm-diffusion process (Watts et al., 2021). Lack of institutional accommodation has always put smallholders on the worst end of changes brought about by new sustainability regulations such as EUDR.

While assistance from major players in the palm oil supply chain and increased self-awareness from governments are often expected to drive sustainability improvements, the logic of certification fails to adequately recognize the diversity of local capabilities. Instead of acknowledging the varying capacities of local stakeholders to implement sustainability governance, discussions rarely address the differing positions of smallholders in achieving certification (Hutabarat et al., 2019). A significant challenge arises from the assumption that the transformation from traditional farming practices to certified sustainable practices can be broadly achieved among smallholders. The diverse starting points of smallholders critically influence their ability to benefit from certification, particularly in financial terms. Those who are better prepared and more familiar with practices aligned to certification requirements are naturally positioned to gain greater advantages. The lack of addressing this situation creates disincentives for smallholders in implementing certification.

The interregional institutional framework that evolves in the relations between the EU and Southeast Asian countries has not yet been able to facilitate transitioning processes for different levels of palm oil producers. This has been the major weakness of the international norm diffusion mechanism as regards developing a stronger EU sustainability leadership. The externalization of economic costs and environmental costs associated with smallholder-based palm oil production remains an unsolved issue. Facilitating a significant scope of smallholders' equal economic opportunity across the palm oil value chain as a form of building stronger power/influence of the EU as a norm promoter is a gap that deters significant progress. Simultaneously, the current institutional arrangement that advocates for the implementation of sustainability criteria has not been able to provide a solid ground for smallholders to gain a significant economic leverage that allows sustainability norm diffusion to precipitate in the smallholders-driven value chain. This has been well documented in previous studies, which ended by advocating for facilitating mechanisms provided by the EU as the promoter of the new sustainability regulations (Melati et al., 2024). This has created major structural drawbacks to the localization of the EGD.

Agro-Extractivism as Dominant Development Mode of Production

Previous studies emphasized how major palm oil producing countries are economies relying on agro-extractivism as the source of national economic growth. The contemporary palm oil economy landscape in Southeast Asian countries is being shaped by food security and energy discourse that is supported by the role of palm oil production driven by national policy interventions. Moreover, the economic roles of palm oil accommodate the very wide spectrum of social beneficiaries. Palm oil is accessible to the poor, making it an inseparable part of food security practices at the community level (Kiatmanaroch & Sriboonchitta, 2014).

While there is an asymmetric dependence of Southeast Asian countries on the palm oil economy that creates complex domestic political economic settings, the underlying characteristics of the palm oil political economy in Southeast Asian member countries are the consistent dependence of the government on the sources of income from the agro-extractive industry. This tendency remains a persistent feature of the agro-industrial development sector, with the increasing intervention in the national production structure coming from the uneven exposure to technological and other capital-driven industrial innovations. Over the last three decades, there has been a continued expansion of the palm oil industry in terms of reconsolidating land use for an effective and concentrated production scheme. This has been followed by market-led intervention sustained by political regimes that demand a stronger flow of investment to support domestic industrialization (Rasiah, 2018).

The mutual dependence between political regimes and the palm oil production system, furthermore, is very well recognized as a political economic context in which normative transformation may encounter a significant structural challenge. The resonance of the environment-development debate is continuously present in the context of political elites' practices. This is mainly related to how to win the support of the political constituents standing at a polarizing position as regards to the controversial impacts of adopting sustainability policies (Warburton, 2017). Such context, in fact, cannot be explained merely by looking at international sustainability norm-diffusion processes as a problem of compliance by norm takers.

There have been strong political claims by leaders in Southeast Asian palm oil-producing countries, signifying that the EGD poses a threat to the sovereign states, given its scale of influence on the policy institutions and material bases of Southeast Asia's palm oil economy. The resignation of the Indonesia Palm Oil Company Association (GAPKI) from the RSPO scheme is an epitome of structural resilience in which Indonesia, as major palm oil producer, seeks to reclaim its sovereign power in the source of dealing with international sustainability norm diffusion (Schouten & Hospes, 2018). It highlighted the reinstatement of state sovereignty amidst the pluralization of the transnational sustainability regime.

Global Structure of Palm Oil Production/Consumption

From the viewpoint of a Coxian structure, changes in social relations of production and changes in the forms of state have historically coevolved with changes in world order. The utilization of palm oil has been increasingly diverse, as has been its international consumption and production pattern. The role of emerging economic powers, namely India and China, has substantially influenced the global consumption pattern of palm oil. This has also been recently facilitated by the increasing demand for palm oil-based biofuel from Europe. This has also implied the need for obtaining feedstock from various sources of biofuel, among which palm oil becomes the strategic resource (Mohamad & Ab-Rahim, 2024). The emergence of a massive scale of palm oil production in Southeast Asia, therefore, is part of the emerging global division of labour among global vegetable oil producing countries.

After the EU issued the EU Directives on Renewable Energy in 2003, the global market for biofuel surged. The growth of Crude Palm Oil (CPO) production and export was encouraged by its demand and price, which were competitive with other edible oils, such as soybean, sunflower, rapeseed, and coconut oils. Palm oil is used mostly in food products and manufacturing industries. It is a ready substitute for other vegetable oils for cooking, such as soybean, corn, canola, and cottonseed oils, depending on price and ability (Mohamad & Ab-Rahim, 2024). Palm oil production in Southeast Asian countries has developed its resilience when it comes to maintaining the marketability of land-efficient sources of vegetable oil production for global market demand.

In this regard, deforestation and other environmental problems associated with palm oil production are hardly a responsibility attached to palm oil-producing countries per se. It is worth noting that such problematization is part of the historical dependence of the EU on palm oil feedstock for biofuel and edible oil use, which is now being transformed by applying a discriminatory treatment to unsustainable palm oil production sources based on the EUDR criteria. How the EGD/EUDR may substantially transform this global structure of dependence, therefore, remains an issue related to the transformation of the global division of labour (Waters et al., 2024). At the global level, the exclusion of palm oil from the global sustainable commodity market has created various problems in the relations between the EU and trading partners. The path through which the transition from unsustainable to sustainable vegetable oil production may take place is also still under-explored. The introduction of EGD/EUDR hardly takes such existing limits of the global palm oil production structure into serious consideration. It is not only Indonesia and Malaysia that need to be disciplined, but the whole global structure of palm oil production/consumption that must be transformed accordingly so it will be able to shift to globally desirable sustainability goals.

Conversely, a series of crises has significantly undermined the EU's ability to impose its regulatory framework on the global stage (Meunier & Nicolaidis, 2019). Escalating geopolitical tensions have further exacerbated this decline by disrupting the material flows of critical resources, such as energy and food, to the EU. These challenges have heightened the difficulty for the EU in promoting and enforcing non-material objectives, including sustainability norms and values. As the capacity to assert such normative agendas diminishes, there has been a noticeable shift towards more pragmatic approaches, prioritizing access to productive forces driven by economic considerations.

Conclusion

The making of the EGD as international sustainability norms needs to be understood as a product of dialectical relations between international norm diffusion and the structural political economic context in which they emerge and gain a foothold. The structural context is being shaped by asymmetric dependence, industrial stratification, and market specialization that situate different segments of palm oil actors in different levels of power leverage when responding to the introduction of the sustainability norms. Albeit inexplicit, these structural contexts determine the conditions of norm diffusion and its constitutive localization. The political economic structure that sustains the palm oil economy in Southeast Asian countries reflects political endeavours to navigate the structural constraints embedded in the unequal power relations in the local, national, and global palm oil economy and value chain. This also demonstrated the mutually constitutive relations between norm promoters and their structural conditions. The EU, as norm makers, continuously reconstructs the normative orientation and practices relevant to the economic landscape and everyday industrial practices of palm oil producing countries against the backdrop of uneven access and control to benefit offered by the global vegetable oil market.

Reference List

Acharya, A. (2009). *Whose Ideas Matter? Agency and Power in Asian Regionalism*. Cornell University Press.

Almeida, D. V., Kolinjivadi, V., Ferrando, T., Roy, B., Herrera, H., Marcela, M.V., & Van Hecken, G. (2023). The "Greening" of Empire: The European Green Deal as the *EU First* Agenda. *Political Geography*, 105, 1–10.

Brack, D. (2023). *The EU Deforestation Regulation Analysis*. Tropical Forest Alliance.
Bradford, A. (2012). The Brussels Effect. *Northwestern University Law Review*, 107(1), 1–69.
Bryant, R. L., & Bailey, S. (1997). *Third World Political Ecology*. Routledge.
Busch, J., Amarjargal, O., Taheripour, F., Austin, K., Siregar, R., Koenig, K., & Hertel, T. (2022). Effects on Demand-Side Restriction on High-Deforestation Palm Oil in Europe on Deforestation and Emissions in Indonesia. *Environmental Research Letters*, 17(1), 1–12.
Chain Reaction Research. (2022, July 8). *EU Deforestation Regulation: Implications for the Palm Oil Industry and Its Financers*. https://chainreactionresearch.com/report/eu-deforestation-regulation-implications-for-the-palm-oil-industry-and-its-financers/.
Chikh M'hamed, S. (2022). *The European Green Deal: Perspectives for the EU-Asia Relationship*. Konrad Adenauer Stiftung.
Cortell, A., & James, W. (2000). Understanding Domestic Impact of International Norms: A Research Agenda. *International Studies Review*, 2(1), 65–87.
Cox, R. (1987). *Production, Power, and World Order: Social Forces in the Making of History*. Columbia University Press.
EIAS. (2024, March 29). *Balancing Environmental and Socioeconomic Priorities: EU-ASEAN Relations and the Deforestation Regulation*. https://eias.org/policy-briefs/balancing-environmental-and-socioeconomic-priorities-eu-asean-relations-and-the-deforestation-regulation/.
ERT. (2024). *Single Market Obstacles: Technical Studies*. https://ert.eu/wp-content/uploads/2024/02/ERT-Single-Market-Obstacles_Technical-Study_WEB.pdf.
Hapsari, M. (2012). *The Political Ecology of Oil Palm Expansion in Indonesia: Structure and Transformation in a Globalizing World* [Doctoral dissertation, Nagoya University].
Harvey, D. (2010). *A Companion to Marx's Capital*. Verso.
Hasan, F., Ahmad, T., Hidayat, A., & Zubaidah, D. (2022). *Implications and Response to EU Deforestation-Free Supply Chain Regulation*. INDEF Policy Brief No. 6.
Hegde, N. G. (2024). Support of Spirituality and Traditional Culture to Achieve Sustainable Development Goals. *Journal of Rural Advancement*, 12(1), 50–59.
Hereau-Morales, J., Segarra, A., & Valderrama, C. (2023). The European (Green?) Deal: A Systematic Analysis of Environmental Sustainability. *Sustainable Development*, 32(1), 1–15.
Hutabarat, S., Slingerland, M., & Dries, L. (2019). Explaining the "Certification Gap" for Different Types of Oil Palm Smallholders in Riau Province, Indonesia. *Journal of Environment and Development*, 28(3), 253–281.
Indonesia Palm Oil. (2022, November 9). *EU Deforestation Regulation will "Increase Poverty" Says Indonesian Palm Oil Association*. www.indonesiapalmoilfacts.com/eu-deforestation-regulation-will-increase-poverty-says-indonesian-palm-oil-association/.
Indonesia Palm Oil. (2023, January 18). *Anger Growing in ASEAN's Capitals as EU Parliament Committee Votes on Deforestation Regulation*. www.indonesiapalmoilfacts.com/anger-growing-in-asean-capitals-as-eu-parliament-committee-votes-on-deforestation-regulation/.
Kiatmanaroch, T., & Sriboonchitta, S. (2014). Dependence Structure between Crude Oil, Soybeans and Palm Oil in ASEAN Region: Energy and Food Security Context. In S. Songsak, V. Huynh, & V. Kreinovich (Eds), *Modeling Dependence in Econometrics*. (pp. 329–341). Springer.
Kissack, R. (2010). *Effective Multilateralism: The European Union, International Organisations, and Politics of Decision Making*. Palgrave Macmillan.
Klotz, A. (1995). *Norms in International Relations: The Struggle against Apartheid*. Cornell University Press.
Krause, K. (1998). *Culture and Security: Multilateralism, Arms Control, and Security Building*. Frank Cass.
Krungsri Research. (2024). *EUDR: Ensuring that Exports to the EU are Deforestation Free*. Research Intelligence.

Melati, K., Jintarith, P., & Haeun, L. (2024). *Finding a Place for Smallholder Farmers in EU Deforestation Regulation.* Stockholm Environment Institute Brief.

Meunier, S., & Nicolaidis, K. (2019). The Geopoliticization of European Trade and Investment Policy. *JCMS: Journal of Common Market Studies*, 57(S1), 103–113. https://doi.org/10.1111/jcms.12932.

Mohamad, A.H.H., & Ab-Rahim, R. (2024). Europe Union Ban on Palm Oil: The Trend of Palm Oil Competitiveness and the Co-Integration on the Soybean and Rapeseed Oil. *International Journal of Business and Society*, 25(1), 260–283.

Muthu, U., Unnithan, U., & Santhanam, P. (2023). Technology as an Enabler for Smallholder Inclusion and European Union Deforestation Free Regulation (EUDR). In N. Kaliappen, N. Zakaria, & A. Mustaffa (Eds), *Proceedings of the 8th International Case Study Conference (ICSC)* (pp. 349–355). Universiti Utara Malaysia, Sintok, Kedah, Malaysia. e-ISSN: 2756-8482.

Rasiah, R. (2018). Innovation Policy, Inputs, and Outputs in ASEAN. In M. Ambashi (Ed), *Innovation Policy in ASEAN* (pp. 285–286). Economic Research Institute for ASEAN and East Asia.

Risse, T., Ropp, S.C., & Sikkink, K. (1999). *The Power of Human Right: International Norms and Domestic Change*. Cambridge University Press.

Schouten, G., & Hospes, O. (2018). Public and Private Governance in Interaction: Changing Interpretations of Sovereignty in the Field of Sustainable Palm Oil. *Sustainability*, 10(12). https://doi.org/10.3390/su10124811.

Siddi, M. (2020). *The European Green Deal Assessing Its Current State and Future Implementation.* FIAA Working Paper 114.

Solidaridad. (2023, April 12). *Briefing Paper: Implications of the EU Deforestation Regulation (EUDR) for Oil Palm Smallholders.* www.solidaridadnetwork.org/wp-content/uploads/2023/04/Briefing-paper-EUDR-and-palm-oil-smallholders.pdf.

Tropical Forest Alliance. (2023). *Navigating EUDR and Rounding Up Recent Updates.* Indonesia Regional Policy Brief No. 6.

Verhaeghe, E., & Rancilovic-Suominen, S. (2024). Transformation or More of the Same? The EU's Deforestation-Free Products Regulation through a Radical Transformation. *Environmental Science Policy*, 158, 1–10.

Warburton, E. (2017). Resource Nationalism in Indonesia: Ownership Structures and Sectoral Variations in Mining and Palm Oil. *Journal of East Asian Studies*, 17(3), 285–312.

Waters, K., Altiparmak, S., Shutters, S., & Thies, C. (2024). The Green Mirage: The EU's Complex Relationship with Palm Oil Biodiesel in the Context of Environmental Narratives and Global Trade Dynamics. *Energies*, 17(2). https://doi.org/10.3390/en17020343.

Watts, J., Pasaribu, K., Irawan, S., Tacconi, L., Martanila, H., Wiratama, C., Musthofa, F., Sugiarto, B., & Manvi, U. (2021). Challenges Faced by Smallholders in Achieving Sustainable Palm Oil Certification in Indonesia. *World Development*, 146. https://doi.org/10.1016/j.worlddev.2021.105565.

Wurzel, R., & Conelly, J. (Eds). (2011). *The European Union as a Leader in International Climate Change Politics*. Routledge.

Zbuchea, A. (2022). Traditional Crafts. A Literature Review Focused on Sustainable Development. *Culture. Society. Economy. Politics*, 2(1), 10–27. https://doi.org/10.2478/csep-2022-0002.

6 The Legal Implications of the European Union Deforestation Regulation towards Environmental Governance in Indonesia

Agus Suntoro, Laely Nurhidayah, Binov Handitya and Dinna Dayana La Ode Malim

Introduction

The European Parliament adopted the European Union (EU) Climate Change Law in June 2021, which sets a very ambitious target to reduce emissions by 55% by 2030 and achieve climate neutrality by 2050. The EU New Green Deal is a package of policy initiatives that aims to set the EU on the path to a green transition, with the goal of reaching climate neutrality by 2050. The European Union Deforestation Regulation (EUDR) is a key element of the EU Green Deal. The EUDR, which took effect on 29 June 2023, stipulates that starting operators and traders must ensure that the production and procurement of key commodities comply with the legal sourcing regulations of the country of origin. Manufacturers, operators, and traders must adhere to due diligence requirements for each shipment, including providing the geo-coordinates of the exact locations where the commodities were sourced. Under EUDR, seven commodities, including soy, beef, palm oil, wood, cocoa, coffee, and rubber, must have been produced by the deforestation policies of their country of origin, be deforestation-free, and be covered by a due diligence statement. The overall aim of this regulation is to mitigate forest and biodiversity loss as well as land degradation.

The implementation of the EUDR in Indonesia, which is the world's largest producer of palm oil and a major producer of wood, coffee, and rubber, poses significant challenges for producers, companies, and government agencies. The regulation imposes an obligation on companies that want to export commodities to EU member countries to demonstrate that the products are not derived from deforestation or forest degradation (Mei et al., 2022). EU agencies and environmental non-governmental organizations (NGOs) consider the expansion of oil palm plantations in Indonesia a key driver of deforestation. In addition, it is claimed that the expansion of oil palm plantations has created conflict and tension with Indigenous people (Tamano, 2023). Oil palm plantations have been established in Indonesia without respect for the rights of Indigenous peoples and local communities (Mei et al., 2022). International standards, such as the United Nations Declaration on the Rights of Indigenous Peoples, were later adopted by the Roundtable on Sustainable

DOI: 10.4324/9781003783176-8

Palm Oil (RSPO) as principles. The Indonesian Palm Oil Farmers Association/APKI stated that EUDR will impact small farmers rather than big corporations, as corporations are already familiar with RSPO certification. In addition, oil palm plantations are now subject to the government's moratorium policy, as stipulated by Presidential Instruction No. 5/2019, which imposes a moratorium on new palm plantation licenses and aims to improve the governance of primary forests and peat lands.

Environmental law and governance are crucial in complying with EUDR regulations. This chapter will examine the legal implications, challenges, and compliance of Indonesia's current environmental laws and policies to align with EUDR obligations. The methodology for this research is a comparative legal analysis, complemented with case studies at the local level. Comparative legal analysis is a research method that examines how laws and legal systems of different jurisdictions are similar and different. This chapter found that several laws and regulations conflict with the EUDR, including Job Creation Law No. 11/2020 (also known as the Omnibus Law), and have significant implications for increasing deforestation by shortening the environmental impact assessment (EIA) process. In addition, the Ministry of Environment and Forestry Regulation No. P24/2020 allows forest areas to be used for food estates. In addition, overlapping land tenure and conflict are widespread despite the One Map policy programme. This has caused smallholders and Indigenous people difficulty meeting the traceability due diligence under EUDR. On the other hand, some regulations align with and comply with EUDR, including a permanent moratorium that ends the issuance of new permits in primary forests and peatlands covering areas of over 66 million hectares and a social forestry programme. This chapter is divided into six sections: first is an introduction; second is a review of EUDR, trade, and climate justice; third is on the legal implications of EUDR on Indonesia's Trade and Climate Agenda Folu Net Sink 2030; fourth is on the challenges to the compliance of EUDR; fifth is on the opportunities of the compliance of EUDR based on Indonesian environmental governance and policy; and finally a conclusion.

EUDR, Trade, and Climate Justice

The EUDR aims to eliminate deforestation and forest degradation, as the world loses 10 million hectares of forest each year. Deforestation and forest degradation increase greenhouse gas emissions through forest fires, permanently eliminating the capacity to sequester carbon and substantially reducing biodiversity, disease resistance, and pest resistance. The Intergovernmental Panel on Climate Change (IPCC) noted in 2019 that deforestation globally accounts for 11% of greenhouse gas emissions (European Commission, 2024). For a long time, numerous attempts to develop a multilateral forest governance regime have been unsuccessful, resulting in a persistent deficit in global forest management. Due to sovereignty concerns, this governance failure can be partly attributed to developing countries' historical opposition to initiatives that would impose trade restrictions on forest products or establish a global forest convention. The unilateralism of the EUDR can be justified by the lack of a worldwide forest convention and by the failure of the Voluntary Partnership Agreement on Forest Law Enforcement, Governance, and Trade (VPA FLEGT) to stop deforestation.

The effectiveness of EUDR in addressing deforestation is questionable because it lacks the capacity to address the main drivers of tropical deforestation. Another limitation is that the EUDR adopts an EU-driven definition of deforestation based solely on consumption while ignoring the financial sector and the need for accountability of European trading companies operating globally (Muradian et al., 2025). The EUDR has also raised concerns about climate justice. The EUDR's requirements for traceability and compliance can exacerbate existing inequalities within the agricultural sector. Smallholder farmers, who often lack the resources to meet the stringent EU standards, may be excluded from lucrative markets, leading to economic disenfranchisement (Wood et al., 2018; Shrivastava & Bhaduri, 2019). This exclusion undermines their livelihoods and perpetuates cycles of poverty and inequality, which are central concerns of climate justice (Ogunbode et al., 2023). As such, the EUDR must be accompanied by measures that support smallholders and promote inclusive economic development, ensuring that the transition to sustainable practices does not come at the expense of vulnerable populations.

The controversy on the EUDR intersects with broader discussions about global trade and environmental governance. Critics argue that such regulations can be perceived as neocolonial, imposing Western standards on developing countries without considering their unique socio-economic contexts (Gilbert, 2024; Gomes & Merida, 2024). This perspective aligns with the concept of climate justice, which advocates for including diverse voices in decision-making processes and recognizing local knowledge and practices in environmental governance (Newell et al., 2021; Harris et al., 2019). The implementation of the EUDR has had a significant impact on Indonesia's legal system, particularly in terms of natural resource regulation, international trade, and national legal sovereignty. The legal implications of the EUDR are that it may conflict with the principles of the rule of law and non-intervention. These legal consequences include changes in legal status, the emergence of rights and responsibilities, the implementation of punishments, and changes to the legal system (Cadman et al., 2024). According to the principles of the rule of law and non-intervention in international law, every country has the right to control its affairs, including natural resource management (Raimi & Davicino, 2024). However, the EUDR de facto places external legal pressure on Indonesia to change domestic practices and regulations in order to comply with EU standards without a balanced multilateral negotiation process, resulting in a shift from the principle of national legal sovereignty to a form of regulatory imperialism in which supranational legal powers (the EU) dictate the national legal practices of developing countries such as Indonesia. Furthermore, the implementation of the EUDR creates legal hurdles and numerous issues or conflicts that arise during its application, interpretation, or enforcement (McDermott et al., 2025). Challenges in harmonizing environmental and trade regulations, as the EUDR mandates that all export products (seven commodities) be deforestation-free and comply with country-of-origin rules (Oliveira et al., 2024).

Although Indonesia already has legal instruments such as the Timber Legality Assurance System (SVLK) and ISPO (Indonesian Sustainable Palm Oil), the EU considers these standards inadequate. We argue this leads to a unilateral norm conflict between national law and international standards. According to legal pluralism theory, such overlap between domestic and international rules necessitates harmonization rather than subordination (Mensah, 2021). Otherwise, legal disruption will harm Indonesia's bargaining position in the global supply chain. With pressure from the EUDR, the Indonesian government may be forced to review, eliminate, or adjust much environmental, spatial planning, and forestry legislation that does not meet EUDR requirements. Worse, it may allow judicial scrutiny of specific regulations in both the Supreme Court and the Constitutional Court. According to the idea of legal change, the EUDR is an external factor that causes national legal reform, potentially undermining a regulation's democratic legitimacy. In the trade sector, the EUDR has the potential to change the legal structure of Indonesia's international trade, including aspects such as export licensing, supply chain compliance, and legal protection for small business actors (Carodenuto et al., 2025), as well as force Indonesian administrative law to adapt by increasing the capacity of legality audits and information transparency (Pham et al., 2025). This is unavoidable since Indonesia will naturally be urged to adopt compliance with supranational regulations (EU) through the acts or attitudes of persons, legal entities, or institutions that are by applicable worldwide legal standards.

Implications of the EUDR on Trade and Indonesia's Diplomatic Response

Global Forest Watch reports that the rate of Indonesian primary forest loss in 2021 decreased by 25%, or 200,000 hectares, compared to 270,000 hectares of primary forest land in 2020, equivalent to 208 metric tonnes (mt) of carbon emissions. However, Indonesia's cumulative deforestation in 2021 of 202,905 hectares is still fourth among tropical countries, after Brazil (1,548,657 hectares), Congo (499,059 hectares), and Bolivia (291,379 hectares) (Mutia, 2022). According to the Research Centre of the Indonesian Ministry of Environment and Forestry, deforestation in Indonesia generally occurs through the conversion of forests into oil palm plantations and industrial crops, peatland burning, and poor land-use governance. The most considerable deforestation occurred in oil palm plantations, reaching 23%. Even in 2019, more than 3 million hectares of forest area were allocated for oil palm production – although plantations can legally operate in production forests, they also cross conservation and protection forests (Sarren, 2022). The government is responsible for a high rate of deforestation, especially in the plantation and palm oil industries. These companies control 60% of oil palm plantations, distributed among state-owned companies (10%), public companies listed on the Indonesian and foreign stock exchanges (25%), and hundreds of unlisted Indonesian-owned private companies (25%) (Li, 2024).

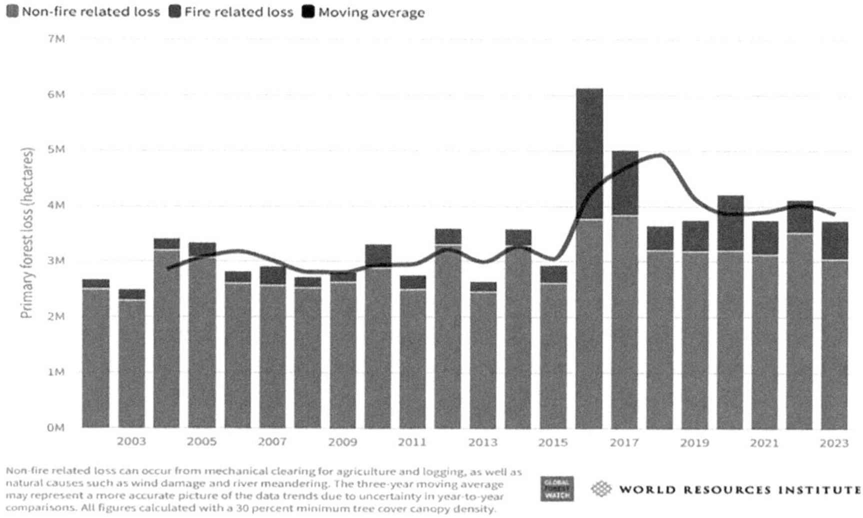

Figure 6.1 Indonesia primary forest lost 2023

Source: Figure by World Resources Institute.

Economic Impact on Commodities

Indonesian Palm Oil Association (GAPKI) Positive Campaign Chairman Edi Suhardi said the EUDR would impact the Indonesian palm oil industry, but not significantly. GAPKI and the government can diversify the market into non-traditional regions, such as South Asia and Africa. Large palm oil companies have the resilience to EUDR implementation by improving certification procedures and trade requirements. Meanwhile, small-scale oil palm farmers will be significantly affected by the qualifications and requirements set out in the EUDR (Suhardi, 2024). In the 2023 report of the Central Statistics Agency (BPS), palm oil commodity exports reached 28,628,000 tonnes with an economic value of US$25.07 billion. The largest markets are India and China, followed by the United States and European countries, especially the Netherlands, Spain, and Italy (Figure 6.2). The statistical data show a downward trend in palm oil exports to several European countries over the past several years (BPS, 2024).

Another commodity potentially affected by the EUDR is cocoa exports. Data from the Central Bureau of Statistics 2017–2021 shows that cocoa exports dominate Asia (India, China, and Malaysia), the United States, and several European countries. Indonesian cocoa is used as a raw material for chocolate-based food and beverage products, including chocolate candy, biscuits, wafers, bread, and ice cream. According to World Atlas, since 2022, Indonesia has become the third-largest cocoa producer in the world, with a total production of 739,483 tons,

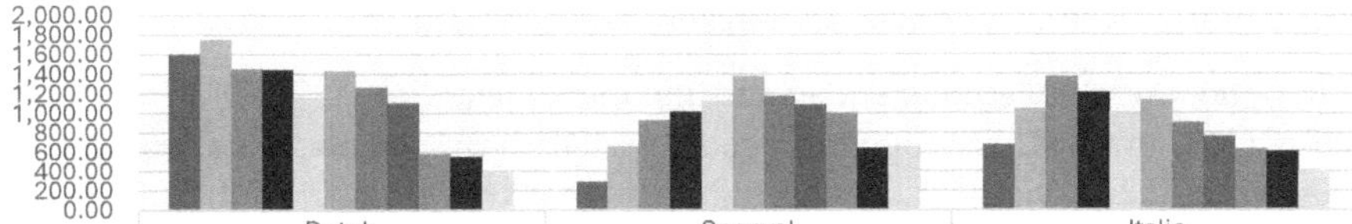

	Dutch	Spanyol	Italia
2012	1,601.20	287.9	672.9
2013	1,747.80	659.2	1,042.80
2014	1,451.40	924.2	1,369.10
2015	1,441.40	1,011.20	1,204.30
2016	1,157.40	1,127.00	1,012.30
2017	1,428.60	1,377.50	1,128.50
2018	1,262.30	1,170.90	899.8
2019	1,103.70	1,086.10	753.4
2021	580.1	994.8	622.9
2022	551.5	636.7	595.8
2023	392.8	655.1	401.4

Figure 6.2 Indonesian palmoil export data to several EU countries (in thousand tons).
Source: The National Statistics Agency of Indonesia, 2024, modified by the author.

after the Ivory Coast, in first place, with 2.2 million tons, and Ghana, with 800 thousand tons. According to data from the Directorate General of Plantations of the Ministry of Agriculture in the 2020–2022 national superior plantation statistics report, cocoa production has averaged over 700,000 tonnes per year in the last five years. The islands of Sulawesi and Sumatra are the largest cocoa producers, accounting for almost 80% of total production (Syafira, 2023). However, the area of cocoa plantations in Indonesia has been decreasing. For example, in 2018, the area of cocoa plantations reached 1.61 million hectares; in 2022, it will be 1.42 million hectares, a decrease of 11.79%. The decline in cocoa plantation area is due to land conversion for other commodities that are more economical compared to efforts to prevent deforestation (BPS, 2023).

Head of the specialization and industry department of the Indonesian Coffee Exporters Association (AEKI), Moelyono Soesilo, said that exporters remain optimistic that Indonesian coffee can be exported amidst the EUDR implementation plan, even though Europe has been one of the main markets, with 85,000 tonnes, or 25% of exports, worth US$230 million/year. Italy, for example, will still need robusta coffee from Indonesia to strengthen espresso blend production. If the EUDR is applied carelessly, the Italian coffee industry will suffer (Rachmawati, 2023). The Central Bureau of Statistics notes that European countries such as Germany, the Netherlands, the UK, Belgium, and Italy import Indonesian coffee. Coffee has become a necessity and a way of life, and in the Netherlands, the average person drinks four cups of coffee daily. Meanwhile, after exporting coffee from Indonesia, Belgium exports green and roasted coffee beans to Western European countries (Samosir, 2013).

Diplomatic Responses of the Indonesian Government

The Indonesian government is against the implementation of EUDR. Indonesia's efforts to unite ASEAN countries against EUDR have postponed its implementation until 2026. The coordinating minister for economic affairs of the Republic of Indonesia, Airlangga Hartato, stated that the EUDR had raised many concerns and objections from various circles and countries because the discussion did not involve commodity-producing countries such as those that produce timber, palm oil, coffee, cocoa, soybeans, rubber, and cattle. In addition, the EUDR is considered unaccommodating to smallholders and ignores the regulations of producing countries with sustainable palm oil certification schemes. In addition, as the world's leading palm oil producers, Indonesia and Malaysia have held discussions with the EU and agreed to form a Joint Task Force (JTF) to discuss the impact of the EUDR. In the JTF, the five areas of discussion are the involvement of smallholders in the commodity supply chain; the gap analysis between EUDR provisions and national standards (ISPO and MSPO); traceability tools from exporting countries; and country benchmarking for personal data protection (CMfEA, 2024).

Indonesia has held a JTF; of course, it is also necessary to encourage and accelerate the completion of negotiations on the I-EU CEPA (Indonesia-European Union Comprehensive Economic Partnership Agreement) with the EU. The ASEAN-EU FTA negotiations must be part of regional consolidation between ASEAN countries with trade interests with the EU and other forms of support from 20 like-minded countries for the EUDR (Wignaraja, 2014; Ariyasajjakorn et al., 2009). Several gap analyses exist between the EUDR and Indonesian regulations, especially in implementing sustainable standards through ISPO. One of the gap analyses is related to the definition of forest (Cosimo et al., 2024), termination date limits, geoinformation (Vasconcelos et al., 2024), permitted deforestation in the area (Berning & Sotirov, 2024), new planting requirements (Oliveira et al., 2024), some EUDR information related to legal requirements (Radosavljević et al., 2024), traceability aspects (Vander Wilde et al., 2023), the ISPO mass balance supply chain system, and others (Ministry of Agriculture, Directorate General of Plantations, 2024; Pareira, 2023).

Indonesian diplomacy concerning the EUDR has been conducted intensively across multiple levels. This initiative commenced with the issuance of the First Joint Letter by the Indonesian Embassy in Brussels, in collaboration with 13 other like-minded countries, on 27 July 2022. The letter articulated the perspective of commodity-producing nations, asserting that the EU's approach to mitigating deforestation is fundamentally flawed (Verhaeghe & Ramcilovic-Suominen, 2024). The EU is encouraged to pursue an alternative route, emphasizing the need for substantial, sincere, and constructive dialogue on the issues outlined previously before implementing the proposed regulation (Johnston et al., 2025; Noordwijk et al., 2025).

Furthermore, the joint letter from the EU on its proposal for a regulation on deforestation-free products to the World Trade Organization (WTO) was submitted by Indonesia and Brazil regarding the impact of the soybean supply chain

(Schilling-Vacaflor & Gustafsson, 2024; Lüpke et al., 2025). This joint letter was disseminated exclusively to the Agriculture Committee to ensure transparency in the application of the EUDR, as documented in the official records of the WTO Agriculture Committee dated 28 November 2022. The Indonesian delegation also articulated objections in the WTO and the Council of Palm Oil Producing Countries (CPOPC) forums. These objections were subsequently communicated directly by President Joko Widodo to President Ursula von der Leyen of the European Commission during a bilateral meeting at the G7 Summit in Hiroshima on 21 May 2023 (Dharmawan, 2023).

In another diplomatic effort, on 30–31 May 2023, Indonesia and Malaysia conducted a joint diplomatic mission to Brussels (Hasna, 2025), the seat of government of the EU, to have direct dialogue with policymakers in the European Commission and members of the European Parliament involved in the formulation of the EUDR (Arnidhya, 2025). The Joint Mission agreed on a consultative mechanism (JFT) between Indonesia, Malaysia, and the EU (Muradian et al., 2025). This step also reflects diplomatic efforts to find solutions that balance the interests of palm oil producers with the European Union's environmental sustainability goals. The meeting resulted in the formation of the Ad Hoc JFT on EUDR to review the situation of related commodities in Indonesia and Malaysia within the scope of the EUDR for the EU market Joint Press Release: The Second Meeting of the Ad Hoc Joint Task Force on the EUDR (2024). In addition, the Indonesian Embassy in Brussels, together with CPOPC, took the initiative to hold a meeting on 24–25 October 2023 to discuss readiness to face the implementation of the EUDR, which has the potential to impose additional burdens on the palm oil industry and smallholders (Johnston et al., 2025; Parra-Paitan et al., 2024) through increased export administration burdens (Partzsch et al., 2023).

Internally, to strengthen Indonesia's diplomatic posture in addressing the EUDR challenge, the Ministry of Environment and Forestry has asked all Forest Utilisation Business Licenses (PBPH) to overlay the European Union Forest Observatory (EUFO) map with the PBPH Map and the PBPH Working Map. The Indonesian government is tak(ing anticipatory steps to advance diplomacy and harmonize definitions and methods with the EUFO Global Forest Map (GFM) map (Sahuri et al., 2024) to better understand forest cover and deforestation. Regulatory Technical Standars (RTS) has also been made by the Indonesian Government (KLHK) to harmonize with the Global Forest Watch (GFW) Map published by the World Research Institute (Sulistyorini, 2024).

Threats of EUDR Implementation

Disparities between the Job Creation Law and the EUDR

Job Creation Law No. 11/2020 (the Omnibus Law) has sparked much debate about its impact, including in the environmental context. One of the main criticisms is the reduction in the environmental impact assessment Analisis Mengenai Dampak Lingkungan Hidup (AMDAL) process. The elimination of AMDAL is feared to increase the risk of deforestation and other environmental damage, mainly due to the acceleration in issuing permits for development projects, which can only be reduced through effective policy interventions (Alix-García & Millimet, 2023). Meanwhile, several countries have implemented industry-wide policies to regulate activities that impact pollution reduction and increase conservation (Kotchen & Segerson, 2020), including cap-and-trade programmes (Weyant, 2017). Simplifying the AMDAL process could lead to reduced oversight of the environmental impacts of these projects.

The Omnibus Job Creation Law No. 11/2020 is inconsistent with the EUDR because of differences in approaches to deforestation and environmental management. However, it does not seem easy to synchronize all climate laws and policies, as each uses different indicators (Eskander et al., 2021). The differences between the Job Creation Law and the EUDR can be traced as follows:

1. **Relaxation of AMDAL (Environmental Impact Analysis).** The Job Creation Law simplifies the AMDAL process and speeds up the process of granting project permits, which can potentially trigger deforestation. Meanwhile, EU regulations prohibit products linked to deforestation from entering the European market, creating tensions because companies in Indonesia may not meet EU standards. Globally, corporations often ignore the impact of environmental damage on productivity and the utility of the company's work (Annicchiarico et al., 2022).
2. **Forest Protection and Sustainability.** The EUDR specifically targets imports of commodities that contribute to deforestation, such as palm oil and timber, as well as other commodities, such as soy, beef, cocoa, coffee, and natural rubber. EUDR also includes livestock products, which are globally responsible for around 67% of deforestation for feed land (Funke et al., 2022). According to Amania (2020), the Job Creation Law is seen as providing leeway for investments that could harm Indonesia's forests, which is contrary to the EU's goal of reducing the global footprint of deforestation.

The EU, through its regulations, encourages partner countries to implement higher sustainability standards. Rather than being a progressive and beneficial regulation (Hsiang et al., 2019), the Job Creation Law is considered to weaken environmental regulations in Indonesia (Ruhiyata et al., 2022), which has the potential to cause trade friction with the EU because products from Indonesia may no longer meet the sustainability criteria set by the EUDR.

These two regulations, although aimed at improving the economy, have different priorities regarding environmental protection, which can lead to potential conflicts, especially in the context of trade and sustainability (Harjono, 2021). Several articles in the Job Creation Law No. 11 of 2020 are considered to conflict with the EUDR, especially those related to the relaxation of environmental rules (Wagner, 2020). The following articles are often highlighted and can be explained in the table below.

Disparities between Sustainable Commodity Certification ISPO and EUDR

Despite some alignment between ISPO and EUDR, gaps exist that require ISPO to be harmonized with EUDR. The Indonesian Ministry of Agriculture has issued the

Table 6.1 Provisions of the Job Creation Law No. 11 of 2020 relating to the context of EUDR. Modified by Author

Article	*Terms*	*Issue*
Article 22 and Article 23	Simplification of Environmental Licensing Processes	These articles regulate the acceleration of permits for development projects, including in the forestry and plantation sectors, which have the potential to cause deforestation. However, their relaxation is considered inconsistent with EUDR regulations emphasizing forest protection with stricter standards.
Article 24	AMDAL	Simplifying the AMDAL process in the Job Creation Law is considered to reduce supervision of environmental impacts, including deforestation. It is considered to conflict with the EUDR, which prioritizes caution because products from areas affected by deforestation have the potential to be banned from the EU market.
Article 110A and Article 110B	Environmental Sanctions	These articles relax administrative sanctions for violators of environmental regulations, especially for companies involved in activities that cause deforestation. The EU, through this regulation, emphasizes the importance of ensuring that imported products do not originate from areas experiencing deforestation and have passed strict environmental standards.
Article 29	Forest Area	This article allows for changes in the status of forest areas for other activities, including infrastructure development or other economic projects. This could facilitate the transfer of forest land, potentially increasing deforestation, and is contrary to the EUDR.

ISPO policy, which aims to increase the competitiveness of Indonesian palm oil on the world market, reduce greenhouse gas emissions, and address environmental and social labour issues. The legal basis for compliance by palm oil companies in Indonesia is the Minister of Agriculture No. 38 Regulation of 2020, which sets criteria for legality, environmental management, plantation management, and social responsibility. Table 6.2 is the table of similarities and differences between EUDR and ISPO. Comparison between EUDR and ISPO regulations, focusing on aspects like geolocation, deforestation-free, legality, traceability, risk assessment, and other areas.

Several components are missing or held back from ISPO regarding geolocation information for smallholder plantations less than 25 hectares due to slow tenure-legalization processes and a lack of human and financial resources. In addition, ISPO does not have an operational information technology (IT) system that could be linked to the data platforms for the plantation business permit Ijin Usaha Perkebunan (IUP) and cultivation registration certificate Surat Tanda Daftar

Table 6.2 Comparison between EUDR and ISPO regulation. Modifications by the Author.

No	Instrument	Aspect	EUDR	ISPO
1	Geolocation	Format Data	Latitude/Longitude (6 decimals) + for polygon> ha plots	Data from IUP (large plantations) and STD-B (smallholders).
2	Geolocation	Availability	Mandatory for all production plots	Available for large plantations (> 25 ha); limited for smallholders
3	Deforestation-Free	Forest Definition	FAO: Canopy cover > 10%, tree height > 5 m, area > 0.5 ha	Based on the official "Kawasan Hutan" (Forest Area) and 2018 moratorium
4	Deforestation-Free	New Plantation Ban	No deforestation after 31 December 2020	Prohibits opening natural forests/peatlands for plantations > 25 ha
5	Legality	Land Right	Compliance with national laws (land use permits, environmental licenses)	Location permits, HGU/HGB, STD-B, and land dispute resolution
6	Legality	Human Rights	FPIC, labour rights, anti-corruption	FPIC is required only for large plantations, no rules for smallholders
7	Traceability	Supply Chain Model	Segregated supply chains for end products	Mass balance (mixing certified and non-certified products)
8	Traceability	Transaction Data	Full traceability from farm to consumer	Transaction records exist but lack digital integration
9	Risk Assessment (EUDR Article 10)	Audit Reports	Public audit reports for compliance verification	Certification Body (CB) audit reports are not publicly available
10	Risk Assessment (EUDR Article 10)	Complaints Mechanism	Complaints from communities/independent observers	ISPO Dispute Resolution Team exists but lacks transparency
11	Other Areas	Certification Coverage	Mandatory for all EU-bound products	Mandatory for all plantations by 2025; only 1% of smallholders are certified
12	Other Areas	Public Registry	EU due diligence information system	No centralized registry for certified entities

Budidaya (STDB). In addition, regarding Deforestation-free information, ISPO does not follow the EUDR/Food and Agriculture Organization (FAO) forest and deforestation definitions, and the new planting requirements prohibiting the development of new plantations on natural forest and peatland do not apply to plantations less than 25 hectares. Regarding legal information, ISPO does not provide details on the human rights protected under international law in the production area's legal status. Information on free, prior, and informed consent (FPIC) is unavailable to smallholders.

Regarding traceability, having smallholder geolocation information is difficult without an operational IT system. To confirm with Risk Assessment Article 10 of the EUDR, the information connecting palm oil to the production area is unavailable for smallholders. Risk assessment under EUDR requires various checks, including those related to indigenous rights and supply chain complexity. ISPO has some relevant data but lacks public reports and clear complaint mechanisms. EUDR legislation covers a broad range of laws, including human and labour rights. ISPO covers some aspects for companies but not for smallholders. The gap here is the lack of human rights and of coverage for smallholders. Traceability in EUDR needs full supply chain transparency. ISPO's mass balance allows mixing and lacks a functional IT system.

The EUDR implementation delay time gap until 2026 opens opportunities for Indonesia to develop strategies for ISPO to meet the EUDR requirements with several key adaptations to address the gaps that exist above, especially for incorporating the information of smallholders, which currently is lacking, and the law and legislation applicable to address human rights and FPIC.

Based on ISPO's compliance with EUDR regulations, it has the potential to meet several requirements, particularly those related to human rights, the environment, and social aspects. However, there are several areas where ISPO could be strengthened to more closely align with EUDR standards, namely differences in forest definitions, Indigenous peoples' rights, the implementation of new systems and infrastructure, and employment. Implementing the EUDR also has the potential to burden farmers with costs, technical challenges, and the time required to learn the new system, necessitating several changes (Hasan, 2023).

Opportunities

Being a state party to various international agreements obligates Indonesia to comply with international standards and principles, including environmental rights. However, ensuring that the EUDR complies with Indonesian national law is complicated because it does not originate from the parent covenant text of economic, social and cultural rights or civil rights. Therefore, Weling believes that a more detailed study is needed, and which ones should be implemented progressively according to resource availability (O'Connell et al., 2014). Therefore, to ensure the principle of sustainability, especially the right to a good and healthy environment, the state must take immediate action by drafting laws and regulations, policies, programmes, action plans, and so on to realize this right (Diokno, 1999). Thus, EUDR, from a legal and political perspective, should be an opportunity for Indonesia to align policies, regulations, and work programmes to save humans, the environment, and biodiversity.

One Map Policy

Indonesia's forests cover 120.3 million hectares, or nearly two-thirds of the country's land area, consisting of 22.9 million hectares of conservation forest, 29.6 million hectares of protected forest, 26.8 million hectares of limited production forest, 29.2 million hectares of regular production forest, and 12.8 million hectares of convertible production forest (Wardojo & Masripatin, 2002). The Ministry of Environment and Forestry estimates that 17.6 million–24.4 million hectares of forest area have conflicts in the form of overlapping State Forest claims and claims of Indigenous peoples or other local communities, village/village development, and the existence of other sector licenses that are in practice located in forest areas (MoFE, 2020). The Consortium for Agrarian Reform reported that overlapping licenses and forest area claims are among the causes of conflict in communities. In 2023, there were 212 agrarian conflicts, a 12% increase compared to the previous year. Most conflicts occurred in plantation/agribusiness areas (108 or 44%), while in forestry areas, 17 conflicts (7%). Conflicts in forestry areas reached 77.487 hectares across 28 villages in Indonesia, affecting 10,900 households (Consortium for Agrarian Reform, 2023).

These conflicting interests, compounded by the absence of a single national reference map with all georeferenced data on spatial use, have led to conflicts over land ownership. In December 2010, then-President Susilo Bambang Yudhoyono pushed for the initiation of a single map of Indonesia, triggered by differences in forestry data between the Ministry of Forestry and the Ministry of Environment in the context of REDD+. Finally, in 2016, Presidential Regulation No. 9 on the Acceleration of One Map Policy Implementation was issued, expected to fulfil the one map principle, which refers to one geospatial reference, one standard, one database, and one geoportal (Presidential Regulation of the Republic of Indonesia No. 9/2016, 2016). Preparing one forestry map (part of a single map of Indonesia) aims to digitize data and information on primary and secondary forests, including peatlands, to eliminate multiple licenses, overlaps, and area claims. These efforts established the Geospatial Information Agency Badan Informasi Geospasial (BIG) through Presidential Regulation No. 94/2011 (Shahab, 2016).

One map policy addresses the forestry sector's overlapping land use and land conflict. For example, in Kalimantan alone, 19.3% – or 10.4 million hectares – of the island's 53.98 million hectares of land were subject to overlapping land use, although similar issues also occurred within the boundaries of the village or district. Massive land-use changes have sparked widespread conflicts over control and access to these lands. Conflict is partly due to the overlapping claims by local Indigenous peoples, the state, and companies over forest lands and concession areas that have occurred since the late 1980s under the regime of former President Soeharto.

Overlapping claims have disadvantaged smallholders and Indigenous people. It creates difficulties with traceability because of overlapping land claims, bureaucratic confusion, and unofficial fees imposed by unregistered smallholders. This lack of clarity regarding land ownership and use rights hampers these groups' ability to meet the EUDR's due diligence requirements, thereby exacerbating their challenges in accessing international markets (Fisher et al., 2018). One Map Policy faces many socio-political, technical, and administrative challenges. The challenge is undeniable when it comes to recognizing indigenous customary forests. The process of recognizing customary forests is slow due to limited mapping at the village level. Of the approximately 74,000 villages across Indonesia, only 19% have been mapped. Despite the challenges of the One Map Policy, it offers hope, as it will produce an improved map with a new database that will also include participatory maps of Indigenous territories. This will help Indigenous people and smallholders meet the obligation to trace their products.

Social Forestry Programme

Environmental scientists believe that tree planting has been an important aspect of forestry history and an effective solution to ecological problems, as promoted by the People's Republic of China in the 1950s to support national development (Li & Liu, 2020). Some forest management models are deliberately designed to respond to environmental changes, particularly those affecting forest resources (Hashida & Lewis, 2019), and to enhance forests' ecological and economic potential (Brock, 2018). Social forestry, as an alternative to community-based forest management, aims to create a carbon sequestration market for climate mitigation and provide higher incentives, encouraging companies and landowners to voluntarily convert land into forests because of the benefits of higher wood prices (Favero & Mendelsohn, 2014). According to Nordhaus (2014), incentives can be among the driving factors in economic variables, helping measure the effectiveness of policies aimed at addressing the impacts of climate change, including the quality of the forestry environment.

Agroforestry is one of the best agricultural management practices on forest land through planning, continuous measurement (Alix-García & Millimet, 2023), provision of techniques, technology, monitoring, and success testing (Lavelle, 2022). It is important to select specific partners based on their interest in participating by providing development rights on forest land so that they can optimize potential and support ecosystem recovery, as well as maximize land restoration and protection efforts (Kroll et al., 2019).

Conservation partnerships prioritize the development and empowerment of communities around forest areas (Hartoyo et al., 2020) in efforts to rehabilitate and conserve natural resources and ecosystems (Prayitno, 2020). Through this programme, the economies of communities around the forest can grow, and illegal activities can be significantly reduced. This programme is running well, as seen in several buffer villages of Way Kambas National Park (Safitri et al., 2023), Rantau Malam Village, Bukit Baka Bukit Raya National Park (Situmorang et al., 2022), Pesawaran Village, Tahura Wan Abdul Rachman Rachman (Wati Amelda et al., 2022), Mantehage Island, Bunaken National Park area (Wijaya et al., 2022), Negeri Masihulan, Manusela National Park (Faizah et al., 2024), and the Fostered Village of the Cycloop Mountains Nature Reserve conservation area (Gaol et al., 2022).

Another form of social forestry initiated by the government is the Community Forestry programme that allows communities to manage forest land legally (Mulyadin et al., 2016) to benefit from wood products through the implementation of integrated trees and crops (Dewi et al., 2018). Increasing commercial harvests can enhance community perceptions of tropical forests, both locally and nationally. In addition, this can also provide incentives to maintain forest resources rather than converting land and can strengthen the ecological aspects of human interaction with forests (Palmolina, 2014). Community involvement like this can optimize forest land by implementing agroforestry based on community socio-economic conditions, such as community preferences and pattern adoption (Puspasari et al., 2017). Furthermore, this programme is part of an effort to increase exports of commodities such as coffee and chocolate. Thus, it is undeniable that expanding the planting area necessitates changes in the forest's functions. To avoid loss of forest function, the most developed planting system is a multi-strata canopy (Sanudin et al., 2016).

In certain forest areas, customary forests are controlled and managed by customary law communities from generation to generation. Recognition of customary law communities provides space for their utilization of natural resources and for sustainable forest management (Dewi et al., 2020). For customary communities, forests have become a source of life and a place to live that must be maintained (Pratama et al., 2022). However, in some places, customary land control involves land claimants using labour to change, maintain, and cultivate the land, even to improve the land through investment in the field or by building non-agricultural income streams on the land (Barrett et al., 2023).

Another form of social forestry, namely the Village Forest, is a forest area that is not burdened by permits, managed by the village, and utilized for community welfare (Masluki & Mutmainnah, 2023). For example, planting coffee under the forest canopy requires minimal maintenance and no agricultural chemicals (Perfecto et al., 2019). Examples of successful coffee planting include the Punik-Punik Hamlet in Sumbawa, Nusa Tenggara Barat (NTB) province, which has developed various types of local coffee through a social forestry business model (Hafizh et al., 2023). Another Wiji Mertiwi Mulyo Petungkriyono Farmer Group has also obtained permission from the East Pekalongan Forest Management Unit (KPH) Perhutani to manage coffee plants in the Petungkriyono forest (Ikbal, 2019). Before becoming coffee cultivators, most of the community worked as loggers. In addition, there is social forestry in Central Java and a Kemuning forest coffee plantation in Kemuning Village, Temanggung (Azi, 2019). Forest management like this is an effort to shift forestry development from a state-based to a community-based model (Rifan, 2019).

Conclusion

Indonesia's commitment to reducing deforestation and forest degradation is showing mixed signals. Some regulations support reducing deforestation through permanent moratoria on converting primary forests and peatlands to other uses, such as an oil palm plantation moratorium, a social forestry programme, and a map policy. However, other regulations can accelerate deforestation, such as the 2020 omnibus job-creation law and a regulation allowing forests to be converted into food estates. The EU's anti-deforestation regulation of 29 June 2023, which will come into effect in December 2025, will significantly impact smallholders and Indigenous people who cannot prove traceability and geolocation. Given the gaps between Indonesia's certification under ISPO and EUDR, Indonesia needs to address how smallholders meet EUDR requirements despite ongoing negotiations and delays in its implementation. Indonesia faces greater challenges in meeting EUDR requirements due to existing gaps and limited timeframes. To comply with the EUDR regulation, the government of Indonesia should revise the Omnibus Law on Job Creation regarding EIA and strictly apply integrated suitability assessment and the selection of food crops before converting forests into a food estate programme. In addition, the government should improve the One Map Policy to include recognition of indigenous customary rights and to help smallholders comply with the due diligence and traceability required for EUDR implementation. Harmonizing EUDR and environmental governance in Indonesia is challenging; it requires the government's political will to revise regulations to support sustainability and local implementation. Further negotiation with the EU is needed to request assistance with compliance with smallholders' EUDR requirements.

References

Alix-García, Jennifer, & Daniel L. Millimet. (2023). Remotely Incorrect? Accounting for Nonclassical Measurement Error in Satellite Data on Deforestation. *Journal of the Association of Environmental and Resource Economists*, 10 (5), 1149–1404. https://doi.org/10.1086/723723

Amania, N. (2020). Problems of the Job Creation Law in the Environmental Sector. *Syariati Jurnal Studi Alquran Dan Huku*, 6 (2), 209–210. https://doi.org/10.32699/syariati.v6i02.1545

Annicchiarico, Barbara, Stefano Carattini, Carolyn Fischer, & Garth Heutel. (2022). Business Cycles and Environmental Policy: A Primer. *Environmental and Energy Policy and the Economy*, 3 (1), 221–253. https://doi.org/10.1086/717222

Ariyasajjakorn, D., P. James, S. R. Gander, & Stephen E. Reynolds. (2009). ASEAN FTA, Distribution of Income, and Globalization. *Journal of Asian Economics*, 20 (3), 327–335. https://doi.org/10.1016/j.asieco.2009.02.009

Arnidhya, Nur Zhafira. (2025). Coordinating Ministry for Economic Affairs: Indonesia Awaits EU Response Regarding EUDR Negotiations, July 3, 2025. *Antara News Agency*. https://www.antaranews.com/berita/4940721/kemenko-ekonomi-indonesia-nantikan-respons-ue-terkait-negosiasi-eudr/

Azi, Muhammad Rafi'Ul. (2019). *Abundance and Pattern of Space Use by Bird Community (Aves) in Coffee Plantation Management Under Forest Stands in Kemuning Forest*. University of Gadjah Mada. https://etd.repository.ugm.ac.id/penelitian/detail/176287

Barrett, Christopher B., Ariel Ortiz-Bobea, & Trinh Pham. (2023). Structural Transformation, Agriculture, Climate, and the Environment. *Review of Environmental Economics and Policy*, 17 (2), 195–216. https://doi.org/10.1086/725319

Berning, Laila, & Metodi Sotirov. (2024). The Coalitional Politics of the European Union Regulation on Deforestation-Free Products. *Forest Policy and Economics*, 158 (103102). https://doi.org/10.1016/j.forpol.2023.103102

BPS. (2023). *Indonesia Cocoa Statistic*. Jakarta. https://doi.org/ISSN2714-8440.

BPS. (2024). *Palm Oil Exports by Major Destination Countries, 2012–2023*. Indonesia. https://www.bps.go.id/en/statistics-table/1/MTAyNiMx/exports-of-palm-oil--by-major-countries-of-destination--2012-2024.html

Brock, E. K. (2018). Sudden Change as an Unwelcome Experiment: Lessons on Time from Forest Management. *Environmental History*, 23 (1), 157–163. https://doi.org/10.1093/envhis/emx131

Cadman, Tim, Kate Macdonald, Edward Morgan, Sean Cadman, Sikha Karki, Matthew Dell, Gregory Barber, & Upama Koju. (2024). Forest Conversion and Timber Certification in the Public Plantation Estate of NSW: Implications at the Landscape and Policy Levels. *Land Use Policy*, 143 (107179). https://doi.org/10.1016/j.landusepol.2024.107179

Carodenuto, Sophia, Claire Cutler, Sokhna Dieng, E. Marshall, A. Adams, & William Thompson. (2025). Formalization through Contracts: Implications for Power in Smallholder Cocoa Supply Chains. *Geoforum*, 164 (104323). https://doi.org/10.1016/j.geoforum.2025.104323

The Consortium for Agrarian Reform. (2023). *Decades of Agrarian Crisis: The Legacy of Nawa Cita and the Future Agrarian Reform After 2024 Political Change*. Jakarta, Indonesia. https://www.kpa.or.id/2024/01/dekade-krisis-agraria-warisan-nawacita-dan-masa-depan-reforma-agraria-pasca-perubahan-politik-2024/

Coordinating Ministry for Economic Affairs. (2024). Wave of Opposition to the Implementation of the European Union on Deforestation-Free Regulation (EUDR). *Ekon.go.id*.

Cosimo, Luiz Henrique Elias, Mauro Masiero, Aynur Mammadova, & Davide Pettenella. (2024). Voluntary Sustainability Standards to Cope with the New European Union Regulation on Deforestation-Free Products: A Gap Analysis. *Forest Policy and Economics*, 164 (103235). https://doi.org/10.1016/j.forpol.2024.103235

Dewi, Indah Novita, San Afri Awang, Wahyu Andayani, & Priyono Suryanto. (2018). Characteristic of Farmer and Contribution of Community Forestry to Farmer's Income InKulon Progo. *Jurnal Ilmu Kehutanan*, 12 (1), 86–98. https://doi.org/10.22146/jik.34123

Dewi, Septya Hanung Surya, I. Gusti Ayu Ketut Rachmi Handayani, & Ulfatun Fatma Najicha. (2020). Position and Protection of Indigenous Peoples in Inhabiting Customary Forests. *Journal Legislatif*, 4 (1), 79–92. https://journal.unhas.ac.id/index.php/jhl/article/view/12322

Dharmawan. (2023). Jokowi Hopes Indonesia-EU CEPA Negotiations Will Be Completed Soon, May 22, 2023, *Presidential Advisory Council of the Republic of Indonesia*. https://wantimpres.go.id/id/newsflows/jokowi-harapkan-negosiasi-indonesia-eu-cepa-segera-rampung/

Diokno, Maria Socorro I. (1999). A Rights-Based Approach towards Budget Analysis. *World*, 38.

Eskander, Shaikh, Sam Fankhauser, & Joana Setzer. (2021). Global Lessons from Climate Change Legislation and Litigation. *Environmental and Energy Policy and the Economy*, 2 (1), 44–82. https://doi.org/10.1086/711306

European Commission. (2024). *The European Green Deal*. https://doi.org/10.5771/9783748918882

Faizah, Rohny M. Maail, & Henderina Lelloltery. (2024). The Strategy of Conservation PartnershipDevelopment by Giving Access to Non-Timber Forest Products (NTFPs) Resin Collection in Manusela National Park. *Jurnal Penelitian Kehutanan*, 18 (1), 176–188. https://doi.org/10.30598/makila.v18i1.12459

Favero, Alice, & Robert Mendelsohn. (2014). Using Markets for Woody Biomass Energy to Sequester Carbon in ForestsUsing Markets to Sequester Carbon in Forests. *Journal of the Association of Environmental and Resource Economists*, 1 (1/2), 75–95. https://doi.org/10.1086/676033

Fisher, M. R., Moeliono, M., Mulyana, A., Yuliani, E. L., Adriadi, A., Judda, J., & Sahide, M. A. K. (2018). Assessing the New Social Forestry Project in Indonesia: Recognition, Livelihood and Conservation? *International Forestry Review*, 20 (3), 346–361.

Funke, Franziska, Linus Mattauch, Inge van den Bijgaart, H. C. J. Godfray, Cameron Hepburn, David Klenert, Marco Springmann, & Nicolas Treich. (2022). Toward Optimal Meat Pricing: Is It Time to Tax Meat Consumption? *Review of Environmental Economics and Policy*, 16 (2), 219–240. https://doi.org/10.1086/721078

Gaol, Chandra I. Lumban, Janviter Manalu, & Basa T. Rumahorbo. (2022). The Development Strategy of the Community Empowerment Based Conservation Program with Fostered Village Models and Conservation Partnerships in the Cycloop Mountains Nature Reserve. *Jurnal Kehutanan Papuasia*, 8 (2), 356–372. https://doi.org/10.46703/jurnalpapuasia.Vol8.Iss2.369

Gilbert, C. L. (2024). The EU Deforestation Regulation. *EuroChoices*, 23 (3), 64–70.

Gomes, C. B. A., & Merida, C. (2024). Global Environmental Governance and the Reflexes of The European Union Anti-Deforestation Regulation on Brazilian Agribusiness: Governança Global Ambiental e os reflexos do Regulamento Antidesmatamento da União Europeia sobre o agronegócio brasileiro. *Concilium*, 24 (12), 118–143.

Hafizh, Muhammad Akasah, Ahmad Yamin, & Umar. (2023). Village Fund Management Strategy through BUMDes In Supporting the Development of Coffee Commodities in Batu Dulang Village. *Prosiding Seminar Nasional Manajemen Inovasi*, 5 (1), 82–105. https://conference.uts.ac.id/index.php/SEMAI/article/view/324

Harris, J. E., Rodenhouse, N. L., & Holmes, R. T. (2019). Decline in Beetle Abundance and Diversity in an Intact Temperate Forest Linked to Climate Warming. *Biological Conservation*, 240, 108219.

Harjono, Dhaniswara K. (2021). *Business Law Review of Law Number 11 of 2020 Concerning Job Creation*. Jakarta: UKI Press. ISBN 978 623 6963 25 8. http://repository.uki.ac.id/4527/

Hartoyo, Didin, Kukuh Setyo Pambudi, & Erti Fadhilah Putri. (2020). Conservation Partnerships and the Future of Papua's Forests. *Jurnal Dinamika Sosial Budaya*, 22 (2), 148–157. http://dx.doi.org/10.26623/jdsb.v22i2.2871

Hasan, Fadhil. (2023). Unraveling ISPO and EUDR Conformity. *Indef*. https://indef.or.id/publikasi/mengurai-kesesuaian-ispo-dan-eudr/

Hashida, Y., & David J. Lewis. (2019). The Intersection between Climate Adaptation, Mitigation, and Natural Resources: An Empirical Analysis of Forest Management. *Journal of the Association of Environmental and Resource Economists*, 6 (5), 853–1037. https://doi.org/10.1086/704517

Hasna, Alma A. (2025). Indonesian Government's Efforts in Facing the European Union's Zero Deforestation Policy Regarding the Palm Oil Sector in 2023. *Global Insights Journal*, 2 (1). https://doi.org/10.36859/gij.v2i1.2478

Hsiang, S., Paulina Oliva, & Reed Walker. (2019). The Distribution of Environmental Damages. *Review of Environmental Economics and Policy*, 13 (1), 83–103. https://doi.org/10.1093/reep/rey024

Ikbal, H. (2019). *Sustainable Empowerment: A Portrait of Empowerment by SwaraOwa NGO in Sokokembang Forest Community*. University of Diponegoro. https://eprints.undip.ac.id/75261/1/COVER.pdf

Johnston, C., Jinggang Guo, & Jeffrey P. Prestemon. (2025). The European Union Deforestation Regulation: Implications for the Global Forest Sector. *Forest Policy and Economics*, 173 (103462). https://doi.org/10.1016/j.forpol.2025.103462

Kotchen, M. J., & Kathleen Segerson. (2020). The Use of Group-Level Approaches to Environmental and Natural Resource Policy. *Review of Environmental Economics and Policy*, 14 (2), 173–193. https://doi.org/10.1093/reep/reaa002

Kroll, Stefanie A., Richard J. Horwitz, David H. Keller, Bern W. Sweeney, John K. Jackson, & Lin B. Perez. (2019). Large-Scale Protection and Restoration Programs Aimed at Protecting Stream Ecosystem Integrity: The Role of Science-Based Goal-Setting, Monitoring, and Data Management. *Freshwater Science*, 38 (1), 23–39. https://doi.org/10.1086/701756

Lavelle, Peter B. (2022). Placing the Science of Agriculture in Early Twentieth-Century China. *Isis*, 113 (4), 816–828. https://doi.org/10.1086/722410

Li, Cheng, & Yanjun Liu. (2020). Selling Forestry Revolution: The Rhetoric of Afforestation in Socialist China, 1949–61. *Environmental History*, 25 (1), 62–84. https://doi.org/10.1093/envhis/emz081

Li, T. M. (2024). Securing Oil Palm Smallholder Livelihoods without More Deforestation in Indonesia. *Nature Sustainability*, 7 (4), 387–393. https://doi.org/10.1038/s41893-024-01279-w

Lüpke, Heiner von, Bence Mármarosi, Charlotte Aebischer, Egor Trushin, Martha Bolaños, Thomas Webb, Eros Nascimento, Djoko Suroso, & Gustavo Breviglieri. (2025). Does

International Climate Finance Contribute to the Adoption of Zero Deforestation Policies? Insights from Brazil and Indonesia. *Forest Policy and Economics*, 174 (103480). https://doi.org/10.1016/j.forpol.2025.103480

Masluki, M., & M. Mutmainnah. (2023). Utilization of Social Forestry Areas through Good Agricultural Practices (Gap) for Coffee Farmers in Latimojong and West Suli Districts, Luwu Regency. *Journal Abdimas Langkanae*, 3 (1), 64–76. https://doi.org/10.53769/jpm.v3i1.158

McDermott, Constance L., et al. (2025). Equity in Unilateral Value Chain Policies: A Monitoring Framework for the EUDR and Beyond. *Forest Policy and Economics*, 174 (103469). https://doi.org/10.1016/j.forpol.2025.103469

Mei, Lan, Helen Newing, Oda Almås Smith, Marcus Colchester, & Angus McInnes. (2022). *Identifying the Human Rights Impacts of Palm Oil: Guidance for Financial Institutions and Down- Stream Companies. Forest People Programme*. London, England. https://globalcanopy.org/wp-content/uploads/2022/08/FPP-Palm-Oil-Report-FINAL52.pdf

Mensah, Linda. (2021). Legal Pluralism in Practice: Critical Reflections on the Formalisation of Artisanal and Small-Scale Mining (ASM) and Customary Land Tenure in Ghana. *The Extractive Industries and Society*, 8 (4), 100973. https://doi.org/10.1016/j.exis.2021.100973

Ministry of Agriculture, Directorate General of Plantations, 2024, "Indonesian Government Firmly Declares ISPO as Proof of Plantation Sovereignty, Pushes for Official Recognition from the European Union", https://ditjenbun.pertanian.go.id/pemerintah-indonesia-tegas-nyatakan-ispo-bukti-kedaulatan-perkebunan-dorong-pengakuan-resmi-dari-uni-eropa/

MoFE. (2020). Forest Management Unit. *Www.Menlhk.go.id*.

Mulyadin, Raden Mohamad, S. Surati, & Kuncoro Ariawan. (2016). Study of Community Forest as Source of Income: A Case in Gunungkidul Regency, Yogyakarta. *Jurnal Penelitian Sosial Dan Ekonomi Kehutanan*, 13 (1), 13–23. https://dx.doi.org/10.20886/jsek.2016.13.1.13-23

Muradian, Roldan, et al. (2025). Will the EU Deforestation-Free Products Regulation (EUDR) Reduce Tropical Forest Loss? Insights from Three Producer Countries. *Ecological Economics*, 227. https://doi.org/10.1016/j.ecolecon.2024.108389

Mutia, A. (2022). Indonesia's Primary Forest Loss Trend Declines in Last 5 Years. *Katadata.co.id*.

Newell, P., Srivastava, S., Naess, L. O., Torres Contreras, G. A., & Price, R. (2021). Toward Transformative Climate Justice: An Emerging Research Agenda. *Wiley Interdisciplinary Reviews: Climate Change*, 12 (6), e733.

Noordwijk, Meine van, Beria Leimona, & Peter A. Minang. (2025). The European Deforestation-Free Trade Regulation: Collateral Damage to Agroforesters? *Current Opinion in Environmental Sustainability*, 72 (101505). https://doi.org/10.1016/j.cosust.2024.101505

Nordhaus, W. (2014). Estimates of the Social Cost of Carbon: Concepts and Results from the DICE-2013R Model and Alternative Approaches Estimates of the Social Cost of Carbon. *Journal of the Association of Environmental and Resource Economists*, 1 (1/2), 273–312. https://doi.org/10.1086/676035

O'Connell, R., Aoife Nolan, Colin Harvey, Mira Dutschke, & Eoin Rooney. (2014). *Applying an International Human Rights Framework to State Budget Allocations*. London: Routledge, Taylor & Francis Group.

Oliveira, Susan E. M. Cesar de, Jaqueline C. Visentin, Bruna F. Pavani, Paulo D. Branco, Marcello de Maria, & Rafael Loyola. (2024). The European Union-Mercosur Free Trade Agreement as a Tool for Environmentally Sustainable Land Use Governance. *Environmental Science & Policy*, 161 (103875). https://doi.org/10.1016/j.envsci.2024.103875

Palmolina, M. (2014). The Roles of Non-Timber Forest Products in the Development of Community Forestry in Menoreh Hills (A Case of Hargorejo Village, Kokap, Kulon Progo Regency, Yogyakarta). *Jurnal Ilmu Kehutanan*, 8 (2). https://doi.org/10.22146/jik.10170

Parra-Paitan, Claudia, Patrick Meyfroidt, Peter H. Verburg, & Erasmus K. H. J. zu Ermgassen. (2024). Deforestation and Climate Risk Hotspots in the Global Cocoa Value Chain. *Environmental Science & Policy*, 158 (103796). https://doi.org/10.1016/j.envsci.2024.103796

Pareira, S. P. (2023). Achieving Indonesian Palm Oil Farm-To-Table Traceability Through ISPO-RSPO Harmonization. *Modernizing Indonesia's Agriculture*, 220. https://repository.cips-indonesia.org/publications/560227/achieving-indonesian-palm-oil-farm-to-table-traceability-through-ispo-rspo-harmonization

Partzsch, Lena, Lukas Maximilian Müller, & Anne-Kathrin Sacherer. (2023). Can Supply Chain Laws Prevent Deforestation in the Democratic Republic of the Congo and Indonesia? *Forest Policy and Economics*, 148 (102903). https://doi.org/10.1016/j.forpol.2022.102903

Perfecto, Ivette, M. Estelí Jiménez-Soto, & John Vandermeer. (2019). Coffee Landscapes Shaping the Anthropocene Forced Simplification on a Complex Agroecological Landscape. *Current Anthropology: Patchy Anthropocene: Frenzies and Afterlives of Violent Simplifications*, 60 (s20), S236–S250. https://doi.org/10.1086/703413

Pham, Thu Thuy, Thi Kim Hong Tang, & Andrew Lowe. (2025). Policy Forum: Opportunities and Challenges for Vietnamese Companies to Source Sustainable Timber from Africa, and Implications for Future Implementation of the EU Deforestation Regulation. *Forest Policy and Economics* 170 (103387). https://doi.org/10.1016/j.forpol.2024.103387

Pratama, Muhammad Risky Surya, Arum Ayu Lestari, & Rimas Intan Katari. (2022). Fulfillment of Rights for Indigenous Peoples by the State in the Field of Customary Forests. *Jurnal Hukum IUS QUIA IUSTUM*, 29 (1), 189–210. https://doi.org/10.20885/iustum.vol29.iss1.art

Prayitno, D. E. (2020). Conservation Partnerships as an Effort to Resolve Tenurial Conflicts in Conservation Area Management in Indonesia. *Jurnal Hukum Lingkungan Indonesia*, 6 (2), 184–209. https://doi.org/10.38011/jhli.v6i2.175

Presidential Regulation of the Republic of Indonesia No. 9/2016. (2016). Accelerating the Implementation of One Map Policy at the Map Accuracy Level of Scale 1:50,000. *Indonesia*. https://peraturan.bpk.go.id/Details/38518/perpres-no-9-tahun-2016

Puspasari, Eny, Christine Wulandari, Arief Darmawan, & Irwan Sukri Banuwa. (2017). Social Economic Aspects Agroforestry System in the Forest Community Work Area (Hkm) District West Lampung, Lampung Province. *Jurnal Sylva Lestari*, 5 (3), 95–103. http://dx.doi.org/10.23960/jsl3595-103

Ogunbode, C. A., Pallesen, S., Böhm, G., Doran, R., Bhullar, N., Aquino, S., . . . & Lomas, M. J. (2023). Negative Emotions about Climate Change are Related to Insomnia Symptoms and Mental Health: Cross-Sectional Evidence from 25 Countries. *Current Psychology*, 42 (2), 845–854.

Rachmawati, D. (2023). Coffee Exports to Europe Sell Well, No Worries About Anti-Deforestation Law. *Bisnis.com*.

Radosavljević, Maja, Todora Rogelja, Mauro Masiero, Dragan Čomić, Branko Glavonjić, & Davide Pettenella. (2024). Institutional and Actor-Oriented Factors Influencing Timber Legality in Selected Western Balkan Countries: Multiple Case Study of Croatia, Montenegro, Serbia, Slovenia and the Republic of Srpska (Bosnia and Herzegovina). *Forest Policy and Economics*, 166 (103261). https://doi.org/10.1016/j.forpol.2024.103261

Raimi, Daniel, & Alana Davicino. (2024). Securing Energy Sovereignty: A Review of Key Barriers and Opportunities for Energy-Producing Native Nations in the United States. *Energy Research & Social Science*, 107 (103324). https://doi.org/10.1016/j.erss.2023.103324

Rifan, M. (2019). Designing the Anatomy of Forest Management by Village Communities. *PANGRIPTA: Jurnal Ilmiah Kajian Perencanaan Pembangunan*, 2 (2), 1–12. https://doi.org/10.58411/cwzm3h89

Ruhiyata, Sandy Gustiawan, Imamulhadi Imamulhadib, & Yulinda Adharani. (2022). Regional Authority in Protection and Management of the Environment Post-Application of the Copyright Law. *Bina Hukum Lingkungan Journal*, 7 (1), 39–58. https://doi.org/10.24970/bhl.v7i1.298

Safitri, Intan Maharani, Susni Herwanti, Indra Gumay Febryano, Rudi Hilmanto, K. Kuswandono, & R. Rusdianto. (2023). Factors that Encourage the Community Labuhan

Ratu Vii Village to Participate in the Conservation Partnership in Way Kambas National Park. *Jurnal Belantara*, 6 (2), 147–156. https://doi.org/10.29303/jbl.v6i2.895
Sahuri, Sahuri, Lina Fatayati Syarifa, Andrea Akbar, Radite Tistama, Suroso Rahutomo, & Aprizal Alamsyah. (2024). Strategi Menghadapi Regulasi Bebas Deforestasi Uni Eropa (EUDR) Pada Karet Alam Berkelanjutan. *Warta Perkaretan*, 43 (1). https://doi.org/10.22302/ppk.wp.v43i1.958
Samosir, Sry Lestari. (2013). Coffee Export Potential from Indonesia to Europe. *Ukmindonesia.co.id.*
Sanudin, San Afri Awang, Ronggo Sadono, & Ris Hadi Purwanto. (2016). Progress of Community Forest in Lampung Province. *Journal Manusia Dan Lingkungan*, 23 (2), 276–283. https://doi.org/10.22146/jml.725
Sarren, S. (2022). Vanishing Act: Deforestation in Indonesia. *Earth.org.*
Schilling-Vacaflor, A., & Maria-Therese Gustafsson. (2024). Integrating Human Rights in the Sustainability Governance of Global Supply Chains: Exploring the Deforestation-Land Tenure Nexus. *Environmental Science & Policy*, 154 (103690). https://doi.org/10.1016/j.envsci.2024.103690
Shahab, N. (2016). *Indonesia : One Map Policy*. Open Government Partnership.
Shrivastava, M. K., & Bhaduri, S. (2019). Market-Based Mechanism and 'Climate Justice': Reframing the Debate for a Way Forward. *International Environmental Agreements: Politics, Law and Economics*, 19 (4), 497–513.
Situmorang, Aon, Emi Roslinda, & Gusti Hardiansyah. (2022). Conservation Partnership as an Effort to Empower the Rantau Malam Village Community. *Jurnal Lingkungan Hutan Tropis*, 1 (1), 269–282. https://jurnal.untan.ac.id/index.php/jlht/article/view/60672/75676595899
Suhardi, E. (2024). GAPKI: EUDR Will not Cause Significant Impact to RI. *CNBC Indonesia.*
Sulistyorini, Indah. (2024). Real Facts on Indonesia's Forest Cover: Indonesia's Diplomatic Modalities to Face the EUDR Challenge, April 29, 2024. *Kontan Daily*. https://adv.kontan.co.id/news/fakta-riil-tutupan-hutan-ri-modalitas-diplomasi-indonesia-hadapi-tantangan-eudr
Syafira, Nur Halimah. (2023). These are the Provinces that Produce the Most Cocoa in Indonesia. *Indonesiabaik.id.* 2023.
Tamano, Muhammad Alrasyid. (2023). Indonesian Palm Oil Industry: Environment Risk, Indigenous Peoples, and National Interest. *Law and Humanities Quarterly Reviews*, 2 (4). https://doi.org/10.31014/aior.1996.02.04.93
Vander Wilde, Calli P., Joshua P. Newell, Dimitrios Gounaridis, & Benjamin P. Goldstein. (2023). Deforestation, Certification, and Transnational Palm Oil Supply Chains: Linking Guatemala to Global Consumer Markets. *Journal of Environmental Management*, 344 (118505). https://doi.org/10.1016/j.jenvman.2023.118505
Vasconcelos, André A., Mairon G. Bastos Lima, Toby A. Gardner, & Constance L. McDermott. (2024). Prospects and Challenges for Policy Convergence between the EU and China to Address Imported Deforestation. *Forest Policy and Economics*, 162 (103183). https://doi.org/10.1016/j.forpol.2024.103183
Verhaeghe, Elke, & Sabaheta Ramcilovic-Suominen. (2024). Transformation or More of the Same? The EU's Deforestation-Free Products Regulation through a Radical Transformation Lens. *Environmental Science & Policy*, 158 (103807). https://doi.org/10.1016/j.envsci.2024.103807
Wagner, I. (2020). The Progress and Regression of the Transformation of the Regulations Concerning Environmental Impact Analysis in Indonesia. *Diktum: Jurnal Ilmu Hukum*, 8 (2), 144–166. https://doi.org/10.24905/diktum.v8i2.103
Wardojo, Wahjudi, & Nur Masripatin. (2002). Trends in Indonesian Forest Policy. *Policy Trend Report*, 77–87.
Wati Amelda, Mira, Hari Kaskoyo, Rini Nurindarwati, Qurniati Rommy, & Eny Puspasari. (2022). Contribution of Agroforestry and Factors Affecting Income of the Conservation

Partnership Group at Wan Abdul Rachman Grand Forest Park. *Jurnal Rimba Lestari*, 2 (1), 15–23. https://doi.org/10.29303/rimbalestari.v2i1.1412

Weyant, J. (2017). Some Contributions of Integrated Assessment Models of Global Climate Change. *Review of Environmental Economics and Policy*, 11 (1), 115–137. https://doi.org/10.1093/reep/rew018

Wignaraja, G. (2014). The Determinants of FTA Use in Southeast Asia: A Firm-Level Analysis. *Journal of Asian Economics*, 35, 32–45. https://doi.org/10.1016/j.asieco.2014.10.002

Wijaya, Pandu, Hengki Djemie Walangitan, & Wieske Chriesti Rotinsulu. (2022). Tenurial Conflict Resolving Strategies Through Conservation PartnershipIn Bunaken National Park(Mantehage Island Case Study). *Agrisosioekonomi:Jurnal Transdisiplin Pertanian (Budidaya Tanaman, Perkebunan, Kehutanan, Peternakan, Perikanan), Sosial Dan Ekonomi*, 18 (3), 803–10. https://doi.org/10.35791/agrsosek.v18i3.44723

Wood, S. A., Tirfessa, D., & Baudron, F. (2018). Soil Organic Matter Underlies Crop Nutritional Quality and Productivity in Smallholder Agriculture. *Agriculture, Ecosystems & Environment*, 266, 100–108.

7 Developing Sustainable Finance Taxonomies in the European Union and ASEAN

Convergence or Contestation?

Apolline Simons and Lena Rethel

Introduction

One of the key challenges for both the Association of Southeast Asian Nations (ASEAN) and the European Union (EU) is the question of how to finance the green transition, with recent estimates putting the figure of global funding required as high as exceeding US$9 trillion annually. As a result, the topic of green finance – or sustainable finance more broadly – is increasingly gaining traction in academic and policy circles. Indeed, finance features prominently in the EU Green Deal, with a target of 30% of investments to contribute to climate objectives. In this drive, the EU taxonomy regulation plays an important role as it is thought to be key to mobilizing private sector investment "in green and sustainable projects" (European Commission, 2019).

More generally, taxonomies – that is, classification systems that identify and categorize the impact of economic activities on the environment – have emerged as important tools in the green transition. In focusing on regional-level efforts to develop sustainable finance taxonomies, this chapter examines commonalities and differences between the regulatory frameworks for sustainable finance developed in ASEAN and the EU.

While in practice sustainable finance in Southeast Asia frequently emulates mainstream financial market norms and adopts elements from mainstream products and policies, in this chapter we highlight instances of innovation via adaptation and paradigmatic contestation in the taxonomy case. To this end, we mobilize Acharya's framework of norm localization and subsidiarity, forms of norm-taking and norm-making, as we explain in more detail in the next section. We argue that the ASEAN taxonomy framework, particularly in how it situates itself vis-à-vis its European equivalent, displays features of both norm localization and norm subsidiarity.

The remainder of this chapter is divided into four main sections. The next section introduces the key concepts and methods on which we draw in this chapter. This is followed by a section in which we sketch the development of the ASEAN taxonomy. Thereafter, we present our data analysis and key findings in relation to how the ASEAN taxonomy, at the time of writing in its third version, compares to the EU taxonomy. Before concluding, we discuss the key insights derived from this study and important limitations.

DOI: 10.4324/9781003783176-9

Key Concepts and Methods

In this section, we present the key concepts and methods on which our chapter draws.

Key Concepts

The development and publication of both the ASEAN and the EU taxonomies happen in the context of a hierarchical financial system (Alami et al., 2022). In particular, in the area of green finance, there exists a hierarchical system of norm production that, to date, is dominated by the EU. As a result, when comparing the ASEAN and EU taxonomies and their evolution, we must take into account the power dynamics that both arise from and shape this process of norm-making. This should not obscure the agency of non-hegemonic actors, including ASEAN, as we discuss in more detail elsewhere (Simons & Rethel, 2025).

In this chapter, we focus in particular on dynamics of convergence and contestation between the ASEAN and EU taxonomies. To do so, we mobilize Acharya's conceptual framework of norm localization and subsidiarity. These concepts challenge the widespread assumption that norm diffusion is a one-sided, top-down transmission where a (usually Western) norm-giver diffuses a norm that might then be accepted or rejected by an (often non-Western) norm-taker. Instead, norm diffusion elicits dynamic, multidirectional responses, in which subordinated actors in the global (financial) system still exert agency in how they adopt and adapt new rules or propose entirely new ones (Acharya, 2004, p. 240, 2011, p. 96).

First, non-local norms are rarely adopted as-is; instead, they are adapted and joined with other elements that more clearly reflect regional norms and realities. This process of "norm localization" reinterprets external norms to align with a local context through a series of adaptive processes, emphasizing the agency of local actors. Norm localization also depends on normative compatibility with local cultural, political, and socio-economic precepts: in adapting foreign norms, a process of "cultural selection" takes place (Acharya, 2004, pp. 245–246; for the case of green finance policies specifically, see Larsen, 2022). Norm localization creates coherence between conflicting ideas.

Second, in seeking to adapt foreign norms in ways that make them usable for local actors, some aspects of the foreign norm might be changed to such an extent – and supplemented with such significantly new ideas – that it results in the creation of entirely new norms, going beyond adaptation or localization of foreign norms. This is where Acharya's concept of "norm subsidiarity" comes into play. Whereas localization, while stressing agency, is still a process of norm-taking, norm subsidiarity has local actors rejecting norms and/or making new norms. Acharya ascribes a specific strategic intent to this process, notably to "preserve their [regional actors'] autonomy from dominance, neglect, violation, or abuse by more powerful central actors" (Acharya, 2011, p. 97).

Like Acharya, we focus on Southeast Asia as a particularly salient site of processes of norm localization and subsidiarity. The norms we examine through the lens of Acharya's concepts, are green taxonomies – specifically the three versions of the ASEAN taxonomy published to date: the initial release in 2021, the updated second version in 2023, and the third version published in April 2024 (referred to as ASEAN-1, ASEAN-2, and ASEAN-3, respectively) – as well as the EU taxonomy, including its major delegated acts (Climate Delegated Act 2021, Disclosures Delegated Act 2021, and Environmental Delegated Act 2023).

Qualitative Content Analysis

Our goal is to examine commonalities and differences between the ASEAN and EU taxonomies in three areas: their design, measurement approach, and the underlying understanding of (green) finance on which the documents build. To do so, we compare the content of the texts (the design and thresholds used) and then analyze the documents using software-assisted Qualitative Content Analysis (QCA) with the software NVivo 10. We first used exploratory methods (cluster analysis by word-similarity) before proceeding with the QCA. The approach was inductive, with categories emerging from several rounds of coding. We ended up with 23 parent categories across both documents. That way, the underlying positions on finance and sustainability in the EU taxonomy, ASEAN-1, ASEAN-2, and ASEAN-3 could be measured, and instances of convergence and persistent divergence could be tracked thematically.

To understand how these competing visions of the taxonomy are articulated, the documents were subjected to a further round of coding, where the interaction between relevant excerpts was coded. For example, if a sentence mentioning ASEAN's diversity is immediately followed and grammatically linked to a sentence that says that this is why the taxonomy needs to be flexible, then the first sentence (code: "diversity stakeholders/MS") and the second sentence (code: "flexibility taxonomy") are coded as having a "connected" relationship. If a sentence mentions that a science-based, rigorous measurement is ideal (code: "evidence-based & rigorous") but that this is problematic because it makes it less accessible to some member states where data availability is more limited (code: "importance inclusion"), then the relationship is coded as "conflictual."

Taxonomy Design Features

Since the emergence of the first green and sustainable financial products in the mid-2000s, there has been significant momentum towards the further institutionalization of the market. A key role is played by sustainable finance taxonomies. These frameworks define unified standards of sustainability for financial instruments such as green bonds or the Islamic variant, sukuk, by rating the activities underlying these investments. They might be used by private actors who wish to invest in sustainable finance, but are also frequently the basis for public investment targets or support the formulation of further green policies (Larsen, 2022). Potentially, sustainable finance taxonomies offer clarity about what is to be considered "green" and can thus make the investment in such activities more transparent, easier, and less costly.

Effectively, though, as we illustrate in this chapter, taxonomies can be shaped by different understandings of what constitutes (green) finance. For taxonomies to matter, they need to be able to influence wider financial norms. This form of financial knowledge-making is therefore also shaped by the broader power-structures in finance; they constitute an important site in which financial norm-making power is reproduced or challenged. Interestingly, the United States, as the dominant rule-maker in global finance, has been largely absent from this space, given domestic political contestation around the green transition. This has left a gap in leadership that benefited the EU – but arguably also gave some autonomy to Asian policymakers (Larsen, 2022).

From the mid-2010s onwards, several East and Southeast Asian countries began work on developing green taxonomies, with China and Malaysia at the forefront. However, a watershed moment was the publication of the EU taxonomy in 2020 (Regulation 2020/852). As Larsen (2022) highlights, the EU published its taxonomy later than several other actors. Nevertheless, it has substantial standard-setting power. Once the EU had published its taxonomy, the playing field changed: "After the EU begins standard setting, countries across the world are exposed to isomorphic pressure and gradually start rolling out policies, either as guidelines or as voluntary, which all converge on the institutionalized norms" (Larsen, 2022, p. 366).

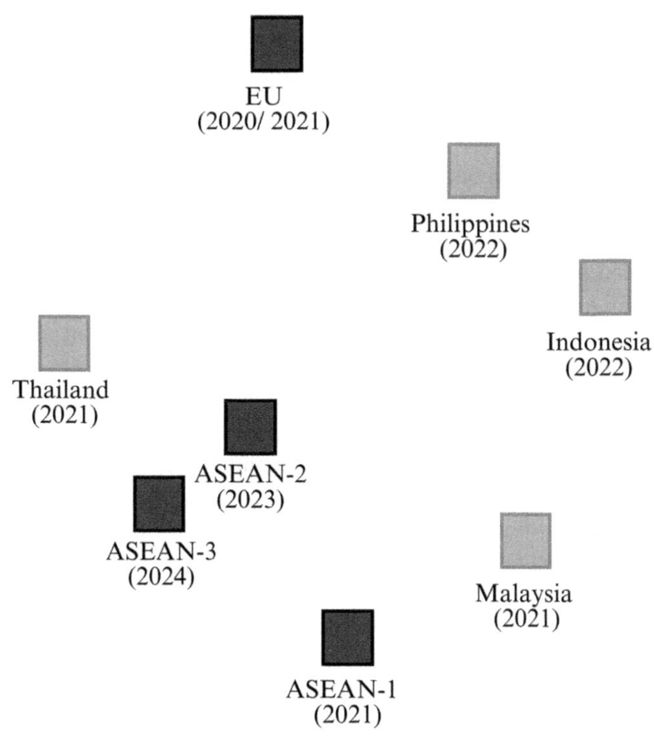

Figure 7.1 Items clustered by word similarity

The timeline of taxonomy development, therefore, is quite important. The first version of the ASEAN taxonomy was developed largely in parallel with the EU taxonomy and published the year after the main document of the EU taxonomy was released; later versions of the ASEAN taxonomy were published after the EU taxonomy had acquired full legal standing. This means that these latter versions of the ASEAN taxonomy, published in March 2023 and April 2024, respectively, had to contend with the existence of a more "dominant" foreign taxonomy in a way the first version did not have to.

Figure 7.1 illustrates the relative similarity of Southeast Asian taxonomies and where they stand vis-à-vis the EU taxonomy by using cluster analysis, which groups taxonomies together according to how similar their word usage is. It shows significant divergence between the EU taxonomy and the first version of the ASEAN taxonomy. This divergence diminishes in subsequent versions of the ASEAN taxonomy.

Table 7.1 summarizes key features of the EU and ASEAN taxonomies. A close look at their design and approach to measurement reveals both instances of convergence and of (enduring) divergence. All versions of the taxonomy contain an essential criterion: the "Do No Significant Harm" (DNSH) principle. This criterion originates from an older EU directive (Regulation (EU) 2019/2088) and excludes investments into activities that are environmentally beneficial in some ways but harm the environment in other ways. Where the ASEAN taxonomy diverges from the EU taxonomy is by introducing a second general principle: the importance of "Remedial Measures to Transition" (RMT), measures meant to reduce, minimize, or remedy environmental harm caused by activities. These measures allow harmful activity to receive an improved sustainability classification if remediation takes place

The ASEAN taxonomy uses a traffic light system; so, for example, a harmful activity that remedies some of the environmental harm it causes would be classified as "amber" instead of "red." ASEAN-2 adds a further essential criterion, "social aspects," which include "Respect Human Rights, Prevention of Forced and Child Labour and Impact on People Living Close to Investments" (ASEAN Taxonomy Board [ATB], 2023, p. 1). While the EU taxonomy also mentions principles such as respect for human rights or the necessity to take negative social externalities into account, these are featured much less prominently and constitute minimal safeguards, focusing mostly on human and labour rights.

In this instance, despite a core element being directly adopted from the EU taxonomy with little initial modification, the added criteria significantly change the DNSH principle, in so doing localizing the EU DNSH norm. The added remedial measure greatly limits the effect of the DNSH principle and changes its meaning to such an extent that ASEAN-2 even considers it a "unique feature and a global first for a regional taxonomy" (ATB, 2023, p. 3). The addition of social aspects from ASEAN-2 onwards further changes the nature of the ASEAN taxonomy: from regulatory framework for climate-related issues to sustainability framework. While the adoption of the DNSH principle is more adaptive, the inclusion of a traffic light system from the outset in ASEAN-1 and the granting of an equal footing

Table 7.1 Comparison of key taxonomy features

	EU Taxonomy (inc. Delegated Acts 1 & 2)	*ASEAN-1*		*ASEAN-2*		*ASEAN-3*	
General objectives and essential criteria	Environmental objectives	Environmental objectives		Environmental objectives		Environmental objectives	
	DNSH: the pursuit of one goal of the taxonomy cannot lead to negative outcomes for other goals of the taxonomy	DNSH		DNSH		DNSH	
		RMT: can improve the grade of an activity even if it causes harm		RMT		RMT	
				'Social Aspects'		'Social Aspects'	
Approach to classifying and measuring activities	Focused on technical screening criteria:	Two-tiered approach		Two-tiered approach		Two-tiered approach	
		Plus Standard:	Foundation Framework:	Plus Standard:	Foundation Framework:	Plus Standard:	Foundation Framework:
	'Science-based'; mostly quantitative	Generally quantitative	Qualitative	Generally quantitative	Qualitative	Generally quantitative	Qualitative
	'The technical screening criteria . . . should build, where relevant, on existing Union law, best practices', EU Delegated Act 1, §5	No details about measuring method	More accessible decision tree to classify activities	Indicators: mostly GHGs and GVA	Decision tree	Indicators: mostly GHGs and GVA	Decision tree
				Initially focused on the energy sector		Sectors added: transportation and storage; construction and real estate	

to both environmental objectives and social aspects from ASEAN-2 onwards can be understood as cases of norm subsidiarity. As a result, the ASEAN taxonomy embodies a different, arguably more holistic understanding of sustainable finance that connects it to its social and developmental context.

The other central design feature relates to the measurement method. While the EU has a focus on thresholds and quantitative measurements (the "Technical Screening Criteria"), the ASEAN taxonomy lays out a two-tiered system with a more stringent, quantitative option (the "Plus Standard") and a more lenient, qualitative, and inclusive option (the "Foundation Framework").

In ASEAN-1, the details of the frameworks and their measurement system are not yet set in stone. Several options are explored, especially for the Plus Standard. While greenhouse gas (GHG) emissions and gross value added (GVA) are set up to be the main quantitative measurement tools, details about their use are not yet present. The other tier, namely the Foundation Framework, uses a more qualitative decision tree (for illustration, see e.g., ATB, 2023, p. 42). The decision tree classifies activities according to broad criteria such as "supporting climate change mitigation," "transitioning away from high carbon activities" or "mitigating harm" (ATB, 2021, p. 43). If there exists a "concrete plan . . . to implement remedial measures to address residual harm within 5 years," an activity might be classified as "amber" (ATB, 2023, p. 36).

In the two later versions of the ASEAN taxonomy, the same two-tiered system – Plus Standard and Foundation Framework – is kept, but with more details about the measurements successively added. Thus, in ASEAN-2 the more quantitative "Plus Standard" is being equipped with clear thresholds for the energy sector, to which ASEAN-3 further adds the sectors of transportation and storage and construction and real estate. In this instance, we can see straightforward adoption of key thresholds from the EU document. For example, in the ASEAN-2 taxonomy, the threshold used to determine whether an energy-producing activity (such as power generation) can be seen as "green" under ASEAN's traffic light system is 100 g CO_2e/kWh. This same threshold is found in the EU taxonomy for activities related to electricity production and use (EU Technical Expert Group, 2020). As such, the content of the Plus Standard seems to align more closely with the EU taxonomy.

However, the Foundation Framework remains firmly different with its inclusive and qualitative approach. It asks "guiding questions" depending on the type of activity, which leads to a categorization in "green," "amber," and "red" while integrating the remedial criteria. Harmful activities might still be considered green if there are measures set out to address the harm caused. Once more, we see both instances of localization and norm subsidiarity; however, in this instance, norm subsidiarity is separate from the localized norm, not building upon it.

This approach makes it possible to overcome challenges that are more prevalent in Southeast Asia, such as lack of data, and thus make the methodology more widely usable, even though there is a clear trade-off as far as specificity and rigorousness of measurement are concerned. This dual tool differs from the EU approach and

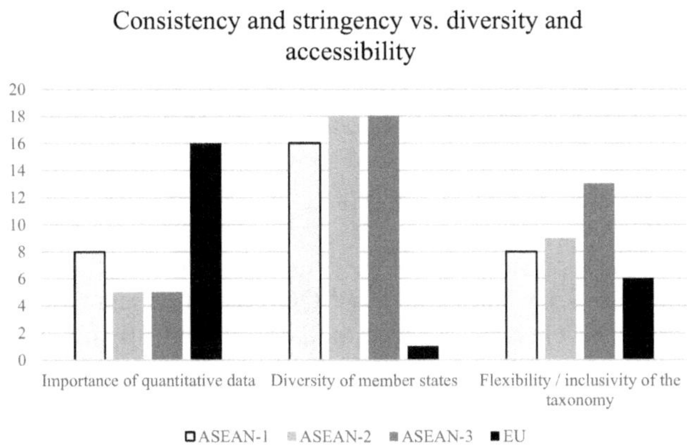

Figure 7.2 Inclusivity

challenges – or at least offers an alternative – to the EU's insistence that a highly accurate, quantitative approach is necessary to legitimize the taxonomy. In this instance, again, a localized norm is combined with an original component. Effectively, this leads to a rather distinctive, more nuanced approach to classifying economic activities in terms of their environmental impact: "the ASEAN Taxonomy has taken an innovative approach to enable it to be effective, practical, and usable. The two-tiered approach of having a Foundation Framework and a Plus Standard achieves the dual requirements of inclusivity and credibility" (ATB, 2023, p. 48).

Taxonomy Outlook

Figures 7.2–7.4 highlight important differences between the ASEAN and EU taxonomies in their outlook. We focus on three dimensions in particular: their inclusivity, understandings of the economy as embodied in the taxonomy texts, and the way the environment is presented.

More specifically, the first dimension coalesces around the question of whether to prioritize consistency and stringency or to prioritize accessibility for a diverse range of actors, which requires some flexibility. The second dimension relates to what understanding of the role of the market underlies the taxonomies, distinguishing two approaches: a conventional approach on the one hand and a socially minded, critical approach on the other hand. Finally, the taxonomies differ along a third dimension: the understanding of the environment that prevails in the documents – either a narrower, emission-centric "climate" approach or a broader, holistic, and localized approach. Our comparative analysis shows how the EU diverges from ASEAN-1 and the extent to which this divergence persists in ASEAN-2 and ASEAN-3.

Regarding the first dimension, the ASEAN taxonomy emphasizes inclusivity, while the EU taxonomy focuses on consistency and compliance above flexibility, as depicted in Figure 7.2. Indeed, this emphasis on inclusivity has been a core feature of the design of the ASEAN taxonomy, including the introduction of the Foundation Framework, as we discussed above, which also is a response to specific challenges that ASEAN member states may face, such as lack of data (ATB, 2023, pp. 13, 16, 32).

These contending perspectives on the imperative to be rigorous versus the need to be inclusive also show strongly in our QCA results. Figure 7.2 highlights significant emphasis on the need to accommodate the diversity of member states and embrace flexibility and hence inclusivity in all three versions of the ASEAN taxonomy. For the EU it is the opposite; here the focus rests on the importance of stringent, quantitative data.

To further corroborate this point, we have pulled out key quotes from the ASEAN taxonomy. For example, ASEAN-2 states that "[t]he economic situations of the AMS also differ significantly, with varying stages of development and economic structures" (ATB, 2023 p. 15). ASEAN-3 makes a similar point, highlighting "the range of financial sector maturity levels that exist across the region" (ATB, 2023, p. 18). ASEAN-3 further emphasizes that "[t]he inherent diversity throughout the region necessitates an *inclusive* approach to development, regional progress, and cooperation" (ATB, 2023, p. 15; our emphasis). Such an approach is realized through the two-tiered approach to measurement: "A 'one-size-fits-all' taxonomy will not provide an inclusive solution for ASEAN. The FF [Foundation Framework] and PS [Plus Standard] were developed to ensure the inclusive treatment of users from diverse economic backgrounds" (ATB, 2023, p. 22).

There are also some differences between ASEAN-1 and the more recent versions: the mention of international pressures and the necessity to align with other norms and taxonomies is very present in the second version. The influence of the EU taxonomy is stated very clearly: "The ASEAN Taxonomy has drawn on learning from and intends to be interoperable with the EU Taxonomy, as well as other taxonomies (i.e., national taxonomies in ASEAN)" (ATB, 2023, p. 15) and the ASEAN taxonomy as well as national ASEAN member states' taxonomies "also need to reflect the expectations of international investors" (ATB, 2023, p. 15). Nonetheless, as Figure 7.2 shows, ASEAN's inclusive approach persists, and while the necessity of interoperability is acknowledged, it is also clearly stated that "where relevant, – the taxonomy – will be tailored according to ASEAN's unique circumstance" (ATB, 2024, p. 3).

Regarding the second dimension, Figure 7.3 highlights how the relationship between the economy, finance, and the environment is understood markedly differently in the EU and ASEAN taxonomies. ASEAN-1 often frames the economy as damaging to the environment, whereas the EU taxonomy mostly talks about the potential in using market mechanisms to protect the environment. More generally, the ASEAN taxonomy is less in line with financial orthodoxy, although this declines over successive versions. This more critical approach to the economy is perhaps best summarized by the following quote: "The ASEAN Member states

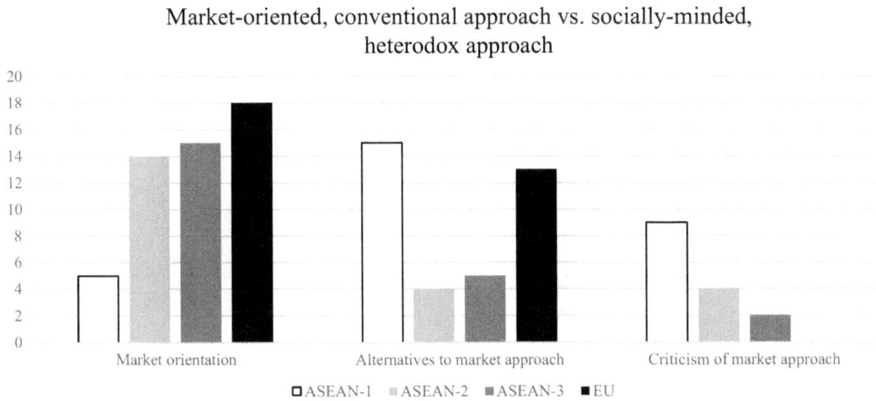

Figure 7.3 Understandings of the economy

(AMS) have seen rapid economic growth, but it has come with a heavy price. Economic development, with the focus on industrialization, has brought about environmental impacts (water pollution, extraction of natural resources, and poor sanitation)" (ATB, 2021, p. 8).

While some central topics in the ASEAN taxonomy, like the insistence on the importance of transparency and the occasional mention of the importance given to quantitative data, align with financial orthodoxy, we also found competing themes that challenge financial orthodoxy. There are frequent mentions of the responsibility finance bears in climate change, the necessity to have the market align with sustainable goals, and more generally the necessity for systemic change.

In particular, ASEAN-1 highlights that the taxonomy "must be able to facilitate transformative systemic changes in the real economy" (ATB, 2021, p. 49) and, more generally, that "there is a need to decouple economic growth from resource use and environmental impact" (ATB, 2021, p. 27). By contrast, the EU taxonomy embodies a more orthodox understanding of finance and economics. While there is some mention of the importance of a "circular economy," this does not challenge the market-based and profit-maximizing understanding of finance; instead, the focus is on improving capital flows and avoiding negative effects of the taxonomy for the financial system ("it is crucial to remove obstacles to the efficient movement of capital into sustainable investments").

In both ASEAN-2 and ASEAN-3, we see tenets of economic orthodoxy becoming progressively more present with more market and technology optimism. Mentions of an alternative view of the link between market and environmental imperatives are still present but less explicit, although there remains an emphasis on "sustainable and inclusive growth" and an awareness of the role of industrialization as responsible for wide-ranging environmental and social issues (see e.g. ATB, 2023, pp. 15, 29). Importantly, outright criticism of the market as it relates to climate still persists in successive versions of the ASEAN taxonomy, which is

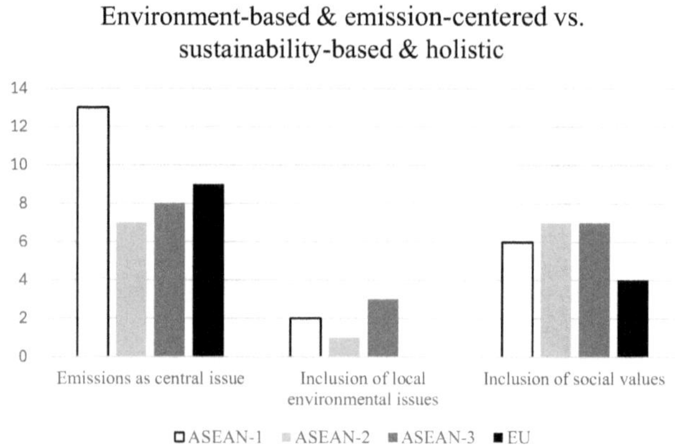

Figure 7.4 Understandings of "greenness"

not the case for the EU taxonomy. The convergence between the two frameworks is therefore incomplete.

The final dimension is depicted in Figure 7.4: What does environmental protection mean, and which concept of sustainability is put forward? There are fewer differences regarding this dimension than perhaps expected, with a strong focus on emission reduction overall. Nonetheless, the ASEAN taxonomy adopts a broader understanding that also includes further environmental issues such as air pollution and water use (see e.g., ATB, 2023, p. 15). The EU taxonomy occasionally mentions environmental issues such as biodiversity preservation and reforestation but heavily focuses on GHGs, to such a degree that even where other environmental issues such as deforestation are mentioned, it is mainly through the lens of how they affect GHGs. Diverging from the EU taxonomy, the ASEAN taxonomy focuses more on sustainability issues that are localized, which the EU taxonomy does not do. At least potentially, the ASEAN taxonomy thus presents a more holistic understanding of "greenness," including a broader range of issues and highlighting different levels of application: both global and localized. More prominently, and as already discussed when it comes to the design, the ASEAN taxonomies link the environmental issues to social issues, pointing to a broader sustainable (rather than just environmental) standard.

Figure 7.5 presents the results of the second round of coding that focused on the interactions between relevant excerpts, once more pointing to significant differences between the EU and ASEAN taxonomies. The figure shows the extent to which these interactions are connected or conflictual, with both types of interactions being present in the documents. In particular, we see that there are some points of tension where specific priorities of the ASEAN taxonomy are seen to clash directly with mainstream financial expectations or European green finance norms on topics such as inclusivity versus methodological rigour, for example.

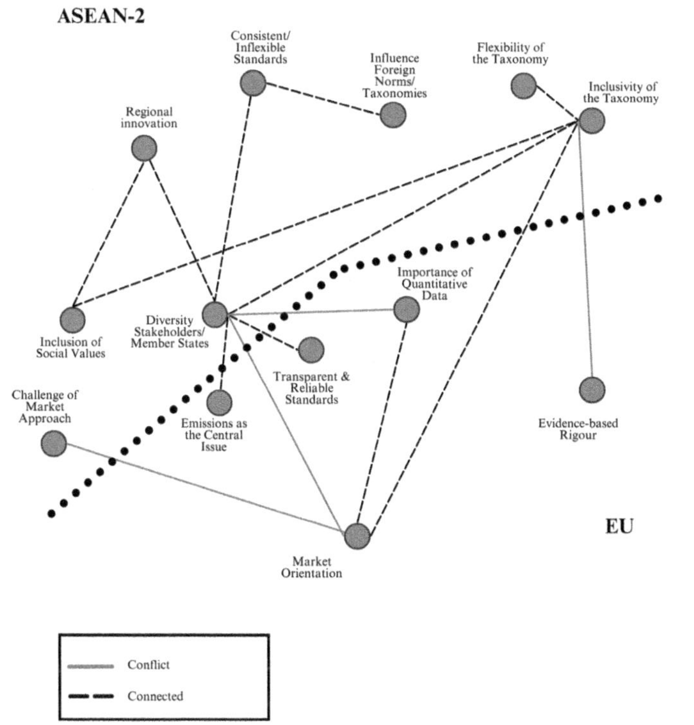

Figure 7.5 Relationships between codes

Discussion of Findings and Limitations of This Study

In several instances, the ASEAN taxonomy privileges flexibility in its approach to setting sustainable finance norms. In contrast to the EU taxonomy's inflexible, quantitative approach, the ASEAN taxonomy proposes a more flexible and inclusive two-tiered approach, creating space for mitigation of harmful activities. And regarding the broader expectation that ASEAN align with international (especially European) green standards, the taxonomy makes the argument that the diversity of ASEAN and the specific challenges it faces, both economically and ecologically, are more important or at least as important as international norms. These are important ASEAN innovations, resulting in a distinctive taxonomy framework, which integrates elements from the EU taxonomy sparingly via localization ("Do No Significant Harm" principle, some specific thresholds in the quantitative Plus Standard Framework) within a design tailored to its own challenges.

However, this does not mean that innovation in and through the ASEAN taxonomy is not a result of regional limitations, such as the lack of data or the limited coercive capabilities of ASEAN's decision-making structure. It is very clear that

ASEAN policymakers had to compromise between their ambitions, and the pressures exerted on the region regarding finance and its subordinate position. It also does not mean that ASEAN has created a particularly radical taxonomy from an ecological standpoint. On the contrary, the possibility of remediation as well as other stipulations not discussed in the empirical section, such as the permissive coal phase-out scheme, potentially allow for more environmental harm.

Indeed, the EU taxonomy, while drawing more heavily from the principles and from the language of financial orthodoxy, is still likely to produce a more stringent, more "green" taxonomy. The EU includes mechanisms for verification and enforcement that are much stricter and go further in excluding harmful activities. This reflects the EU's higher degree of institutional power and centralization. However, through the taxonomy and its selective incorporation, modification, and innovation beyond EU norms, ASEAN policymakers have asserted non-dominant agency in financial norm-making. The ASEAN taxonomy represents a workable compromise for a region and an organization facing various challenges in the face of the increasingly hegemonic influence of (Western/EU) financial environmental norms that is not uncontroversial.

Conceptually, looking at the taxonomies through the lens of "norm localization" and "norm subsidiarity" therefore makes it possible to understand the ASEAN taxonomies as composite products, combining elements from the EU taxonomy with distinctive ideas developed at both national and regional local levels. Such an approach is especially important in the face of the significant normative and material power of the EU Green Deal.

First, as our analysis showed, the elements from the EU taxonomy incorporated into the ASEAN taxonomy were not simply adopted but adapted to better fit ASEAN norms and realities, including divergence between ASEAN and the EU on topics such as market-centered versus state-centered approaches and different concepts of environment and ecology, as discussed above. The selective engagement with certain European norms also depended on these norms' compatibility with the ASEAN cultural, political, and socio-economic positions. It very well fits Acharya's concept of "cultural selection" (Acharya, 2004, pp. 245–246). The taxonomy case shows how the process of norm diffusion, far from only being a unilateral, top-down process of (usually Western) norm export towards (often non-Western), passive norm-takers instead is a multidimensional process which elicits more complex, interdependent dynamics.

In seeking to adapt European norms in ways that make them usable for ASEAN actors, however, some elements of the taxonomy were changed to such an extent and supplemented with such significantly new ideas that the result was very much the creation of new norms, such as with the two-tiered ASEAN design. Thus, the ASEAN taxonomy process went significantly beyond the adaptation or localization of European sustainable finance norms. In Acharya's terms, this second process goes beyond localization, which is still a process of norm-taking. It fits the concept of norm subsidiarity: creating entirely new norms and affirming ASEAN and ASEAN member states' autonomy vis-à-vis the EU. The attempt to export, via the EU taxonomy and EU Green Deal more generally, European norms to other regions, a process that inevitably affirms EU power, is partly rejected, even though the interoperability of taxonomies is a significant concern for ASEAN.

The concept of norm subsidiarity suggests further that this form of subordinate norm innovation may be externalized – that is, diffused beyond its area of origin. While we see important instances of diffusion within ASEAN as more and more member states develop their own sustainable finance taxonomies, to date evidence of the diffusion of specific ASEAN taxonomy norms beyond the region is limited (Simons & Rethel, 2025). Nonetheless, the prioritization of principle-based over measurement-based approaches pioneered by ASEAN can also be detected in other Global South taxonomies, with Brazil, Colombia, Mexico, and South Africa, for instance, embracing a similar, principle-led approach.

Regarding specific norms, these have found a foothold mainly within the ASEAN region. Thus, following the release of ASEAN-1, both Indonesia and Thailand published taxonomies that featured a traffic light system. Likewise, the Philippines incorporated a Foundation Framework in their subsequently released taxonomy. Even though the diffusion of norms central to the ASEAN taxonomy has to date been largely restricted to ASEAN member states, its innovations nevertheless challenge hegemonic understandings of (sustainable) finance at both normative and practical levels. Returning to Acharya (2011, p. 101), norm subsidiarity in the taxonomy space thus also can be seen as challenging the "consensual normative order" that the EU is trying to achieve through its Green Deal.

Conclusion

In this chapter, we focused on the financial aspect of the EU Green Deal and its importance for Southeast Asia by contrasting the EU sustainable finance taxonomy with efforts to develop an ASEAN-wide sustainable finance taxonomy, which, at the time of writing, is in its third version. Even though there has been some convergence over time, with both the second and third versions of the ASEAN taxonomy emphasizing the importance of interoperability of taxonomies, specifically referencing the EU taxonomy, our findings suggest that fundamental differences persist. These include (i) an emphasis on the importance of recognizing the diversity of member states in the ASEAN taxonomies versus regulatory consistency, if not uniformity, in the EU; (ii) a focus on socio-economic development in ASEAN versus market conformism in the EU; and (iii) a broader understanding of what constitutes sustainable finance increasingly oriented at adaptation and local environmental issues in ASEAN versus a narrower emissions-centrism in the EU.

As such, we suggest that the development of sustainable finance regulations in Southeast Asia is at least partly an instance of non-hegemonic agency in financial norm-making, contesting the hegemonic position of the EU as a sustainable finance norm-maker. The particular features of the ASEAN taxonomy show that the region has been neither passive in its reception of outside norms nor delegated to a role of being merely a norm-taker: it exerted agency in its adaptation of EU norms and proposed entirely independent norms.

Reference List

Acharya, A. (2004). How Ideas Spread: Whose Norms Matter? Norm Localization and Institutional Change in Asian Regionalism. *International Organization*, 58(2), 239–275.

Acharya, A. (2011). Norm Subsidiarity and Regional Orders: Sovereignty, Regionalism, and Rule-Making in the Third World. *International Studies Quarterly*, 55(1), 95–123.

Alami, I., Alves, C., Bonizzi, B., Kaltenbrunner, A., Koddenbrock, K., Kvangraven, I., & Powell, J. (2022). International Financial Subordination: A Critical Research Agenda. *Review of International Political Economy*, 30(4), 1360–1386.

ASEAN Taxonomy Board. (2021). *ASEAN Taxonomy for Sustainable Finance Version 1*, accessed at: https://asean.org/book/asean-taxonomy-for-sustainable-finance/.

ASEAN Taxonomy Board. (2023). *ASEAN Taxonomy for Sustainable Finance Version 2*, accessed at: https://asean.org/wp-content/uploads/2023/03/ASEAN-Taxonomy-Version-2.pdf.

ASEAN Taxonomy Board. (2024). *ASEAN Taxonomy for Sustainable Finance Version 3*, accessed at: www.theacmf.org/images/downloads/pdf/ASEAN-Taxonomy-Version-3.pdf.

Commission Delegated Regulation 2021/2139. *Commission Delegated Regulation (EU) 2021/2139 of 4 June 2021 Supplementing Regulation (EU) 2020/852 of the European Parliament and of the Council by Establishing the Technical Screening Criteria for Determining the Conditions under Which an Economic Activity Qualifies as Contributing Substantially to Climate Change Mitigation or Climate Change Adaptation and for Determining Whether That Economic Activity Causes No Significant Harm to Any of the Other Environmental Objectives*, accessed at: http://data.europa.eu/eli/reg_del/2021/2139/oj/eng.

EU Technical Expert Group. (2020). *Final Report of the Technical Expert Group on Sustainable Finance*, accessed at: https://finance.ec.europa.eu/document/download/9101b639-ebe5-413e-9c86-3e291722899e_en?filename=200309-sustainable-finance-teg-final-report-taxonomy_en.pdf.

European Commission. (2019). *Finance and the Green Deal*, accessed at: https://commission.europa.eu/strategy-and-policy/priorities-2019-2024/european-green-deal/finance-and-green-deal_en.

Larsen, M. L. (2022). Driving Global Convergence in Green Financial Policies: China as Policy Pioneer and the EU as Standard Setter. *Global Policy*, 13(3), 358–370.

Regulation 2020/852. *Regulation (EU) 2020/852 of the European Parliament and of the Council of 18 June 2020 on the establishment of a framework to facilitate sustainable investment, and amending Regulation (EU) 2019/2088*, accessed at: https://eur-lex.europa.eu/legal-content/EN/TXT/?uri=CELEX:32020R0852.

Simons, A., & Rethel, L. (2025). Subordinated Agency and the Grafting of Sustainable Finance Regulations in Southeast Asia. *International Affairs*, 101(5), 1679–1699.

8 Finding Loopholes in the Forest

How Nickel Companies Abuse Discursive Ambiguity on Deforestation

Nadia Fausta Azhara

Introduction

Over 90 countries around the world have set their commitments to achieving net-zero emissions to keep the global temperature rise limited to 1.5°C above pre-industrial levels (Climate Watch, 2024). The European Union (EU) has committed to achieving net-zero emissions by 2050, as outlined in the EU Green Deal (EGD) document. The EGD, launched in 2019, is the EU strategy for tackling climate and other environment-related challenges, focusing on eight key areas ranging from climate ambition, energy, circular economy, resources, pollution, biodiversity, food, and mobility (European Commission, 2020).

One of the key areas in the EGD is "Accelerating the shift to sustainable and smart mobility," intending to reduce 90% in transportation emissions by transitioning to cleaner transportation alternatives (European Commission, 2020). Even though the EGD does not directly mention the use of electric vehicles, the document mentions that the acceleration of the net-zero transition requires 13 million zero- and low-emission vehicles roaming around Europe in 2025 or 30 million zero-emission cars by 2030 (Fetting, 2020), with support from about 1 million public recharging and refueling stations (European Commission, 2020).

Transitioning from fossil-fueled vehicles to electric vehicles sounds promising, as electric vehicles are claimed to be 17%–30% lower in carbon emissions (European Environment Agency, 2024). Currently, two-thirds of global electric vehicle stocks are using batteries, while the rest are hybrid with fossil fuel (ASEAN, 2019). Nickel is an important component in batteries, which makes the batteries run farther than those that do not use nickel. During Tesla Battery Day 2020, Andrew Baglino, a Tesla Executive, said that "nickel is the cheapest material and has the highest energy density," which is why the material is chosen to make electric vehicles possible (Ackerman et al., 2024). Furthermore, nickel from Indonesia is close to the earth's surface; therefore, it is relatively cheaper to extract nickel from Indonesia than from Canada or Russia (The Wall Street Journal, 2023).

As Figure 8.1 shows, Indonesia is the biggest nickel producer in the world since nickel production rose by 60% in 2022 (Jong, 2023), with nickel reserves accounting for 20.6% of the global total (Nadig, 2024).

DOI: 10.4324/9781003783176-10

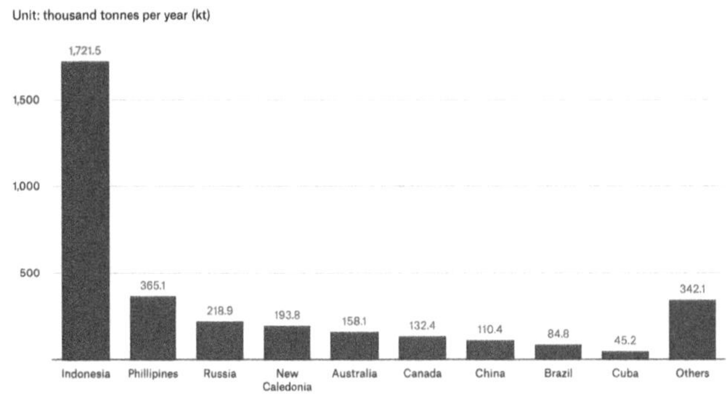

Figure 8.1 Ten largest nickel-producing countries in 2023

Source: Nadig, 2024.

Along with the growing global demand for electric vehicles, nickel production in Indonesia rose to 60% in 2022, accounting for half of global production (Jong, 2023). The development of the nickel industry in Indonesia comes with a cost of forest loss as nickel concessions need to expand. The nickel industry expansion happens, especially after the Indonesian government imposed the nickel ore export ban policy in late April 2022, requiring nickel ore to be processed first and have added value before exporting (International Energy Agency, 2023b). The expansion of nickel processing requires a bigger area, which often entails sacrificing forests and biodiversity. A report under Mighty Earth (Brown & Harris, 2024) stated that deforestation caused by 329 nickel mines in Indonesia is up to 76,031 hectares. In a broader sense, The TreeMap (2024) estimated that a total of 721,000 hectares of forests, including 150,000 hectares of primary forest, had been cleared from 2001 until December 2023.

Even if nickel companies legally have permits to use or clear certain areas for the expansion of their concessions, investors are looking beyond legal compliance and digging deeper into the environmental, social, and governance (ESG) aspects. In this case, environmental impact, biodiversity, and deforestation are receiving investors' attention. With investors increasingly focusing on ESG aspects, companies are trying to build good corporate branding around it to attract investors (Azhara, 2023).

The problem arises when investors are calling for action to "no deforestation," and companies claim that they have complied with the relevant regulations on the matter, yet the definitions and understanding of deforestation that they use differ from one another. Some understand that only primary forests are off-limits to be cut down, while others understand that deforestation's definition includes both primary and secondary forests. There are also differences in the terminology used to refer to primary and secondary forests. The details of these categories and definitions are explained in the following sections.

The different definitions, or even the absence of mutual understanding, blur the line between investors' and/or other stakeholders' (e.g., CSOs and the general public) expectations and the companies' compliance claim. The different definitions referred to by different actors in various contexts and occasions may lead to a discursive ambiguity. This happens when different actors use the same "deforestation" word but mean different things regarding the "loss of the forest." Some actors may discuss the "deforestation" definition from the legal permit and business approach, some may approach this through environmental issues, and others may see it as necessary to support the global agenda in the energy transition. The discursive ambiguity becomes more significant since the differences in definitions and meaning-making are institutionalized through regulations and policies as well as reflected in discursive practices through seminars, workshops, meetings, and media releases.

This chapter explains how deforestation, meaning-making, and forest categorization influence how the corporate image of the nickel industry is perceived in accelerating sustainable mobility. By learning about discursive ambiguity on deforestation, this chapter calls for various stakeholders (e.g., investors, government, CSOs, the general public, media, NGOs, *et cetera*) to be critical in observing and driving nickel companies to be responsible and transparent – to hold them accountable in sustainability issues, specifically in the deforestation issue in this case.

Additionally, studying discourse analysis allows companies to open an inclusive and just dialogue with their stakeholders, addressing the different understandings of deforestation. This is important to avoid counterproductive debates based on claims standing on different grounds. Moreover, within the EGD document, the EU wants to increase its climate ambition, among others, through reliable, comparable, and verifiable information to reduce the risk of greenwashing. In this case, discourse analysis plays a role in addressing what has been taken for granted and not maintaining the status quo, where the loophole caused by the discursive ambiguity is neglected in achieving a net-zero transition.

Problem Statement

Different Definitions of Forest Types and Deforestation

Prior to talking about deforestation, it is helpful if we understand the meaning of forest and its various classifications. Since we are talking in the context of nickel mining in Indonesia, this chapter accentuates the forest classifications defined by the Ministry of Environment and Forestry of the Republic of Indonesia, as Table 8.1 shows.

The devil is in the details. These forest classifications are significant for understanding the technical issues in differentiating and defining, for instance, the type of forest a nickel concession is located in or near. Understanding the type of forest will help the government and the company to decide what type of action they need to take to protect the forest and what kind of activities are allowed or not allowed in the area. However, if we are talking in the context of deforestation, two forest classifications are more commonly used, namely primary and secondary forests.

Table 8.1 Forest classification by the Indonesian Ministry of Environment and Forestry

Forest Classifications	*Definition*
Forest	An ecosystem unit in the form of an expanse of land containing biological resources dominated by trees in a natural environment, which is inseparable from one another
Forest Area	A certain area designated by the government to be maintained as a permanent forest
State Forest Area	A certain area determined by the government to be maintained as permanent forest is located on unencumbered land
Customary Forest Area	An area of customary law communities located within a forest area that has been designated by the government and/or excluded from the state forest area
Conservation Forest	A forest area with certain characteristics, which has the main function of preserving the diversity of plants and animals and their ecosystems
Protection Forest	A forest area that has the main function of protecting life support systems to regulate water management, prevent flooding, control erosion, prevent seawater intrusion, and maintain soil fertility
Production Forest	A forest area that has the main function of producing forest products.
Permanent Production Forest	A forest area whose main function is to produce forest products and whose existence is maintained as permanent forest
Convertible Production Forest	A production forest area that can be spatially reserved for development outside of forestry activities and can be made into a permanent production forest
Permanent Forest	A forest area consisting of conservation forest, protection forest, and permanent production forest

Source: Permen LHK No. 7/2021 presented in a table by the author

The Food and Agriculture Organization (FAO) describes the primary forest as a "naturally regenerated forest of native tree species, where there is no visible indication of human activities and the ecological processes are not significantly disturbed" (Food and Agriculture Organization, 2020). According to various documents of the Ministry of Environment and Forestry of Indonesia (KLHK),[1] primary forest is "all forest appearances that do not show traces of logging/disturbance" (Susetyo, 2021).

FAO describes the secondary forest as "forests regenerating largely through natural processes after significant removal or disturbance of the original forest vegetation by human or natural causes at a single point in time or over an extended period, and displaying a major difference in forest structure and/or canopy species composition" (FAO, n.d.). A similar tone comes from KLHK, which defines secondary forest as "natural forests that have been encroached upon by concession rights and altered in structure through the regrowth of trees" (Kompas, 2011).

In the context of forest utilization for the nickel industry, Government Regulation 22/2021 on the Implementation of Forestry (Pemerintah Republik Indonesia, 2021) imposes an obligation for mining companies to obtain a Forest Utilization Permit or Borrow and Use Permit from KLHK (Kementerian Lingkungan Hidup dan Kehutanan, 2021). The type of forest that can be converted for development outside forestry is a production forest, unlike a permanent forest, which has to be protected (Kementerian Lingkungan Hidup dan Kehutanan, 2016). To ground this discussion further, outlining different deforestation definitions is necessary, as discussed in the following.

According to KLHK, deforestation is "the permanent change of forested land into non-forested land as a result of human activities" (Indonesian National Carbon Accounting System, n.d.). Whereas the Accountability Framework Initiative (AFi) defines deforestation as the "loss of natural forest as a result of (i) conversion to agriculture or other non-forest land use; (ii) conversion to a tree plantation; or (iii) severe and sustained degradation." Based on this definition, the loss of natural forest is considered to be deforestation regardless of whether it is legal or not (Accountability Framework Initiative, n.d.a). In this sense, even though the mining concession has the Forest Utilization Permit to clear production forest, AFi still considers this to be deforestation. While KLHK does not clearly state which type of forest is included in the deforestation definition, AFi mentions that natural forests in the deforestation definition include primary and secondary forests (Accountability Framework Initiative, n.d.b).

The European Union Deforestation Regulation (EUDR) defines deforestation as "the conversion of forest to agricultural use" (European Commission, n.d.a). The EUDR does not regulate the mining industry as of now and states that logging in concessions can never qualify as deforestation but rather qualifies as degradation, which means "structural changes to forest cover, taking the form of the conversion of primary forest or naturally regenerating forest into plantation forest or into other wooded land and the conversion of primary forest into planted forests" (Fern, 2023).

Based on these definitions, we can see that there are different understandings of whether both losses in primary and secondary forests can be considered deforestation or only the loss in the primary forest. In contrast, the loss of secondary forest can be considered as a production forest fulfilling its purpose. Another different takeaway is whether certain criteria in losing forest coverage are considered deforestation or degradation. These different definitions are being communicated by different actors and shape the conduct of others in the context of the mining industry.

Conceptual Framework

Discourse Analysis

Every social practice has meanings that shape and influence what we do (Hajer & Versteeg, 2006, p. 44). Discourse governs the way a topic can be meaningfully talked about and reasoned about, as well as influences how ideas are put into practice and used to regulate the conduct of others (Hall, 2013, p. 29).

Different discourses lead to different courses of action; thus, the ascription of meaning in discourse constitutes and changes the world (Jorgensen & Phillips, 2002, p. 6). The way the Indonesian Ministry of Environment and Forestry, nickel companies, non-governmental organizations (NGOs), and other civil society organizations give meaning to forests and deforestation affects how they regulate and control the conduct of others in terms of non-deforestation practices. These meanings are channeled through a particular set of routines and mutually accepted rules and norms that are situational to the historical, cultural, and political context (Hajer & Versteeg, 2006, pp. 176–177). The way these meanings are communicated is also significant, whether this happens in informal but common discussions among actors or is being formally institutionalized through regulations that eventually are accepted to shape the social conduct. If the regulations cover nickel companies that have permits, may clear production forests, and do not deem this as deforestation, this discourse sustains as a regime of truth and will have real consequences to become "true" in terms of having real effects (Hall, 2013, p. 33).

However, discourse is about where meaning comes from, and it is constantly evolving, context-related, ever-challenged, and debatable. This is why deforestation, meaning that which is considered true by one regulation, may be challenged by another meaning communicated by civil society. Discourse governs the way a topic is given meaning and reasoned about and influences how it is put into practice to regulate the conduct of others. To sum it up, discourse is "an ensemble of ideas, concepts, and categories through which meaning is given to social and physical phenomena, which is produced and reproduced through an identifiable set of practices" (Hajer & Versteeg, 2006, p. 175).

Category Analysis

The various types of forests constitute the meaning-making of deforestation. This means that different types of forest can determine whether the loss of a forest is considered deforestation, forest degradation, or mere land utilization. Those different meanings (loss as deforestation, degradation, or land utilization) also depend on who defines the forest type. This premise is reflected in the category analysis, popularized by Yanow (2003).

Essentially, Yanow (2003) describes that categories are intended to separate, and in interpretive research, this type of analysis can be helpful to observe how meanings and values shape categories and vice versa, how categories shape different meanings and values. There is power in naming categories. Category builds boundaries between elements that are different and should not be mixed. Using category analysis in this case also makes the "unseen" be seen or recognized, digging deeper into the deforestation discursive ambiguity in the nickel industry.

Only after we take categories into our main consideration do we understand how the power of naming categories has performative effects in reality. For instance, if Entity A considers the loss of secondary forest deforestation, while Entity B considers it as forest degradation or land utilization, then there will be different implications in terms of responsibility. When the meaning-making of deforestation by Entity B is institutionalized, nickel companies that clear forests can justify their actions and can still claim that they are not doing deforestation. However, categories and categorizations are not universal and potentially change across settings and time.

Research Design and Method

This is qualitative research using interpretative methodology for digging deeper into discursive ambiguity on deforestation, with the case study of the nickel industry in Indonesia. Choosing this case was significantly related to my previous professional experience as a sustainability consultant for the private sector in Indonesia and briefly as a sustainability specialist at one of the nickel companies in Indonesia.

Addressing the discursive ambiguity on deforestation in the nickel industry is a timely case study as the energy transition becomes a global agenda (IEA, 2024a), and it endorses the emerging electric vehicle industry (IEA, 2024b), in which nickel is one of the battery components. The case study is also relevant to the EGD policies and regulations, especially the EU Battery Regulation (European Commission, n.d.b) and the Critical Raw Materials Act (CRMA) (European Commission, n.d.c), expecting the nickel industry throughout the supply chain to implement the responsible sourcing aspect in their operations. Both regulations take into account, among others, environmental protection, public disclosure of sourcing practices, ESG risks, and overall sustainable supply chain.

Data Collection

As interpretive research, this study collected secondary data from both the linguistic (texts and spoken words) and indirect observation of the non-linguistic (practice) aspect, such as behaviour, tone of speaking, how each actor performs their roles, sequence and organization of actions, et cetera. Deforestation discourse is present in the regulation, discussions, conversations, and various forms of publication, which this study traced and analyzed the discursive formation and reflected critically on the current discursive practice in the Indonesian nickel industry.

Preparation includes understanding the situation of the nickel industry in Indonesia. My positionality smoothens out the way to grasp a better understanding and know the right keywords to search for during the literature review. Working briefly as a sustainability specialist at one of the Indonesian nickel companies made me question the deforestation discourse revolving around the industry. Similarly, the experience also helped me to familiarize myself with the important keywords that are significant to accessing the information necessary for this study.

Keywords (both in Indonesian and English) used to searchfor information and data in this research include: *Indonesian nickel mining, electric vehicle industry in Indonesia, energy transition, nickel downstreaming, Indonesian government priorities on nickel production, deforestation in Indonesia, deforestation regulation in Indonesia, EU Green Deal, EU Deforestation Regulation*, and *discourse analysis*.

This study uses secondary data that is publicly available, including fifteen news articles, nine academic publications, three regulations, thirteen other reports or documents, and two public webinars retrieved throughout June 2024–July 2025.

Data Analysis

The collected data is analyzed using discourse analysis and referring to category analysis as explained below. The primary data is analyzed by referring back to previous or existing studies on the relevant topic for data triangulation to ensure the trustworthiness of the analysis of the data gathered.

Discourse Analysis

Deriving from different meanings imposed on types of forests and deforestation itself, this chapter presents interpretative research to observe the meaning-making in forests and deforestation that is often taken for granted. Using discourse analysis, one can learn how meaning embedded in language in use may shape and reflect our societal conduct. In discourse analysis, the language-in-use includes both written and spoken in various forms of communication (Jorgensen & Phillips, 2002, p. 13). Discourse analysis is useful for this research to understand how language-in-use in discursive practices constructs reality, influences perceptions, and maintains or even challenges existing power structures.

As discussed previously, there are various types of forest classifications and differences in deforestation meanings. This is highly related to discourse analysis, where meaning-making influences how ideas are put into practice and is used to regulate the conduct of others.

Category Analysis

Category analysis by Yanow (2003) is referred to in data analysis, especially to understand how nickel companies leverage the formal forest categorization by the regulator. In such analysis, we refer to how category analysis provides six dimensions or aspects (Yanow, 2003, p. 16) in organizing the analysis of the case, which are:

1. Understand the **similarities and differences** that construct the categories;
   This relates to what indicators are used to identify what is similar within a category and what the different aspects a category has that the others don't.
2. Knowing the **order and logic of the organizing** principles underlying the categories;
   This is about what the basis is for making indicators to differentiate each category and what this implies and organizes.
3. Observing the **point of view** embodied in the categories;
   Determining which characteristics are relevant to the category-making, for instance, the forest coverage or forest purposes.

4. Identifying the **frames** that highlight certain features and divert from other features in creating the categories;

   Framing helps with the sense-making of the categorization. In this case, the frame that can be used is the implication of the forest categorization on whether its loss is considered deforestation or not.
5. Understanding that framing expresses collective **ways of seeing and knowing**;

   By making those categories, it imposes collective knowledge of meaning and how people understand that different forest categories influence the implications of responsibilities to protect or restore.
6. **Communicating the tacit knowledge**.

Finally, how this knowledge is put into practice and becomes material. For instance, the production forest category is communicated and understood as a type of forest that can be utilized for other purposes.

Results

As described earlier in the introduction, different actors impose different meanings on forest types and deforestation. There is ambiguity where different approaches to the deforestation discourse with various meaning-making remain unaddressed, leading to differences between what the nickel companies can claim and the public's expectations of them regarding their environmental responsibility.

In Indonesia, a nickel company may legally operate as long as it acquires a Forest Lending and Utilization Permit from KLHK. This permit allows them to convert designated production forests into mining facilities. Additionally, a Land Use Permit in Protected Forest Areas also allows companies to have mining activities but not to open mining concessions (World Resources Institute, 2013). Legally, nickel companies can make claims that their mining activities are compliant with the legal requirements and the laws that are applicable in Indonesia. Indirectly, if we take into consideration KLHK's definition of deforestation, mining activities and concessions can be considered as deforestation because they cause changes of forested land into non-forested land as a result of human activities (Indonesian National Carbon Accounting System, n.d.). Yet, production forests are still legally allowed to be converted (Kementerian Lingkungan Hidup dan Kehutanan, 2016).

Nickel companies often carefully communicate their activities through reports or press releases. Touching upon deforestation discourse, nickel companies do not make any confirmation or even deny that their operations cause "widespread deforestation" (Harita Nickel, 2024). They would rather bring up their compliance with national regulations and environmental permit requirements for their operations (Vale Indonesia, 2023; Trimegah Bangun Persada, 2023). Hiding behind legality, wiping out deforestation is an elephant in the room.

Furthermore, the executive director of the Indonesian Mining Association stated, "If mining activities are carried out properly, there will be no problem with deforestation" (Pandu, 2023). He also highlighted the importance of returning post-mining land in forest areas to its designated purpose as production forests or protected forests. This adds to another meaning-making in the deforestation discourse; if deforested land is reclaimed eventually, then it is not considered a deforestation problem.

Quite contrary to nickel industry practices in Indonesia, the Dutch Association of Investors for Sustainable Development (VBDO) and its knowledge partner, Rainforest Foundation Norway (RFN), developed an investor expectation. This document consists of three expectations for corporate action towards enhanced social and environmental due diligence. Among those three expectations, one is for nickel companies to adopt a time-bound commitment to having a deforestation-free nickel supply chain, having measures to eliminate deforestation in the supply chain by 2025 as the latest cut-off date (VBDO, 2024).

Within the investor expectation document, VBDO and RFN refer to AFi's definition of deforestation, which considers both losses in primary and secondary deforestation. When the investor association acknowledges AFi's definition, investors are expecting companies to address forest-clearing activities as deforestation, regardless of whether such activities are legal or not. Based on this, nickel companies in Indonesia and the investor association example have different approaches to embedding meanings in deforestation, yet these differences remain unaddressed clearly in discussions or communication between companies and the public/investors.

It is significant to acknowledge and address this discourse ambiguity, especially when investors play a crucial role in enabling the companies' activities – financially. Ignoring this loophole may enable broader environmental destruction or lead to endless debate while standing on different grounds. This loophole happens, for instance, when the investors trust and support companies' "on paper" claims and commitment towards non-deforestation, although what the companies claim and what investors expect are different. The investor expectation document approaches deforestation discourse from an environmental perspective and data on what's happening in the field, whereas the companies respond from a legal and current business perspective. While they argue over different meanings of what is considered deforestation and what is not, and choose whichever definition supports their approaches, this unaddressed difference widens the discourse ambiguity and hinders us from finding solutions to a just energy transition.

Discussion

This section examines how the dominant narrative constructs the conduct of the nickel industry in Indonesia. It further explores how this unquestioned narrative can legitimize performative actions, even as deforestation continues to occur on the ground.

Through discourse analysis, one can learn how certain narratives construct the ways in which deforestation discourse is ascribed to certain meanings by different actors. The way the meaning is being communicated also constructs reality. When nickel companies communicate that they do not cause widespread deforestation and are compliant with the applicable regulations and are doing rehabilitation in the post-mining areas, the narrative is manifested not only through verbal communication but also in writing. The narrative is legitimized through companies' reports and formally institutionalized through permits retrieved from the government.

Deforestation for nickel mining in Indonesia is also permissible and supported by collective narratives on clean energy transition at the global and national levels (International Energy Agency, 2023a; Pertamina, n.d.). If not critically studied and communicated, indirectly, EGD may also contribute to this narrative, since EGD supports the accelerating shift to sustainable and smart mobility – which can be achieved through the provision of zero- and low-emission vehicles and public recharging and refueling stations (Fetting, 2020; European Commission, 2020).

The EU Battery Regulation and the CRMA emphasize responsible sourcing, transparent supply chains, and sustainable battery life cycles, from the mining process until disposal (European Commission, n.d.b; European Commission, n.d.c). As a part of EGD, these regulations encourage the private sector to assess the potential risks coming from their supply chain, including environmental risks in the battery sector (Bauer, 2024), which may encourage nickel companies to show that they are compliant by avoiding environmental risks. If the understanding of what "environmental risks" or "responsible sourcing" entails is not critically communicated, there would be no clarity on what was considered "compliant." The EGD may support the narrative that the companies' non-deforestation legal claim is true, regardless of what happens in the field.

Additionally, the Indonesian government supports nickel downstream, with export values claimed to surge up to 745% in 2022 compared to 2017, and is deemed to increase the national economic development (Administrator, 2023). Given the importance of the nickel industry to Indonesia's economic development, the government also attributes the nickel mining and processing activities as "national strategic projects (PSN)" (Anwar, 2020), which then strengthens the dominant discourse communicated by nickel companies – not acknowledging land clearing as deforestation. Nickel companies often deliver the narrative of land clearing activities alongside their rehabilitation plans and environmental impact assessments that are aligned with the regulations (Harita Nickel, 2024; Trikarinaputri, 2024). Given this shaped conduct, nickel companies can justify their activities regardless of the deforestation they cause.

Deriving from category analysis, categories shape different meanings and values, and vice versa (Yanow, 2003). Nickel companies benefit from the forests formally categorized by regulation as production forests that are permitted for companies to borrow and use the land for their productive activities, from which companies can gain maximum benefits. Such regulation provides framing and sense-making to society, communicating that production forests can be used as productive non-forestry activities. This communicated way of seeing and knowing may influence the implications of companies' responsibilities and the justification of deforestation.

The prevailing and widely accepted narrative highlights the critical importance of the energy transition from fossil fuels to sustainable energy sources. This is strongly supported by the EGD (Widuto, 2023), which is driving a significant surge in the global nickel production to meet the demand for electric vehicle batteries. Marginalizing the fact that the nickel mining industry is also using massive amounts of fossil fuel and coal in its operations (Walhi Sulteng, 2024), contributing to more emissions and loss of biodiversity from deforestation (Climate Rights International, 2024). This highlights that "language has the capacity to make politics, create symbols and signs that can shift power balances and can impact on institution and policy-making" (Hajer, 2006). If nickel mining and processing continue to be framed as essential to the global energy transition, shielded under the label of "national strategic projects (PSN)," while overlooking broader environmental impacts, particularly deforestation, such practices will remain permissible. As this narrative has been institutionalized, the balance of power shifts in favour of nickel companies, enabling them to sustain their operations with limited accountability.

Discourse governs how a topic can be talked about and reasoned about, and influences how ideas are put into practice to regulate the conduct of others (Hall, 2013, p. 29). As long as the dominant narrative frames land clearing for nickel mining and processing activities as something other than deforestation – justified by future plans of rehabilitation – we will continue to enable an energy transition that tolerates the act of deforestation, which releases back the stored carbon into the atmosphere and contributes to climate change (Ali, 2022).

Critical thinking is essential given the discourse ambiguity surrounding deforestation among key actors in the nickel industry – namely the nickel companies, investors, and regulators. Amidst the massive local and international initiatives to promote both energy transition and non-deforestation, it is important to critically assess nickel companies' claims of compliance with non-deforestation. Without such scrutiny, these claims pose risks to legitimizing performative compliance, enabling business-as-usual practices under the guise of responsible and sustainable operations.

Performativity is repeated performance or actions that result in constructed realities (de Vries et al., 2014). In this case, repeated claims from nickel companies, stating that their activities comply with relevant regulations and standards, construct a good corporate image that those companies do not deviate from their responsibilities as stipulated by regulations and standards. "What" they claim to be compliant with is something that we have to pay attention to. Questioning corporate actions enables a better understanding of what these actors actually stand for, and highlights the discrepancies between their meaning-making of non-deforestation and the one promoted by the investor association.

With EGD, the existing discursive ambiguity should be used as an entry point to foster two-way dialogues and consultations on what EGD policies and regulations – particularly the EU Battery Regulations and the CRMA – mean by responsible mining and sustainable supply chains, including whether there is a particular non-deforestation standard required. Without such clarity, companies may compete to appear compliant on paper, only to satisfy the EU market requirements. There is a risk that the EGD, despite its normative commitment to no-deforestation, ends up legitimizing the institutionalized deforestation in the nickel industry. This dynamic potentially serves to build the EU's image as the "first climate-neutral region"

(European Commission, 2020), at the hidden expense of environmental degradation in the Global South.

While we take the companies' claims of non-deforestation for granted, deforestation continues to occur in Indonesia. Mighty Earth (2024) reported that Indonesia's nickel mines are responsible for more than 80,000 ha of forest clearing, of which 2,654 ha of production forests were reportedly cleared without a Borrow and Use Permit. Compounding the issue, Mighty Earth wrote that more than half a million hectares of forests are within nickel concessions and at risk for deforestation. An Indonesian NGO on conservation, Auriga Nusantara, also pointed out that forests surrounding nickel-processing plants are disappearing twice as fast. The rising number of nickel smelters in Indonesia in the past decade, from 3 to 30, has caused a 234% increase in deforestation (IUCN NL, 2024).

Studying deforestation discourse and addressing the discourse ambiguity encourages nickel companies to disclose and communicate their claims, commitments, and compliance more comprehensively. Addressing the meaning-making of no-deforestation can also be accompanied by the companies' targets of rehabilitation, progress, evidence-based data, monitoring, and evaluation. Discourse analysis may help companies, investor associations, and possibly other actors see eye-to-eye when they talk about no deforestation and prevent performative actions resulting from taken-for-granted deforestation discourse communicated and institutionalized through regulations, standards, claims, permits, compliance, certifications, and commitments.

Conclusion

The institutionalized transition towards sustainable and smart mobility, driven by EGD and other global energy transition agendas, is indirectly supported through the promotion of electric vehicles. In this regard, the provision of electric vehicle batteries inevitably requires land clearing. However, the companies, regulators, investors, and other actors may take for granted how different actors make sense of deforestation and how the dominant discourse shapes social conduct. The key takeaway of this study is that discourse analysis offers valuable insights into how different actors make sense of deforestation discourse and interpret it through discursive practices, such as making corporate claims, issuing press releases and reports, engaging in discussions, or demonstrating compliance with regulations.

Nickel companies in Indonesia leverage government-issued permits to obtain nickel concessions, which often result in land clearing and deforestation. Moreover, many of these concessions are designated as PSN, potentially giving them a more favourable and prioritized position within the national development agenda. Up to the completion of this study, regulators had not publicly addressed or held nickel companies accountable for deforestation. This situation shows that even though, by regulatory definition, opening forest areas regardless of their legality is considered deforestation because there is a forest loss, the corporate claims and companies' meaning-making of deforestation are taken for granted. Nickel companies demonstrated claims, institutionalized within their official reports and press releases, that their activities do not cause major deforestation issues because they comply with the law and regulations, will do rehabilitation, do carbon offsetting outside their companies' sites, and what they do supports the global agenda for energy transition in transportation and is a part of PSN.

The institutionalization creates a dominant discourse (Buizer & Kurz, 2016, p. 50) that deforestation for developing the nickel industry is a necessary measure to boost the national economic growth, support the energy transition, and eventually achieve the net-zero emission agenda. The dominant, taken-for-granted discourse shapes practices by normalizing the continuation of nickel companies' operations, largely because they are perceived as compliant with regulations and engaged in forest rehabilitation, despite ongoing deforestation on the ground. The prevailing and widely accepted narrative reinforces the urgency of transitioning from fossil fuels to sustainable energy sources, while often sidelining the environmental costs embedded in that transition. This situation is strongly supported by the EGD (Widuto, 2023), driving a significant surge in global nickel production to meet the growing demand for electric vehicle batteries, regardless of deforestation activities.

This limited desk study highlights what we need to bring to the table when discussing EGD, specifically related to energy transition in transportation by resourcing raw materials from Indonesia. Addressing the taken-for-granted meaning-making of deforestation across actors in the context of the nickel industry in Indonesia is crucial. Future studies can involve interviews with different actors to deepen the insights into the meaning-making of deforestation and how it is embodied in discursive practices in which each actor participates. Another deforestation discourse study can also dig deeper into a case-by-case study related to conflicts between companies and the community.

Last but not least, the study will be enriched by continuing the discussion on green colonialism, where shifting towards less-polluting transportation is a means to making the EU the first climate-neutral continent in the world by 2050 (European Commission, 2020) at the cost of deforestation in developing countries (Reyes, 2024).

Note

1 Regulation of the Director General of Forestry Planning and Environmental Management Number P. 1/VII-IPSDH/2015, Document FREL (Forest Reference Emissions Level) 2016, SNI 8033, 2014, and SNI 7645–1, 2014.

Reference List

Accountability Framework Initiative. (n.d.a). *Deforestation Definitions*. Retrieved August 2024, from Accountability Framework Initiative: https://accountability-framework.org/use-the-accountability-framework/definitions/deforestation/

Accountability Framework Initiative. (n.d.b). *Natural Forest Definitions*. Retrieved August 2024, from Accountability Framework Initiative: https://accountability-framework.org/use-the-accountability-framework/definitions/natural-forest/

Ackerman, D., Chakrabarti, M., & Skoog, T. (2024, March 14). *The Promise of Nickel: Power and Prosperity in Indonesia.* Retrieved July 2025, from WBUR: www.wbur.org/onpoint/2024/03/14/nickel-power-prosperity-indonesia-green-metal-energy

Administrator. (2023, July 8). *Nickel Export Value Surges by 745%.* Retrieved November 2024, from Indonesia.Go.Id Portal Informasi Indonesia: https://indonesia.go.id/kategori/editorial/7255/nickel-export-value-surges-by-745?lang=2

Ali, A. (2022, October 11). *The Impact of Deforestation on Carbon Storage.* Retrieved November 2024, from Visual Capitalist: www.visualcapitalist.com/sp/the-impact-of-deforestation-on-carbon-storage/

Anwar, M. C. (2020, November 23). *Jadi Proyek Strategis Jokowi, Luhut Kebut Hilirisasi Nikel.* Retrieved November 2024, from CNBC Indonesia: www.cnbcindonesia.com/news/20201123175700-4-204024/jadi-proyek-strategis-jokowi-luhut-kebut-hilirisasi-nikel

ASEAN. (2019). *ASEAN Fuel Economy Roadmap for Transport Sector 2018–2025: With Focus on Light-Duty Vehicles.* Jakarta: ASEAN Secretariat.

Azhara, N. F. (2023). *Sustainable Development Discourses in Sustainability Reporting Practice in Indonesia* [Master's thesis]. https://edepot.wur.nl/637923

Bauer, T. (2024, January 29). *EU Critical Raw Materials Act Introduces New Supply Chain Obligations for Large Companies.* Retrieved July 2025, from University of Oxford: https://blogs.law.ox.ac.uk/oblb/blog-post/2024/01/eu-critical-raw-materials-act-introduces-new-supply-chain-obligations-large

Brown, D., & Harris, J. (2024). *From Forest to Electric Vehicles.* Mighty Earth.

Buizer, M., & Kurz, T. (2016). Too hot to handle: Depoliticisation and the discourse of ecological modernisation in fire management debates. *Geoforum*, 48–56.

Climate Rights International. (2024). *Nickel Unearthed: The Human and Climate Costs of Indonesia's Nickel Industry.* Climate Rights International.

Climate Watch. (2024, January). *Net-Zero Tracker.* Retrieved from Climate Watch Data: www.climatewatchdata.org/net-zero-tracker

de Vries, J. R., Roodbol-Mekkes, P., Beunen, R., Lokhorst, A. M., & Aarts, N. (2014). Faking and forcing trust: The performance of trust and distrust in public policy. *Land Use Policy*, 282–289.

European Commission. (2020, January 15). *The European Green Deal.* Retrieved from European Commission: https://commission.europa.eu/strategy-and-policy/priorities-2019-2024/european-green-deal_en

European Commission. (n.d.a). *Deforestation Regulation Implementation.* Retrieved July 2025, from European Commission: https://green-forum.ec.europa.eu/nature-and-biodiversity/deforestation-regulation-implementation_en

European Commission. (n.d.b). *Batteries.* Retrieved July 2025, from European Commission: https://environment.ec.europa.eu/topics/waste-and-recycling/batteries_en

European Commission. (n.d.c). *Critical Raw Materials Act.* Retrieved July 2025, from European Commission: https://single-market-economy.ec.europa.eu/sectors/raw-materials/areas-specific-interest/critical-raw-materials/critical-raw-materials-act_en

European Environment Agency. (2024, June 24). *Electric Vehicles.* Retrieved from European Environment Agency: www.eea.europa.eu/en/topics/in-depth/electric-vehicles

FAO. (n.d.). *What Are Secondary Forests.* Retrieved August 2024, from FAO: www.fao.org/4/J0628E/J0628E16.htm#:~:text=Secondary%20forests%20are%20forests%20regenerating,and%2For%20canopy%20species%20composition

Fern. (2023). *What is the EU Regulation on Deforestation-Free Products?* Retrieved August 2024, from Fern: www.fern.org/fileadmin/uploads/fern/Documents/2023/What_is_the_EU_Regulation_on_deforestation_free_products_and_why_should_you_care.pdf

Fetting, C. (2020). *The European Green Deal.* Vienna: ESDN.

Food and Agriculture Organization. (2020). *Terms and Definition.* Retrieved from Food and Agriculture Organization: https://openknowledge.fao.org/server/api/core/bitstreams/531a9e1b-596d-4b07-b9fd-3103fb4d0e72/content

Hajer, M. (2006). Doing discourse analysis: Coalitions, practices, meaning. *Asia Pacific Journal of Human Resources*, 65–74.

Hajer, M., & Versteeg, W. (2006). A decade of discourse analysis of environmental politics: Achievements, challenges, perspectives. *Journal of Environmental Policy & Planning, 7*(3), 175–184.

Hall, S. (2013). *Representation: Cultural Representations and Signifying Practices*. London: Sage and Open University.

Harita Nickel. (2024, May 3). *Harita Nickel's Response to BBC Inquiry*. Retrieved from TBP Nickel: https://tbpnickel.com/media/press-release/media-statement/harita-nickel-response-to-bbc-inquiry

IEA. (2024a, November 11). *Chairs' Summary and Call to Action: COP29-IEA High-Level Energy Transition Dialogues*. Retrieved July 2025, from International Energy Agency: www.iea.org/news/chairs-summary-and-call-to-action-cop29-iea-high-level-energy-transition-dialogues

IEA. (2024b, June 6). *Electric Vehicles*. Retrieved July 2025, from International Energy Agency: www.iea.org/energy-system/transport/electric-vehicles

Indonesian National Carbon Accounting System. (n.d.). *Definitions*. Retrieved August 2024, from Indonesian National Carbon Accounting System: http://incas.menlhk.go.id/methodology/definitions/

Initiative for Responsible Mining Assurance. (n.d.). *IRMA Mining Standards*. Retrieved July 2025, from Initiative for Responsible Mining Assurance: https://responsiblemining.net/irma-mining-standard/

International Energy Agency. (2023a, September). *Progress in the Clean Energy Transition*. Retrieved November 2024, from International Energy Agency: www.iea.org/reports/net-zero-roadmap-a-global-pathway-to-keep-the-15-0c-goal-in-reach/progress-in-the-clean-energy-transition

International Energy Agency. (2023b, December 12). *Prohibition of the Export of Nickel Ore*. Retrieved from International Energy Agency: www.iea.org/policies/16084-prohibition-of-the-export-of-nickel-ore

IUCN NL. (2024, July 18). *Nickel Rush in Indonesia: Deforestation Rates Double Around Nickel-Processing Plants*. Retrieved July 2025, from IUCN National Committee of the Netherlands: www.iucn.nl/en/news/nickel-rush-in-indonesia-deforestation-rates-double-around-nickel-processing-plants/

Jong, H. N. (2023, July 3). *Indonesia's Coal Burning Hits Record High – and 'Green' Nickel is Largely Why*. Retrieved from Mongabay: https://news.mongabay.com/2023/07/indonesias-coal-burning-hits-record-high-and-green-nickel-is-largely-why/

Jorgensen, M., & Phillips, L. J. (2002). *Discourse Analysis as Theory and Method*. London: SAGE Publication Ltd.

Kementerian Lingkungan Hidup dan Kehutanan. (2016). *Permen LHK No. 51/2016 tentang Tata Cara Pelepasan Kawasan Hutan Produksi yang Dapat Dikonversi*. Retrieved from Kementerian Lingkungan Hidup dan Kehutanan: https://ksdae.menlhk.go.id/assets/news/peraturan/P.51_MENLHK_2016_TATA_CARA_PELEPASAN_KAWASAN_HUTAN_PRODUKSI_YANG_DAPAT_DIKONVERSI_.pdf

Kementerian Lingkungan Hidup dan Kehutanan. (2021). Permen LHK No. 7/2021 tentang. *Perencanaan Kehutanan, Perubahan Peruntukan Kawasan Hutan dan Perubahan Fungsi Kawasan Hutan, Serta Penggunaan Kawasan Hutan*. https://jdih.menlhk.go.id/new2/uploads/files/2021pmlhk007_menlhk_06102021120659.pdf

Kompas. (2011, January 12). *Kumpulan Berita Lingkungan Hidup*. Retrieved from Perpustakaan MENLHK: http://perpustakaan.menlhk.go.id/pustaka/images/docs/kompas_12_januari_2011_Izin_di_Kawasan_Hutan_Dievaluasi.pdf

Mighty Earth. (2024, April 16). *Nickel Industry Costs Lives and Livelihoods in Indonesia's Last Nomadic Sea Tribe*. Retrieved from Mighty Earth: https://mightyearth.org/article/from-forests-to-electric-vehicles/

Nadig, S. (2024, March 25). *Top Ten Nickel-Producing Countries in 2023.* Retrieved from Mining Technology: www.mining-technology.com/features/top-ten-nickel-producing-countries-in-2023/

Pandu, P. (2023, July 13). *Expansion of Nickel Mining Triggers Deforestation of 25,000 Hectares.* Retrieved from Kompas.id: www.kompas.id/baca/english/2023/07/13/en-ekspansi-pertambangan-nikel-picu-deforestasi-seluas-25000-hektar

Pemerintah Republik Indonesia. (2021). *Peraturan Pemerintah Nomor 22 Tahun 2021 tentang Penyelenggaraan Perlindungan dan Pengelolaan Lingkungan Hidup.* Retrieved from Database Peraturan BPK: https://peraturan.bpk.go.id/Details/161852/pp-no-22-tahun-2021

Pertamina. (n.d.). *Energy Transition.* Retrieved November 2024, from Pertamina: www.pertamina.com/en/energy-transition

Reyes, J. J. (2024, November 11). *Greener on the Other Side? Perspectives on Green Colonialism.* Retrieved from Heinrich Boll Foundation: https://th.boell.org/en/2024/11/11/-green-colonialism

Susetyo, P. D. (2021, April 27). *Memahami Definisi Tutupan Hutan.* Retrieved from Forest Digest: www.forestdigest.com/detail/1126/beda-hutan-primer-dan-hutan-sekunder

The TreeMap. (2024, August 13). *Indonesia's Mining Crossroads: New Map Unveils Opportunities for Environmental Monitoring.* Retrieved August 2024, from Linkedin: www.linkedin.com/pulse/indonesias-mining-crossroads-new-map-unveils-opportunities-y46fc/?trackingId=bCP2oa2jRSEasAorpsZLAA%3D%3D

Trikarinaputri, E. (2024, August 27). *Penjelasan Lengkap Bos Vale soal Tuduhan Praktik Dirty Nickel di RI.* Retrieved November 2024, from Tempo: www.tempo.co/arsip/penjelasan-lengkap-bos-vale-soal-tuduhan-praktik-dirty-nickel-di-ri-15426

Trimegah Bangun Persada. (2023). *Sustainability Report.* Retrieved from TBP: https://tbp-nickel.com/sustainability/sustainability-report

Vale Indonesia. (2023). *Sustainability Report.* Retrieved from Vale: https://vale.com/in/indonesia/laporan-keberlanjutan

VBDO. (2024, February 20). *VBDO.* Retrieved from Investor Expectations for Enhanced Social and Environmental Due Diligence in Nickel Supply Chains of the Electric Vehicle (EV) Industry: www.vbdo.nl/wp-content/uploads/2024/02/Investor-Expectations-Statement-on-nickel-supply-chains-20_02_2024.docx.pdf

Walhi Sulteng. (2024, March 19). *Ambisi Hilirisasi Nikel dan Masifnya penggunaan Energi Fosil Batubara di Sulawesi Tengah.* Retrieved November 2024, from Walhi Sulawesi Tengah: https://walhisulteng.org/ambisi-hilirisasi-nikel-dan-masifnya-penggunaan-energi-fosil-batubara-di-sulawesi-tengah/

The Wall Street Journal. (2023, June 13). *Inside Indonesia's Explosive Rise into the Global EV Supply Chain | WSJ* [Video]. YouTube. Retrieved July 27, 2024, from www.youtube.com/watch?v=Kg-gJ9wPYsI&t=83s

Widuto, A. (2023, November). *Energy Transition in the EU.* Retrieved November 2024, from European Parliament: www.europarl.europa.eu/RegData/etudes/BRIE/2023/754623/EPRS_BRI(2023)754623_EN.pdf

World Resources Institute. (2013, October 16). *How to Change Legal Land Use Classifications to Support More Sustainable Palm Oil in Indonesia.* Retrieved from World Resources Institute: www.wri.org/research/how-change-legal-land-use-classifications-support-more-sustainable-palm-oil-production

Yanow, D. (2003). *Constructing 'race' and 'ethnicity' in America: Category-making in public policy and administration.* M.E. Sharpe.

Part 3

Environmental and Social Impacts – Controversies and Opportunities

9 From Green Transition to Green Grabbing

The Impact of Democratic Regression at Indonesia's Geothermal Frontier

Yogi Setya Permana

Introduction

How does green grabbing manifest in a country experiencing democratic regression, one that has not fully devolved into authoritarianism but has not yet attained the stability characteristic of a mature liberal democracy? Is it analogous to the practices seen in authoritarian regimes that predominantly employ coercion and violence as methods of dispossession, enforce land grabs, and suppress resistance (Dell'Angelo et al., 2017; Gurol et al., 2024)? This chapter aims to address these increasingly pertinent questions in the context of the global agenda surrounding the energy transition. It explores the tension within the geothermal project in Poco Leok, Nusa Tenggara Timur (NTT), Indonesia, to illuminate the relationship between green grabbing and democratic regression. This connection has been largely neglected in existing scholarly discourse. Furthermore, this case study highlights that the European Union Green Deal (EGD), as the European Union's (EU) package of green policy measures, lacks a contextual approach, failing to consider the political and administrative contexts and processes, such as democratic reform or regression.

Over the past decade, a vigorous debate has emerged regarding the intersection of environmental sustainability initiatives and the emergence of grievances, particularly phenomena known as "green grabbing." This discussion critically examines how sustainability efforts can inadvertently lead to the appropriation of resources and land under the pretence of conservation, raising various socio-economic and environmental justice concerns (Fairhead et al., 2012). However, the connection between green grabbing and democratic regression remains inadequately examined in the current literature. Linking green grabbing to democratic regression could provide scholars and policymakers with deeper insights into how environmental policies and projects might inadvertently bolster authoritarian tendencies, elite dominance, and social inequalities within a non-dictatorial or non-authoritarian country.

Current research often overlooks how green grabbing intersects with the context of democratic regression. There is a notable lack of studies that detail the mechanisms through which the context of democratic regression, occurring globally (Diamond, 2021), facilitates green grabbing. Consequently, this study poses

DOI: 10.4324/9781003783176-12

the question: How does the process of green grabbing unfold, and what specific mechanisms underlie the appropriation in a country experiencing democratic regression? In this context, democratic regression refers to a country that has not yet devolved into authoritarianism but has also not reached the maturity typical of liberal democracy. Thus, this study aims to link the discussions of green grabbing and democratic regression to provide new insights into the energy transition policy, specifically through an examination of geothermal investment in Indonesia as a case study.

Indonesia, situated in the Ring of Fire, possesses vast untapped geothermal resources and has made significant investments in this sector as part of its energy transition towards achieving net-zero emissions by 2060. This aligns with the EGD and is supported by the Just Energy Transition Partnership (JETP), which has pledged US$ 21.6 billion from developed countries and financial institutions to support Indonesia's transition from fossil fuels to renewable energy. However, geothermal projects funded through this global initiative have sparked controversy, resistance, and societal tension, especially as civic space shrinks and grassroots and Indigenous communities face marginalisation (Warburton & Aspinall, 2019; Adiprasetio et al., 2024). A critical examination of these projects is urgently needed, particularly in Indonesia, one of the world's largest democracies, currently facing democratic regression despite its key role in renewable energy development.

Using Indonesia's geothermal investment project in Poco Leok, East Nusa Tenggara Province, as a case study, this study argues that two mechanisms facilitate "green grabbing" within the context of Indonesia's democratic regression, a term that refers to the decline of democratic governance and the erosion of democratic institutions. The first mechanism involves a stringent institutional framework that allows unchecked investments in renewable energy. This framework undermines environmental impact assessments by limiting public participation and oversight, as demonstrated by Law 21/2014 concerning geothermal investment and the Omnibus or Job Creation Law 6/2023. The second mechanism is the criminalisation of people who oppose geothermal projects, such as Indigenous peoples and journalists acting as watchdogs. These two elements operate within Indonesia's legal frameworks, granting legal status to land appropriation practices that are otherwise illegitimate while casting resistance to investment projects as illegal actions. Therefore, this study demonstrates that a country undergoing democratic regression exhibits specific mechanisms that facilitate green grabbing, which differ from those observed in authoritarian regimes. In contexts of democratic regression, green grabbing activities often occur within existing legal frameworks, lending the resource appropriation process a superficial sense of legitimacy. This issue is illustrated by the geothermal power plant initiative in Poco Leok, where local communities face heightened risks as their rights and resources are marginalised under the guise of promoting environmental sustainability. This geothermal investment project extends extraction activities even into conservation areas, jeopardising the sustainability of land waterscapes, biodiversity, food-producing lands, and other vital sources of livelihood for the people.

This chapter will be structured into five distinct sections. The first section will offer an overview of the existing literature on green grabbing and democratic regression, enabling us to explore the potential relationship between these two concepts. The second section will focus on geothermal projects in Indonesia, examining both the policymaking processes and their implementation at the ground level. In the following section, I will analyse the ecological and social impacts associated with geothermal investments, as well as the friction and resistance encountered, particularly in the case of Poco Leok, East Nusa Tenggara. Subsequently, I will link the Poco Leok case to the broader discussion of green grabbing and democratic regression, explicitly addressing how this study can help bridge the knowledge gap. Finally, the fifth section will provide concluding remarks, reflecting on Indonesia's energy transition and its implications for the debate on EGD, as well as discussing the expectations regarding the EU as a significant investor in geothermal projects in Indonesia.

Connecting Green Grabbing and Democratic Regression

Green grabbing and democratic regression may initially seem like disparate areas of literature; however, it is entirely possible to draw connections between the two. This study specifically employs the term "regression" instead of "backsliding," as the latter term emphasises the active undermining of democracy by identifiable political actors during specific episodes or phases. In contrast, "regression" broadens the scope to encompass all forms of democratic decline, including gradual and structural weakening (Bermeo, 2016; Gerschewski, 2021). Democratic regression suggests that the erosion of democratic quality occurs slowly, through a long-term decline, whereas backsliding is concerned with particular events or moments that precipitate a decline in democratic practice (Bermeo, 2016; Gerschewski, 2021). The democratic system is experiencing a gradual erosion, evident in the proliferation of legislation that serves to entrench the interests of predatory elites while simultaneously curtailing opposition to prevailing policies. This trend reflects a systemic manipulation of legal frameworks that undermines the integrity of democratic processes and stifles dissent.

This study proposes that democratic regression serves as a necessary condition for facilitating green grabbing. Democratic regression fosters conditions conducive to green grabbing by eroding democratic governance, marginalising local participation, consolidating authority, and legitimising the appropriation of resources under the guise of environmental initiatives (Anugrah, 2023; Busscher, 2018). This dynamic results in the dispossession and further marginalisation of vulnerable communities, all framed as part of green development efforts (Busscher, 2018). To elucidate the relationship between these concepts and demonstrate how this study can expand our understanding of green grabbing more broadly, I will first outline our current knowledge of green grabbing and provide a conceptual explanation of democratic regression.

The term "green grabbing" has emerged to describe land appropriation practices that utilise purported "green" credentials to justify the acquisition of land under the guise of sustainability or environmental protection (Fairhead et al., 2012, p. 238). In this context, appropriations refer to the transfer of ownership, rights, and control over resources that were previously held by the public or private entities – or even those not subject to ownership – into the hands of more powerful stakeholders, often at the expense of the poor (Fairhead et al., 2012, p. 238). The environmental agendas invoked as justifications for these appropriations can encompass a variety of initiatives, including biodiversity conservation (Büscher & Fletcher, 2018; Holmes, 2014), wildlife protection (Green & Adams, 2015), biocarbon sequestration, biofuels (McCarthy et al., 2012), ecotourism (Wieckardt et al., 2022; Rocheleau, 2015), and renewable energy (Siamanta, 2019; Dunlap, 2020). A distinguishing feature of green grabbing compared to traditional land grabbing is the broader and more varied array of actors involved (Fairhead et al., 2012). This contemporary form of appropriation engages a diverse set of participants, including pension funds, venture capitalists, international donors, commodity traders, consultants, geologists, academics, geographic information system service providers, business entrepreneurs, ecotourism companies, military actors, and green activists.

Franco and Borras (2019) identified a connection between climate change politics and land grabbing, which is particularly evident in dam projects for hydropower along the Salween River in mainland Southeast Asia. They argue that the impact of climate change politics may result in the displacement or dispossession of more individuals from their land than the actual effects of climate change itself (Franco & Borras, 2019, p. 193). Additionally, they emphasise the "repackaging" strategy, which is illustrated by the Myanmar government's approach to rebranding existing initiatives, such as the construction of large-scale hydropower dams and the expansion of its general forest conservation areas, as components of a climate change mitigation and adaptation campaign. Those who oppose the dam project have consequently been characterised as being against climate change mitigation efforts (Franco & Borras, 2019, p. 196).

Numerous studies have documented the phenomenon of "green grabbing" within the expanding literature on political ecology related to renewable energy development. The establishment of wind farms in various countries is often mired in controversy due to the exclusion of local communities from decision-making processes, instances of top-down governance, political corruption, green militarisation, and adverse effects on livelihoods, culture, and ecosystems (Siamanta, 2019). Similarly, in the realm of hydropower, researchers have observed that its expansion leads to alterations in land and water availability, depriving riverside communities of numerous interconnected livelihood benefits (Rousseau, 2020). In Turkey, the populist authoritarian government has leveraged the narrative of climate mitigation to advance geothermal projects, resulting in environmental injustice, heightened grievances, and increased inequality (Ozen, 2024). Ozen's work makes an important contribution by illustrating how an authoritarian populist regime can exploit the transition to renewable energy to create new avenues for capital accumulation for its allies, who are instrumental in both the financial and political support of its dominance, all while jeopardizing highly fertile farmlands and the rural livelihoods that depend on them (Ozen, 2024, p. 1593). Consequently, it is not surprising that the existing academic literature on the social acceptance of renewable energy has yet to reach a consensus regarding the factors that influence support or acceptance of such projects (Enserink et al., 2022).

From the existing literature, we have found limited explanations regarding the practice of green grabbing in countries experiencing democratic regression. These countries have not yet descended into authoritarianism but have also not attained the maturity of a fully developed democracy, similar to Indonesia. How does the green grabbing process unfold in such contexts, and what are the specific mechanisms through which appropriation occurs? To address this inquiry, we must first conceptually grasp the notion of democratic regression.

For nearly a decade and a half, the world has been experiencing a democratic recession (Diamond, 2021). A small illustration of this global phenomenon can be seen in the publication patterns of the journal *Democratization*, which has focused on the study of democratisation since its inception in 1994. Beginning in the mid-2000s, there has been a significant rise in articles and special issues addressing challenges to democracy promotion, including concepts such as "defective democracy," "hybrid regimes," "dynamics of authoritarian politics," and "authoritarian innovations" (Croissant & Haynes, 2020, p. 2). Notably, the percentage of articles in the *Democratization* journal that explored issues related to democratic transition and consolidation declined from 72% in 2005 to 57% in 2015. Conversely, the proportion of articles focusing on democratic breakdown and authoritarianism rose from 7.5% to 23.5% during the same period (Croissant & Haynes, 2020, p. 2).

The term "democratic regression" refers to the state of a democratic regime that experiences a decline in quality, representing a negative trajectory for democracy, which results in a transformation within the democratic framework (Tomini & Wagemann, 2018, p. 688). In this context, a country has neither entirely succumbed to an authoritarian regime nor achieved the status of a liberal democracy. Nations facing democratic regression typically do not endure military coups or authoritarian rule without electoral processes. Instead, the erosion of democratic principles is often enacted by presidents or elected officials who gradually undermine institutional checks, political opposition, media independence, and the oversight functions of civil society (Diamond, 2021, p. 22). These democratically elected leaders exploit the existing legal framework to serve their interests, which has detrimental implications for the health of democracy (Gerschewski, 2021). They may accomplish this by appointing judges who align with their viewpoints and suppressing dissenting voices. Over time, this results in an accumulation of power over the judiciary, and a weakening of judicial independence, all under the pretext of acting in the interest of the populace. Consequently, this leads to restrictions on opposition rights and violations of civil liberties and political rights (Gerschewski, 2021, p. 10). Notable examples, such as South Korea under Presidents Lee Myung-bak and Park Geun-hye, illustrate how laws can be manipulated for less democratic ends. In South Korea, the decline of democracy occurred through various legal strategies employed by the government, including the misuse of criminal defamation laws, electoral regulations, and the National Security Law (Gerschewski, 2021, p. 10).

Within the previously discussed theoretical framework, the relationship between green grabbing and democratic regression can be observed through the gradual deterioration of existing democratic institutions. In a country like Indonesia, the emergence of new policies and regulations appears to favour elite control over resources and exacerbate dispossession, particularly by employing the renewable energy narrative to facilitate land grabbing. Regulations enacted by the executive branch, with the backing of the legislative body, legitimise land grabbing while marginalising the rights of local communities. It illustrates how this predatory legal framework serves as a tool to suppress community opposition, even in a state that cannot be classified as formally authoritarian.

Overview of the Geothermal Extraction in Indonesia

As a region situated along the Ring of Fire, Indonesia boasts 127 active volcanoes scattered throughout its archipelago (Alhusni et al., 2023). This geological feature provides the country with immense potential for geothermal energy. It is estimated that Indonesia holds approximately 40% of the world's geothermal resources (Koons, 2024). As a result, the nation has a significant geothermal capacity of up to 24 GW, distributed across more than 350 geothermal sites (Alhusni et al., 2023). As of early 2024, Indonesia operates 16 geothermal power plants, generating nearly 2.4 GW of electricity, positioning it as the second-largest producer of geothermal power globally, behind the United States (Koons, 2024). However, this production figure is still relatively small compared to Indonesia's potential. According to the General Plan for National Energy (RUEN), the Indonesian government plans to expedite the development of geothermal energy to achieve a capacity of 7.2 GW by 2025, necessitating an investment of US$15 billion (Koty, 2022). By 2035, the government aims to further increase geothermal power to 9.3 GW (Koty, 2022). Consequently, the Indonesian government is actively pursuing international funding to secure investment for geothermal development as part of its efforts to accelerate the transition to green energy.

The rise in investment is already making an impact. On 16 November 2022, the Government of Indonesia and the International Partners Group (IPG) launched JETP Indonesia during the G20 Summit in Bali. The IPG is co-led by the governments of Japan and the United States, and includes Canada, Denmark, the EU, Germany, France, Norway, Italy, and the United Kingdom. Indonesia's recent adoption of the JETP aims to secure over $20 billion from a blend of domestic and international sources, particularly from the EU, to advance its renewable energy sector, with a special emphasis on geothermal energy. With an initial commitment of $20 billion, JETP Indonesia represents the largest energy transition financing package in the world to date (JETP Secretariat, 2023). In November 2023, the JETP Secretariat published the Comprehensive Investment and Policy Plan (CIPP) document, outlining the short-term implementation strategy for JETP in Indonesia. The document identifies geothermal development as the highest priority (Ahdiat, 2023).

Geothermal exploitation in Indonesia has its roots in the Dutch colonial era, beginning at the Kamojang crater in West Java during the 1920s. However, it was not until the 1970s that the Indonesian government gave serious attention to developing geothermal resources (Alhusni et al., 2023, p. 3). In that decade, with assistance from various countries, Indonesia conducted a comprehensive geothermal inventory that culminated in Presidential Decree 16/1974, which tasked Pertamina with exploring geothermal resources in Java and Bali. Significant discoveries were made at Kamojang, leading to the establishment of a small power plant in 1978, followed by a 30-MW plant in 1979 (Alhusni et al., 2023, p. 3). Further explorations revealed four active geothermal fields: Kamojang, Salak, Darajat, and Lahendong, which foreign donors and the Indonesian government funded. By 1997, Pertamina had assessed 250 geothermal prospects, identifying 70 suitable for electricity generation and entering Joint Operating Contracts (JOCs) for 10 of these sites. The Asian financial crisis of 1997–1998 resulted in project cancellations and a decline in private investment. In response to these challenges, Presidential Decree 76/2000 ended Pertamina's monopoly, allowing regional governments to oversee geothermal projects (Alhusni et al., 2023, p. 3). In 2002, Pertamina and the State Electricity Company (PLN) established PT Geo Dipa Energi to manage geothermal fields and power plants. Today, PT SMI (*Sarana Multi Infrastruktur*) serves as the institution appointed by the Indonesian government to manage the JETP fund for geothermal development in Indonesia.

The Indonesian government has designed its geothermal development project to encourage the involvement of private companies. In 2003, Indonesia enacted Law No. 27/2003 on Geothermal Energy, which permitted private sector participation in geothermal energy initiatives. This law was built upon the earlier Presidential Decree 76/2000 and introduced an auction process for securing Geothermal Mining Permits (IUP). It empowered both central and local governments to conduct exploration surveys and drilling, utilising the data to establish Geothermal Working Areas (GWAs) for auction purposes. In 2014, Geothermal Law No. 21/2014 replaced Law No. 27/2003, officially categorising geothermal energy as renewable rather than mining activity. This change allowed geothermal projects to be carried out in conservation areas, fostering expectations of significant growth. However, this shift has opened a Pandora's box, leading to heightened resistance against geothermal exploitation in various regions of Indonesia, including Poco Leok in East Nusa Tenggara Province. The classification of geothermal as a non-mining activity was further affirmed by the Omnibus Law enacted in 2020 and then in 2023, which aimed to boost both foreign and domestic investment by streamlining regulatory requirements for business permits and land acquisition. In the following section, I will delve deeper into the friction and conflicts arising from geothermal exploitation in Indonesia, using the case of Poco Leok in East Nusa Tenggara as the case study.

The Story of Resistance in Poco Leok, East Nusa Tenggara Province

Based on their observations of geothermal exploitation worldwide, Greiner et al. (2023, p. 2) highlighted that geothermal energy development has a substantial landscape footprint, which is more significant than that of other energy resources, despite its lower numerical land-use footprint for facilities and pipelines. This process necessitates boreholes and extensive pipelines to transport steam or hot water to power plants, creating physical barriers for activities such as livestock herding and altering local environments (Greiner et al., 2023, p. 2). Additionally, infrastructure such as roads and power lines is required, along with treatment facilities for contaminated thermal water. Emissions, noise, and micro-earthquakes resulting from drilling and water reinjection can adversely affect the surrounding area. Consequently, geothermal development has the potential to impact the livelihoods of vulnerable rural communities, leading to criticism and resistance from residents who perceive it as a "harm industry" (Greiner et al., 2023, p. 2). A similar situation is also evident in Indonesia.

According to records from CELIOS, an Indonesian non-governmental organisation (NGO) dedicated to sustainable environmental advocacy, 15 geothermal power sites in Indonesia are believed to be problematic (Kumparan Bisnis, 2024). First, emissions from H2 gas and waste produced by power plants are adversely affecting the crops of residents, contributing to drought conditions. Since all geothermal sites are located in mountainous regions, their operations have a direct impact on the livelihoods of local farmers who rely on agriculture. Consequently, there has been a significant decline in crop productivity. Second, geothermal exploitation has led to water pollution, primarily due to inadequate management of geothermal steam. This mismanagement has resulted in fracking, which creates fissures in rock layers, allowing water contaminated with chemicals to seep into the environment. Finally, there are conflicts over land related to geothermal exploration and extraction, such as those observed in Poco Leok, NTT.

The expansion of geothermal exploitation at Poco Leok, financed by a €150 million loan, reflects the Indonesian government's designation of Flores Island as a Geothermal Island in 2017. Located in East Nusa Tenggara, Flores Island is geologically situated within a volcanic ring of fire, endowing it with significant geothermal potential that attracts investment in this sector. Consequently, the government plans to advance geothermal development in several additional locations around Flores Island, including Wae Sano, West Manggarai, Mataloko, Ngada, and Ulumbu, in addition to ongoing efforts in Poco Leok.

The conflict in Poco Leok, located in East Nusa Tenggara Province, originated from the planned expansion of the Ulumbu Geothermal Power Plant, which has been in operation since 2012. This facility currently generates 10 MW of electricity (Wicaksono, 2023). To enhance geothermal power production capacity, the PLN expanded its exploitation zone to include the Poco Leok region, which is home to 14 traditional communities across 3 villages. The geothermal project in the Poco Leok Mountains encompasses 60 drilling points, situated within 13 traditional communities spanning Lungar, Mocok, and Golo Muntas Villages (Susabun, 2023). This development aims to increase electricity production by 40 MW, significantly boosting the original production capacity by four times (Wicaksono, 2023). The financing for this geothermal exploitation expansion is provided by Kreditanstalt für Wiederaufbau (KfW), the German Development Bank, as part of Germany and the EU's commitment to accelerate the clean energy transition in the Global South and developing countries. The agreement between the Indonesian government, represented by PLN and KfW, was established in October 2018, stipulating debt funding of €150 million.

With the progression of the geothermal project development plan in the Poco Leok area, the Indigenous communities residing in the Poco Leok Mountains are increasingly vocal in their rejection and opposition to these exploitative activities. They fear that the geothermal project will lead to the loss of their land, the destruction of local animal and plant habitats, and damage to the surrounding water systems. Furthermore, they are concerned about the potential health and safety risks posed by the geothermal industry waste (Wicaksono, 2023). The first physical confrontations erupted in early 2023 when the government attempted to survey the land designated for the geothermal project, accompanied by military and police forces. This land mapping encroached upon the Lingko Tanggong area, a sacred customary land for the Indigenous people of Poco Leok, which the government had earmarked as one of the drilling sites (Wicaksono, 2023). The Indigenous communities, united in their opposition, blocked the government's efforts to mark the drilling land, resulting in physical clashes. Nine Indigenous individuals were injured in the altercations, including four women (Floresa, 2023).

In July 2023, the Indigenous community of Poco Leok, supported by a coalition of civil society groups, submitted a letter to the KfW requesting the cancellation of funding for a geothermal project in their region. In response, KfW acknowledged the concerns raised by the Indigenous people and indicated that follow-up steps would be taken. However, they asserted that they had no direct involvement in the geothermal project and had delegated the responsibility for its planning, implementation, and operation to PLN. KfW maintained that it bore no responsibility for the developments in Poco Leok, citing that full authority over the project rested with the Indonesian government (Wicaksono, 2023). Civil society activists and members of the Indigenous community expressed deep disappointment with KfW's response, arguing that the organisation should not overlook the situation in Poco Leok (Wicaksono, 2023).

The ongoing rejection and resistance of residents towards geothermal project development have been accompanied by the criminalisation of Indigenous individuals who oppose these initiatives. In October 2023, seven members of the Poco Leok Indigenous community were taken by police for questioning at their headquarters. The individuals were bewildered by the police's actions, as they were merely expressing their opinions and defending their customary territory; however, these actions were deemed criminal (PPMAN, 2023). The police alleged that the seven Indigenous individuals violated laws related to the 2014 and 2023 geothermal regulations, as well as the Omnibus Law on natural resource investment, by obstructing government officials engaged in work related to the geothermal project (PPMAN, 2023). They are facing potential prison sentences of one year and four months. In response, several civil society organisations and the Catholic Church in Flores have reported this criminalisation case against Indigenous people to the National Human Rights Commission in Jakarta in pursuit of justice.

Physical clashes erupted once again on 2 October 2024, as government officials and PLN entered Poco Leok to survey residents' land and identify drilling locations. The situation saw a significant deployment of police and military forces to secure the operation. This confrontation led to injuries among dozens of Indigenous people. Additionally, three residents and one journalist were taken into custody

(WALHI, 2024). The journalist, who serves as the editor-in-chief of Floresa News, had actively reported on the Indigenous community's opposition to the geothermal project in Poco Leok. He alleged that he was subjected to torture and physical abuse by the police during his arrest while covering the residents' protests on 2 October 2024 (Bria & Ardin, 2024). A coalition of media and advocacy groups expressed their deep concern over the arrests of both residents and the journalist, viewing it as an attempt at criminalisation by the police (Belseran, 2024).

In September 2024, an independent team commissioned by KfW visited Poco Leok to engage with the Indigenous people in response to the ongoing controversy surrounding the land acquisition process. The Indigenous residents reported that the government and PLN's approach was rife with coercion, manipulation, and a lack of transparency. Some residents were compelled to accept the government's compensation, while others stated that 369 households, comprising 1,592 people, rejected the development of the Poco Leok geothermal project (Floresa, 2024). This figure stands in sharp contrast to PLN's claims regarding the number of individuals who consented to the project's construction. Additionally, the Indigenous community conveyed to the KfW team that their refusal to accept the geothermal project was rooted in a profound attachment to their living environment, which they refer to as the five main elements. These elements include *lingko* (customary farm), *mata wae* (springs), *compang* (altars for ancestral offerings), *natas* (village yards), and *mbaru gendang* (traditional houses). As a result, they feel unable to relocate, as their cultural heritage, passed down through generations, is deeply intertwined with their land (Floresa, 2024).

The process of acquiring residents' land revealed the government's and PLN's utilisation of religious narratives to tame the opposition. Given that the majority of East Nusa Tenggara's residents are Catholic, PLN consultants engaged in communications often invoked the authority of the Catholic Church in NTT. They referenced the Laudato Si document (Floresa, 2022). This document, issued by the Pope in 2015, articulates the Catholic Church's perspective on environmental stewardship. The consultants consistently highlighted that geothermal development is in harmony with the Pope's message, emphasising its environmentally friendly nature. During various public meetings, PLN consultants distributed booklets featuring excerpts from the Laudato Si document. However, they included additional phrases regarding geothermal energy that were not part of the original text: "The use of fossil fuels, diesel, and coal for power plants is highly polluting to the environment and health. Renewable geothermal energy is the preferred choice as it is more environmentally friendly and sustainable in the long term (-trans. English)." This explicit reference to geothermal energy does not appear in the version of the Laudato Si document translated by the Indonesian Bishops' Conference (Floresa, 2022). Moreover, the Ruteng Diocese Church has repeatedly refuted PLN's assertions that they have endorsed the development of the geothermal project (Floresa, 2022).

Exploring the Relationship between Indonesia's Democratic Regression and Green Grabbing

The decline of democracy in Indonesia has become a significant topic of discussion among analysts and observers, both within the country and internationally.

According to the 2021 Freedom House index, Indonesia is categorised as partly free, a status that has remained unchanged since 2013 (freedomhouse.org). The Economist has classified Indonesian democracy as flawed since 2006 (Economist Intelligence Unit, 2021), noting the presence of free elections but highlighting serious shortcomings in governance, political culture, and civic participation. Recent scholars have raised alarms regarding the state of democracy in Indonesia, employing terms such as "regression" (Power & Warburton, 2020), "authoritarian innovation" (Mietzner, 2020), and "illiberal democracy" (Diprose et al., 2019). Citizens' rights often hinge on their access to the state (Berenschot & van Klinken, 2018), with marginalised groups, particularly the urban poor, facing challenges like unwarranted evictions (Wilson, 2019). Moreover, the formal representation system tends to favour upper-class voters, inadequately reflecting the interests of grassroots communities (Warburton & Aspinall, 2019).

Signs of a decline in the quality of democracy are evident in Indonesia through the emergence of broader illiberal trends affecting civil liberties, particularly in the laws and regulations governing them. Notable examples include the 2008 Law on Electronic Information and Transactions (ITE) and the Criminal Code, which dates back to the colonial era. There is increasing evidence that individuals in positions of power, including high-level politicians, are utilising these laws to suppress and mitigate criticism from citizens, opposition figures, and anti-corruption activists (Warburton & Aspinall, 2019, p. 260). This regression in democratic practices also adversely affects the efforts of activists and ordinary citizens engaged in environmental protection (Tomsa & Bax, 2023). Environmental activists and those affected by land grabs face restrictions on their freedom of expression and inadequate legal protections. As a result, conservationists and advocates for land reform find it challenging to tackle corruption in the forestry and mining sectors or address the ecological impacts of infrastructure projects. Speaking out can lead to severe repercussions, including threats to personal safety and property (Tomsa & Bax, 2023, p. 751). Mietzner (2024) argues that Indonesian democracy is unlikely to succumb to authoritarianism, even in the face of a significant decline. He identifies two key factors: first, the dispersion of power is so extensive that achieving monopolisation would be challenging. Second, this power distribution has fueled intense rivalry among the elite, thwarting any attempts to restore a personalist autocracy. Nonetheless, it is essential to acknowledge that elites have cooperated in undermining democracy as long as a foundational framework for the competitive rotation of power remains in place (Mietzner, 2024).

Two key factors facilitate green grabbing within the context of Indonesia's democratic regression, as exemplified by the Poco Leok case. First, a draconian institutional framework exists that promotes unchecked investment in renewable energy. This framework undermines environmental impact assessments by eliminating public participation and oversight, thereby compromising the integrity of the assessments. It is evident in Law 21/2014 regarding geothermal investment and the Omnibus Job Creation Law 6/2023. Second, there is a troubling trend of criminalising Indigenous peoples who oppose geothermal projects, as well as journalists who act as watchdogs. I argue that these two elements form the basis for suppressing opposition to the geothermal development in Poco Leok. This suppression occurs within the existing legal framework, enabling the labelling of resistance by opposition groups as illegal activities. This situation highlights a significant feature of democratic regression: those in power exploit the legal system to serve their interests, which has detrimental consequences for democracy (Gerschewski, 2021). Such actions result in the restriction of the opposition's rights and violations of civil liberties and political rights (Gerschewski, 2021, p. 10). Therefore, it is evident that democratic regression not only poses a threat to civil rights but also facilitates the green grabbing process, making it increasingly easier to quell opposition to the advancement of projects like this one.

Law 21/2014 on geothermal energy was subsequently reinforced by Law 6/2023, known nationally as the "Omnibus Law," aimed at job creation. The implementation of these two legal frameworks reveals a significant challenge in curtailing land grabbing driven by interests in renewable energy development. This regulatory approach raises serious concerns, particularly as classifying geothermal exploitation as a non-mining activity can have adverse effects on both the environment and the lives of local communities. Geothermal projects can be established across Indonesia, including in production forest areas, protected forest areas, conservation forests, water bodies, and even on customary lands (CELIOS & WALHI, 2024, p. 9). The facilitation of exploitation, extending even to conservation areas and customary lands, undermines efforts towards environmental sustainability and justice. This situation threatens biodiversity, causes landscape destruction, and exacerbates environmental pollution resulting from industrial activities. Moreover, the designation of customary lands for geothermal operations has resulted in escalating land conflicts, as exemplified by the situation in Poco Leok.

Auriga Nusantara, an Indonesian NGO dedicated to environmental protection, has reported at least 155 cases of threats against environmental defenders in Indonesia between 2015 and 2024. The incidence of these threats has shown a rising trend, particularly during the second term of President Joko Widodo's administration. Auriga Nusantara compiled this data by gathering information from public sources and communicating directly with the victims and other stakeholders aware of the threats (Auriga Nusantara, 2024). The threats to environmental defenders are widespread across all major islands of Indonesia. Since 2018, Auriga has been documenting cases faced by these defenders from 2014 to 2024. Out of the 155 documented incidents, the highest number occurred in Java (42 cases), followed by Sumatra (40 cases), Sulawesi (25 cases), and Kalimantan (25 cases). Bali and Nusa Tenggara reported 16 cases, while the Maluku Islands and Tanah Papua reported 5 and 2 cases, respectively.

There are six distinct types of threats faced by environmental defenders: criminalisation, physical violence, intimidation, murder, arson, and deportation. In Indonesia, criminalisation is the most prevalent threat, accounting for 64% of all cases (Auriga Nusantara, 2024). This form of criminalisation is not solely limited to formal court verdicts; it also includes situations where individuals are labelled as suspects by the police under various legal charges. An example of this can be seen with the Poco Leok Indigenous community and journalists from Floresa. This issue of criminalisation is particularly concerning due to the broad authority granted to police investigators, who are not required to ensure that all suspects are brought before a court of law.

The series of draconian laws and criminalisation in contemporary Indonesia are indicators of democratic regression and serve as enablers of green grabbing practices. Unlike green grabbing in authoritarian regimes, which often relies on violence and coercive measures, Indonesia's energy transition policies provide a legal framework that legitimises such practices, as illustrated by the Poco Leok case. This case illustrates that environmental protection initiatives, often framed as renewable energy development, can have detrimental effects, including marginalising residents and exacerbating inequality, due to a lack of deliberative and democratic decision-making processes. The Poco Leok case ultimately benefits a select few who gain access to electricity while undermining the livelihoods of the community residing in the area where the resource is extracted.

Conclusion and Implication for the Debate on EGD

Based on this study, I conclude that the literature on green grabbing should consider the context of democratic regression that has occurred globally. Countries experiencing democratic regression exhibit distinct mechanisms that facilitate green grabbing, which differ from those found in authoritarian regimes. In democratic regression contexts, green grabbing activities operate within existing legal frameworks, granting the process of resource appropriation a veneer of legality. Consequently, opposition resistance is often deemed illegal. This criminalisation strategy has become a prevalent tactic employed by governments and corporations to suppress dissent from environmental defenders, such as Indigenous peoples and journalists, as seen in the Poco Leok case. Additionally, this study emphasises that entities like the EU or KfW Germany, as debt funders, should not ignore or act irresponsibly regarding the disputes and conflicts that arise. Funders play a complicit role in large-scale projects that significantly affect local livelihoods in recipient countries.

This study highlights that the global trend of democratic regression can accelerate instances of green grabbing in various regions. It is mainly because the narratives surrounding environmental protection initiatives – such as the energy transition, which is currently on the global agenda – are susceptible to exploitation by elite political interests. Therefore, policymakers, donor agencies, experts, and civil society activists must adopt a more critical stance and incorporate political assessments when evaluating investments in energy transition projects. The pursuit of a green energy transition must be accompanied by a commitment to uphold democratic and equitable standards throughout the process.

The geothermal project in Poco Leok plays a vital role in contextualising the ongoing discussions surrounding the EGD. As discussed in Chapter 1 of this volume, the EGD is frequently portrayed as a neutral, linear, and rational policymaking process. However, this portrayal often obscures the complex power dynamics and political struggles inherent in both the design and implementation of such policies (Chapter 1, pp. 6–7). A central argument presented in this book is the lack of attention given to power-related questions – both concerning societal dynamics and institutional implementation capacity – especially in the Southeast Asian context. This analytical gap is evident in the Poco Leok case, where European financial institutions appear to have underestimated the contentious and politically charged environment surrounding energy transition projects at the local level.

While geothermal development is advocated as a form of clean energy, in countries like Indonesia – where democratic institutions are fragile and accountability mechanisms are weak – such initiatives can exacerbate grievances and provoke local resistance. International actors must acknowledge that domestic political configurations, including elite interests, state capacity, and the dynamics of civil society, significantly influence the implementation of policy in Southeast Asia. Consequently, the practical and just execution of EGD-aligned policies necessitates a nuanced, context-sensitive approach that prioritises the political and administrative realities on the ground. Without this understanding, relying solely on technical and financial solutions will be inadequate to ensure equitable and environmentally sound outcomes for local communities.

Reference List

Adiprasetio, J., et al. (2024). Shrinking civic space and the media: How Indonesian media frame environmental issues. *Journal of Civil Society*, *20*(1), 1–20.

Ahdiat, A. (2023). *Skenario investasi transisi energi JETP, terbesar untuk panas bumi*. Databoks – Katadata.co.id. https://databoks.katadata.co.id/ekonomi-makro/statistik/4f55da2093b52fb/skenario-investasi-transisi-energi-jetp-terbesar-untuk-panas-bumi

Alhusni, H., et al. (2023). Geothermal business outlook in Indonesia. In *Proceedings of the 48th workshop on geothermal reservoir engineering* (pp. 6–8). Stanford University.

Anugrah, I. (2023). Land control, coal resource exploitation and democratic decline in Indonesia. *TRaNS: Trans-Regional and National Studies of Southeast Asia*, *11*(2), 195–213.

Auriga Nusantara. (2024). *Status pembela lingkungan di Indonesia 2014–2023: Ancaman kian tinggi, saatnya negara hadir*. https://auriga.or.id/press_release/detail/50/status-pembela-lingkungan-di-indonesia-2014–2023-ancaman-kian-tinggi-saatnya-negara-hadir

Belseran, C. J. (2024). *Soroti kekerasan di proyek panas bumi Poco Leok, koalisi: Lindungi masyarakat*. Mongabay Indonesia. www.mongabay.co.id/2024/10/10/soroti-kekerasan-di-proyek-panas-bumi-di-poco-leok-koalisi-lindungi-masyarakat/

Berenschot, W., & van Klinken, G. (2018). Informality and citizenship: The everyday state in Indonesia. *Citizenship Studies*, *22*(2), 95–111. https://doi.org/10.1080/13621025.2018.1445494

Bermeo, N. (2016). On democratic backsliding. *Journal of Democracy*, *27*(1), 5–19.

Bria, Y., & Ardin, A. (2024, October 4). Kronologi Pemred Floresa ditangkap-disiksa saat liput demo tolak geotermal. detikBali. https://www.detik.com/bali/nusra/d-7571853/kronologi-pemred-floresa-ditangkap-disiksa-saat-liput-demo-tolak-geotermal

Büscher, B., & Fletcher, R. (2018). Under pressure: Conceptualising political ecologies of green wars. *Conservation and Society*, *16*(2), 105–113.

Busscher, N. A. (2018). *Land grabbing and its environmental justice implications* [Master's thesis, University of Groningen]. Rijksuniversiteit Groningen.

CELIOS & WALHI. (2024). *Geothermal di Indonesia: Dilema potensi dan eksploitasi atas nama transisi energi*. CELIOS-WALHI. https://www.walhi.or.id/uploads/buku/ID%20CELIOS%20x%20WALHI%20Geothermal%202024.pdf

Croissant, A., & Haynes, J. (2020). Democratic regression in Asia: Introduction. *Democratization*. https://doi.org/10.1080/13510347.2020.1851203

Dell'Angelo, J., et al. (2017). The tragedy of the grabbed commons: Coercion and dispossession in the global land rush. *World Development*, *92*, 1–12. https://doi.org/10.1016/j.worlddev.2016.11.005

Diamond, L. (2021). Democratic regression in comparative perspective: Scope, methods, and causes. *Democratization*, *28*(1), 22–42. https://doi.org/10.1080/13510347.2020.1807517

Diprose, R., et al. (2019). Two decades of Reformasi in Indonesia: Its illiberal turn. *Journal of Contemporary Asia*, *49*(5), 691–712. https://doi.org/10.1080/00472336.2019.1637922

Dunlap, A. (2020). Bureaucratic land grabbing for infrastructural colonization: Renewable energy, L'Amassada, and resistance in southern France. *Human Geography*, *13*(2), 109–126.

Economist Intelligence Unit. (2021). *Democracy index 2021: The China challenge*. www.eiu.com/n/campaigns/democracy-index-2021/

Enserink, M., et al. (2022). To support or oppose renewable energy projects? A systematic literature review on the factors influencing landscape design and social acceptance. *Energy Research & Social Science*, *91*, 102740.

Fairhead, J., et al. (2012). Green grabbing: A new appropriation of nature? *Journal of Peasant Studies*, *39*(2), 237–261.

Floresa. (2022, November 3). *PLN catut nama lembaga Gereja Katolik dan kutip ensiklik Laudato Si', diduga untuk loloskan proyek geothermal Poco Leok*. Floresa. https://floresa.co/reportase/peristiwa/51511/2022/11/03/pln-catut-nama-lembaga-gereja-katolik-dan-kutip-ensiklik-laudato-si-diduga-untuk-loloskan-proyek-geothermal-poco-leok

Floresa. (2023, June 22). *Pengukuran lahan proyek geothermal Poco Leok, Flores dikawal ketat aparat, protes warga direspons dengan represi*. Floresa. https://floresa.co/reportase/mendalam/54221/2023/06/22/pengukuran-lahan-proyek-geothermal-poco-leok-flores-dikawal-ketat-aparat-protes-warga-direspons-dengan-represi

Floresa. (2024, September 5). *Dikunjungi tim independen bank asal Jerman, warga Poco Leok nyatakan tolak serahkan ruang hidup, minta stop danai proyek geotermal*. Floresa. https://floresa.co/reportase/mendalam/67454/2024/09/05/dikunjungi-tim-independen-bank-asal-jerman-warga-poco-leok-nyatakan-tolak-serahkan-ruang-hidup-minta-stop-danai-proyek-geotermal

Franco, J. C., & Borras, S. M. Jr. (2019). Grey areas in green grabbing: Subtle and indirect interconnections between climate change politics and land grabs and their implications for research. *Land Use Policy*, 84, 192–199

Freedom House. (2022). *Freedom in the world 2022*. https://freedomhouse.org/report/freedom-world

Gerschewski, J. (2021). Erosion or decay? Conceptualizing causes and mechanisms of democratic regression. *Democratization*, *28*(1), 43–62.

Green, K. E., & Adams, W. M. (2015). Green grabbing and the dynamics of local-level engagement with neoliberalization in Tanzania's wildlife management areas. *Journal of Peasant Studies*, *42*(1), 97–117.

Greiner, C., et al. (2023). The political ecology of geothermal development: Green sacrifice zones or energy landscapes of value? *Energy Research & Social Science*, *99*, 103063.

Gurol, J., et al. (2024). *Authoritarian power and contestation beyond the state. Globalizations*, 21(6), 1009–1022. doi: 10.1080/14747731.2022.2162290

Holmes, G. (2014). What is a land grab? Exploring green grabs, conservation, and private protected areas in southern Chile. *Journal of Peasant Studies*, *41*(4), 547–567.

JETP Secretariat. (2023). *Comprehensive Investment and Policy Plan*. Just Energy Transition Partnership Indonesia. https://jetp-id.org/storage/official-jetp-cipp-2023-vshare_f_en-1700532655.pdf

Koons, E. (2024, February 28). *Indonesia's untapped geothermal energy potential*. Energy Tracker Asia. https://energytracker.asia/geothermal-energy-indonesia/

Koty, A. C. (2022, July 28). *An overview of Indonesia's geothermal energy sector*. ASEAN Briefing. https://www.aseanbriefing.com/news/an-overview-of-indonesias-geothermal-energy-sector/

Kumparan Bisnis. (2024, September 17). *Riset CELIOS: 15 pembangkit listrik tenaga panas bumi di Indonesia bermasalah*. Kumparan. https://kumparan.com/kumparan-bisnis/riset-celios-15-pembangkit-listrik-tenaga-panas-bumi-di-indonesia-bermasalah-23XhrBAmqvc

McCarthy, J. F., et al. (2012). Trajectories of land acquisition and enclosure: Development schemes, virtual land grabs, and green acquisitions in Indonesia's outer islands. *Journal of Peasant Studies*, *39*(2), 521–549. https://doi.org/10.1080/03066150.2012.671768

Mietzner, M. (2020). Authoritarian innovations in Indonesia: Electoral narrowing, identity politics and executive illiberalism. *Democratization*, *27*(6), 1021–1036. https://doi.org/10.1080/13510347.2019.1704266

Mietzner, M. (2024). The limits of autocratisation in Indonesia: Power dispersal and elite competition in a compromised democracy. *Third World Quarterly*. https://doi.org/10.1080/01436597.2024.2317970

Ozen, H. (2024). Why is 'clean' energy opposed? The resistances to geothermal energy projects in Turkey. *Environment and Planning E: Nature and Space*, 7 (4), 1580-1600. https://doi.org/10.1177/25148486241254684

PPMAN. (2023, October 4). Hentikan upaya kriminalisasi masyarakat adat Poco Leok. Perhimpunan Pembela Masyarakat Adat Nusantara. https://ppman.org/ppman-hentikan-upaya-kriminalisasi-masyarakat-adat-poco-leok/

Power, T., & Warburton, E. (Eds.). (2020). Democracy in Indonesia: From stagnation to regression? ISEAS–Yusof Ishak Institute.

Rocheleau, D. E. (2015). Networked, rooted and territorial: Green grabbing and resistance in Chiapas. *Journal of Peasant Studies*, *42*(3–4), 695–723. https://doi.org/10.1080/03066150.2014.993622

Rousseau, J. F. (2020). When land, water and green-grabbing cumulate: Hydropower expansion, livelihood resource reallocation and legitimisation in southwest China. *Asia Pacific Viewpoint*, *61*(1), 134–146.

Siamanta, Z. C. (2019). Wind parks in post-crisis Greece: Neoliberalisation vis-à-vis green grabbing. *Environment and Planning E: Nature and Space*, *2*(2), 274–303.

Susabun, A. (2023, March 8). Was-was panas bumi rusak ruang hidup warga Poco Leok. Mongabay Indonesia. https://mongabay.co.id/2023/03/08/was-was-panas-bumi-rusak-ruang-hidup-warga-poco-leok/

Tomini, L., & Wagemann, C. (2018). Varieties of contemporary democratic breakdown and regression: A comparative analysis. *European Journal of Political Research*, *57*(3), 687–716.

Tomsa, D., & Bax, N. (2023). Democratic regression and environmental politics in Indonesia. *Asian Studies Review*, *47*(4), 740–760.

WALHI. (2024, October 3). Poco Leok kembali memanas: Tarik mundur aparat, hentikan intimidasi dan kekerasan pada warga Poco Leok dan jurnalis. https://www.walhi.or.id/poco-leok-kembali-memanas-tarik-mundur-aparat-hentikan-intimidasi-dan-kekerasan-pada-warga-poco-leok-dan-jurnalis

Warburton, E., & Aspinall, E. (2019). Explaining Indonesia's democratic regression. *Contemporary Southeast Asia*, *41*(2), 255–285.

Wicaksono, R. A. (2023, August 11). Warga minta perluasan geothermal Ulumbu ke Poco Leok dihentikan. Betahita. https://betahita.id/news/detail/9104/warga-minta-perluasan-geothermal-ulumbu-ke-poco-leok-dihentikan.html?v=1708734193

Wieckardt, C. E., et al. (2022). Environmentality, green grabbing, and neoliberal conservation: The ambiguous role of ecotourism in the Green Life privatised nature reserve, Sumatra, Indonesia. *Journal of Sustainable Tourism*, *30*(11), 2614–2630.

Wilson, I. (2019). Urban poor activism and political agency in post – new order Jakarta. In M. Mietzner & B. Muhtadi (Eds.), *Activists in transition* (pp. 99–116). Cornell University Press. https://doi.org/10.7591/cornell/9781501742477.003.0006

10 Are Small Farmers Doomed? A Techno-Political Analysis of the European Union Deforestation Regulation's Effect on Palm Oil Supply Chains in Malaysia

Pieter E. Stek and Asad Ata

Introduction

Malaysia, as the world's second-largest producer and exporter of palm oil, is one of the countries that has significant exposure to the new European Union Deforestation Regulation (EUDR). The stated purpose of the EUDR is to "guarantee that the products EU citizens consume do not contribute to deforestation or forest degradation worldwide" (European Commission, 2023) and the regulation prohibits the import of cattle, cocoa, coffee, oil palm, rubber, soya, and wood unless they can be verified to be "deforestation-free" (Regulation (EU) 2023/1115, 2023).

The production of palm oil is a significant source of income for many rural communities across the tropical climate zone (Ogahara et al., 2022). Since the early 2000s, there has been a movement towards the development and implementation of environmental and social standards for palm oil. This movement has been led by the Roundtable on Sustainable Palm Oil (RSPO), an organization founded by large palm oil producers, traders, buyers, and an environmental organization. The RSPO introduced its first certification system in 2007 and, in 2019, launched a separate standard aimed at small farmers (RSPO, 2019).

Like the RSPO, the EUDR can be viewed as a "tripartite standards regime" (TSR), linking standard-setting, certification, and accreditation activities and enabling the development of a market for sustainable products (Fouilleux & Loconto, 2017; Hatanaka et al., 2012; Loconto et al., 2012). Although the EUDR is a public policy measure, it gives rise to a chain of private-sector activities to ensure compliance, and has a material impact on producers located outside the European Union (EU). Given that the certification of small producers has been a persistent problem for TSRs (Fouilleux & Loconto, 2017), such problems will likely persist for the EUDR.

Within the specific context of palm oil, researchers note that sustainability standards for small farmers "do not respond to many key challenges, nor build upon smallholder advantages for both socio-economic and environmental benefits" (Ogahara et al., 2022, p. 9). This conclusion has also been drawn more broadly with regards to sustainability standards for small- and medium-sized enterprises

DOI: 10.4324/9781003783176-13

(SMEs), especially those in developing countries. As described by Sommers (2017), the adoption of sustainability standards:

> requires managerial and technical skills as well as the financial means for investments, both of which SMEs systemically lack. Hence, the spread of standards could exclude SMEs from international production and from lucrative markets.
>
> (Sommer, 2017, p. 2)

As EUDR implementation comes into focus, the problem of small producers is highlighted once more, although it echoes a long-running discourse on how small producers fit within Malaysia's agricultural landscape. Colonial administrators in Malaysia during the 1930s already problematized small palm oil farmers' lack of organization and the critical role of middlemen dealers (Pakiam, 2021). In that sense, today's EUDR may seem uncomfortably close to the colonial discourse of that era.

The aim of this study is threefold. First, it provides a theoretical framing of the EUDR from the perspective of TSRs and, more broadly, the development of palm oil sustainability standards. Second, the study addresses the specific challenges of the palm oil supply chain for small producers in Malaysia, showing how EUDR traceability, as it is currently envisaged, is unworkable for small producers (section 3). Third, the study outlines how reframing palm oil production and deforestation from a territorial lens could offer an outcome that achieves the goals of the EUDR and would allow small producers to remain in the supply chain (section 4).

The final section (section 5) provides a brief discussion of the research findings and their implications. The issues and framing of small palm oil producers in Malaysia and the EUDR, and the solutions to overcoming related challenges, may also apply for different TSRs, different commodities, and different geographies.

TSRs in Palm Oil

Defining TSRs

TSRs emerge as a specific regulatory regime once a voluntary sustainability standard is developed. TSRs combine the socio-technical standards with certifications and accreditations, creating a specific but integrated standards regime (Fouilleux & Loconto, 2017; Hatanaka et al., 2012; Loconto et al., 2012).

The standard at the core of the TSR is developed by a Standard Development Organization (SDO), which consists of experts and interested parties who create the standard (Fouilleux & Loconto, 2017; Loconto et al., 2012). Examples of SDOs include the International Standards Organization (ISO), a non-governmental organization (NGO) based in Geneva, Switzerland, which sets international technical industrial standards. In the field of palm oil, there is the RSPO, which is a NGO based in Kuala Lumpur, Malaysia.

SDOs work with Certifying Bodies (CBs) whose task is to audit organizational processes, products, or services to ensure they meet the standard. CBs are in turn monitored by Accreditation Bodies (ABs), who verify if the standard developed by the SDOs is being certified correctly (Fouilleux & Loconto, 2017). In the case of RSPO standards for palm oil, its AB is Assurance Services International, a private company based in Bonn, Germany.

> TSRs are notably different from government regulation, both in how decisions are made, as well as in their scope and role. TSRs typically involve voluntary private standards and they often occur in a trans- national setting (Fouilleux & Loconto, 2017).

As explained by Busch (2011):

> TSRs differ from state-based modes of governance in that they are often a cobbled-together network of persons, organizations, and things, rather than being constructed on a formal hierarchy of status relations. TSR may be granted special status by nation-states, or they may be an entirely private form of governance, subject to state laws about contracts, fraud, and so forth, but not the subject of any special legislation. (p. 221)

Technical standards also have a number of important functions in the technical and economic spheres. They are an important channel for the diffusion of knowledge, as they encourage the formation of a scientific consensus on a particular topic and subsequently support the dissemination of best practices in terms of technical design, safety, environment, and functionality. From an economic perspective, standards help enhance equipment interoperability and lower transaction costs by providing transparent information about a product, thereby facilitating trade (Egan, 2002; Loconto et al., 2012). Standards, therefore, not only give rise to a TSR but also help to create a market for a specific kind of product, such as *sustainable* palm oil.

Standards Regimes and Technologies of Governance

Viewed more broadly, standards regimes can be viewed as a 'technology of governance' (Bowker & Star, 2000; Espeland & Stevens, 2008; Schweber, 2017). "Governance comprises the means used to influence behavior, the production of resources, and the distribution of resources" (Davis et al., 2012, p. 78). More specifically: "To govern, in this sense, is to structure the possible field of action of others" (Foucault, 1983, p. 221).

TSRs can be framed as a "technology of governance" because they go beyond the sphere of what is traditionally regarded as government, a phenomenon Foucault calls "governmentality" (Foucault, 1983; Hunt & Wickham, 1994; Schweber, 2017). Increasingly, the "techniques and tactics of domination" (Foucault, 1980, p. 102) used by governments are adapted and applied to other social settings. As Schweber (2017, p. 295) explains, "whereas in earlier power/knowledge regimes were associated with the exercise of power by specific actors in specific types of institution (e.g., the courts, prison, the military, schools), under neoliberalism they have (also) permeated other aspects of everyday life."

Further examples of technologies of governance include military intervention, fund transfers, the adoption and use of legal instruments, publication of scientific reports, advertising campaigns, and educational programmes. Each of these technologies involves the application of different types of resources, both tangible, in terms of funds and personnel, and intangible, in terms of status and information (Davis et al., 2012).

International environmental standards are an area where self-regulation often occurs due to a "governance void" (Rasche, 2012, p. 679) on the part of the state, as states are unable or unwilling to establish and agree on a credible international regulatory framework. In response to this, non-state actors, sometimes in collaboration with governments and intergovernmental organizations, create their own environmental standards (Collard et al., 2016; Terlaak, 2007).

Of particular concern is the tendency of environmental standards to become "closed" (certification and reporting) as opposed to "open" (principle-based). While both "open" and "closed" standards have advantages and disadvantages, there appears to be a natural social-organizational tendency towards closed standards (Bowker & Star, 2000; Christensen et al., 2017). Closed standards often exclude criteria that are not quantitative (Schweber, 2017), exclude ethical considerations (Kärreman & Alvesson, 2010), and exclude dissenting or different views; "when discussion is thwarted, a particular view of reality is maintained at the expense of equally plausible ones, usually to someone's advantage" (Deetz, 1992, p. 188).

A community of practice (or "social world") is created by the persons setting standards. who have a shared understanding about the subject matter. Membership of such a community depends to a large extent on one's knowledge of the standards, as well as being part of a consensus about the meaning of the activities being undertaken (Bowker & Star, 2000; Schweber, 2017). In this sense, the standards that are created primarily reflect the interests and shared beliefs of members of the community. In her review of voluntary environmental standards, Schweber (2017) notes:

> often taken for granted calculations contained in standards and techniques serve to filter, rank, distinguish and reward particular arrangements over others, with potentially significant implications for the effect of the techniques in which they are embedded.
>
> (p. 295)

For this reason, Christensen et al. (2017) emphasize the need for the open discussion and contestation of environmental standards, particularly when standards developed for multinational corporations are applied to SMEs to ensure that all aspects important to SMEs are adequately incorporated into the standard.

The EUDR as a TSR

Although the EUDR is formally a domestic regulation that only applies to EU-based firms, the EUDR has extraterritorial effects as a technology of governance. EU importers pass traceability requirements on to their suppliers, who are located outside the Union, thus generating the measure's extraterritorial effect.

As the EUDR is currently defined, its primary requirement is traceability of deforestation-sensitive products to their location of production, defined as a geospatial point or polygon. This spatial traceability should enable an EU importer to document and verify whether a crop was grown on recently deforested land (European Commission, 2023).

In this sense, the EU can be viewed as an SDO, with the EUDR as a due diligence standard based on certain principles and norms related to climate change, biodiversity, and deforestation. The EUDR is similar to an RSPO standard in the sense that it describes a range of due diligence requirements that private-sector actors must interpret and implement. Therefore, the EUDR appears to give rise to a chain of CBs and ABs that work to ensure the traceability of the supply chain. Where the EUDR is different from a voluntary private-sector standard such as the RSPO, is that the EU actively engages foreign governments, and that the EUDR is an extension of broader EU trade diplomacy. This last aspect expresses itself in the use of a "country risk classification," whereby different due diligence requirements are applied to different countries based on an assessment by the EU, which appears to be primarily influenced by EU political-economic concerns (Sotirov et al., 2017; McDermott & Sotirov, 2018). The role of trade diplomacy is also reflected in how the EU engages with its trading partners.

For example, the EU and Malaysia are currently in administrative-level consultations about palm oil supply chains as part of the *KAMI* project.[1] One of the aims of the consultation is to explore amending the Malaysian Sustainable Palm Oil (MSPO) standard to bring it in line with the EUDR (MSPO & EFI, 2024). In this sense, the MSPO, which is being funded by the Malaysian government, is trying to become a CB within the tripartite framework. One could argue that the European Forestry Institute (EFI), which engages on the technical aspects of the EUDR, acts as the AB. The EFI is also managing the KAMI project.

Although the EUDR does not completely fit within the TSR framework because it is a public policy measure and not a voluntary private-sector standard, it is nevertheless a technology of governance that attempts to impose certain behaviour on actors elsewhere – in this case, the behaviour of the Malaysian palm oil supply chain. The influence of the EUDR is greater than the size of the EU itself, as other economic partners may follow similar traceability and no-deforestation requirements in future, as the EU is often a pioneer in developing environmental regulations (Bradford, 2020; Hidayat, 2024).

The assumption that the EUDR is fixed, and producer countries like Malaysia must adapt, also indicates the economic power imbalance that exists between Malaysia and the EU. Malaysia's position in this regard appears to be weakening further, as artificial palm oil production technology is reaching a stage whereby large-scale commercial production may soon become viable (Hidayat, 2024).

Small Farmers in Malaysia's Palm Oil Supply Chain

According to the Malaysian Palm Oil Board (MPOB), there are approximately 215,000 independent smallholders in Malaysia cultivating approximately 822,073 ha of land. Their output represents 28% of the palm oil production in Malaysia (MSPO & EFI, 2024). Before discussing the specific structure of the supply chain in Malaysia, we briefly discuss how small palm oil farmers have been impacted by sustainability certification schemes.

Background: Small Palm Oil Farmers and Sustainability Certification

Sustainable palm oil standards were developed to mitigate some of the negative environmental and social effects of palm oil production. Negative environmental impacts mainly include deforestation, biodiversity loss, and increases in greenhouse gas emissions due to land-use changes and harmful agricultural practices (Abood et al., 2015; Carlson et al., 2013; Vijay et al., 2016). However, small farmers are generally found to be more biodiversity-friendly than large plantations, although they are still far less biodiverse than forests (Dhandapani et al., 2020; Razak et al., 2020).

Small producers have traditionally been marginalized in global palm oil value chains: while accounting for approximately 30% of global production, it is typically lower-yielding, and small farmers claim a much smaller share of around 6% of the total value chain (Ogahara et al., 2022; Rijk et al., 2021). The low yields achieved by small farmers are often attributed to poor or insufficient inputs, including poor-quality planting material, wrong application of fertilizer, herbicides, and insecticides, and poor-quality soils (Ogahara et al., 2022). Nevertheless, palm oil often brings in more income than other crops, and therefore it plays an important role in rural economies (Ogahara et al., 2022).

It is important to note that the narrative of low yields among small farmers is contested by some authors, who note that small farms can meet, or even exceed, the yields obtained by large corporate plantations, highlighting their autonomy and ability to learn and adapt to changing circumstances (Li & Semedi, 2021).

A solution to small farmers' problems is often seen in the formation of farmer groups (cooperatives, associations, etc.). These groups can improve farmers' bargaining power (Bennett et al., 2019; Raharja et al., 2020) and lower the transaction costs of sustainability certification schemes by certifying groups of farmers at the same time and by disseminating good agricultural practices to their members as a way to also improve yields (Ogahara et al., 2022). It is important to note that organizing farmers is not a new issue, especially in Johor. A need to organize small farmers in the area was already noted by British colonial administrators during the 1930s (Pakiam, 2021).

In order to get sustainability certification, small farmers need to join an organization that is capable of disseminating good agricultural practices and carrying out internal audits and record-keeping to ensure that the sustainability standards are being followed (Hidayat et al., 2015). The cost of such an organization is high relative to farmers' income levels, and the return on investment is uncertain (Dharmawan et al., 2021; Kunz et al., 2019; Tey et al., 2021). Due to insufficient demand for sustainable palm oil, smallholders typically do not receive a large price premium for certified palm oil (Apriani et al., 2020; Martens et al., 2020).

Joining a certification organization also creates dependence, as small farmers can only use licensed suppliers and sell to licensed mills, and depend on the organization to maintain their certification (Hidayat et al., 2015). The certifying organization, which is often an NGO, exerts significant influence over the small farmers, which is a situation that is not sufficiently addressed by certification schemes (Ogahara et al., 2022).

An alternative to using certification organizations is a jurisdictional approach, whereby the government takes over the role of the certification organizations. This approach exists under the MSPO standard and is now also being tried in the Malaysian state of Sabah for RSPO certification. In Sabah, the statewide certification process is being led by the Sabah Forestry Department and financially supported by several international donors. The jurisdictional approach effectively converts the voluntary RSPO standard into a mandatory standard for Sabah, an action that also raises a number of legal and political concerns (Colchester, 2020).

Regardless of whether group or jurisdictional certifications are used, the cost of certification for small farmers is typically borne by external parties (donors or governments), and therefore acts as a social programme for small farmers aimed at achieving positive socio-economic and environmental outcomes.

Small Farmers and Big Mills

Independent small farmers typically sell their fresh fruit bunches (FFBs) to dealers and not directly to a mill. This system of middlemen exists because Malaysia's palm oil sector is primarily organized around large plantations, which are owned and operated by large, vertically integrated business groups. Given the relatively high quality of rural road infrastructure, these firms operate highly efficient, large-capacity mills, which are able to process FFBs from a relatively large catchment area. It is not unusual for mills to take on FFBs from small farmers when they have excess capacity.

Dealers play a critical role in providing small farmers with access to the mills. Their role includes aggregating FFBs from multiple farmers to ensure they can get processing slots at the mill. However, dealers can also help to arrange transportation and can sell fertilizer and pesticides to farmers, along with small amounts of commercial credit. Dealers might also have relationships with large plantations, who have an account at the mill, and have their FFBs processed under the plantation's quota. The typical supply chain from small farmer to the mill is shown in Figure 10.1, below

The presence of dealers poses significant challenges from the perspective of supply chain traceability because the collection centres fulfill a largely unofficial role within the supply chain. In other regions, such as in Nigeria or Sumatra, mills tend to be smaller, and farmers deliver FFBs directly to mills. In Peninsular Malaysia, small farmers *cannot* sell directly to mills, and they are therefore forced to use middlemen, which increases the complexity of the supply chain:

"As dealers are not certified and as they are not required to pass relevant information on the area of FFB production to the mill, tracing palm oil back to the plot of land on where FFBs were cultivated is not possible. Additionally, the smallholders and mills that dealers transact with can change frequently, further complicating the situation" (MSPO & EFI, 2024, p. 21).

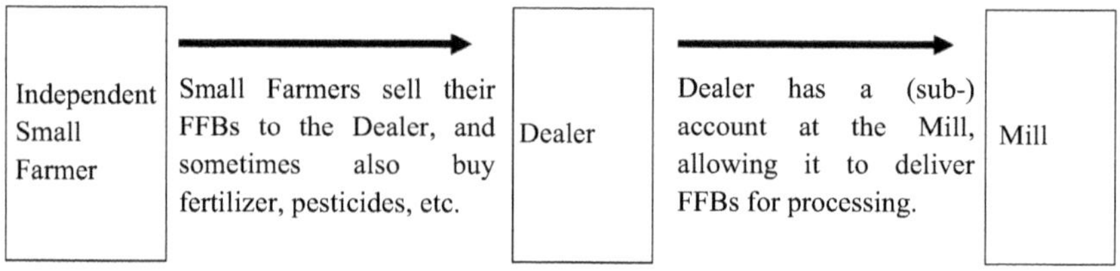

Figure 10.1 Typical palm oil supply chain from small farmer to mill in peninsular Malaysia

Table 10.1 Four chains of custody in supply chains, adapted from RSPO (RSPO, 2024)

Chain of Custody	*Supply Chain Implementation*	*Comments*
Identity preservation	Each product can be traced to a specific producer (farm)	Accepted under EUDR, difficult for palm oil due to large-scale mills
Segregation	Certified and non-certified products have completely separate supply chains	Accepted under EUDR
Mass balance	Certified and non-certified products are collected together, but with bookkeeping to verify the origin of certified products	Not accepted under EUDR
Book-and-claim	Certified products enter the non-certified supply chain, but suppliers get a certificate ("claim") that they can sell to buyers seeking certified products	Currently used for smallholder RSPO certification; not accepted under EUDR

In terms of their spatial location, dealers are typically located within 1–10 km from collection centres, with an average of 5.77 km (Bok et al., 2022; Kannan et al., 2017). In Peninsular Malaysia, mills are typically located 5–10 km from oil palm farms. Locations beyond 10 km are typically not preferred due to high transportation costs (Shevade & Loboda, 2019).

Viewed from the four chains of custody models (see Table 10.1), identity-preserved custody is not feasible for small farmers due to the large scale of mills. It is not possible to process a single batch of FFBs from a single farm at a large mill. Segregated supply chains are uneconomical in mill catchment areas with certified and uncertified production because they would require the replication of collection and transportation infrastructure. However, this problem is solved if all production within the mill catchment area is certified. As this has not happened, mass balance systems are currently being explored through collaborations between collection centres and certification organizations. However, mass-balance methods have been rejected under current EUDR proposals. Book-and-claim systems are currently used by the RSPO and MSPO, as small RSPO-certified farms are still in the minority, making it the most viable approach to ensuring traceability. Book-and-claim is also not acceptable under EUDR rules.

To illustrate the challenges of traceability within the current supply chain, consider that FFBs are sometimes left by the roadside for collection. FFBs are then picked up by a truck, which may drive directly to the mill or transfer the FFBs to other trucks. Transportation sometimes occurs at night due to lower temperatures, less traffic, and less police enforcement against truck overloading. Once the truck arrives at the mill, carrying FFBs from various farms, the bunches are inspected and might then be declared under the main account of another party, such as a large plantation, from where the FFBs did not originate.

Dealing with the Dealers

Even if transparency and traceability at the mill gate are improved, logistics providers would need to verify the precise origin of FFBs. While dealers can know where they collected their cargoes, they may be unable to reliably verify the specific farm of origin for the FFBs. Transparently declaring the origin of FFBs to the mill or on a publicly accessible traceability system could also harm the commercial position of dealers. Dealers, like any business, are never keen to disclose their client and supplier lists, along with their turnover, to their competitors, clients, and the wider public.

The way in which dealers operate is complex, opaque, and informal, and this presents an important weakness from a supply chain compliance perspective. Dealers could potentially be used to mask the origins of FFBs so that they can enter a "deforestation-free" supply chain, something that has happened in the past with MSPO- and RSPO-certified palm oil (Kusumaningtyas, 2018; Low, 2024).

In response to these challenges, the MSPO has recently developed a dealer standard under MS2530:2022 Part 4–3, which will be implemented from January 2025. However, this standard also has significant gaps. A joint report issued by KAMI, an intergovernmental palm oil working group between Malaysia and the EU, notes the lack of "a traceability reporting module/interface for dealers" and the lack of an "interface for EU operators to register and access EUDR-relevant information for their due diligence statements, such as geolocation and immediate supplier information" (MSPO & EFI, 2024). Thus, it must be concluded that even if the MSPO standard for dealers were implemented widely in January 2025, it would not make dealers EUDR compliant.

Due to the absence of traceability for small farmers, the report concludes that: "certified palm oil is likely to be derived from lower-complexity supply chains and further information could potentially be available in audit reports" (MSPO & EFI, 2024). The "high-complexity" involved in tracing FFBs produced by small farmers will likely lead EU buyers and the mills they source from to remove dealers and small farmers from their supply chain to avoid potential compliance liabilities.

High Complexity, High Cost, and High Corruption?

While it is theoretically possible to design a traceable and highly complex supply chain, experience with other sustainable agriculture certification schemes suggests that the cost of compliance tends to be relatively high for independent small producers, placing them at a further disadvantage. As a result, small producers are forced to enter a cooperative, thus surrendering their independence, and will face an increase in their costs if compliance is not subsidized in some way.

Complex certification and supply chain schemes are also vulnerable to fraud, as is the case with the EU's own common agricultural policy (Giannakas & Fulton, 2002). It is therefore possible that EUDR compliance for small farmers will be costly and nevertheless lead to significant abuse.

Sustainability Standards as a Force for Producer Consolidation

The EUDR is based on a relatively simple concept: that the EU should not import products that lead to deforestation. The way in which this goal has now been operationalized is by attempting to trace a product's origin, which is not always easy, especially in Malaysia's highly complex supply chain that includes independent small farmers.

The consequence of this operationalization, as with many other sustainability standards, is that small producers are placed at a disadvantage within global sustainable supply chains. Small producers must either accept higher costs of compliance due to their lack of scale, or they must accept being locked out of leading export markets.

While producer countries like Malaysia experience a degree of political mobilization against externally imposed sustainability standards, and express a need to modify them to protect the interests of small producers, these efforts are not always effective in practice. Malaysia's domestic palm oil standard, MSPO, has had specific facilities for independent smallholders for more than two decades.

The MPOB began a small farmer outreach and upgrading scheme, *Tunjuk Ajar dan Nasihat Sawit* (TUNAS), in 2002, which aimed to organize smallholders into groups (Sustainable Palm Oil Clusters, SPOCs). SPOCs were served by a TUNAS agent, or SPOC manager. The SPOC manager is essentially a government employee who manages between 500 and 2,000 smallholders. Each independent small farmer automatically belongs to a local SPOC. As of January 2019, there were 162 SPOCs with a total of 262,724 members covering 1,015,524 ha (Kannan et al., 2021). The MPOB has gradually begun to certify SPOCs, achieving 30% coverage in July 2020 and 74% by mid-2024 (BERNAMA, 2024). However, the registration rates of small farmers within SPOCs may be lower, with a figure of 24.82% cited for May 2020 (Bok et al., 2022).

Concerns have also been raised about the high number of farmers per SPOC manager and that there are cases of non-compliance within SPOCs that have achieved MSPO certification. A significant factor in non-compliance is related to record-keeping and traceability, which again highlight the complexity challenges posed by certification (Kannan et al., 2017, 2021).

Compliance issues for certified small producers, a relatively low certification rate until recently, and occasionally contradictory data suggest that domestic smallholder certification efforts remain incomplete and lack international credibility.

While this outcome is likely due to a lack of resources, underinvestment in smallholder certification also reflects a lack of policy priority.

The status quo, whereby compliance requirements have a greater negative effect on small producers, implicitly favours large producers. Large producers have a comparative advantage in obtaining sustainability certification and account for more than 70% of national output. This places them in a preferred position to fulfill export orders and removes small producers from the export market. Hence, the influence of sustainability standards is unlikely to influence total exports: orders could simply shift from small producers to large producers.

The likely result of these structural disadvantages suffered by small producers is consolidation. Small producers will exit the market, either by cultivating different crops or by selling land to nearby large plantations. This future course of action benefits larger producers, who can expand their acreage and reduce competition. Hence, large producers have a vested interest in stricter sustainability standards, and they may quietly welcome the imposition of the EUDR and similar policies while not seriously prioritizing smallholder compliance efforts.

Conclusion: From Anti-Deforestation to Consolidation

Taken at face value, the EUDR has laudable environmental goals: to prevent deforestation, which threatens the world's carbon sinks and biodiversity. However, as a side effect, the EUDR could permanently exclude small farmers from sustainable supply chains, even if the vast majority of these farmers do not grow their crops in recently deforested areas. Implementation of the EUDR could mean that only large plantations or farmers' cooperatives can have access to EU markets, which was not the intent of the regulation and which has rightly raised the concerns of affected countries such as Malaysia. Is the EUDR "fair" if it systematically excludes small farmers?

The problem of small producer traceability in highly complex supply chains is not unique to Malaysia or to palm oil: it can be found in countries and sectors around the world (Dietz et al., 2021; Mithöfer et al., 2017). While sustainability standards are not explicitly designed to exclude small producers, they are typically designed with the needs of larger lead producers in mind and are difficult and relatively costly to implement for small producers (Sommer, 2017). In the case of the EUDR, the geocoding of individual farms may be feasible. However, tracing FFBs from farm to mill in a complex, competitive, multilayered, and dynamic supply chain is very difficult.

The response to this challenge seems typical of TSRs: the joint consultation between the EU (SDO and AB) and the Malaysian government (CB) does not challenge the standard itself but proposes that in response to the problem of complexity, every layer and actor in the supply chain should become certified, even if the economic and practical viability of doing so is unclear. The default position is that small producers are "the problem" that must be controlled through certification and that the MSPO standard needs "improvement."

It is telling that the SPOC and territorial approaches to certification are not even mentioned in documents about the EUDR co-published by the MSPO, the "inventor" of the SPOC (MSPO & EFI, 2024). The single-minded focus on traceability highlights the strength of the standards and knowledge regime that has already emerged around the EUDR. Together with the European Parliament and the European Commission, the certifiers and accreditors, along with large producers, have built a techno-political regime that has successfully co-opted Malaysian public organizations such as the MSPO and MPOB.

Without strong push-back from actors outside of the TSR – politicians, civil society, academics, and small farmer organizations, both in Europe and in producer nations – the EUDR will continue to develop as a closed standard whose practicality and economic viability are highly doubtful for independent small farmers and whose high degree of complexity makes it susceptible to fraud.

An alternative approach is to insist that the EUDR must become a more open standard, whereby the EU and local actors can renegotiate its implementation based on the specific local context of small and large producers (Christensen et al., 2017). This approach should preserve the fundamental anti-deforestation goal of the EUDR while seeking collaboration and co-regulation with regards to implementation by incorporating both the views of the regulator (EU) and the regulated parties (small farmers) (Rouvière & Caswell, 2012).

In Malaysia's case, the territorial approach to palm oil certification via SPOCs already offers a potential avenue for monitoring deforestation, while offering a simpler system of traceability. Instead of trying to trace 262,724 small farms, the goal would be to trace and monitor 162 SPOCs.

However, given the apparent strength of the coalition that has already developed between Malaysian regulators, large plantations, and EU institutions over the EUDR, such a simplified and lower-cost traceability regime is highly unlikely to be adopted.

Note

1 https://efi.int/partnerships/kami/malaysia

Reference List

Abood, S. A., Lee, J. S. H., Burivalova, Z., Garcia-Ulloa, J., & Koh, L. P. (2015). Relative contributions of the logging, fiber, oil palm, and mining industries to forest loss in Indonesia. *Conservation Letters*, *8*(1), 58–67.

Apriani, E., Kim, Y.-S., Fisher, L. A., & Baral, H. (2020). Non-state certification of smallholders for sustainable palm oil in Sumatra, Indonesia. *Land Use Policy*, *99*, 105112. https://doi.org/10.1016/j.landusepol.2020.105112

Bennett, A., Ravikumar, A., McDermott, C., & Malhi, Y. (2019). Smallholder oil palm production in the Peruvian Amazon: Rethinking the promise of associations and partnerships for economically sustainable livelihoods. *Frontiers in Forests and Global Change*, *2*. www.frontiersin.org/articles/10.3389/ffgc.2019.00014

BERNAMA. (2024, July 24). *Only 74 Pct Oil Palm Smallholders Achieve Mspo Certification – Kpk*. BERNAMA. www.bernama.com/en/news.php?id=2321277

Bok, C. H., Lim, C. H., Ngan, S. L., How, B. S., Ng, W. P. Q., & Lam, H. L. (2022). Life cycle assessment and life cycle costing analysis for uncertified and Malaysia sustainable palm oil – MSPO-certified independent smallholders. *Journal of Cleaner Production*, *379*, 134646. https://doi.org/10.1016/j.jclepro.2022.134646

Bowker, G. C., & Star, S. L. (2000). *Sorting Things Out: Classification and Its Consequences*. MIT Press.

Bradford, A. (2020). *The Brussels Effect: How the European Union Rules the World*. Oxford University Press.

Busch, L. (2011). Food standards: The cacophony of governance. *Journal of Experimental Botany*, *62*(10), 3247–3250. https://doi.org/10.1093/jxb/erq439

Carlson, K. M., Curran, L. M., Asner, G. P., Pittman, A. M., Trigg, S. N., & Marion Adeney, J. (2013). Carbon emissions from forest conversion by Kalimantan oil palm plantations. *Nature Climate Change*, *3*(3), Article 3. https://doi.org/10.1038/nclimate1702

Christensen, L. T., Morsing, M., & Thyssen, O. (2017). License to critique: A communication perspective on sustainability standards. *Business Ethics Quarterly*, *27*(2), 239–262.

Colchester, M. (2020, June). Preliminary findings from a review of the jurisdictional approach initiative in Sabah. *Forest Peoples Programme*, 1–7.

Collard, R.-C., Dempsey, J., & Rowe, J. (2016). Re-regulating socioecologies under neoliberalism. In S. Springer, K. Birch, & J. MacLeavy (Eds.), *The Handbook of Neoliberalism*. Routledge.

Davis, K. E., Kingsbury, B., & Merry, S. E. (2012). Indicators as a technology of global governance. *Law & Society Review*, *46*(1), 71–104.

Deetz, S. (1992). *Democracy in an Age of Corporate Colonization: Developments in Communication and the Politics of Everyday Life*. SUNY Press.

Dhandapani, S., Girkin, N. T., Evers, S., Ritz, K., & Sjögersten, S. (2020). Is intercropping an environmentally-wise alternative to established oil palm monoculture in tropical peatlands? *Frontiers in Forests and Global Change*, *3*. www.frontiersin.org/articles/10.3389/ffgc.2020.00070

Dharmawan, A. H., Mardiyaningsih, D. I., Rahmadian, F., Yulian, B. E., Komarudin, H., Pacheco, P., Ghazoul, J., & Amalia, R. (2021). The Agrarian, structural and cultural constraints of smallholders' readiness for sustainability standards implementation: The case of Indonesian sustainable palm oil in East Kalimantan. *Sustainability*, *13*(5), Article 5. https://doi.org/10.3390/su13052611

Dietz, T., Grabs, J., & Chong, A. E. (2021). Mainstreamed voluntary sustainability standards and their effectiveness: Evidence from the Honduran coffee sector. *Regulation & Governance*, *15*(2), 333–355. https://doi.org/10.1111/rego.12239

Egan, M. (2002). Setting standards: Strategic advantages in international trade. *Business Strategy Review*, *13*(1), 51–64. https://doi.org/10.1111/1467-8616.00202

Espeland, W. N., & Stevens, M. L. (2008). A sociology of quantification. *European Journal of Sociology/Archives Européennes de Sociologie*, *49*(3), 401–436.

European Commission. (2023). *Regulation on Deforestation-Free Products*. https://environment.ec.europa.eu/topics/forests/deforestation/regulation-deforestation-free-products_en

Foucault, M. (1980). Power/knowledge, brighton. *Harvester Press*, *206*, 381–393.

Foucault, M. (1983). The subject and power. In H. L. Dreyfus & P. Rabinow (Eds.), *Michel Foucault: Beyond Structuralism and Hermeneutics* (Second Edition, pp. 208–228). The University of Chicago Press.

Fouilleux, E., & Loconto, A. (2017). Voluntary standards, certification, and accreditation in the global organic agriculture field: A tripartite model of techno-politics. *Agriculture and Human Values*, *34*(1), 1–14. https://doi.org/10.1007/s10460-016-9686-3

Giannakas, K., & Fulton, M. (2002). The economics of decoupled farm payments under costly and imperfect enforcement. *Canadian Journal of Agricultural Economics/Revue Canadienne d'agroeconomie*, *50*(3), 297–315. https://doi.org/10.1111/j.1744-7976.2002.tb00339.x

Hatanaka, M., Konefal, J., & Constance, D. H. (2012). A tripartite standards regime analysis of the contested development of a sustainable agriculture standard. *Agriculture and Human Values*, *29*(1), 65–78. https://doi.org/10.1007/s10460-011-9329-7

Hidayat, F. (2024, April 30). *Indonesia and Malaysia: Palm Oil Under Pressure from Substitutes and EU Deforestation Regulation*. FULCRUM. https://fulcrum.sg/indonesia-and-malaysia-palm-oil-under-pressure-from-substitutes-and-eu-deforestation-regulation/

Hidayat, K. N., Glasbergen, P., & Offermans, A. (Eds.). (2015). Sustainability certification and palm oil smallholders' livelihood: A comparison between scheme smallholders and independent smallholders in Indonesia. *International Food and Agribusiness Management Review*. https://doi.org/10.22004/ag.econ.208400

Hunt, A., & Wickham, G. (1994). *Foucault and Law: Towards a Sociology of Law as Governance*. Pluto Press.

Kannan, P., Basaruddin, N. H., Hashim, K., Abu Bakar, H., Omar, W., Khairil, S. N., Mohd Salleh, Z., & Mansor, N. H. (2017). Monitoring and reporting of oil palm fresh fruit bunch (FFB) transactions among independent smallholders and dealers: An analysis of a case study in Selangor, Malaysia. *Oil Palm Industry Economic Journal*, *17*(2), 68–81.

Kannan, P., Hanani, M., Rahman, N., Say Peng, T., & Mazlan, S. (2021). A review on the Malaysian sustainable palm oil certification process among independent oil palm smallholders. *Journal of Oil Palm Research*, *33*, 171–180.

Kärreman, D., & Alvesson, M. (2010). Understanding ethical closure in organizational settings – the case of media organizations. *Ethics and Organizational Practice: Questioning the Moral Foundations of Management*, 57–80.

Kunz, Y., Otten, F., Mardiana, R., Martens, K., Roedel, I., & Faust, H. (2019). Smallholder telecoupling and climate governance in Jambi Province, Indonesia. *Social Sciences*, *8*(4), Article 4. https://doi.org/10.3390/socsci8040115

Kusumaningtyas, R. (2018). External concerns on the RSPO and ISPO certification schemes. *Online*. https://www.foeeurope.org/sites/default/files/euus_trade_deal/2018/report_profundo_rspo_ispo_external_concerns_feb2018.pdf (Last Accessed: May 2021).

Li, T. M., & Semedi, P. (2021). *Plantation Life: Corporate Occupation in Indonesia's Oil Palm Zone*. Duke University Press.

Loconto, A., Stone, J. V., & Busch, L. (2012). Tripartite standards regime. In *The Wiley-Blackwell Encyclopedia of Globalization*. John Wiley & Sons, Ltd. https://doi.org/10.1002/9780470670590.wbeog919

Low, C. C. (2024, May 10). *Mkini Submits List of Oil Palm Projects Breaching MSPO Rules to Minister*. Malaysiakini. www.malaysiakini.com/news/705188

Martens, K., Kunz, Y., Rosyani, I., & Faust, H. (2020). Environmental governance meets reality: A micro-scale perspective on sustainability certification schemes for oil palm smallholders in Jambi, Sumatra. *Society & Natural Resources*, *33*(5), 634–650.

McDermott, C. L., & Sotirov, M. (2018). A political economy of the European Union's timber regulation: Which member states would, should or could support and implement EU rules on the import of illegal wood? *Forest Policy and Economics*, *90*, 180–190. https://doi.org/10.1016/j.firpol.2017.12.015

Mithöfer, D., Roshetko, J. M., Donovan, J. A., Nathalie, E., Robiglio, V., Wau, D., Sonwa, D. J., & Blare, T. (2017). Unpacking 'sustainable' cocoa: Do sustainability standards, development projects and policies address producer concerns in Indonesia, Cameroon and Peru? *International Journal of Biodiversity Science, Ecosystem Services & Management*, *13*(1), 444–469. https://doi.org/10.1080/21513732.2018.1432691

MSPO, & EFI. (2024). *Joint Gap Assessment of the EUDR Information Needs and Information Availability from the Malaysian Sustainable Palm Oil (MSPO) Certification*. European Forest Institute. https://efi.int/sites/default/files/files/flegtredd/KAMI/MSPO_Joint_Gap_Assessment.pdf

Ogahara, Z., Jespersen, K., Theilade, I., & Nielsen, M. R. (2022). Review of smallholder palm oil sustainability reveals limited positive impacts and identifies key implementation and knowledge gaps. *Land Use Policy*, *120*, 106258. https://doi.org/10.1016/j.landusepol.2022.106258

Pakiam, G. K. (2021). "Not the oil of the country": Smallholders and British Malaya's oil palm industry, 1929–1941. *Agricultural History*, *95*(1), 69–103.

Raharja, S., Marimin, Machfud, Papilo, P., Safriyana, Massijaya, M. Y., Asrol, M., & Darmawan, M. A. (2020). Institutional strengthening model of oil palm independent smallholder in Riau and Jambi Provinces, Indonesia. *Heliyon*, *6*(5). https://doi.org/10.1016/j.heliyon.2020.e03875

Rasche, A. (2012). Global policies and local practice: Loose and tight couplings in multi-stakeholder initiatives. *Business Ethics Quarterly*, *22*(4), 679–708.

Razak, S. A., Saadun, N., Azhar, B., & Lindenmayer, D. B. (2020). Smallholdings with high oil palm yield also support high bird species richness and diverse feeding guilds. *Environmental Research Letters*, *15*(9), 094031. https://doi.org/10.1088/1748-9326/aba2a5

Regulation (EU) 2023/1115 of the European Parliament and of the Council of 31 May 2023 on the Making Available on the Union Market and the Export from the Union of Certain Commodities and Products Associated with Deforestation and Forest Degradation and Repealing Regulation (EU) No 995/2010 (Text with EEA Relevance), 150 OJ L (2023). http://data.europa.eu/eli/reg/2023/1115/oj/eng

Rijk, G., Wiggs, P. C., & Piotrowksi, M. (2021). *FMCGs, Retail Earn 66% of Gross Profits in Palm Oil Value Chain*. Washington, DC: Chain Reaction Research. https://chainreactionresearch.com/files/wp-content/uploads/2021/06/fmcgs-retail-earn-66-of-gross-profits-in-palm-oil-value-chain.pdf

Rouvière, E., & Caswell, J. A. (2012). From punishment to prevention: A French case study of the introduction of co-regulation in enforcing food safety. *Food Policy*, *37*(3), 246–254. https://doi.org/10.1016/j.foodpol.2012.02.009

RSPO. (2019). *RSPO Independent Smallholder Standard*. Roundtable on Sustainable Palm Oil (RSPO). https://rspo.org/wp-content/uploads/RSPO_ISH_Standard_2019-English.pdf

RSPO. (2024, July 1). *Supply Chains*. Roundtable on Sustainable Palm Oil (RSPO). https://rspo.org/as-an-organisation/certification/supply-chains/

Schweber, L. (2017). Jack-in-the-black-box: Using Foucault to explore the embeddedness and reach of building level assessment methods. *Energy Research & Social Science*, *34*, 294–304. https://doi.org/10.1016/j.erss.2017.08.005

Shevade, V. S., & Loboda, T. V. (2019). Oil palm plantations in Peninsular Malaysia: Determinants and constraints on expansion. *PLoS One*, *14*(2), e0210628. https://doi.org/10.1371/journal.pone.0210628

Sommer, C. (2017). *Drivers and Constraints for Adopting Sustainability Standards in Small and Medium-Sized Enterprises (SMEs)* (Working Paper No. 21/2017). Discussion Paper. www.econstor.eu/handle/10419/199511

Sotirov, M., Stelter, M., & Winkel, G. (2017). The emergence of the European Union timber regulation: How Baptists, Bootleggers, devil shifting and moreal legitimacy drive change in environmental governance of global timber trade. *Forest Policy and Economics*, *81*, 69–81. https://doi.org/10.1016/j.forpol.2017.05.001

Terlaak, A. (2007). Order without law? The role of certified management standards in shaping socially desired firm behaviors. *Academy of Management Review*, *32*(3), 968–985.

Tey, Y. S., Brindal, M., Djama, M., Hadi, A. H. I. A., & Darham, S. (2021). A review of the financial costs and benefits of the roundtable on sustainable palm oil certification: Implications for future research. *Sustainable Production and Consumption*, *26*, 824–837. https://doi.org/10.1016/j.spc.2020.12.040

Vijay, V., Pimm, S. L., Jenkins, C. N., & Smith, S. J. (2016). The impacts of oil palm on recent deforestation and biodiversity loss. *PLoS One*, *11*(7), e0159668. https://doi.org/10.1371/journal.pone.0159668

11 Navigating the Labyrinth

Challenges and Opportunities for Southeast Asia's Palm Oil Smallholders under the European Union Green Deal

Iman K. Nawireja, Eusebius Pantja Pramudya, Ghilandy Ramadhan and Maharani Hapsari

Introduction

The "Green New Deal (GND)" has rapidly become a key global policy for climate change mitigation strategies. The European version of the GND, the European Union Green Deal (EGD), is the first public pledge to reduce greenhouse gas emissions by at least 55% relative to 1990 levels by 2030 (Almeida et al., 2023; Regulation (EU) 2023/851, 2023). With these ambitious objectives in mind, the European Union (EU) increasingly adopts unilateral domestic measures (Deringer et al., 2019), as exemplified by the enactment of the European Union Deforestation Regulation (EUDR) – the main component of the EGD – targeting cocoa, cattle, rubber, soy, wood, palm oil, and coffee. Due to its unilateral nature, the impacts reach far beyond EU borders (Hadjiyianni, 2017).

This chapter focuses on oil palm smallholders who account for around 30%–40% of global production (Byerlee et al., 2017; Euler et al., 2016; Rijk et al., 2021), comprise 40% of the total area in Indonesia and Malaysia (de Vos et al., 2023; Ellis-Petersen, 2018; Jelsma, Slingerland, et al., 2017), and more than 75% in Thailand (Jensen et al., 2019; Leng & Tamilwanan, 2024). They are underrated in many ways, such as the low share of profits generated across the value chain and low achievement on Roundtable on Sustainable Palm Oil (RSPO) certification (Ogahara et al., 2022). Moreover, although they contributed 6% of the global value chain, the relative profit share is negligible (Rijk et al., 2021). Although their position in the global value chain is marginal, smallholder oil palm production is crucial for rural livelihood (3 million farmers depend on it) (Ogahara et al., 2022). Moreover, their role in sustainable palm oil is significant. As Li (2024, p. 387) stated, "Independent smallholders who grow oil palm on their own land could secure rural livelihoods without increasing forest loss."

Since smallholders are already overwhelmed by various certification schemes, pledges, commitments, and government regulations at different levels, implementing EUDR means increasing the complexity of governance at the farm level. As new schemes and measures are introduced, smallholders face an unending labyrinth of governance transformation, which they must navigate.[12] Those measures

DOI: 10.4324/9781003783176-14

are often developed without direct input from smallholders (Cheyns, 2014), risking them being left behind in the process and raising concerns about access to the market for palm oil that cannot strictly adhere to the EUDR requirements. Since the EUDR could significantly reshape the landscape of smallholders' oil palm governance in Southeast Asia, understanding the challenges and opportunities of the EUDR for smallholders' palm oil governance is crucial for the future of palm oil in the region. Against this backdrop, the questions put forward in this chapter are: (1) What factors contribute to the smallholder's ability to comply with the requirements of the EUDR? (2) In what ways do the smallholders adapt (and possibly transform their practices) due to the increasing complexity of sustainability oil palm governance with the advent of EUDR?

The enactment of EUDR gives rise to differing environmental, economic, and social implications for a wide range of oil palm actors, including, but not limited to, smallholders, companies, intermediaries, and governments at various levels: who benefits, who controls, and how the changes affect existing social and institutional arrangements. In our case, when considering adaptation – and potential transformation due to EUDR – it is helpful to view smallholder governance as comprising interactions among multiple entities, processes, and interactions, with the capabilities of exhibiting "emergent properties," a range of outcomes that are more or less desirable (Wright & Meadows, 2012). Concurrently, the palm oil industry can be considered a "complex" in which actors of multiple localities with diverse goals interact to shape the overall sector, an arrangement increasingly recognized as an assemblage (O'Reilly et al., 2024).

In the following section, we briefly describe the study's design and the data analysis used in this chapter. Next, we explain the nature of EUDR, including its history and its relationship with other schemes, followed by reviews of smallholder palm oil governance in Southeast Asian countries, with particular attention to Indonesia, Malaysia, and Thailand. Based on the findings of these two sections, we present the challenge of EUDR for smallholders. The chapter concludes with possible avenues for future palm oil smallholders in Southeast Asia.

Methods

This chapter draws upon the literature on oil palm smallholder governance in Indonesia, Malaysia, and Thailand and data derived from qualitative and quantitative sources. It uses grey and peer-reviewed literature (industry reports, policy papers, news articles, and academic papers), conversational interviews with smallholders in Indonesia, company officials, and experts in oil palm. Deriving various cases from existing certification schemes (e.g., RSPO, ISPO, MSPO), pledges, and commitments, we identified how palm oil smallholders in Southeast Asia engage with these schemes. Based on those experiences, we infer the possible trajectory of EUDR implementation. Due to limited resources, the review is based on English and Bahasa (Indonesian/Malay) language materials. Other sources in two major languages, Thai and Tagalog, were excluded from the analysis due to the above reasons and because the number of smallholders in the Philippines is small compared to the three big oil-producing countries.[3] This coincides with the availability of materials, mainly concentrated in Indonesia and Malaysia – this is understandable given the sheer scale of this industry in those two countries (Leng & Tamilwanan, 2024).

Assemblage Thinking for Understanding Smallholder Palm Oil Governance in Southeast Asia

For the sake of analytical clarity, this chapter uses assemblage thinking (Briassoulis, 2017, 2019), zooming into diverse and dynamic elements of oil palm smallholders' governance that provide favourable and constraining conditions for implementing EUDR. These interactions lead to the emergence of diverse intended and unintended outcomes (emergent properties), that the smallholders have to navigate. More specifically, using assemblage thinking, the chapter seeks to reveal the precise impact of the EUDR framework on oil palm smallholders in Southeast Asia and to identify possible challenges to complying with the EUDR and to inclusive EUDR implementation.

Assemblage Thinking

To govern, according to Foucault, is an activity of guiding, shaping, and intervening in the conduct of people to secure the 'welfare of the population, the improvement of its condition, the increase of its wealth, longevity, health, etc.' (Foucault, 1991, p. 100). In the case of EUDR, the EU takes the responsibility to reduce deforestation, greenhouse gas emissions, human rights abuse, non-compliance with existing local regulations, labour abuses, and land conflicts among smallholder palm oil global value chains while maintaining the status of oil palm as a source of livelihoods through domestic measures.

Palm oil governance has evolved from national to the rising influence of subnational and international governance, all with varying degrees of environmental, social, and economic impacts and implications for the smallholders. As such, the palm oil industry can be conceptualized as an assemblage because it is a "complex" (Cramb & McCarthy, 2016) where multiple actors from different regions utilize different modes of production (combining capital, land, and labour) connected through value chains across the regions, manifested in a discernible pattern of economic, social, and environmental outcomes that give the industry its shape (O'Reilly & Varkkey, 2024). Unlike the classical approach, which looks for causal relationships among variables, assemblage thinking allows insight into the dynamic interactions among diverse components (physical and non-physical) and the multifaceted impact of EUDR on smallholders (see Figure 11.1).

While its use in other fields, such as city studies, proliferated long ago, assemblage thinking in oil palm started in the late 2000s (Li, 2007). The theoretical origin of the *assemblage* can be traced back to two main lineages: the majority view refers to Deleuze and Guattari's *agencement* (Deleuze et al., 1988), noting that assemblage is not the perfect translation of the original French word *agencement*,

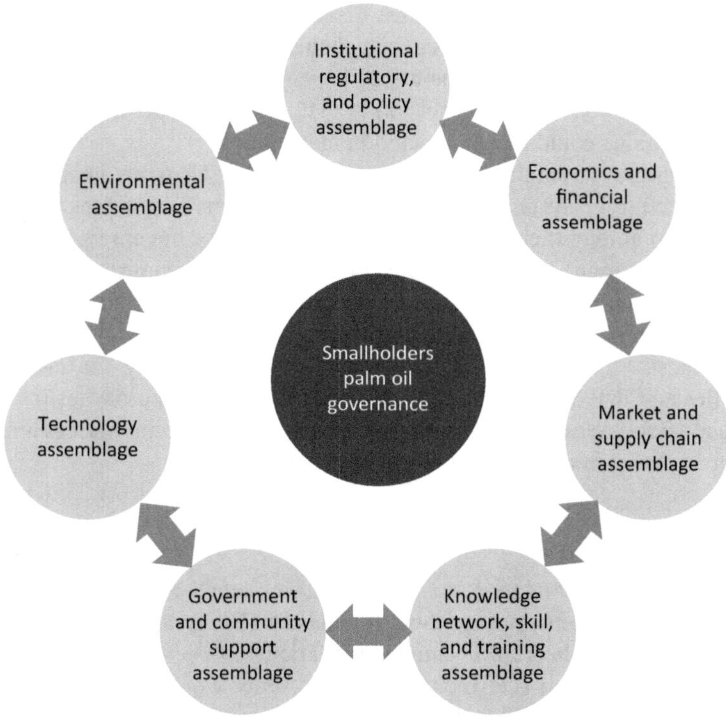

Figure 11.1 Assemblage of oil palm smallholders governance in Southeast Asian countries

(De Landa, 2010) and the minority goes up to Foucault (Freeman, 2017). Deleuze defines assemblage as: "It is a multiplicity which is made up of many heterogeneous terms and which establishes liaisons, relations between them across ages, sexes and reigns – different natures. Thus, the assemblage's only unity is that of co-functioning: it is a symbiosis, a 'sympathy'. It is never filiations which are important but alliances, alloys; these are not successions, lines of descent, but contagions, epidemics, the wind." (Deleuze et al., 1987, p. 69).

In other words, an assemblage organizes diverse entities to work collaboratively over a specific duration of time (Müller & Schurr, 2016). In Deleuze and Guattari's thinking, the assemblage is not governed by a single organizing principle or predetermined hierarchy; instead, every entity holds a similar ontological status. This does not mean the world is flat; the hierarchy results from the organizing mode. Moreover, Deleuze and Guattari do not attempt to develop a system of ideas that would constitute a theory. Instead, they propose a provisional analytical tool consisting of five components: the assemblage is relational, productive, heterogeneous, dynamic de-territorialization and re-territorialization, and characterized by desire (Müller, 2015). Assemblages do not inherently dictate or alter the characteristics of their individual components – which retain a certain degree of autonomy – making it possible for them to simultaneously engage in different roles of several assemblages. Consequently, De Landa (2006) contrasts assemblages with totalities, wherein each element is entirely defined by its relational status within the entirety. In assemblages, components are dependent, as they are neither essential nor entirely arbitrary. This does not imply that anything is permissible, but rather that configurations could be constructed in many ways.

To summarize, assemblage thinking considers how elements integrate to form a larger structure or system. Even though the elements might look like there is no connection among them, their combination facilitates the emergence of something new and unique. This interconnected whole is external to the component. Assemblage-based approaches focus on the practice of interaction between human and non-human entities, avoiding assumptions about power and social structure. They emphasize the essential nature of "relations of exteriority" in linking different entities and determining their shape and effect. These approaches treat power and social structure as emergent properties of the processes involving human and non-human actors in constructing the assemblages.

Emergent Properties

The most important characteristic is that the assemblage consists of emergent properties that exist independently of their interactions (De Landa, 2016), in the sense that they are established from emergent relationships between the components but are external to them (De Landa, 2006). In other words, the heterogeneity in assemblage thinking provides the foundational diversity and complexity needed for emergent outcomes to occur, linking the two concepts closely.

G.H. Lewes coined "emergent" in his multivolume *Problems of Life and Mind* (Ablowitz, 1939; Lewes, 1875). The label was initially created to denote whole properties (systemic quality) in which their individual components, in isolation, cannot satisfactorily explain the system's novel properties as a whole (emergent properties). According to Schmidt (2012, p. 236), 'the macrophenomena's characteristic is emergent, arising casually from but not explainable by microphenomena. This non-reducible thesis contrasts with micro-reductionist theories (Buchmann, 2015; Mayr, 2003). In this sense, smallholder oil palm can be considered an assemblage because it is a multicomponent system involving agroecological and socio-economic factors, such as companies, smallholders, government, infrastructure, cultural practices, and technology (heterogeneity), that are not operated through centralized control or a predictable trajectory.

Smallholder palm oil governance is their own property, emerging from dynamics of interaction between social-ecological systems in landscapes of oil palm production and livelihoods. Although it cannot be understood by examining element properties, summing or averaging at the individual level, in principle, its behaviour can be deduced from the properties and behaviour of its parts as long as we correctly understand the parts' interactions (Crick, 1995). Thus, emergent phenomena should be assumed to occur at the macro-level instead of micro-level processes that facilitate the emergence (Goldstein, 1999). Assessing the dynamics of oil palm smallholder governance required a detailed analysis of processes across different spatial and temporal scales, along with interactions between drivers, including policy shifts.

Results

EU Green Deals

The EUDR was formally enacted in May 2023 and will become operative on December 30, 2024. As for the micro and small firms, the implementation will be on June 30, 2025. However, it was later decided on November 14, 2024, that the EUDR would be delayed until December 30, 2025, for large companies, while for micro and small firms, the due date is June 30, 2026.[4] The EUDR governs EU international and internal commerce in forest-risk commodities and seeks to mitigate the EU's contribution to deforestation and forest degradation instigated by the EU (Köthke et al., 2023). According to this ruling, traders or operators seeking to export to or import to Europe must demonstrate that their products:

(a) have not originated from recently deforested regions or contributed to forest degradation or deforestation after December 31, 2020;
(b) have been produced in compliance with the application regulation of the country of origin;
(c) have been covered by a due diligence statement, a mandate to the operator to establish a due diligence system to prevent commodities or productions that do not comply with the aforementioned requirements above (a and b), which includes risk assessments and mitigations of any non-negligible risk.

In general, the EUDR will be implemented following the sequence as shown in Figure 11.2.

The ruling stated that due diligence is irreplaceable, although other schemes, such as RSPO, can support risk assessment (Article 10.2.j). Since point (b) emphasizes the regulations in producing countries, mandatory schemes such as Indonesia Sustainable Palm Oil (ISPO) in Indonesia and Malaysian Sustainable Palm Oil (MSPO) in Malaysia could gain prominence. On the contrary, voluntary schemes such as RSPO and Thai-Good Agricultural Practices (GAP) could be less relevant. However, since due diligence is still to be carried out and most certification schemes are intended for the EU/US market, they could become disincentives to

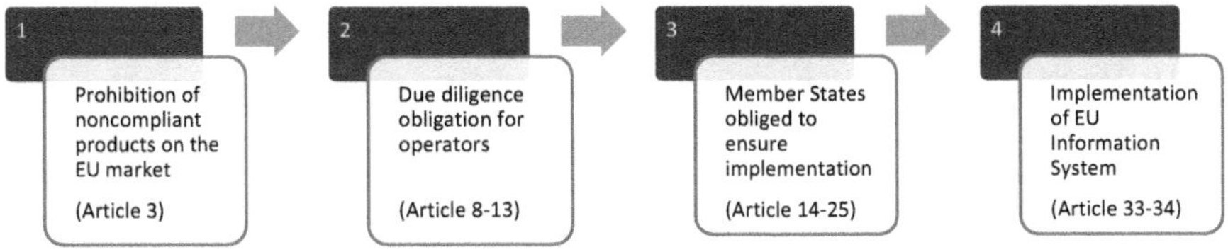

Figure 11.2 The main pillars of EUDR implementation

both voluntary and, to a lesser degree, mandatory certification, unless harmonizations are made. RSPO, for example, assigned a consultant to assess the gap in the RSPO to comply with the EUDR requirement (RSPO, 2023). Indonesia made a significant move by revising the Presidential Regulation on the national certification scheme, which now opens up room for accelerating smallholder mapping, land titling, and development, where a dedicated website was set up under the Ministry of Agriculture's online portal. Similarly, the Malaysian government also committed to assisting smallholders in meeting the EUDR deadline.[5] Even so, this effort still leaves a void on issues of legality and traceability across vast and diverse types of smallholders (Fisher et al., 2024).

However, the EUDR is not without its critics. Southeast Asian countries, including Singapore, have called for a postponement. Most of them are concerned about the "geolocation tag" requirement to identify the product's origin, which needs to be detailed in six decimal Global Positioning System (GPS) coordinates, verifiable by regulators or companies on recently deforested land. However, the EU relies on the flawed Global Forest Cover 2020 map developed by the EU's Joint Research Centre (JRC) to support EUDR implementation. Inaccuracies persist, such as an airport in Riau being categorized as a forest. Similarly, the map overestimates forest area; it is 40% larger than national and other analysts' data. These flaws will make it difficult for farmers to prove they are not planting in recently cleared forests. Even if the company offers to rectify the map, it will only benefit large companies (Rochmyaningsih, 2024).

Implementing such ambitious regulations proved to be a daunting task. For example, due to the concerns raised by EU member states, non-EU countries, traders, and operators that it would be difficult for them to comply with the ruling by the end of 2024, the EU finally agreed to postpone it for one year (December 30, 2025, for large and medium enterprises and June 30, 2026, for small enterprises). This delay is welcomed by the Indonesian Palm Oil Association (GAPKI) and the Malaysian Palm Oil Council (MPOC) as it would give smallholders more time to prepare themselves better.[6] The opposite voice is that "the delay would discourage constructive efforts and lose momentum in supporting good governance,"[7] and only give opportunities for the companies to benefit from deforestation.[8] Also, some companies and NGOs strongly oppose any effort to reopen negotiations on the substance of the EUDR, as it will bring uncertainty to the investment.[9] The recent Indonesian victory over the dispute with the EU on the EU's restriction of oil palm-based biofuel under RED II will likely give Indonesia firmer ground in challenging the EUDR. Combining this with the more cautious stance adopted by the current EU governments makes future EUDR implementation uncertain (Dennison et al., 2024; Meloni, 2025).

However, the delay might only solve part of the problem. For example, Tyson and Meganingtyas (2022, pp. 48–49) stated that Indonesian smallholders "are not a homogenous agricultural group. They are difficult to map and operate under variable conditions, making it challenging to impose any standards. Smallholder cooperatives are often managed by an outside party, such as a plantation company, to increase productivity, gain market access, and improve agricultural practices, as the smallholders lack the capacity and capital to do so independently." In the same vein, a senior campaigner at Kaoem Telapak stated, "The readiness is not solely the responsibility of the smallholders, but also the EU and Indonesian government's readiness and willingness to engage with the smallholders. If you let them face the market by themselves, for sure, the smallholders are not ready."[10]

The Southeast Asia Palm Oil Smallholders

Various terms can define smallholders, sometimes described as peasant cultivators, subsistence farmers, or family farmers, reflecting the various perspectives (social, economic, and spatial determinants) that can be used to analyze them (Nagayets, 2005; Rigg et al., 2016). Moreover, although it is expected to perceive smallholders as owning equal to or less than 2 hectares of land holding (Lowder et al., 2016; Netting, 1993), legal and practical definitions vary across countries or organizations and are sometimes contradictory. For instance, in Indonesia, smallholders are those who manage less than 2 hectares (Law 19/2013) or 25 hectares (Agrarian Law 1960). In Malaysia, smallholders are farmers with 40 hectares or less of land holdings (Kannan et al., 2020); in Thailand, 8 hectares (975 Land Reform Act) (Rigg et al., 2018) or 50 hectares (Thongrak et al., 2023), and in the Philippines, 3 hectares (WorldBank, 2021),[11] while RSPO defines those with less than 50 hectares.[12] The complexity increases if the nature of the smallholders is considered. Still, it can generally be categorized into schemes (linked to the company) and independent or collective landowners (Byerlee & Viswanathan, 2018; Daemeter, 2015; Li, 2024; Vermeulen & Goad, 2006) (Table 11.1).

In general, the smallholders can be classified into "scheme" and "independent."

- Scheme smallholders (also termed as associated/plasma) are those formally bound with a plantation company or POM (palm oil mill). RSPO defined them as "farmers who do not have enforceable decision-making power on how they operate their land and their production practices, and/or the freedom to choose how they use their land, the types of crops to plant, and how they manage them."[13] As such, the scheme smallholders, due to their contractual agreement to sell the FFB to the associated mill, are an integral part of a supply base of the company. In this arrangement, the company provides smallholders with logistical and technical assistance.
- Independent smallholders (ISH) operate without formal association with a company or POM. As such, they have the freedom to plant any crops they choose and manage their farms as they see fit. Another visible feature is that they rely on traders, intermediaries (ramps), subagents, or mills to sell their FFBs – some mills indeed accept ISH FFBs.

The lack of recognition of smallholder heterogeneity results in the neglect of their diverse challenges in meeting compliance requirements, thereby constraining the scope and scale of achievements in initiatives to promote sustainable palm oil practices among them. Jelsma, Schoneveld, et al. (2017) identified distinct clusters of

Table 11.1. Categories of oil palm smallholders in Southeast Asia

No	Types of Smallholders	Indonesia	Malaysia	Thailand	Philippines
1.	Schemes (supported) Smallholders are structurally linked to a company and bound by various schemes, such as contracts, credit/input provisions, or other arrangements to form "patron-client" relationships. Patrons commonly provide support for GAP of farm and cooperative management	(1) Various nucleus-plasma (PIR: *Perkebunan Inti Rakyat*) schemes: PIR *lokal* (1978), Assisted PIR (1984), Special PIR (1984 onwards), Accelerated PIR (1984 onwards), and PIR Trans which replaced the previous schemes. In this scheme, the smallholders were assigned 2 ha of land, and after repaying the debt, they assumed ownership (Vermeulen & Goad, 2006) (2) KKPA (*Koperasi Primer Untuk Anggota*) since 1986 (also known as the one-roof scheme). The members allocated the plots but were not involved in cultivation. They received the payment of the debt incurred from lots of development (Li, 2024; Vermeulen et al., 2006)	The smallholders that received technical support, financial assistance, and market access, under contract or management of government agencies, such as the Federal Land Development Authority (FELDA), Federal Land Consolidation and Rehabilitation Authority (FELCRA), and Rubber Industry Smallholders Development Authority (RISDA) (Vermeulen & Goad, 2006)	Contract farming (Sriboonchitta & Wiboonpoongse, 2008).	Nucleus-plasma schemes, contract farming (Nozawa, 2011)
2.	ISH are farmers who are free to manage their land, self-organized, and self-financed. This means they are not linked through formal agreements with company but possibly receive extensions from government agencies (RSPO, 2023)	(a) Smallholdings of less than 25 ha, which can be: (1) held by customary owners through inheritance or purchase from peers, or (2) held by migrants who acquire the land from customary owners or other migrants. (b) Smallholdings of more than 25 ha, operated without a business permit are commonly owned by wealthy politicians and government employees and are often managed by a manager (Li, 2024)	Those who own oil palm land (or an aggregate amount) of less than 40.46 ha and are assisted through an extension service established by MPOB, known as Tunjuk Ajar dan Nasihat Sawit (TUNAS) (Kannan et al., 2020)	Smallholders (landholdings of less than 50 ha) and average cultivated area of 4 ha (Colchester et al., 2011).	
3.	Collective landowner schemes	(c) Often planted on former agroforest land		Usually less than 8 ha	

smallholders, including small local farmers, medium local farmers, large resident farmers, small migrant farmers, medium migrant farmers, small- and medium-scale peat farmers, and large investor farmers. These groups differ significantly in terms of the contribution of palm oil to their livelihoods, land legality, market access and linkages, and production practices. Such disparities create varied initial conditions for smallholders to bear the certification costs. Worse, their short-term certification benefits sometimes outweigh the costs, further putting more pressure on them (Hutabarat et al., 2018).

Discussion: Challenges and Opportunities for Southeast Asian Palm Oil Smallholders under EUDR

This study set out to assess factors contributing to smallholders' ability, possible challenges to meeting the EUDR requirements, and opportunities from EUDR implementation. For this purpose, we conceptualize smallholders as an assemblage comprised of various elements such as (1) institutional, regulatory, and policy assemblage, (2) economics and financial assemblage, (3) market and supply chain assemblage, (4) knowledge network, skill, and training assemblage, (5) government and community support assemblage, (6) technology assemblage, and (7) environmental assemblage. Assemblage thinking allows us to uncover how the dynamic interaction of these elements creates new challenges and pathways as they adapt to the regulatory shift.

Institutional, Regulatory, and Policy Assemblage

The unilateral nature of EUDR introduced an additional international layer to the prevailing governance structure, forcing the smallholders to comply with the EU's imposed traceability and deforestation-free production requirements. In this regard, EUDR positioned smallholders in the convergence of compliance, that is, international standards, national initiatives, and local authorities' regulations.

The enactment of EUDR thus triggers various responses in Southeast Asian countries. While welcoming the EU commitment to sustainability, Indonesia and Malaysia have voiced concerns about the impact on smallholders (Bagja et al., 2022), leading to differing levels of support that may not align with smallholders' capacity. In Malaysia, frameworks such as MSPO certification could be adapted to meet EUDR standards. However, smallholders still face the challenge of bridging these standards with EUDR requirements. Although the introduction chapter of the EUDR acknowledges the critical role of certification schemes in the risk assessment process for operators, the certification scheme is considered a supporting document and cannot replace due diligence.

The EUDR will make Voluntary Sustainability Certification Schemes (VSCC) (such as RSPO and ISCC (International Sustainability & Carbon Certification)), less relevant to some degree, but increase the relevance of legally mandated certifications (ISPO, MSPO). However, while complementary, a more detailed reading of both standards can be contradictory or at least incompatible. The definition of deforestation in the ISPO standard (based on Indonesian regulations) may not align with the more universal definition adopted by the EUDR. This incompatibility is prone to diplomatic tensions (regulatory imperialism or sovereignty issues) and consequences for international trade (trade restrictions, retaliation, market differentiation). Balancing sovereignty over its domestic sustainability standards and pressure to harmonize with EUDR is a complex task. The South Asian countries could use a multipronged approach, for example, strengthening the ISPO standard, engaging in bilateral/multilateral dialogue such as the Ad Hoc Joint Task Force (JTF) (Godard, 2022), smallholders' capacity building, and market differentiation.

Economics and Financial Assemblage

In 2020, Indonesia shipped 3,381,079 metric tonnes (48%) to the EU, while Malaysia exported 1,793,909 metric tonnes (25%), representing 73% of the total Crude Palm Oil (CPO) tonnage (Zhunusova et al., 2022). Blot and Hiller (2022) estimated that smallholders contributed 1,519,285 metric tonnes to the EU market (Indonesia: 1,404,000 and Malaysia: 115,285 metric tonnes). Although the figure is continuously decreasing, as GAPKI claimed,[14] the influential position of the EU market in setting up the global sustainability standard means that EUDR could serve as a precedent for other markets.

Landholding size and smallholders' links to companies are critical economic factors. The larger the landholders or the more integrated they are into the supply chain (through contractual agreements with the company), the better they are positioned in terms of financial security and access to resources, thereby facilitating compliance. Likewise, independent smallholders or those with smaller landholdings will be more economically vulnerable. Moreover, the availability of premium prices will facilitate compliance with the EUDR. Interviews with RSPO-certified smallholders in Indonesia indicated that RSPO certification (a voluntary certification scheme (VCS)) is preferred over ISPO (a mandatory one) because RSPO provides a premium.

Glasbergen (2018) argues that sustainable change in oil palm should be based on economic sustainability. High premiums and stable prices are preferred as they lead to better products in terms of quality and quantity, and vice versa. Smallholders must be incentivized first to improve products and increase income through training on GAP and better smallholder organization. However, EUDR starts by asserting that "when sourcing products, reasonable efforts should be undertaken to ensure that a fair price is paid to producers, particularly smallholders, to enable a living income and effectively address poverty as a root cause of deforestation." The only mention of smallholders in the text pertains to risk mitigation within the due diligence process. It recommends that companies assist their suppliers, particularly smallholders, in complying with the EUDR through capacity-building and investment; however, this remains optional (Fern, 2023).

Therefore, EUDR puts smallholders in dilemmatic situations: if they are stuck with VSCC certification – which provides incentives to finance the certification process, such as a premium, but is not fully recognized by the EU – then they will undergo a time-consuming and costly due diligence process. Even the most robust certification system, RSPO, still has gaps that must be addressed (RSPO, 2023). Complying with legal requirements, such as land title requirements, can be especially difficult for Indonesian independent smallholders.

Although the EUDR recognizes the significance of international collaboration in addressing deforestation, it fails to provide specific commitments for allocating financial support to producing countries. Along with the EUDR implementation, member states may reduce the allocation of experts and resources to the affected regions on the basis that they are no longer involved in global deforestation (Muradian et al., 2025). Interviews with smallholders found that the primary motive for joining the RSPO is the eligibility for the RSPO premium upon certification. The premium allows them to prepare, finance, and maintain their certificate. It is common among Indonesian smallholders to enter RSPO certification first, before ISPO certification – since the government only recently provided funds for ISPO certification through the Badan Pengelola Dana Perkebunan Kelapa Sawit/The Indonesian Oil Palm Plantation Fund Management Agency (BPDPKS) fund – a model that has been applied long before by the Malaysian government for the implementation of MSPO among smallholders (Nik Ibrahim et al., 2022). Since the EUDR will be applied without a clear financial commitment to smallholders, it could likely discourage them from joining the EUDR.

Market and Supply Chain Assemblage

Indonesia and Malaysia are export-oriented, accounting for over 80% of their CPO, with China, India, and the EU as the leading market destinations. In 2020, according to Zhunusova et al. (2022), Indonesia exported 3,381,079 metric tonnes (48%) and Malaysia 1,793,909 metric tonnes (25%), together accounting for 73% of the volume of EU CPO imports, while Thailand did not export.

At the local level, the market is oligopolistic, with several large corporations playing significant roles in processing and marketing. Due to the nature of FFB processing, smallholders are primarily involved in FFB production, with little engagement in milling and marketing. Mills received FFB from combinations of various sources: owned estates, scheme smallholders, independent smallholders, or third-party suppliers/intermediaries. Many POMs highly depend on third-party suppliers to fill up their processing capacity. In Indonesia, for instance – due to the proliferation of POM without estates – it is common for them to rely on numerous intermediaries to collect FFB from smallholders, often dispersed across distant locations. This mechanism distances mills from direct interaction with smallholders, granting intermediaries the sole interface in the supply chain. Aggregating the FFB from numerous smallholders at this centre compromises the mill's ability to trace the origin and legality of the FFB precisely.[15] Moreover, interactions between smallholders and intermediaries are characterized by informality and trust, with limited documentation (e.g., receipts detailing the quantity/weight of FFB and corresponding payments are often unavailable for review). Additionally, conflicting land claims and bureaucratic roadblocks make full traceability of palm oil difficult.[16] As a result, many palm oil mills are uncertain about the origin of their FFB.

The EUDR requirement affected the market's assemblage by reducing market access. Interviews with companies, NGOs, and smallholders indicate a possible shift in FFB buyers. For example, the company prevents independent smallholders with low capacity from complying and forces them to develop a new marketing channel. Similarly, buyers such as Unilever, which previously bought independent smallholders' RSPO-certified RSPO credit, might shift to EUDR requirements and abandon RSPO/ISCC. If so, the farmers who used to join RSPO certification programmes for the incentive might lose their source of income and abandon certification, increasing the number of unsustainable practices.

A literature review on zero-deforestation value chains found that larger landholders are more likely to participate in global value chains. On the other hand, smallholders are often excluded and are forced to sell their produce in local markets at lower prices (Carlson et al., 2018). As Brandi (2017) found, RSPO-certified trading firms purchase less from smallholders. While smallholders have been excluded from certified oil value chains, they have not been completely cut off from the palm oil market. The domestic Indonesian market, along with China and India, continues to source non-certified palm oil, indicating that the market for smallholders has become more differentiated (Muradian et al., 2025).

Knowledge Network, Skill, and Training Assemblage

Smallholders' ability to comply with EUDR is dependent upon government, community, NGOs, and company support for knowledge sharing and training. In Southeast Asia, these resources vary widely, affecting smallholders' capacities and capabilities towards EUDR compliance in the region. Smallholders who attend training on sustainable practices, organization management, record-keeping, and certification standards regularly find it easier to comply with certification standards. Indonesian case studies indicated that smallholders face challenges in complying with RSPO and ISPO certification requirements (Brandi et al., 2015; Pramudya et al., 2022). Similarly, in Malaysia, MSPO certification was adopted by only 39% of smallholders, compared to 88% of companies (Aziz et al., 2021), while in Thailand, RSPO certification covers only 2.8% of the total planted area.[17] In RSPO, independent smallholders only account for 1.3% of RSPO-certified palm oil (Voora et al., 2020).

Research indicates that smallholders keep facing similar issues after decades of certification. For example, Nawireja and Ross (2010) found that smallholders were unable to comply with documentation requirements and chemical handling as required by the standard. Subsequent research found the same findings (Brandi et al., 2015; Pramudya et al., 2022). Moreover, in the case of RSPO/ISPO in Indonesia, no independent smallholders have achieved certification on their own; they are all assisted by companies or NGOs. These findings indicated that certification knowledge did not flow from one smallholder group to another. The standard requirement is likely too demanding for smallholders to comply with without external assistance to access knowledge networks, skills, and training resources crucial for sustainability standard compliance.

Government and Community Support Assemblage

Various levels of support were given to the farmers in Southeast Asia. Historically, oil palm development in Indonesia and Malaysia was led by large corporations that mimicked the colonial mode of production, aimed at the export market. Support was given to the smallholders, such as the Nucleus Estate Scheme (NES) in Indonesia and FELDA settlements in Malaysia, which are large-scale and transformative in nature and aim to develop rural areas by bringing in new inhabitants. Such schemes were not implemented in Thailand, where oil palm development was the conversion of agricultural areas by smallholders who are relatively independent from large corporations (Nupueng et al., 2022). Again, this gave Thailand's smallholders a stronghold in EUDR, where the governance assemblage during the first phase of oil palm development led to fewer environmental and human rights issues (Leng & Tamilwanan, 2024).

Southeast Asian countries seem to focus on opposing the EUDR instead of preparing the smallholders for readiness. Indonesia and Malaysia have led this opposition since the beginning. Lately, Singapore has jumped on the wagon. Although Singapore is not a producer of commodities of concern under EUDR, as a hub, it could disrupt ASEAN-EU trade.[18] Government support for certification is varied. The Indonesian government, for example, did not put much effort into facilitating RSPO certification among smallholders; the work was mostly done by companies or NGOs.

Technology Assemblage

In the palm oil value chain, the smallholders contribute to production only since large corporations do the processing. As such, in EUDR, there is a need to trace the origin of FFB from the mill to the farmer's lot, which frequently passes through intermediaries and often needs proper documentation. Several technologies exist, such as GPS-enabled devices or blockchain technology for traceability (Hirbli, 2018; Nik Ibrahim et al., 2022). Since the smallholders usually lack expertise and funding, linkage to NGOs or companies for support will be crucial; smallholders with solid ties with external parties will be in better positions than their counterparts to enter into EUDR requirements. In the future, the inclusion of smallholders in technology-led upstream and downstream industries will be an arena where smallholders may strengthen their leverage in the commodity value chain. Given their important roles in technological adoption and reproduction of science-driven technological advancement in oil palm planting and processing, smallholders will be at the forefront of technological innovation. The inclusion of smallholders will also mean that policies related to skill upgrading and skill transfer across palm oil countries will be a strategic arena for smallholders to increase their socio-economic mobilization in expanding their bases of livelihoods.

Environmental Assemblage

The EUDR framework does not forbid the EU from using palm oil. Still, the products will be selectively imported from land certified as low-risk under the EUDR criteria (Tyson & Meganingtyas, 2022). Southeast Asian countries are still open to opportunities by planting on degraded or abandoned land. However, finding such land is increasingly complex, and there is a risk of forest encroachment by the smallholders. Moreover, as in the case of Indonesia, smallholders comprise very diverse farmers' groups operating in very diverse agroecological conditions, making it difficult to map them correctly. As such, the EUDR will affect smallholders variably. Recent evidence suggests that Thailand's oil palm development is rarely linked to direct deforestation since most oil palm expansion occurs by converting rubber, rice, cassava, and sugar cane (Saswattecha et al., 2017). Moreover, the common perception is that the land conversion commonly done by farmers, small processing firms, and minimal support from the government ultimately spares Thailand from deforestation narratives, giving farmers in Thailand a better position compared to Indonesia and Malaysia to claim compliance against EUDR (Leng & Tamilwanan, 2024).

Advocacy and Facilitation Assemblage

Almost no smallholder can achieve certification without external support (from government, NGOs, or companies), indicating the crucial role of facilitation and advocacy assemblages. For example, the certification of the Amanah farmers group in Riau was supported by World Wide Fund for Nature (WWF) Indonesia, the RSPO, the Ministry of Agriculture, the Riau Provincial Government, and Carrefour Foundation International. Similarly, in Thailand, the German Agency for Development Cooperation (GIZ), the Thai government's Office of Agricultural Economics (OAE), and other partner institutes are the main facilitators of the project in Krabi, Surat Thani, and Chonburi provinces. Both projects ended with success (Innocenti & Oosterveer, 2020). Various NGOs' support and government advocacy affect smallholders' ability to influence policy and access supportive networks.

The Way Forward

Viewing the governance of palm oil smallholders as an assemblage makes it possible to reveal the complexity and fluidity of a web of elements that facilitated the emergence of multilayered challenges and opportunities when navigating the EUDR. Smallholders will face challenges complying with complex regulatory requirements, economic/financial/market pressure, land tenure and environmental assemblages, knowledge networks, technical and technological gaps, and advocacy and facilitation assemblages. Moreover, the smallholders will also have to deal with land tenure security, gaps in traceability technology, dependency on the EU market, the EUDR's non-inclusive nature, complex regulatory requirements, and limited resources. As for opportunities, smallholders could benefit from NGO, company, and government partnerships and the innovation of local traceability solutions.

Assemblage thinking emphasizes that these challenges and opportunities are not static. They evolve as components and interactions within the assemblage change, guiding more adaptive and dynamic approaches to support smallholders. Current developments show that although the delay in EUDR implementation creates new challenges and opportunities, it is wise to note that streamlining EUDR requirements, encouraging collaboration among standard bodies, and providing financial and technical assistance are crucial. Including smallholders' voices in the standard setting, facilitating compliance, and providing access to the European market will be crucial in providing avenues for the industry to progress towards a more inclusive and sustainable oil palm industry in Southeast Asia. However, the remaining critical issue is that, without support and facilitation from external parties, especially the national government with structured policy intervention, it is very likely that the smallholders will be unable to comply with the EUDR call to action for stakeholders to support sustainable and inclusive practices.

Notes

1 https://docs.wto.org/dol2fe/Pages/SS/directdoc.aspx?filename=q:/G/AG/GEN213.pdf&Open=True Retrieved October 29, 2024.
2 https://gapki.id/en/news/2023/03/03/ri-to-sue-eus-deforestation-law-atwto/ Retrieved October 29, 2024.
3 The Philippines is excluded because, according to recent data from FAO, its contribution to global palm oil production is less than 0.5% (www.fao.org/faostat/en/#home) Retrieved October 30, 2024.
4 www.preferredbynature.org/news/eudr-postponement-make-most-extra-year Retrieved January 19, 2025.
5 www.bernama.com/en/news.php?id=2349143 Retrieved November 17, 2024.
6 www.ofimagazine.com/news/eudr-delay-confirmed-after-european-parliament-vote Retrieved November 17, 2024.
7 https://news.mongabay.com/2024/11/smallholders-offer-mixed-reactions-to-calls-for-delay-in-eu-deforestation-law/
8 https://news.mongabay.com/short-article/2024/10/225-ngos-call-on-eu-to-reject-delay-to-deforestation-law/ Retrieved November 17, 2024.
9 https://voicenetwork.cc/2024/10/companies-and-csos-oppose-any-calls-to-reopen-the-eudr/ Retrieved November 17, 2024.
10 https://news.mongabay.com/2024/11/smallholders-offer-mixed-reactions-to-calls-for-delay-in-eu-deforestation-law/
11 No updated data is available on the definition of smallholders in the Philippines; however, in 2012, more than 88 percent owned 3 ha or less.
12 https://rspo.org/as-a-smallholder/ Retrieved September 27, 2024.
13 https://rspo.org/as-a-smallholder/ Retrieved September 27, 2024.
14 https://indonesiabusinesspost.com/risks-opportunities/gapki-sees-european-market-as-less-strategic-for-indonesian-palm-oil/ accessed on November 15, 2024.
15 https://rozenbergquarterly.com/is-the-food-industry-concealing-possible-destruction-of-the-tropics-from-the-public/?print=pdf accessed on January 18, 2025.
16 https://news.mongabay.com/2024/08/indonesia-eu-reconcile-forest-data-ahead-of-new-rules-on-deforestation-free-trade/ accessed on January 18, 2025.
17 www.ofimagazine.com/news/thai-oil-palm-smallholders-increase-production-and-income-from-rspo-certification accessed on November 16, 2024.
18 www.indonesiapalmoilfacts.com/indonesia-uniting-asean-against-eudr/ accessed on November 16, 2024.

Reference List

Ablowitz, R. (1939). The Theory of Emergence. *Philosophy of Science*, *6*(1), 1–16. https://doi.org/10.1086/286529

Almeida, D. V., Kolinjivadi, V., Ferrando, T., Roy, B., Herrera, H., Vecchione Gonçalves, M., & Van Hecken, G. (2023). The "Greening" of Empire: The European Green Deal as the EU First Agenda. *Political Geography*, *105*. https://doi.org/10.1016/j.polgeo.2023.102925

Aziz, N. F., Chamhuri, N., & Batt, P. J. (2021). Barriers and Benefits Arising from the Adoption of Sustainable Certification for Smallholder Oil Palm Producers in Malaysia: A Systematic Review of Literature. *Sustainability*, *13*(18). https://doi.org/10.3390/su131810009

Bagja, B., Anjani, S., Jati, E. S. K., Zahra, D. A., & Haniy, S. U. (2022). *Responding to Global Green Call, It's Time for Indonesian Palm Oil Farmers to 'Level Up'*. https://wri-indonesia.org/en/insights/responding-global-green-call-its-time-indonesian-palm-oil-farmers-level

Blot, E., & Hiller, N. (2022). Securing the Position of Smallholders in Zero-Deforestation Supply Chains. In Institute for European Environmental Policy (Ed.), *Policy Briefing*. Brussel.

Brandi, C. A. (2017). Sustainability Standards and Sustainable Development – Synergies and Trade-Offs of Transnational Governance. *Sustainable Development*, *25*(1), 25–34. https://doi.org/10.1002/sd.1639

Brandi, C. A., Cabani, T., Hosang, C., Schirmbeck, S., Westermann, L., & Wiese, H. (2015). Sustainability Standards for Palm Oil: Challenges for Smallholder Certification Under the RSPO. *The Journal of Environment & Development*, *24*(3), 292–314. https://doi.org/10.1177/1070496515593775

Briassoulis, H. (2017). Response Assemblages and Their Socioecological Fit: Conceptualizing Human Responses to Environmental Degradation. *Dialogues in Human Geography*, *7*(2), 166–185. https://doi.org/10.1177/2043820617720079

Briassoulis, H. (2019). Governance as Multiplicity: The Assemblage Thinking Perspective. *Policy Sciences*, *52*(3), 419–450. https://doi.org/10.1007/s11077-018-09345-9

Buchmann, M. (2015). Emergent Properties. In *International Encyclopedia of the Social & Behavioral Sciences* (pp. 433–437). https://doi.org/10.1016/b978-0-08-097086-8.44018-3

Byerlee, D., Falcon, W. P., & Naylor, R. (2017). *The Tropical Oil Crop Revolution: Food, Feed, Fuel, and Forests*. Oxford University Press.

Byerlee, D., & Viswanathan, P. K. (2018). Plantations and Economic Development in the Twentieth Century: The End of an Era? In V. Pinilla & H. Willebald (Eds.), *Agricultural Development in the World Periphery: A Global Economic History Approach* (pp. 89–117). Springer International Publishing. https://doi.org/10.1007/978-3-319-66020-2_4

Carlson, K. M., Heilmayr, R., Gibbs, H. K., Noojipady, P., Burns, D. N., Morton, D. C., Walker, N. F., Paoli, G. D., & Kremen, C. (2018). Effect of Oil Palm Sustainability Certification on Deforestation and Fire in Indonesia. *Proc Natl Acad Sci U S A*, *115*(1), 121–126. https://doi.org/10.1073/pnas.1704728114

Cheyns, E. (2014). Making "Minority Voices" Heard in Transnational Roundtables: The Role of Local NGOs in Reintroducing Justice and Attachments. *Agriculture and Human Values*, *31*(3), 439–453. https://doi.org/10.1007/s10460-014-9505-7

Colchester, M., Sawit, W., & Forest Peoples, P. (2011). *Oil Palm Expansion in South East Asia: Trends and Implications for Local Communities and Indigenous Peoples*. Perkumpulan Sawit Watch; Forest Peoples Programme. www.forestpeoples.org/sites/fpp/files/publication/2011/11/oil-palm-expansion-southeast-asia-2011-low-res.pdf

Cramb, R., & McCarthy, J. F. (2016). *The Oil Palm Complex: Smallholders, Agribusiness and the State in Indonesia and Malaysia*. NUS Press. https://doi.org/10.2307/j.ctv1xz0km.9

Crick, F. (1995). *The Astonishing Hypothesis: The Scientific Search for the Soul*. London: Simon & Schuster Ltd., Touchstone Books.

Daemeter. (2015). *Indonesian Oil Palm Smallholder Farmers: A Typology of Organizational Models, Needs, and Investment Opportunities*. Daemeter Consulting.

De Landa, M. (2006). Chapter 13 Deleuzian Social Ontology and Assemblage Theory. In *Deleuze and the Social* (pp. 250–266). Edinburgh University Press. https://doi.org/doi:10.1515/9780748627080-015
De Landa, M. (2010). *Deleuze: History and Science*. Atropos.
De Landa, M. (2016). *Assemblage Theory*. Edinburgh University Press. www.jstor.org.ezproxy.library.wur.nl/stable/10.3366/j.ctt1bh2hgn
de Vos, R. E., Suwarno, A., Slingerland, M., van der Meer, P. J., & Lucey, J. M. (2023). Pre-Certification Conditions of Independent Oil Palm Smallholders in Indonesia. Assessing Prospects for RSPO Certification. *Land Use Policy*, *130*. https://doi.org/10.1016/j.landusepol.2023.106660
Deleuze, G., Guattari, F. L., & Massumi, B. (1988). *A Thousand Plateaus: Capitalism and Schizophrenia*. Bloomsbury Academic.
Deleuze, G., Parnet, C., Tomlinson, H., & Habberjam, B. (1987). *Dialogues*. Columbia University Press.
Dennison, S., Engström, M., & Hobbs, C. (2024). *Winds of Change: The EU's Green Agenda after the European Parliament Election*. European Council on Foreign Relations. https://ecfr.eu/wp-content/uploads/2024/05/Winds-of-change-The-EUs-green-agenda-after-the-European-Parliament-election-1.pdf
Deringer, H., Lee-Makiyama, H., & Murty, D. (2019). Europe and South-East Asia: Shifting from Diplomacy to Unilateralism. *Policy Brief*, *1*.
Ellis-Petersen, H. (2018). How Palm Oil Ban Has Made the EU a Dirty Word in Malaysia. *The Guardian*. www.theguardian.com/world/2018/apr/26/how-palm-oil-ban-has-made-the-eu-a-dirty-word-in-malaysia
Euler, M., Schwarze, S., Siregar, H., & Qaim, M. (2016). Oil Palm Expansion among Smallholder Farmers in Sumatra, Indonesia. *Journal of Agricultural Economics*, *67*(3), 658–676. https://doi.org/10.1111/1477-9552.12163
Fern. (2023). *What is the EU Regulation on Deforestation-Free Products*? Retrieved September 7, 2024, from www.fern.org/fileadmin/uploads/fern/Documents/2023/What_is_the_EU_Regulation_on_deforestation_free_products_and_why_should_you_care.pdf
Fisher, M. R., Obidzinski, K., Alves, A. M., & Ekaputri, A. D. (2024). Commodities and Global Climate Governance: Early Evidence From the EU Deforestation-Free Regulation (EUDR). *Asia Pacific Issues*, *27*(165).
Foucault, M. (1991). Governmentality. In G. Burchell, C. Gordon, & P. Miller (Eds.), *The Foucault Effect: Studies in Governmentality* (pp. 87–104). University of Chicago Press.
Freeman, R. (2017). Europe in Translation: Governance, Assemblage and the Project Form. In T. Berger & A. Esguerra (Eds.), *World Politics in Translation*. Routledge.
Glasbergen, P. (2018). Smallholders Do Not Eat Certificates. *Ecological Economics*, *147*, 243–252. https://doi.org/10.1016/j.ecolecon.2018.01.023
Godard, G. (2022). *Balancing Environmental and Socioeconomic Priorities: EU-ASEAN Relations and the Deforestation Regulation*. https://eias.org/policy-briefs/balancing-environmental-and-socioeconomic-priorities-eu-asean-relations-and-the-deforestation-regulation/
Goldstein, J. (1999). Emergence as a Construct: History and Issues. *Emergence*, *1*(1), 49–72. https://doi.org/10.1207/s15327000em0101_4
Hadjiyianni, I. (2017). The Extraterritorial Reach of EU Environmental Law and Access to Justice by Third Country Actors. *European Papers*, *2*(2), 519–542. https://hdl.handle.net/1814/51305
Hirbli, T. (2018). *Palm Oil Traceability: Blockchain Meets Supply Chain*. Massachusetts: Massachusetts Institute of Technology, WorldCat. https://dspace.mit.edu/bitstream/handle/1721.1/117800/1051223547MIT.pdf?sequence=1
Hutabarat, S., Slingerland, M., Rietberg, P., & Dries, L. (2018). Costs and Benefits of Certification of Independent Oil Palm Smallholders in Indonesia. *International Food and Agribusiness Management Review*, *21*(6), 681–700. https://doi.org/10.22434/ifamr2016.0162
Innocenti, E. D., & Oosterveer, P. (2020). Opportunities and Bottlenecks for Upstream Learning within RSPO Certified Palm Oil Value Chains: A Comparative Analysis between

Indonesia and Thailand. *Journal of Rural Studies*, *78*, 426–437. https://doi.org/10.1016/j.jrurstud.2020.07.004

Jelsma, I., Schoneveld, G. C., Zoomers, A., & van Westen, A. C. M. (2017). Unpacking Indonesia's Independent Oil Palm Smallholders: An Actor-Disaggregated Approach to Identifying Environmental and Social Performance Challenges. *Land Use Policy*, *69*, 281–297. https://doi.org/10.1016/j.landusepol.2017.08.012

Jelsma, I., Slingerland, M., Giller, K. E., & Bijman, J. (2017). Collective Action in a Smallholder Oil Palm Production System in Indonesia: The Key to Sustainable and Inclusive Smallholder Palm Oil? *Journal of Rural Studies*, *54*, 198–210. https://doi.org/10.1016/j.jrurstud.2017.06.005

Jensen, H. T., Keogh-Brown, M. R., Shankar, B., Aekplakorn, W., Basu, S., Cuevas, S., Dangour, A. D., Gheewala, S. H., Green, R., Joy, E. J. M., Rojroongwasinkul, N., Thaiprasert, N., & Smith, R. D. (2019). Palm Oil and Dietary Change: Application of an Integrated Macroeconomic, Environmental, Demographic, and Health Modelling Framework for Thailand. *Food Policy*, *83*, 92–103. https://doi.org/10.1016/j.foodpol.2018.12.003

Kannan, P., Mansor, N. H., Rahman, N. K., Peng, T. S., & Mazlan, S. M. (2020). A Review on Malaysian Sustainable Palm Oil Certification Process among Independent Oil Palm Smallholders. *Journal of Oil Palm Research*. https://doi.org/10.21894/jopr.2020.0056

Köthke, M., Lippe, M., & Elsasser, P. (2023). Comparing the Former EUTR and Upcoming EUDR: Some Implications for Private Sector and Authorities. *Forest Policy and Economics*, *157*. https://doi.org/10.1016/j.forpol.2023.103079

Leng, K. Y., & Tamilwanan, N. (2024). Thailand's Palm Oil: Evolving from Domestic Smallholder Centrism to Sustainable Exports. In P. O'Reilly & H. Varkkey (Eds.), *Governing the Palm Oil Industry: Perspectives from Southeast Asia and Latin America* (pp. 99–130). Routledge. https://doi.org/10.4324/9781003459606-6

Lewes, G. H. (1875). *Problems of Life and Mind* (Volume 2). Kegan Paul, Trench, Turbner, and Co.

Li, T. M. (2007). Practices of Assemblage and Community Forest Management. *Economy and Society*, *36*(2), 263–293. https://doi.org/10.1080/03085140701254308

Li, T. M. (2024). Securing Oil Palm Smallholder Livelihoods without More Deforestation in Indonesia. *Nature Sustainability*, *7*(4), 387–393. https://doi.org/10.1038/s41893-024-01279-w

Lowder, S. K., Skoet, J., & Raney, T. (2016). The Number, Size, and Distribution of Farms, Smallholder Farms, and Family Farms Worldwide. *World Development*, *87*, 16–29. https://doi.org/10.1016/j.worlddev.2015.10.041

Mayr, E. (2003). *The Growth of Biological Thought: Diversity Evolution and Inheritance* (12th ed.). The Belknap Press of Harvard University Press.

Meloni, S. (2025). What is the Future of the European Union's Once Ambitious Green Agenda? *Earth.org*. https://earth.org/what-is-the-future-of-the-european-unions-once-ambitious-green-agenda/

Müller, M. (2015). Assemblages and Actor-Networks: Rethinking Socio-material Power, Politics and Space. *Geography Compass*, *9*(1), 27–41. https://doi.org/10.1111/gec3.12192

Müller, M., & Schurr, C. (2016). Assemblage Thinking and Actor-Network Theory: Conjunctions, Disjunctions, Cross-Fertilisations. *Transactions of the Institute of British Geographers*, *41*(3), 217–229. https://doi.org/10.1111/tran.12117

Muradian, R., Cahyafitri, R., Ferrando, T., Grottera, C., Jardim-Wanderley, L., Krause, T., Kurniawan, N. I., Loft, L., Nurshafira, T., Prabawati-Suwito, D., Prasongko, D., Sanchez-Garcia, P. A., Schröter, B., & Vela-Almeida, D. (2025). Will the EU Deforestation-Free Products Regulation (EUDR) Reduce Tropical Forest Loss? Insights from Three Producer Countries. *Ecological Economics*, *227*. https://doi.org/10.1016/j.ecolecon.2024.108389

Nagayets, O. (2005, June 26–29). *Small Farms: Current Status and Key Trends*. Future of Small Farms Research Workshop, Wyne College. https://pdf.usaid.gov/pdf_docs/Pnado609.pdf

Nawireja, I. K., & Ross, C. (2010). *Challenges to Certification for Smallholders and Practical Solutions Measurement and Mitigation of Environmental Impact of Palm Oil Production, The Stones Hotel, Bali, Indonesia.* https://icope-series.com/conferences-measurement-and-mitigation-of-environmental-impact-of-palm-oil-production/

Netting, R. M. (1993). *Smallholders, Householders: Farm Families and the Ecology of Intensive, Sustainable Agriculture*. Stanford University Press.

Nik Ibrahim, N. A., Ahmad Tarmizi, A. H., Selvaduray, K. R., & Kuntom, A. (2022). Sustainability and Traceability in the Malaysian Oil Palm Industry. In Y.-Y. Lee, T.-K. Tang, E.-T. Phuah, & O.-M. Lai (Eds.), *Recent Advances in Edible Fats and Oils Technology: Processing, Health Implications, Economic and Environmental Impact* (pp. 425–461). Singapore: Springer. https://doi.org/10.1007/978-981-16-5113-7_16

Nozawa, K. (2011). *Oil Palm Production and Cooperatives in the Philippines* (Volumes 2011–13). University of the Philippines, School of Economics (UPSE).

Nupueng, S., Oosterveer, P., & Mol, A. P. J. (2022). Governing Sustainability in the Thai Palm Oil-Supply Chain: The Role of Private Actors. *Sustainability: Science, Practice and Policy, 18*(1), 37–54. https://doi.org/10.1080/15487733.2021.2021688

Ogahara, Z., Jespersen, K., Theilade, I., & Nielsen, M. R. (2022). Review of Smallholder Palm Oil Sustainability Reveals Limited Positive Impacts and Identifies Key Implementation and Knowledge Gaps. *Land Use Policy, 120.* https://doi.org/10.1016/j.landusepol.2022.106258

O'Reilly, P., & Varkkey, H. (2024). *Governing the Palm Oil Industry Perspectives from Southeast Asia and Latin America.* Taylor & Francis Group. https://public.ebookcentral.proquest.com/choice/PublicFullRecord.aspx?p=31279464

O'Reilly, P., Varkkey, H., & Ali, S. (2024). Palm Oil Governance: A Global Industry Assembled and Reassembled by Many People in Many Places. In P. O'Reilly & H. Varkkey (Eds.), *Governing the Palm Oil Industry: Perspectives from Southeast Asia and Latin America* (pp. 1–22). Routledge. https://doi.org/10.4324/9781003459606

Pramudya, E. P., Wibowo, L. R., Nurfatriani, F., Nawireja, I. K., Kurniasari, D. R., Hutabarat, S., Kadarusman, Y. B., Iswardhani, A. O., & Rafik, R. (2022). Incentives for Palm Oil Smallholders in Mandatory Certification in Indonesia. *Land, 11*(4), 576. www.mdpi.com/2073-445X/11/4/576

Regulation (EU) 2023/851 (2023). https://eur-lex.europa.eu/legal-content/EN/TXT/?uri=CELEX:32023R0851

Rigg, J., Salamanca, A., Phongsiri, M., & Sripun, M. (2018). More Farmers, Less Farming? Understanding the Truncated Agrarian Transition in Thailand. *World Development, 107*, 327–337. https://doi.org/10.1016/j.worlddev.2018.03.008

Rigg, J., Salamanca, A., & Thompson, E. C. (2016). The Puzzle of East and Southeast Asia's Persistent Smallholder. *Journal of Rural Studies, 43*, 118–133. https://doi.org/10.1016/j.jrurstud.2015.11.003

Rijk, G., Wiggs, C., & Piotrowski, M. (2021). *FMCGs, Retail Earn 66% of Gross Profits in Palm Oil Value Chain.* Chain Reaction Research. https://chainreactionresearch.com/wp-content/uploads/2021/06/FMCGs-Retail-Earn-66-of-Gross-Profits-in-Palm-Oil-Value-Chain.pdf

Rochmyaningsih, D. (2024). European Deforestation Rules are Flawed, Scientists Argue. *Science, 385*(6708), 485. https://doi.org/10.1126/science.ads1315

RSPO. (2023). *The RSPO System as a Tool to Help Companies Comply with Requirements of the EU Deforestation Regulatio.* RSPO. https://rspo.org/wp-content/uploads/RSPO-Report-Gap-Analysis-EU-Deforestation-Regulation-05.04.2023-1.pdf

Saswattecha, K., Kroeze, C., Jawjit, W., & Hein, L. (2017). Improving Environmental Sustainability of Thai Palm Oil Production in 2050. *Journal of Cleaner Production, 147*, 572–588. https://doi.org/10.1016/j.jclepro.2017.01.137

Schmidt, R. (2012). *Soziologie der Praktiken: Konzeptionelle Studien und Empirische Analysen.* Suhrkamp. https://books.google.co.id/books?id=MmnBpwAACAAJ

Sriboonchitta, S., & Wiboonpoongse, A. (2008). *Overview of Contract Farming in Thailand: Lessons Learned* (Volume 112). Asian Development Bank Institute (ADBI).

Thongrak, S., Kongmanee, C., & Kiatpathomchai, S. (2023). *Oil Palm Development in Thailand: Trends and Progress of Sustainability Efforts in Palm Oil Production and Procurement*. Faculty of Economics, Prince of Songkla University (PSU).

Tyson, A., & Meganingtyas, E. (2022). The Status of Palm Oil Under the European Union's Renewable Energy Directive: Sustainability or Protectionism? *Bulletin of Indonesian Economic Studies*, *58*(1), 31–54. https://doi.org/10.1080/00074918.2020.1862411

Vermeulen, S., & Goad, N. (2006). *Towards Better Practice in Smallholder Palm Oil Production*. International Institute for Environment and Development.

Vermeulen, S., Nawir, A. A., & Mayers, J. (2006). Rural Poverty Reduction through Business Partnerships? Examples of Experience from the Forestry Sector. *Environment, Development and Sustainability*, *10*(1), 1–18. https://doi.org/10.1007/s10668-006-9035-6

Voora, V., Larrea, C., Bermudez, S., & Baliño, S. (2020). *Global Market Report: Palm Oil*. IISD.

WorldBank. (2021). *Realizing Scale in Smallholder-Based Agriculture: Policy Options for the Philippines*. World Bank. https://documents1.worldbank.org/curated/en/741391625758351866/pdf/Realizing-Scale-in-Smallholder-Based-Agriculture-Policy-Options-for-the-Philippines.pdf

Wright, D., & Meadows, D. H. (2012). *Thinking in Systems a Primer*. Earthscan.

Zhunusova, E., Ahimbisibwe, V., Sen, L. T. H., Sadeghi, A., Toledo-Aceves, T., Kabwe, G., & Günter, S. (2022). Potential Impacts of the Proposed EU Regulation on Deforestation-Free Supply Chains on Smallholders, Indigenous Peoples, and Local Communities in Producer Countries Outside the EU. *Forest Policy and Economics*, *143*. https://doi.org/10.1016/j.forpol.2022.102817

12 Making the European Union Green Deal Benefit the Environment Society of the European Union and ASEAN

Herry Purnomo, Beni Okarda, Lila Juniyanti, Sonya Dyah Kusumadewi and Dyah Puspitaloka

Introduction

Since 2009, trade policies related to palm oil have been a significant focus for the European Union (EU), particularly following the publication of the EU Renewable Energy Directive (RED), which aimed to reduce emissions in the transport sector. In November 2021, the EU proposed a regulation to ensure that products entering the market are compliant with the European Union Deforestation Regulation (EUDR). This proposal states that commodities produced on land deforested after December 31, 2020, will be banned from the EU market. The policy specifically targets commodities such as palm oil, timber, rubber, coffee, and cacao. This initiative has provoked extensive public debate, especially in producing countries like Indonesia and Malaysia. Although the implementation of the EUDR has been postponed, it is now set to take effect in December 2026 for large operators and June 2027 for small enterprises.

Palm oil is a significant trade commodity that contributes to Indonesia's economic development. In 2022, approximately 65% of the country's palm oil production was exported, accounting for 54% of global exports and providing employment for 16.2 million people (Benedict & Heilmayr, 2024). As the world's largest producer and exporter, oil palm contributed 4.5% to Indonesia's gross domestic product. In 2023, the export value of palm oil reached $25.1 billion, with a total volume of 28.2 million tonnes (BPS-Statistics Indonesia, 2025).

Despite facing an economic recession, the agriculture sector consistently grew during the pandemic, achieving a growth rate of 1.75% in 2020 (BPS-Statistic Indonesia, 2020). However, the expansion of oil palm plantations has led to deforestation. Austin et al. (2017) reported that from 1995 to 2015, palm oil development resulted in an annual loss of 117,000 hectares of forest, although this rate has shown a decreasing trend. Furthermore, Purnomo et al. (2020) indicated that palm oil value chains contribute approximately 300 million tonnes of CO_2 equivalent in annual greenhouse gas (GHG) emissions. They propose plausible and quantitative scenarios aimed at reconciling the economic development of palm oil with forest conservation efforts.

DOI: 10.4324/9781003783176-15

Various sustainable oil palm development initiatives have been implemented in Indonesia. The most recent effort is highlighted in Presidential Instruction No. 6/2019, which outlines the National Action Plan for Sustainable Oil Palm Plantations for 2019–2024. Additionally, the Indonesian Sustainable Palm Oil (ISPO) standard and certification system was established under Minister of Agriculture Regulation No. 11/2015.

However, palm oil remains a market-driven commodity. Growing sustainability awareness in the market has become a key factor in governing the global value chain through sustainability standards and certification systems. Public initiatives in importing countries, particularly by the EU through the EUDR, also support sustainable palm oil trade practices. Research by Purnomo et al. (2023) using structural equation modelling (SEM) has demonstrated that global trade has a statistically significant impact on palm oil sustainability in Indonesia.

In 2021, Indonesia published its Long-Term Strategy for Low Carbon and Climate Resilience by 2050 (Indonesia LTS-LCCR 2050), which serves as a national strategy aimed at addressing climate change. One of its key targets is achieving Net FOLU Sink by 2030, focusing on efforts in the forestry and land use sectors (GoI, 2021). Sustainable palm oil trade, particularly through a no-deforestation supply chain, has the potential to contribute significantly to reaching this Net FOLU Sink 2030 target. The EUDR can align with and enhance Indonesia's existing initiatives to support the climate agenda. However, it remains to be seen how the palm oil sector at the national level can adapt to and benefit from the EUDR, as well as the challenges it may face.

We hypothesize that there are ways to adapt to and benefit from new global green deals, such as the EUDR for the palm oil sector in Indonesia and other ASEAN member countries. Indeed, implementing the EUDR may create a trade-off between economic interests and environmental protection. Our modelling effort aims to capitalize on environmental improvements by rewarding zero-deforestation practices while minimizing losses associated with the traditional palm oil economy.

This chapter has four main objectives: (a) to understand the potential impact of the EUDR on the palm oil sector, (b) to develop scenarios illustrating how the palm oil sector can adapt to and benefit from the EUDR, (c) to create a roadmap for implementing these scenarios through a multi-stakeholder process (MSP), and (d) to provide policy recommendations for developing the palm oil sector in the context of EUDR implementation for both EU and ASEAN member countries.

To achieve our goal, we developed a model called the Simulation of Indonesian Palm Oil Sustainability (SIPOS). This model accurately represents palm oil data at the national level and offers scenarios for national policymakers and sustainability leaders to explore various future pathways for oil palm production that meet globally recognized sustainability standards. Additionally, the model facilitates communication among local farmers, governments, traders, and sustainability leaders, ensuring that the global palm oil trade benefits both the environment and the economy.

Framework and Methods

Oil Palm and Forest Landscape

Indonesia's land comprises both forested and non-forested areas. The country has a total land area of 190.5 million hectares, of which 125 million are designated forest areas by law. However, not all designated forest areas are covered in forest. Some portions of these areas are occupied by settlements and crops (including oil palm plantations) or are degraded and deforested. Conversely, there may be forest cover present on lands classified as non-forest. Figure 12.1 illustrates the distribution of forest and non-forest areas.

We adhere to the Food and Agriculture Organization's (FAO) definitions of forest, forest degradation, and deforestation. According to these definitions, a forest is defined as land that has tree crown cover (or an equivalent stocking level) of more than 10% and covers an area greater than 0.5 hectares (ha). The trees in this area should be able to reach a minimum height of 5 meters (m) at maturity in their natural environment. The following classifications are considered forests: forest nurseries and seed orchards that are integral to the forest ecosystem; Forests located in national parks, nature reserves, and other protected areas; plantations primarily intended for forestry purposes, including rubberwood plantations and cork oak stands.

Land mainly used for agricultural practices does not qualify as a forest. Additionally, tree plantations established primarily to produce wood or wood-derived

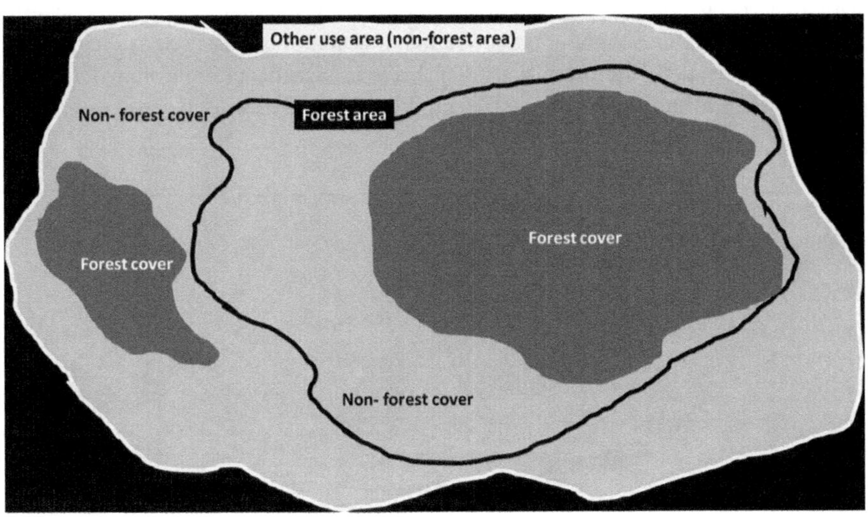

Figure 12.1 Illustration of forest areas and other use areas (non-forest areas)

products are regarded as forests. Conversely, tree plantations focused on producing other goods, such as coconuts or various fruits, are not classified as forests. Similarly, gardens, agroforestry areas, and urban parks do not fall under the forest category. Therefore, it is evident that oil palm plantations do not qualify as forests. The spatial distribution of oil palm plantations in Indonesia is presented in Figure 12.2.

A forest is primarily made up of trees. A tree is a woody plant that typically undergoes regular growth renewal, classifying it as a perennial. Most plants classified as trees feature a single, self-supporting trunk of woody tissue. In many species, this trunk develops secondary limbs known as branches. A tree is a woody perennial plant with a single, usually elongated main stem, often having few or no branches on its lower portion.[1]

Deforestation refers to the process of converting forested areas to other land uses or significantly reducing tree canopy cover to below 10%. Forest degradation involves a decline in the canopy cover or stocking within an existing forest. Afforestation is the act of converting non-forest land into forested areas. In contrast, reforestation is the process of restoring forest formations after a temporary period during which the canopy cover falls below the 10% threshold, whether due to human activity or natural events. The relationships between these terms can be summarized as follows: forest degradation and improvement occur within existing forests, while reforestation happens when forests regrow after experiencing a decline to below 10% canopy cover but are still classified as forests during that time. Deforestation and afforestation represent the transitions between forested and non-forested land uses, as defined by the (FAO, 2003). These conceptual relationships between forest and other land-use classes are shown in Figure 12.3.

Deforestation is the transformation of forested areas into oil palm plantations, which can occur through both legal and illegal means. When forests are converted to oil palm plantations without authorization, this action is classified as illegal deforestation. This type of deforestation often leads to significant environmental consequences, such as habitat loss, decreased biodiversity, and increased carbon emissions.

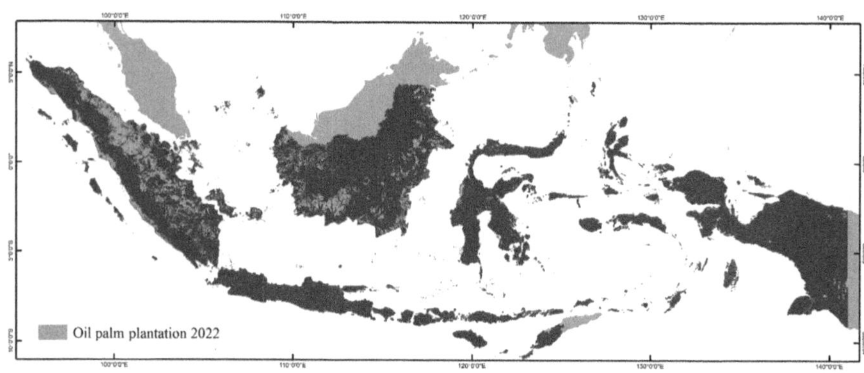

Figure 12.2 Distribution of oil palm concessions and planted oil palm in Indonesia

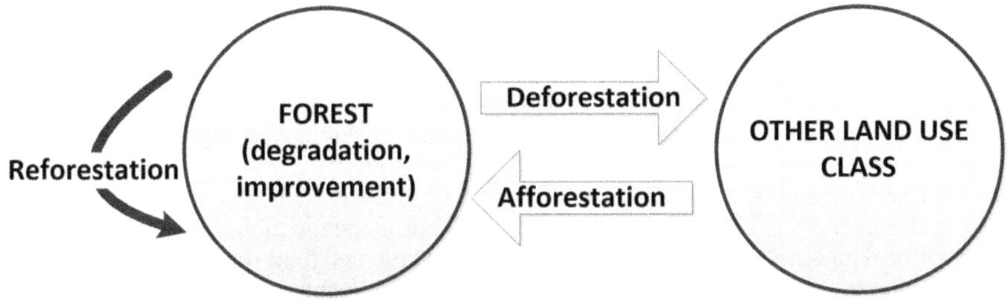

Figure 12.3 Relationship between forest and other land use classes, including agriculture
Source: (FAO, 2003).

Conversely, the conversion of designated convertible production forest (*Hutan Produksi Konversi* or HPK) to oil palm plantations is conducted under legal frameworks and thus is termed legal deforestation. Although this process is sanctioned by law, it still raises concerns regarding the sustainability of land use and the long-term impacts on the ecosystem. Understanding the distinctions between legal and illegal deforestation is crucial for addressing the environmental challenges of oil palm cultivation and developing effective conservation strategies.

Model, Scenario Development, and Verification

We adopted a value chain analysis (VCA) approach combined with systems dynamics modelling (SD) and geographic information systems (GIS). VCA examines the added value of various actors along the supply chain. The VCA process consists of the following steps: (1) mapping the beginning of the value chain, (2) conducting field surveys, and (3) evaluating findings and developing intervention scenarios (Kaplinsky & Morris, 2000). The implementation of SD involves several steps: (1) developing conceptual models, (2) specifying the models, (3) verifying the models, and (4) developing scenarios (Grant et al., 1997). GIS analysis is used to analyze and parameterize the rate of land dynamics associated with oil palm development and to visualize the results of scenarios related to forest cover and land use change. This simulation uses 2022 as the base year and will project it in 30 years of simulation time.

The data incorporated into this model originate from various sources, ensuring a comprehensive and robust representation of real-world conditions. These sources include in-depth GIS analysis, detailed survey results, and credible official data from central government ministries and agencies, as well as from provincial and district governments and their personnel. Additionally, relevant scientific publications contribute valuable insights.

For clarity, Table 12.1 outlines the specific categories of data and the sources utilized throughout the modelling process. This model is designed to closely mirror

Table 12.1 Data and sources used in the model

No	*Classification of Data Type*	*Data Source*
1	Palm oil industry and supply chains	Scientific publications, governments, and surveys
2	Land use and land use change	GIS analysis
3	Biodiversity and CO_2eq. emission	Scientific publication
4	Local and global trade	Research and think-tank organizations
5	Palm oil price and its dynamics	Local government and private sectors
6	Benchmark of palm oil projection	Local government and private sectors

real-world scenarios, and its development employs advanced tools such as the Stella Architect software for system dynamics alongside powerful GIS tools for spatial analysis. Together, these elements create an accurate simulation that aids in understanding complex dynamics within the studied domain.

We tested the model during the TRADE Hub's National MSP workshops.[2] Key stakeholders engaged in identifying essential action pathways using SIPOS as a facilitation tool. From December 2022 to September 2023, three MSPs were held to develop a national roadmap for Indonesian palm oil. The first MSP, a roundtable discussion in December 2022,[3] included 96 participants from 51 institutions. It highlighted the need for collaboration between producer and market countries to halt deforestation, recognizing the EUDR as a potential supportive pathway for Indonesia's FOLU Net Sink 2030 strategy.

In April 2023, a second session featured a high-level dialogue with 450 participants from 258 organizations, stressing the importance of a shared understanding of sustainability and the need for solutions supporting smallholder farmers. A subsequent workshop involved 56 stakeholders in developing the roadmap, culminating in a common vision for sustainable palm oil trade and climate change mitigation. The third MSP, a regional consultation in September 2023, had 602 participants from 270 institutions providing feedback. The final roadmap document was handed over to policymakers in March 2024. These three workshops were used to obtain feedback and justification of the logic and usefulness of SIPOS.

Results

Model Development

Architecture of SIPOS

Figure 12.4 illustrates the architecture of the SIPOS. It consists of three main components: (a) the palm oil supply chains, (b) trade schemes, and (c) output indicators used to evaluate the trade schemes. The trade schemes are designed to enhance the existing palm oil value supply chain and produce output indicators.

The palm oil supply chain includes plantations, palm oil mills, refineries, and markets. Growers cultivate oil palm to produce fresh fruit bunches (FFB), which are then processed by mills into crude palm oil (CPO) and palm kernel oil (PKO).

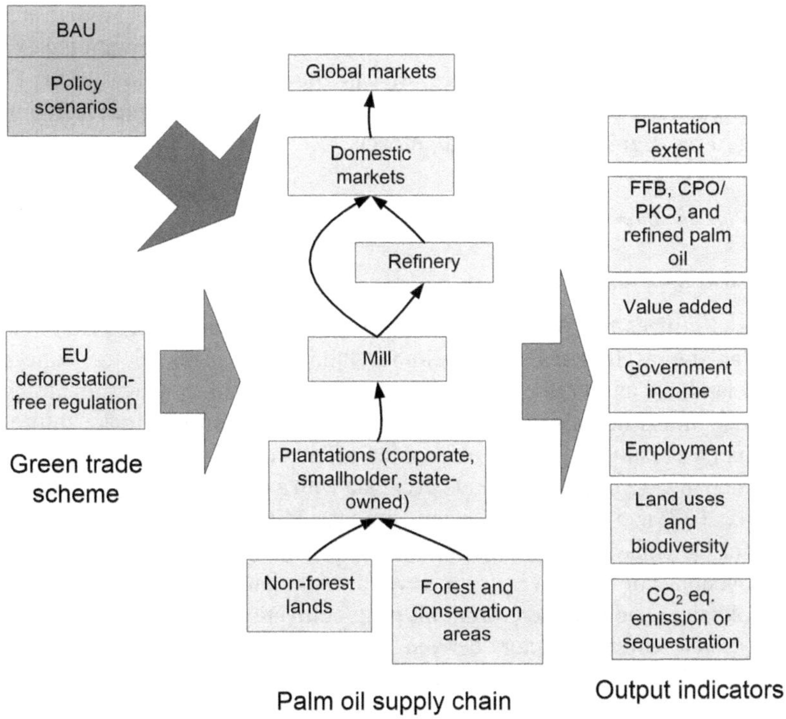

Figure 12.4 The architecture of SIPOS

These oils are further refined into various products, such as cooking oil, oleochemicals, and biodiesel (Mulyani & Las, 2008). These products are distributed in both domestic and global markets, generating revenue that flows back to the refineries, mills, producers, and the government.

The SIPOS model produces several key outputs: (1) the area cultivated with oil palm (in hectares); (2) the production quantities of primary products, such as FFB and CPO or PKO, as well as refined palm oil (RPO), which includes cooking oil, oleochemicals, and biodiesel; (3) the value added for each stakeholder involved; (4) carbon emissions associated with production; (5) employment figures within the palm oil industry; (6) land use and biodiversity impacts; and (7) government revenue generated from the industry.

The indicators discussed in this chapter provide insight into the current landscape under a business-as-usual (BAU) scenario, specifically in the context of the EUDR. These indicators are crucial for understanding the regulatory implications of EUDR, as they primarily focus on factors that directly relate to its objectives, including rates of deforestation, GHG emissions, and various economic dimensions.

In particular, the indicators measuring deforestation offer a quantitative assessment of forest loss and its environmental impact, while those concerning GHG emissions highlight the contributions of different sectors to climate change.

Additionally, the economic indicators included predominantly examine trade volume and value, which encompass both domestic markets and international exports. By analyzing these economic metrics, we can grasp the implications of the EUDR on trade practices and the broader economy, facilitating a comprehensive understanding of the regulation's potential impacts.

SIPOS Specification

(A) OIL PALM LAND RESOURCES

The model utilizes ten years of historical land cover data (2012–2022) obtained from MapBiomas Indonesia (MapBiomas Indonesia – Collection 2 time-series maps of land use and land cover).[4] This data is employed to generate a transition matrix that illustrates historical land cover changes and to estimate future land cover changes resulting from the expansion of oil palm plantations.

Additionally, we overlay the land cover data with a peatland map from PEATMAP (Xu et al., 2018) and spatial designations from the Ministry of Environment and Forestry (MoEF). Emissions resulting from land cover changes are calculated by examining the dynamics of land cover due to new oil palm plantations, carbon sequestration from replanting, and emissions from oil palm cultivation on peatland. Furthermore, we incorporate emission factors derived from the Economic Research Institute for ASEAN and East Asia (ERIA)'s life cycle assessment studies to estimate emissions from the operational activities of plantations, mills, and refineries (ERIA, 2007).

Oil Palm Plantations In the plantation sector, the oil palm life cycle is divided into three stages: planting, maturing, producing FFB, and replanting. This process is represented by a conveyor model. In this model, we set the plantation to begin producing fruit when it reaches five years of age and continue producing until it reaches 24 years, after which it moves to the replanting stage. To better understand the dynamics of different plantation actors, we divided the sub-model into corporate and smallholder plantations. The model will halt the plantation extent once it reaches the maximum area of 44.7 million hectares. We used the most recent statistical data on plantation extent from the Ministry of Agriculture (MoA) as a baseline to simulate plantation growth and palm oil production, projecting the growth based on this same dataset.

(B) MILLS AND REFINERIES

The mills process the FFB from plantations into CPO. In this model, we simplify the calculation by directly converting productivity into CPO. We utilize productivity data from both company and smallholder plantations, sourced from the MoA (Directorate General of Estates, 2022). The mass flow to the mills and refineries is based on supply chain data from 2020, obtained from TRASE.[5] TRASE is an open-data initiative that maps global agricultural supply chains, linking consumer markets, trading companies, and production regions to address deforestation risks.

(C) DOMESTIC AND GLOBAL MARKETS

From the mills, a portion of CPO is exported directly to international markets, while the remaining amount is converted into palm oil derivative products or RPO at refineries before entering the market. The flow of CPO and RPO to both domestic and global markets is tracked using TRASE supply chain data. In 2020, the export ratio for crude palm kernel oil (CPKO) was 16%, and the export ratio for RPO was 53%. For the baseline price, we are using the World Bank's forecast for CPO prices.[6] In 2021, the total export value of oil palm reached US$ 28.7 billion, which accounted for 12% of Indonesia's total export value (Directorate of Distribution Statistics, 2022).

Simulation of BAU Outputs and Verification

BAU OUTPUT INDICATORS

SIPOS can be accessed by the following link.[7] The simulation runs for 30 years, starting from the base year of 2022. According to SIPOS projections, by the end of this period, the total area will reach 22.8 million hectares (MHa). This area will consist of corporate plantations covering 11.8 MHa and smallholder plantations covering 11.0 MHa. As illustrated in Figure 12.5, the gap between the area of corporate and smallholder plantations is expected to narrow over 30 years. This change is attributed to certain moratorium regulations that limit the expansion of

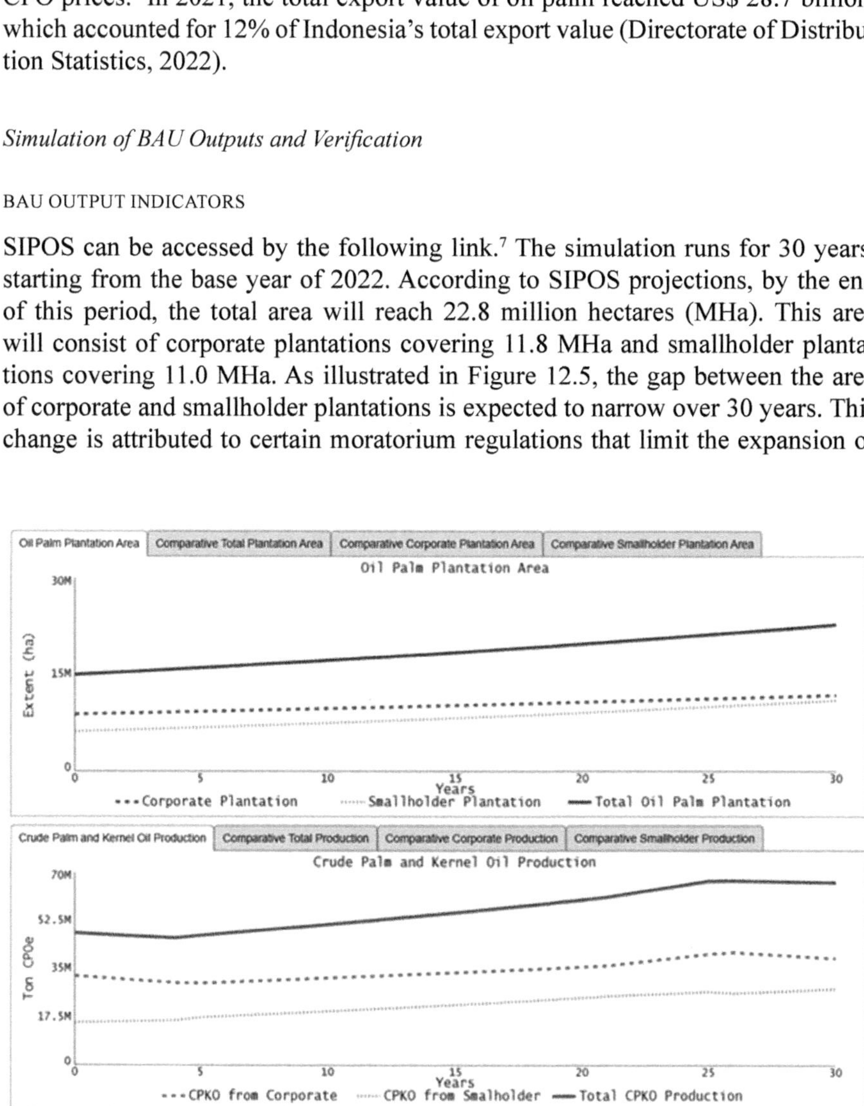

Figure 12.5 Plantation extent (Mha) and crude CPO/PKO production (Mton)

corporate plantations while allowing for smallholder growth. One key regulation is the Moratorium on New Palm Oil Plantation Permits, which was introduced in 2018 to address concerns about deforestation. Although this moratorium expired in 2021, existing laws continue to govern the expansion of palm oil plantations.

CPO and PKO production is projected to reach 66.4 million tonnes, sourced from both corporate and smallholder plantations. The production of crude CPO exceeds that of crude PKO, and corporations produce more than smallholders. The difference in production levels between corporations and smallholders remains consistent, as corporations have higher productivity than smallholders. The crude CPO and PKO produced are processed in mills and sent to refineries to produce RPO.

Figure 12.6 shows the palm oil trade volume, which amounts to 18.9 Mton in 2022 and increases to 26.3 Mton in 30 years of simulation. This number comprises CPKO and RPO exports and domestic trade. In terms of value, it increased from $42.5B to $86.7B, more than double in 30 years. It is also shown that the palm oil export value is greater than the domestic value. It is about 65% of palm oil value that comes from export or international trade. This also underlines the importance of EUDR for Indonesia. EUDR can significantly influence the palm oil trade value for Indonesia and ASEAN-producing countries.

The palm oil industry is undoubtedly lucrative, but it faces several challenges. The EUDR aims to decrease CO_2 emissions by prohibiting trade in commodities linked to deforestation, which is illegal and difficult to track. According to Figure 12.7, the deforestation rate attributed to palm oil was 58,500 hectares in 2022 and has risen to 93,600 hectares annually, an area larger than Jakarta, which

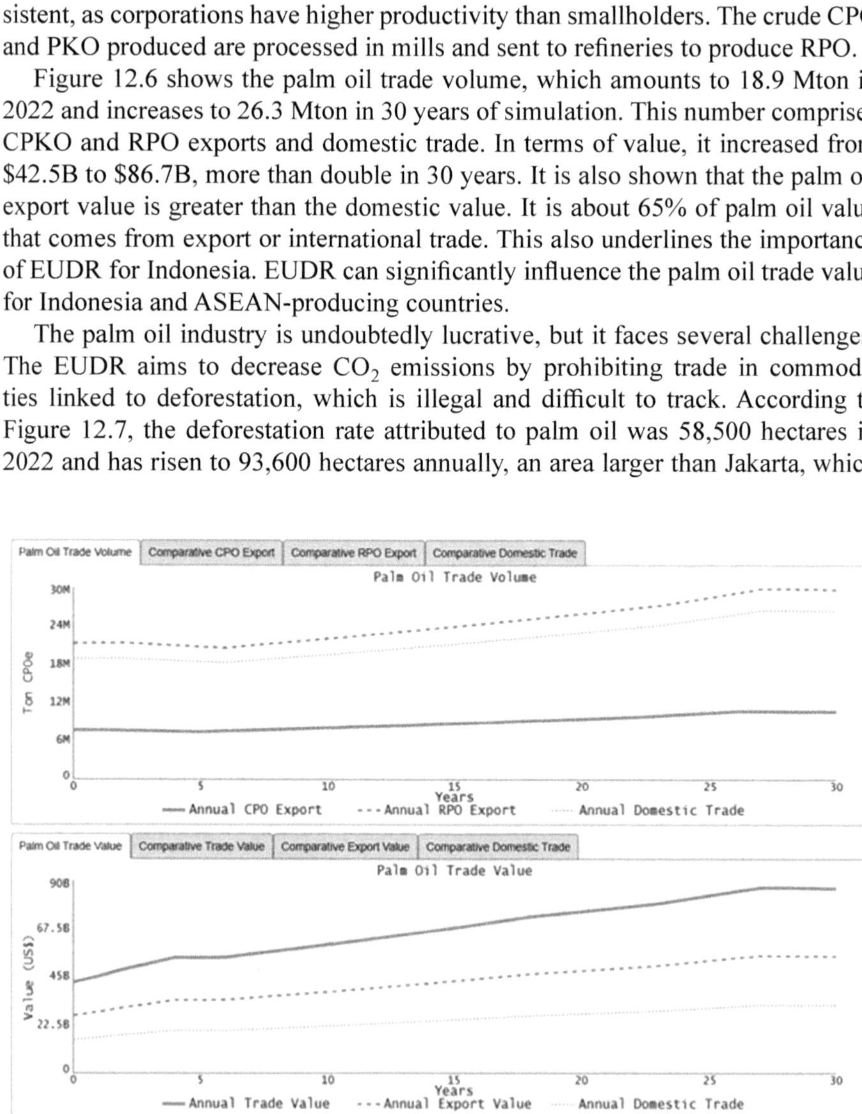

Figure 12.6 Palm oil trade volume (Mton) and value ($B)

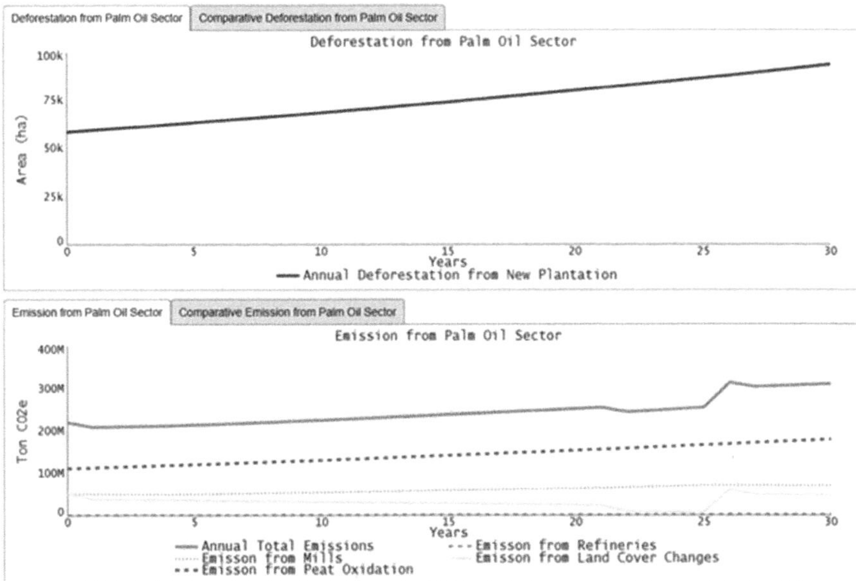

Figure 12.7 Deforestation and CO_2 emission

covers 66,000 hectares. Consequently, CO_2 emissions associated with palm oil have increased from 220 million tonnes to 310 million tonnes per year.

These emissions result from various factors, including peat oxidation, palm oil mills, land cover change, and refineries. Notably, emissions from peatlands represent the largest source of CO_2 emissions in the palm oil sector. Approximately 27% of industrial plantations in Indonesia, mainly oil palm, are established on peatlands. This significant proportion underscores the environmental challenges linked to palm oil cultivation in these carbon-rich and ecologically sensitive regions.

VERIFICATION OF BAU

The SIPOS outputs are verified through several methods. First, they are assessed in various forums, such as TRADE Hub and Scaling Jurisdictional Approach national workshops. During these workshops, key national stakeholders evaluate the logic and acceptability of the SIPOS outputs. We found that 87% of participants believed the outputs were logical and acceptable, while over 89% recognized their potential for usefulness and adoption. The second verification method involves comparing the SIPOS outputs with existing benchmarks, models, or plans from relevant authorities and businesses. Our findings indicate that all government offices – including the MoA, the Presidential Executive Office (KSP), and the Palm Oil Business Association (GAPKI) – expressed interest in increasing trade volumes and values. These results align with the Indonesian Palm Oil Simulation (IPOS) developed by Purnomo et al., 2020.

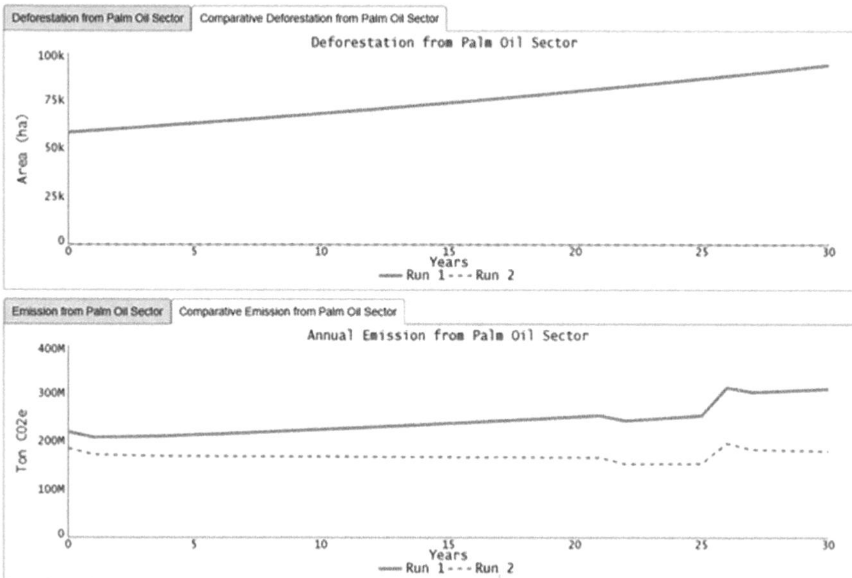

Figure 12.8 Scenario A: Stopping new plantations from illegal and legal conversions and peatland

Scenario Development Implementing No-Deforestation and Legality

The scenario presented here illustrates how EUDR can benefit both the environment and the economy. Figure 12.8 depicts Scenario A, which involves halting new plantations that result from both illegal and legal forest conversion, including on peatland. In this scenario, Indonesia shifts from producing palm oil sourced from deforestation (Run-1) to achieving zero deforestation (Run-2), thereby reducing emissions. During the simulation period, deforestation is projected to decrease from an average of approximately 76,000 hectares to zero. Concurrently, annual emissions are expected to drop from 265 million tonnes to 175 million tonnes, eventually reducing to around 90 million tonnes per year. Under this scenario, Indonesia is still able to expand its palm oil plantations on bare land and non-forest areas.

Scenario A presents a significant challenge, as it is projected to diminish trade value by as much as $10 billion annually. This reduction stems from the opportunity costs of not developing new palm oil plantations in Indonesia. Initially, the impact of not planting for a single year may seem minor; however, the effects compound over time. As each year passes without the establishment of new plantations, the cumulative loss of potential production and income becomes increasingly substantial (see Figure 12.9).

The absence of new palm oil developments not only affects trade value but also limits job creation and economic growth in regions that rely heavily on this industry. For Indonesian palm oil stakeholders – farmers, manufacturers, and exporters – this

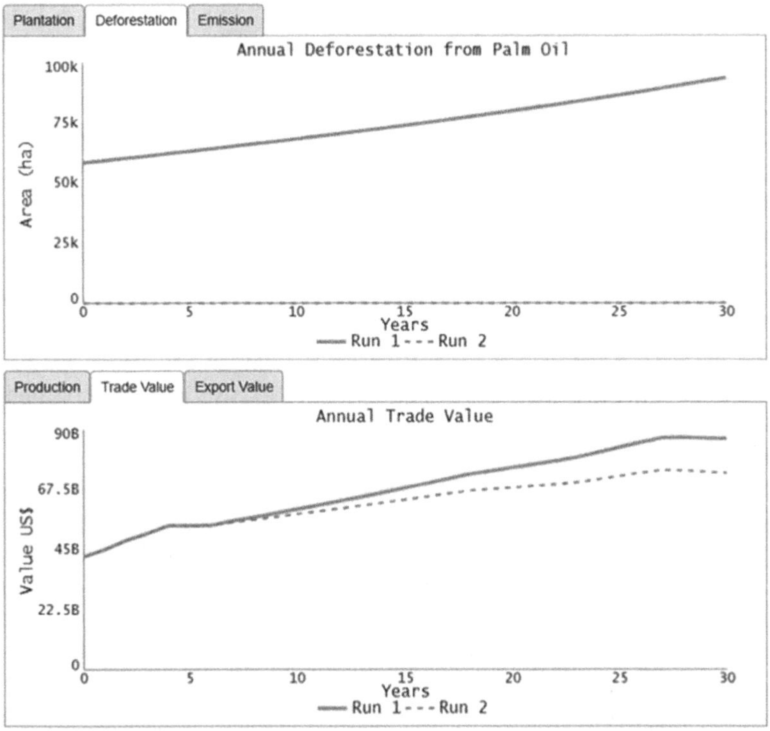

Figure 12.9 Effect of zeroing deforestation and lowering emissions on trade value ($B)

scenario creates an environment of uncertainty and concern. They face the risk of falling behind competitors in the global market, while also grappling with the need to balance economic opportunities with sustainable practices. Ultimately, the objective should be to find a scenario that harmonizes environmental stewardship with economic growth, ensuring that the interests of all stakeholders are addressed while promoting the sustainable development of palm oil agriculture in Indonesia.

1.3.2.2. Maintaining Trade Value while Reducing Deforestation and Emission

Scenario B is centred on the dual goal of halting deforestation and maintaining the economic viability of the palm oil industry. To achieve this, the strategy involves expanding palm oil plantations into areas that are currently devoid of forests, thus avoiding further degradation of existing forested regions. This scenario emphasizes the need for intensification, which refers to increasing productivity on existing plantations rather than expanding into new areas. This approach targets both corporate plantations and smallholder farmers, with a goal of increasing their productivity by 10%.

To support this sustainable intensification, a premium price of 10% above the market rate for palm oil is proposed. This financial incentive is designed to encourage producers to adopt more sustainable practices that enhance yield without further harming the environment. Furthermore, a mechanism for carbon credits will be introduced, allowing producers to earn credits for reducing GHG emissions associated with palm oil production. These carbon credits could generate financial benefits of up to $5 per ton of emissions reduced, providing an additional source of income for the farmers.

In addition to these measures, an ecological fiscal transfer of $50 per hectare will be implemented. This financial initiative incentivizes farmers and landowners to preserve natural landscapes, thus promoting biodiversity and environmental sustainability. Overall, Scenario B seeks to balance ecological preservation with economic performance in the palm oil sector, ensuring that environmental and economic objectives are effectively met. For further details, please refer to Figure 12.10.

Scenario B presents a comprehensive approach to environmental sustainability by focusing on three key outputs: the complete elimination of deforestation, a significant reduction in GHG emissions, and the preservation of palm oil's market value, as illustrated in Figure 12.11. In practical terms, achieving zero deforestation within Scenario B means that there is no occurrence of either legal or illegal deforestation. This is critical for ensuring that ecosystems are preserved and biodiversity is protected. The aspect of legality within this scenario is particularly important, as it entails the prohibition of new palm oil plantations on peatland, which is a vital step towards curbing emissions. Peatland acts as a significant carbon sink, and its protection is essential for minimizing the release of carbon dioxide and other greenhouse gases into the atmosphere.

Importantly, while Scenario B's trade value is projected to surpass that of the current BAU scenario, it is anticipated to be somewhat lower in the long term. This reduction is primarily attributed to the decision not to expand plantation areas to the same extent as in the BAU scenario. Emphasizing sustainability over expansion aligns with the goal of enhancing environmental integrity while still maintaining economic viability in the palm oil sector.

MSP of Roadmap Development

The stakeholders agreed to a shared vision that a sustainable trade system can be realized by respecting smallholders' rights and IPLCs (Indigenous peoples and local communities) and environmental justice with multi-stakeholder collaboration. To achieve the vision, there are eight action tracks as potential pathways; these are #0 Common understanding of sustainability; #1 Sustainable consumption; #2 Production system; #3 Markets; #4 Benefits; #5 Fair system; #6 Access to Finance; and #7 Communication.

Five identified action tracks (#1 and #5) related to the trade system explained in SIPOS. Sustainable consumption is the first relevant action track (#1). This action track to promote and create demand for sustainable palm oil, including in

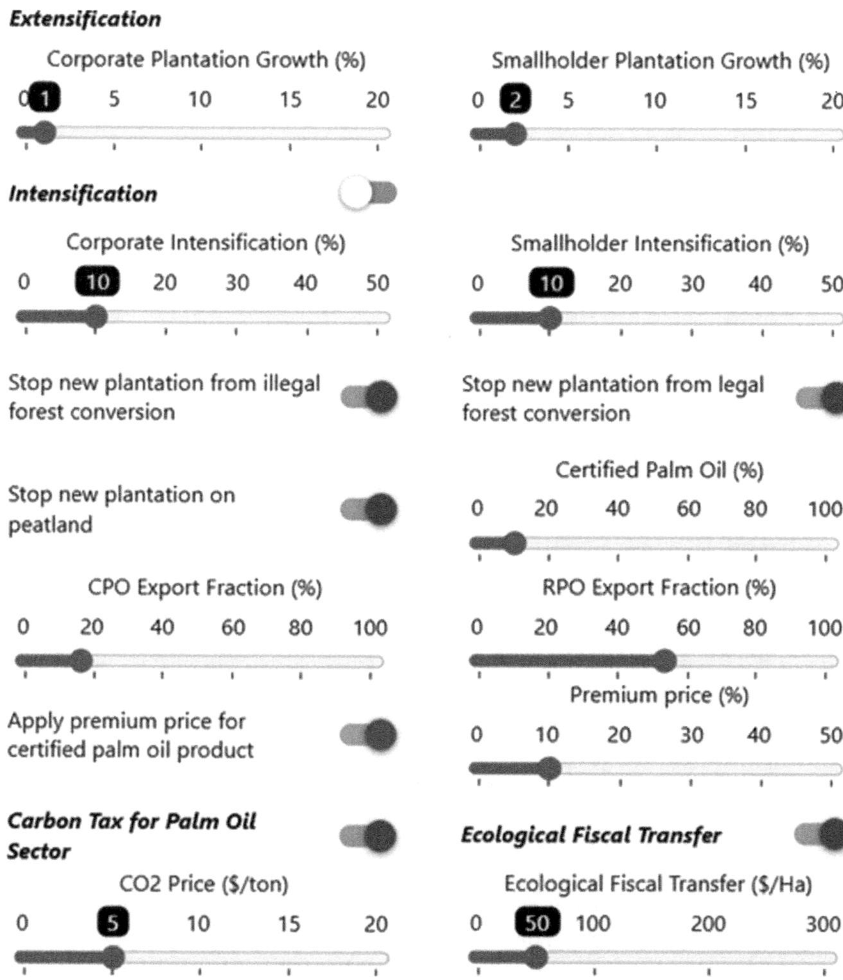

Figure 12.10 Scenario B: Stopping deforestation, intensification, premium price, and payment for environmental services

the domestic market and derivatives industries, was important besides increasing demand for the sustainable export market. The SIPOS model demonstrated this pathway by applying certification rate and export ratio. The second relevant action track is the production system (Action Track #2) to ensure sustainable practices by small- and large-scale producers, including by adopting mandatory and voluntary sustainable standards and enforcement laws against illegal expansion. In SIPOS, this is also simulated through certification and intensification scenarios, including stopping illegal and legal forest conversion.

The Market Action Track (#3) is the third track that was simulated using SIPOS. This track emphasizes the importance of connecting smallholders to sustainable markets

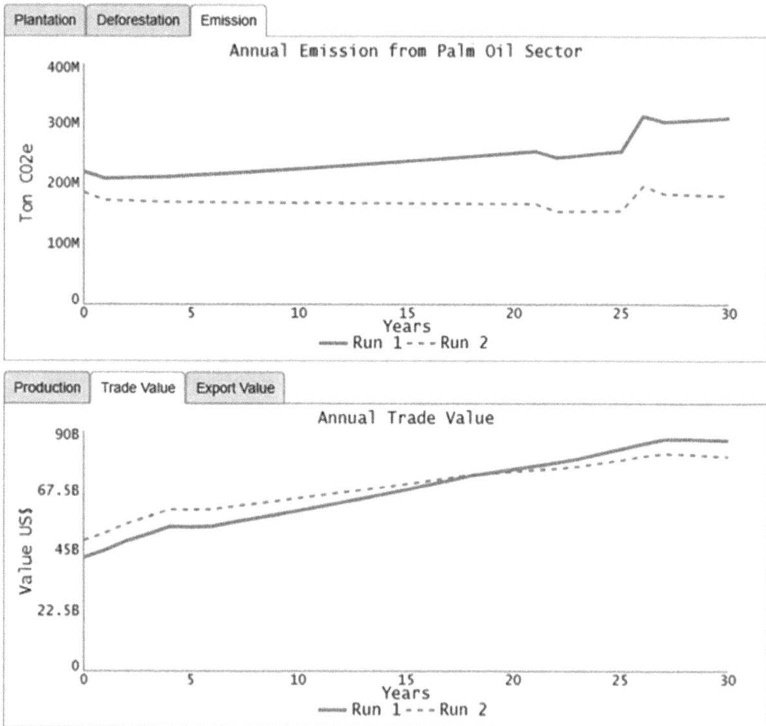

Figure 12.11 The result of Scenario B: Zero deforestation, lower emissions, maintained trade value

and creating incentive schemes for sustainable production. In SIPOS, this action track can be simulated by applying a premium pricing scenario. Action Track #4 focuses on ensuring that benefits are shared among all actors along the value chain. This track was tested in SIPOS by adjusting interventions for smallholders, such as the rate of intensification or extensification. The model showed farmers' income as an output indicator.

The fifth relevant action track for SIPOS is Action Track #5, which promotes a fair system. This track aims to distribute the costs and risks associated with sustainable transformation fairly between producers and consumers. SIPOS was used to analyze these trade-offs by utilizing its output indicators. While emission reductions can benefit both consumers and consumer countries in terms of climate change mitigation, the risks and economic losses cannot fall solely on producer countries, such as Indonesia. SIPOS illustrated these trade-offs through scenario development.

Results

Key Results

The key results are that EUDR can benefit Indonesian palm oil and EU communities with arrangements that are not strange or new for Indonesia and the EU. EUDR benefits Indonesia's environment and the global economy; meanwhile, the palm oil industry can be maintained and increased. This is to counter-argue criticism of EUDR.[8] Legal and illegal deforestation can be avoided. To make EUDR work for the economy, Indonesia should apply ecological fiscal transfer and carbon credit from reduced GHG emissions from the palm oil sector. A mechanism to get payment for carbon credits produced can be carbon trade or tax.

Planting oil palm on peatland can be avoided because it is illegal. In Indonesia, peatland conversion into palm oil plantations is heavily restricted by regulations aimed at protecting these ecologically sensitive areas. Key laws include Presidential Instruction No. 8 of 2015 (imposing a moratorium on new permits for primary forests and peatlands) and amendments to Government Regulation No. 71/2014, which classify peatlands into protected and cultivation zones, with protected areas (e.g., peat deeper than 3 meters) strictly off-limits for development. While limited development is allowed in cultivation zones under strict guidelines, the moratorium on new permits and the ISPO certification further reinforce sustainability standards. Despite these regulations, enforcement challenges and illegal conversions remain a concern, as peatland conversion leads to significant environmental impacts, including carbon emissions and increased fire risks.

However, this is from a producing country's view, like Indonesia. ASEAN countries like Malaysia face a similar position. As a consumer country, the EU has a vast job rewarding EUDR compliance with palm oil commodities. This reward should be in the form of a premium price. Palm oil premium pricing is a strategy where palm oil is priced higher than the market average to reflect compliance with EUDR. It targets consumers who are willing to pay more for EUDR compliance. This approach can compensate for the economic loss due to the efforts to comply with EUDR. It is difficult for EU consumers to work since premium prices usually work for niche markets or luxury segments where exclusivity and reputation are key.

The mechanism to pay more for palm oil that complies with EUDR is vital work for the EU. This can be done by separating products from countries that comply with EUDR and those that do not. Economic incentives must be given not only to governments but also to producers, either corporations or smallholders. The best economic incentives are connected to the products they sell so that they can understand that good products will provide more benefits to them.

Learning from previous evidence about the timber sector is key to EUDR's success. In Indonesia, the Voluntary Partnership Agreement (VPA) under the EU Forest Law Enforcement, Governance, and Trade (FLEGT) Action Plan is pivotal in promoting sustainable forest management and addressing illegal logging. The VPA, which Indonesia and the EU formally signed in 2013, ensures that timber and timber products exported to the EU come from legal sources. Through a long bilateral dialogue between Indonesia and the EU, Indonesia became the first country to issue FLEGT licenses in 2016, a milestone that reflects its commitment to improving forest governance. These licenses ensure that timber products comply with Indonesia's robust timber legality assurance system (SVLK), which tracks timber from harvest to export. By enhancing transparency, reducing illegal logging, and fostering accountability, the VPA and FLEGT licensing system have boosted Indonesia's timber trade credibility and contributed to forest conservation and the livelihoods of local communities.

Generalization and Limitation

This finding highlights the potential for mutual benefits under the EUDR in specific bilateral arrangements, particularly among ASEAN countries, and for commodities like coffee, cocoa, and rubber. The EUDR offers an excellent opportunity to enhance environmental sustainability on a global scale. To address potential economic losses, it is beneficial to explore innovative compensation strategies. These strategies should emerge from collaborative discussions between the EU and ASEAN countries and should be tailored to commodities. Such arrangements can be flexible and adaptable, reflecting the unique needs of different countries and products.

This finding has not yet addressed the problem faced by smallholders regarding traceability. The EUDR mandates that specific commodities, including palm oil, soy, coffee, cocoa, timber, and rubber, must be deforestation-free and legally produced to enter the EU market. A critical aspect of EUDR is commodity traceability, which requires businesses to collect detailed information about the origin of these products, including geolocation data of production areas, ensuring compliance with laws and that they do not originate from deforested land after December 31, 2020. Corporates and smallholders must implement robust traceability systems, map supply chains, conduct risk assessments, and submit due diligence statements to EU authorities. Non-compliance can lead to penalties, including fines of up to 4% of a company's total annual EU-wide turnover. This traceability ensures transparency and aligns production with sustainability and legal standards. In Indonesia, almost half of palm oil production is connected to smallholders. Smallholders commonly have problems proving their traceability.

Science Advancement

The findings prove how system dynamic modelling enlightens the MSP of palm oil roadmap development in Indonesia concerning the EUDR. The modelling shows how the current business model cannot sustain our environment. The scenario of a win-win solution between ASEAN and EU countries exists and is rational. Deforestation and GHG emissions must be halted to sustain our lives on Earth. At the same time, economic and social interests related to deforestation-driven commodities are high. Oil palms provide huge economic returns and employment opportunities to the people. Solutions exist and must be discussed.

Traceability for smallholders is a gap, and a method and tool must be developed. The Center for International Forestry Research and World Agroforestry (CIFOR-ICRAF) is experiencing the platform development of Palm Oil Traceability and Certification (POTRACE).[9] POTRACE provides smallholder oil palm farmers with a reliable platform for tracking the source of FFB from plantations to mills. The goal is to enhance transparency and traceability, ensuring every palm oil supply chain stage is visible and accountable. Using practical and accessible technology enables stakeholders to monitor the location and production of smallholders' palm oil. This ensures that the supply chain is aligned with sustainability practices and standards. By offering these insights, it is aimed to strengthen trust between farmers, consumers, and manufacturers while supporting sustainability in the palm oil industry. The platform is in the piloting process and is committed to continuously enhancing and adjusting it based on feedback and real-world applications. With POTRACE, every step of the process is traceable, helping to promote a more transparent and sustainable palm oil industry. Figure 12.12 shows the POTRACE interface, explaining the traceability of smallholders' palm oil.

Ways Forward

The Green Deal will not be effective if it is endorsed unilaterally.[10] Scenarios for mutual benefits between consumer and producer countries of the Green Deal must be explored and emerged. Indeed, the scenario exists. People in EU and ASEAN countries need to be more deliberative, outline the scenario, and stay away from provocative terms. While the EU countries must recognize the success and progress of ASEAN countries in reducing deforestation, ASEAN countries cannot only raise the issue of trade discrimination by the EU against Indonesia and other producing countries.[11] The genuine and meaningful dialogue between ASEAN and the EU must continue. It will take time before solutions are agreed upon and implemented.[12]

Time is critical. The EU parliament wants to postpone EUDR implementation for only a year and disagrees with a two-year postponement, as suggested by the

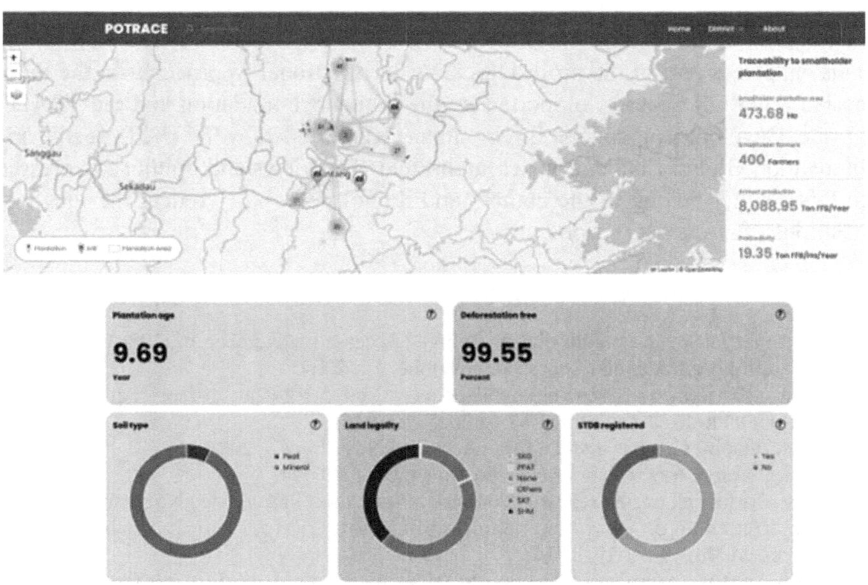

Figure 12.12 Interface of POTRACE

Source: https://data.cifor-icraf.org/potrace/.

European People's Party (EPP).[13] Most producing countries are not fully ready yet to implement EUDR. Therefore, the working group between the EU and ASEAN countries and between the EU and individual country members needs to be strengthened and endorsed. If agreement cannot be achieved with the working groups, then the EUDR will be an effective tool to sustain the environment in producing countries.

Conclusion

The research highlights the potential for mutual benefits under EUDR for Indonesia's palm oil sector and EU communities. EUDR offers environmental and economic advantages, supporting sustainable palm oil production while addressing criticisms of the regulation. By avoiding deforestation, illegal oil plantations on peatlands, and utilizing mechanisms like ecological fiscal transfers and carbon credits, Indonesia can ensure compliance with EUDR while sustaining its palm oil industry. Economic incentives, such as premium pricing for EUDR-compliant products and transparent traceability mechanisms, are essential for success. Smallholder challenges in meeting traceability requirements must be addressed through innovative tools like the POTRACE platform. Collaboration between ASEAN and EU countries is vital to ensure balanced outcomes, with lessons from Indonesia's FLEGT licensing offering insights into promoting sustainability and legality in commodity trade. Continued dialogue and cooperative frameworks are crucial to overcoming implementation barriers, fostering environmental sustainability, and securing economic benefits for producer and consumer countries.

Acknowledgements

This chapter is part of the project "Scaling Jurisdictional Approaches in the Indonesian Palm Oil Sector," supported by the Walmart Foundation and the TRADE (Trade, Development, and the Environment) Hub, funded by the UK Research and Innovation Global Challenges Research Fund. The views and opinions expressed in this chapter belong to the authors and do not necessarily reflect the views or positions of any organizations.

Notes

1 www.merriam-webster.com/dictionary/tree (Accessed November 10, 2024)
2 www.cifor.org/tradehub (Accessed November 15, 2024)
3 www.cifor-icraf.org/event/palm-oil-economy-eu-deforestation-free-regulation-and-folu-net-sink-2030/ (Accessed November 15, 2024)
4 https://mapbiomas.nusantara.earth/ (Accessed November 3, 2024)
5 https://explore.trase.earth/ (Accessed November 5, 2024)
6 www.worldbank.org/en/research/commodity-markets#3 (Accessed November 5, 2024)
7 https://exchange.iseesystems.com/public/cifor-vfi/sipos-eng/index.html#page1 (Accessed November 19, 2024)
8 www.reuters.com/world/asia-pacific/indonesia-presidential-front-runner-prabowo-criticises-eu-deforestation-2023-11–13/ (Accessed November 18, 2024); www.thejakartapost.com/business/2024/08/26/eu-embargo-on-indonesian-palm-oil-a-blessing-in-disguise-prabowo-says.html (Accessed November 18, 2024).
9 https://data.cifor-icraf.org/potrace/ (Accessed November 18, 2024)

10 https://jakartaglobe.id/business/eu-didnt-consult-with-indonesia-before-passing-eudr-minister (Accessed November 10, 2024)
11 www.channelnewsasia.com/asia/malaysia-indonesia-brussels-european-union-deforestation-regulation-palm-oil-3527931 (Accessed November 18, 2024)
12 https://gapki.id/en/news/2024/03/18/ri-eu-parliaments-agree-to-mediate-eudr-dispute (Accessed November 10, 2024)
13 www.euronews.com/green/2024/06/27/epp-environment-lead-calls-for-delay-to-anti-deforestation-law (Accessed November 11, 2024)

Reference List

Austin, K. G., Mosnier, A., Pirker, J., McCallum, I., Fritz, S., & Kasibhatla, P. S. (2017). Shifting patterns of oil palm driven deforestation in Indonesia and implications for zero-deforestation commitments. *Land Use Policy*, *69*(2017), 41–48. https://doi.org/10.1016/j.landusepol.2017.08.036

Benedict, J., & Heilmayr, R. (2024, October 7). *Indonesian palm oil exports and deforestation.* Trase.

BPS-Statistic Indonesia. (2020). *Pertumbuhan Ekonomi Indonesia Triwulan III-2020.* BPS-Statistic Indonesia (Press Release No. 97/11/Th. XXIII).

BPS-Statistics Indonesia. (2025). *Exports of palm oil by major countries of destination, 2012–2024.* Retrieved on November 11, 2025, from https://www.bps.go.id/en/statistics-table/1/MTAyNiMx/exports-of-palm-oil--by-major-countries-of-destination--2012-2024.html

Directorate of Distribution Statistics. (2022). *Indonesia foreign trade statistics exports 2021, Volume 1.* In Hertinmalyana, M. & Sulaiman, H. (Eds.), Sub-directorate of Statistical Compilation and Publication, Directorate of Distribution Statistics, BPS- Statistics Indonesia.

Directorate General of Estates. (2022). *Statistical of national leading estate crops commodity 2021–2023.* In Gartina, D. & Sukriya, L. R. R. (Eds.), Secretariate of Directorate General of Estates, Directorate General of Estates, Ministry of Agriculture.

ERIA. (2007). *Investigation on Sustainable Biomass Utilization Vision in East Asia: Lifecycle Assessment for Biomass-Derived Fuel in Malaysia.* ERIA (Economic Research Institute for ASEAN and East Asia).

FAO. (2003). *Three definitions of forest change processes.* UN Food and Agriculture Organization.

GoI. (2021). *Indonesia Long-term strategy for low carbon and climate resilience 2050.* United Nations Framework Convention on Climate Change.

Grant, W. E., Pedersen, E. K., & Marín, S. L. (1997). *Ecology and natural resource management: systems analysis and simulation.* Addison-Wesley.

Kaplinsky, R., & Morris, M. (2000). *A handbook for value chain research.* Institute of Development Studies, University of Sussex.

Mulyani, A., & Las, I. (2008). Potensi Sumber Daya Lahan dan Optimalisasi Pengembangan Komoditas Penghasil Bioenergi di Indonesia. *Jurnal Litbang Pertanian*, *27*(1), 31–41.

Purnomo, H., Kusumadewi, S. D., Ilham, Q. P., Kartikasara, H. N., Okarda, B., Dermawan, A., Puspitaloka, D., Kartodihardjo, H., Kharisma, R., & Brady, M. A. (2023). Green consumer behaviour influences Indonesian palm oil sustainability. *International Forestry Review*, *25*(4), 449–472. https://doi.org/10.1505/146554823838028210

Purnomo, H., Okarda, B., Dermawan, A., Ilham, Q. P., Pacheco, P., Nurfatriani, F., & Suhendang, E. (2020). Reconciling oil palm economic development and environmental conservation in Indonesia: A value chain dynamic approach. *Forest Policy and Economics*, *111*(December 2019), 102089. https://doi.org/10.1016/j.forpol.2020.102089

Xu, J., Morris, P. J., Liu, J., & Holden, J. (2018). PEATMAP: Refining estimates of global peatland distribution based on a meta-analysis. *Catena*, *160*, 134–140. https://doi.org/10.1016/j.catena.2017.09.010

13 Afterword

Main Points, New Principles, and Future Outlook

Otto Hospes, Arya Hadi Dharmawan, Athiqah Nur Alami and Helen E.S. Nesadurai

Drawing on different theoretical approaches and detailed empirical analyses of key aspects of the European Union Green Deal (EGD), this book unpacks the complex mix of controversies, ambiguities, and opportunities that EGD policies present for Southeast Asian countries and the responses of key stakeholders to these policies. Controversies stem from its unilateral nature, rooted in power imbalances between the European Union (EU) and Southeast Asia, which give rise to perceptions of inequity and create political-economic strains. Meanwhile, ambiguities arise from the EGD's evolving nature and lack of inclusive dialogue and communication in its policy design, leaving room for uncertainties and misinterpretation. Opportunities hinge on its potential as a catalyst for green innovation and in fostering regional collaboration.

If for one thing, our book is a vivid demonstration of the agency of Southeast Asian countries, their governments, and different stakeholders. Not only do different state and non-state actors find different ways to cope with, give meaning to, or outright disqualify EGD policies, but they also manifest their agency in generating their own policies, norms, and rules. This does not mean that there are no controversies, ambiguities, and power conflicts at different levels and in different policy areas within Southeast Asian countries. There are many. However, the fundamental recognition of the agency of Southeast Asian countries and actors by EU agencies and policymakers could help to overcome much of the controversy and ambiguities around the EGD in Southeast Asia, and to identify approaches and projects that can benefit both EU countries and Southeast Asian countries.

Recognizing the agency of Southeast Asian countries and actors implies a critical reconsideration of unilateral and one-size-fits-all approaches. We propose two alternative principles for (re)design and implementation of EU policies aimed at global sustainability transformation: norm subsidiarity and contextual approaches. With the adoption of each principle, we see crucial roles for scholars to support processes of policymaking and implementation.

From Unilateralism to Norm Subsidiarity

The concept of norm subsidiarity derives from the general notion of subsidiarity, which refers to "a principle of locating governance at the lowest possible level – that

DOI: 10.4324/9781003783176-16

closest to the individuals and groups affected by the rules and decisions adopted and enforced" (Slaughter, 2004). Subsidiarity is a key principle of EU lawmaking processes: action is only taken at the EU level when it is more effective than EU countries acting alone at the national, regional, or local level (European Union, 2016). We propose that the EU consider extending this principle to legislation that is aimed at global sustainability transformation. Subsidiarity would then include the principle of locating governance closest to the individuals and groups outside the EU territory that are affected by EU rules and decisions.

Using Slaughter's definition of subsidiarity, we define norm subsidiarity as a principle of locating norms closest to the individuals and groups outside the EU that are affected by EU laws and policies. Southeast Asian countries are not institutional voids and have developed their own policies, regulations, and standards to reduce deforestation, protect biodiversity, and organize climate mitigation and adaptation. Whereas their success in transforming economies and leaving no one behind is not guaranteed, these policies, regulations, and standards are much more tailored to the contexts, values, and economic challenges of Southeast Asian countries. Norm subsidiarity refers to the bottom-up process of developing norms, using local or national ones as the fundament and then building upon these with international ones. Scholars can explore how local and national norms developed by and in Southeast Asian countries can be complemented and reinforced by EGD policies, all having the same ambition: sustainability transformation and green innovation that leave no one behind.

For Acharya (2011), norm subsidiarity is not just about locating norms closest to the individuals and groups affected by rules and decisions of policymakers but also about agency and challenging hegemonic powers. He defines norm subsidiarity as the process "whereby local actors create rules with a view to preserve their autonomy from dominance, neglect, violation, or abuse by more powerful central actors" (p. 97). Different waves of private standards and public regulations from Europe on sustainability have prompted norm subsidiarity in Southeast Asian countries. Understanding such a norm of subsidiarity may help European policymakers and legislators realize that unilateral policymaking is not the way to gain recognition, support, and partnership from governments, businesses, and smallholder associations in Southeast Asia. Acknowledging the norm of subsidiarity is a precondition for building new and true partnerships.

From One-Size-Fits-All to Contextual Approaches

Both the EU and Southeast Asian countries have a lot to gain when adopting a contextual approach to the implementation of EGD policies outside the EU. Context matters for making policies successful and meaningful. A contextual approach can help mitigate much of the controversy surrounding the unilateral design of EGD policies and address ambiguities regarding their implementation in Southeast Asia. A contextual approach can also help the European Commission to upgrade and adapt its Better Regulation guidelines (European Commission, 2021), not only specifying tools and steps to assess the impact of EU policies for EU citizens but also for those affected by these policies outside the EU.

Scholars can play a crucial role in identifying the contextual factors and mechanisms that trigger both intended and unintended outcomes of EGD policies and instruments in Southeast Asian countries. Their analyses can inform the European Commission's efforts to refine its Better Regulation guidelines and, more importantly, support the development of regulations that better anticipate and accommodate non-EU contexts – particularly the realities faced by smallholders and other vulnerable stakeholders beyond the EU. Additionally, scholars can contribute to organizing inclusive, multi-stakeholder consultations at the national level within Southeast Asian countries. These consultations can help map and compare the diverse bodies of knowledge that public authorities and relevant stakeholders draw upon to interpret and apply the terms and norms embedded in EGD policies.

Agenda for Policy Dialogue and Collaborative Action

Using normative subsidiarity and contextual approaches to design, adjust, and implement EGD policies, we see great opportunities for partnerships, projects, and consultations that can benefit both EU and Southeast Asian countries. Drawing from evidence and ways forward presented in the book chapters, we propose the following agenda for policy dialogue and collaborative action:

- Establishing bilateral partnerships, dialogues, and task forces between EU member states and Southeast Asian countries, as well as between the EU and ASEAN, with a clear mandate to co-design country-specific strategies for the implementation of EGD policies in Southeast Asian contexts.
- Exploring ways in which EGD policies and instruments can support and enhance existing initiatives within Southeast Asian countries, particularly under the ASEAN Green Deal. This includes not only EU investment in technical projects related to renewable energy and clean technologies, but also support for social initiatives that empower smallholders and local communities to engage with, adapt, and shape EGD policies in ways that reflect their specific contexts. Such support should enable these actors to understand and comply with EGD requirements on their own terms.
- Organizing inclusive, multi-stakeholder consultations at the national level within Southeast Asian countries to ensure that all those affected by EGD policies – especially smallholders – have a voice in their implementation.
- Making land tenure conditions and the economic realities of smallholders a foundational design principle in the implementation of relevant EGD policies to ensure equity and feasibility.
- Establishing regular policy dialogues between EU agencies and relevant authorities in Southeast Asian countries to explore how adjustment and implementation of EGD policies can be aligned with – and reinforce – existing domestic laws and policies on deforestation prevention, biodiversity conservation, and climate change mitigation and adaptation.

While these actions can really make a difference, the emphasis remains on a better implementation of the EGD. The EGD as a policy or instrument is not really questioned or changed. Southeast Asian governments may consider using different channels and routes to influence or even transform EGD policies. We distinguish three strategies, also seeing important roles for scholars in International Relations in this regard:

The first strategy is to "multilateralize" EGD policies. A concrete step is the formation of joint task forces composed of representatives from both the EU and Southeast Asian countries to discuss and coordinate the implementation of EGD policies within national contexts. The second strategy is to build bilateral relationships and partnership programmes with individual EU member states. These partnerships can yield direct benefits, such as support for technological development and green innovation in Southeast Asia. Indirectly, they also offer diplomatic leverage: when bilateral partners echo Southeast Asian concerns within EU institutions, they help amplify regional voices at the heart of EU policymaking. The third strategy is to use ASEAN as leverage. As a strategic trade partner of the EU, ASEAN represents a powerful platform for collective action and interest articulation. EU–ASEAN councils and partnership dialogues constitute key venues through which Southeast Asian states can collectively negotiate with the EU over the local implementation of EGD policies. When mobilized as a vehicle for collective action, ASEAN's influence should not be underestimated.

Scholars in International Relations – particularly in diplomacy studies – can play a vital role not only in describing and analyzing different strategies but also in providing informed feedback to Southeast Asian governments and diplomats. Such insights can support the strategic design of well-calibrated mixes of diplomatic tools and efforts, thereby enhancing the region's capacity to respond effectively to the challenges posed by the EGD.

The Future of the EGD and What's Next for Southeast Asian States

The future of the EGD and what's next for Southeast Asian states largely hinges on how the EU manages internal and external pressures in both the short and long term. Both internal and external pressures are about economic interests: internal pressures are political voices from EU member states and members of the European Parliament that echo interests of European business, whereas external pressures come from new economic and foreign policies of the United States.

Since its launch in 2019, the EGD has been subject to sustained political contestation within the EU. The corporate sector has consistently expressed concerns to the European Commission and the political leadership of member states regarding the scope, regulatory requirements, and implementation of various EGD policies and instruments. These lobbying efforts have had a discernible impact on the shaping and adjustment of EGD policies. Several EU member states that initially championed the EGD have shifted towards proposing amendments, postponements, regulatory pauses, and simplifications of its policies and instruments. For instance, Germany and France blocked an agreement on the Corporate Sustainability Due Diligence Directive in 2024: the former feared a negative impact on its car industry, and the latter proposed to reduce the scope of the Corporate Sustainability Due Diligence Directive (CSDDD), limiting it to firms with over 5,000 employees and high revenue. The application of the EUDR that was adopted in 2023 has been postponed twice by the European Commission – first to December 2025, then to December 2026.

A pivotal event that altered the trajectory of the EGD was the 2024 European Parliament elections. In their aftermath, "the Commission and centrist majorities in the Parliament and Council pledged to simplify climate policy in a targeted manner and make it more business-friendly" (Jansen & Jäger, 2025). In line with this shift, the newly installed European Commission sought to boost EU competitiveness by announcing the so-called *Omnibus Law* in November 2024, which merges and amends three core policies of the EGD: the Corporate Sustainability Reporting Directive (CSRD), the CSDDD, and the EU Taxonomy Regulation. Another legislative proposal that signals the European Commission's commitment to making EGD policies more business-friendly is the softening of requirements for traders and downstream operators within the EU while maintaining stringent obligations for producers outside the EU under the EUDR (European Commission, 2025).

The simplification and streamlining of EGD policies to serve the interests of the corporate sector reinforce Almeida et al.'s (2023) characterization of the EGD as an "EU-first" policy. The business-friendly adjustments will not mitigate the controversy in Southeast Asia about the EGD as a unilateral regulatory package. Huge challenges will remain, if not increase, for governments, smallholders, and other stakeholders in Southeast Asia on how to implement EGD policies, certainly when more of the burden of collecting data for meeting due diligence requirements is put with producers at the upstream part. For Southeast Asian states and ASEAN, the dilemma in engaging with the EU and the EGD has become increasingly acute. The choice is between adopting a more confrontational strategy that directly challenges the EU's hegemonic regulatory power and frames the EGD in terms of injustice and coloniality *or* intensifying efforts to forge pragmatic partnerships focused on green technology development, sustainable finance, and the selective alignment of EU and Southeast Asian green policy frameworks.

The external pressures on the EU coming from the new economic and foreign policies of the United States since Donald Trump took office in early 2025, may indirectly be of help to Southeast Asian countries in solving this dilemma. His "America First" policies, emphasizing economic nationalism and transactional alliances, have contributed to heightened geopolitical unrest and pose a serious test for the EU as a traditional ally in political, economic, and military terms. This has increased the EU's receptiveness to renewing, deepening, or broadening bilateral trade agreements with Southeast Asian countries and ASEAN (Ministry of Industry and Trade of Vietnam, 2025; Olson, 2025). This again provides opportunities for these countries and associations to engage in policy dialogue with EU institutions on the implementation and adaptation of EGD policies within the region. A blessing in disguise of Trump's transactional approach may be that it prompts the EU to move away from a unilateral stance and revive partnership-based approaches in advancing its business and environmental agenda towards Southeast Asian countries and other parts of the Global South.

Regardless of the future trajectory of the EGD, the most critical asset of Southeast Asian countries, their governments, and societal stakeholders remains their agency to challenge hegemonic power and to generate their own policies, norms, and regulatory frameworks that simultaneously protect the environment and support economic and social development. It is of utmost importance for governments and societal stakeholders in Southeast Asia to cherish, cultivate, and strategically deploy this agency. Such agency enables them not only to withstand and critique global waves of regulatory unilateralism and resurgent mercantilism but also to establish a robust foundation for genuine and much-needed partnerships in an era of growing global disorder.

Reference List

Acharya, Amitav. 2011. Norm Subsidiarity and Regional Orders: Sovereignty, Regionalism, and Rule-Making in the Third World. *International Studies Quarterly* 55, 95–123. https://doi.org/10.1111/j.1468-2478.2010.00637.x

Almeida, Diana Vela, Vijay Kolinjivadi, Tomaso Ferrando, Brototi Roy, Héctor Herrera, Marcela Vecchione Gonçalves, Gert Van Hecken. 2023. The "Greening" of Empire: The European Green Deal as the EU first agenda. *Political Geography* 105, 102925. https://doi.org/10.1016/j.polgeo.2023.102925.

European Commission. 2021. *Better Regulation Guidelines*. https://commission.europa.eu/law/law-making-process/better-regulation/better-regulation-guidelines-and-toolbox_en.

European Commission. 2025. Commission Proposes Targeted Measures to Ensure the Timely Implementation of EU Deforestation. *Press Release*, October 21, 2025. https://ec.europa.eu/commission/presscorner/api/files/document/print/en/ip_25_2464/IP_25_2464_EN.pdf.

European Union. 2016. Principles of Subsidiarity. *EurLEX*. https://eur-lex.europa.eu/EN/legal-content/glossary/principle-of-subsidiarity.html#:~:text=The%20principle%20of%20subsidiarity%20is,States%20remain%20in%20their%20domain.

Jansen, Jannik, Philipp Jäger. 2025. *Europe is Hollowing Out Its Green Deal, Leaving a Vacuum of Political Vision for Others to Exploit*. Policy Position Paper, December 19, 2025. Hertie School, Jacques Delors Centre, Berlin. 20251219_Policy_Position_Green_Deal_Jansen_Jaeger.pdf

Ministry of Industry and Trade of Vietnam, Multilateral Trade Policy Department. 2025. *EU and ASEAN Bolster Trade Ties: Signing CEPA with Indonesia, Aiming to Conclude FTAs with Thailand, the Philippines, and Malaysia by 2027*. Vietnam National Trade Repository (VNTR), October 16, 2025. https://vntr.moit.gov.vn/index.php/news/eu-and-asean-bolster-trade-ties-signing-cepa-with-indonesia-aiming-to-conclude-ftas-with-thailand-the-philippines-and-malaysia-by-2027.

Olson, Stephen. 2025. *As Trump Disrupts International Trade, Southeast Asia Must Look to Europe*. ISEAS Perspectives No. 94, November 21, 2025. www.iseas.edu.sg/wp-content/uploads/2025/10/ISEAS_Perspective_2025_94.pdf.

Slaughter, Anne-Marie. 2004. *A New World Order*. Princeton, NJ: Princeton University Press.

Index

For Product Safety Concerns and Information please contact our EU representative GPSR@taylorandfrancis.com Taylor & Francis Verlag GmbH, Kaufingerstraße 24, 80331 München, Germany

Batch number: 10482778

Printed by Printforce, the Netherlands